FEMINISM AND FILM THEORY

EDITED BY
CONSTANCE PENLEY

ROUTLEDGE • NEW YORK
BFI PUBLISHING • LONDON

First published in 1988 by

Routledge an imprint of Routledge, Chapman and Hall, Inc.
29 West 35 Street
New York, NY 10001

Published in Great Britain by

BFI Publishing
21 Stephen Street
London W1P 1PL

Library of Congress Cataloging-in-Publication Data

Feminism and film theory / [edited by] Constance Penley.
   p. cm.
   Includes bibliographies.
   ISBN 0-415-90107-3; ISBN 0-415-90108-1 (pbk.)
   1. Feminism and motion pictures. 2. Motion pictures—Philosophy.
I. Penley, Constance, 1948–
PN1995.9.W6F45 1988
791.43'01—dc19   88–6595
              CIP

British Library Cataloguing in Publication Data

Feminism and film theory
   1. Cinema films—Feminist viewpoints
   I. Penley, Constance   II. British Film
Institute
   791.43

   ISBN 0–85170–222–8
   ISBN 0–85170–223–6 Pbk

Contents

Acknowledgments

"The Place of Woman in the Cinema of Raoul Walsh," Pam Cook and Claire Johnston, in *Raoul Walsh*, Edinburgh Film Festival publication (1974)

"Dorothy Arzner: Critical Strategies," Claire Johnston, in *The Works of Dorothy Arzner*, British Film Institute publication (1975)

"Approaching the Work of Dorothy Arzner," Pam Cook, in *The Works of Dorothy Arzner*, British Film Institute publication (1975)

"Visual Pleasure and Narrative Cinema," Laura Mulvey, *Screen* 16, no. 3 (Autumn 1975)

"Afterthoughts on 'Visual Pleasure and Narrative Cinema' inspired by *Duel in the Sun*," Laura Mulvey, *Framework* 6, nos. 15–17 (1981)

"Rereading the Work of Claire Johnston," Janet Bergstrom, *Camera Obscura* nos. 3–4 (Summer 1979)

"Feminine Discourse in *Christopher Strong*," Jacquelyn Suter, *Camera Obscura* nos. 3–4 (Summer 1979)

"The Popular Film as Progressive Text—a Discussion of *Coma*" (Parts 1 and 2), Elizabeth Cowie, *m/f* no. 3 (1979); no. 4 (1980)

"Paranoia and the Film System," Jacqueline Rose, *Screen* 17, no. 4 (Winter 1976–77)

"Enunciation and Sexual Difference," Janet Bergstrom, *Camera Obscura* nos. 3–4 (Summer 1979)

"Alternation, Segmentation, Hypnosis: Interview with Raymond Bellour" an excerpt, Janet Bergstrom, *Camera Obscura* nos. 3–4 (Summer 1979). Translated by Susan Suleiman.

"*Caught* and *Rebecca*: The Inscription of Femininity as Absence," Mary Ann Doane, *enclitic* 5, no. 2 (Fall 1981)

"Woman's Stake: Filming the Female Body," Mary Anne Doane, *October* no. 17 (Summer 1981)

"*India Song/Son nom de Venise dans Calcutta désert*: The Compulsion to Repeat," Joan Copjec, *October* no. 17 (Summer 1981)

"The Cinema of Lol V. Stein," Elisabeth Lyon, *Camera Obscura* no. 6 (Fall 1980)

Introduction
The Lady Doesn't Vanish: Feminism and Film Theory

Constance Penley

Over the past five years innumerable people have asked me for a bibliography of feminist film theory or references to articles that could introduce them to the major debates in this energetic and intellectually sophisticated area of cultural study. After sending them to books like Annette Kuhn's *Women's Pictures: Feminism and Cinema*, E. Ann Kaplan's *Women and Film:Both Sides of the Camera*, Kaja Silverman's *The Subject of Semiotics*, or to Julia Lesage's articles in *Jump Cut* since 1974, I would also give them a list of important essays scattered in various British and American journals. More often than not, however, these essays were difficult or even impossible to find because they appeared in small-circulation journals or monographs, many of which are now out of print. The purpose of this volume is to make those articles more readily available.

The choice of essays was not, however, dictated solely by practical considerations. They were also chosen because they represent one distinct and insistently polemical strain of feminist film criticism, one that directly takes up the major issues of film theory as they were formulated in the theoretical ferment of the 1970s, generated and sustained by the interest in semiology, psychoanalysis, textual analysis, and theories of ideology. The introduction attempts to give a sense of the theoretical context in which these articles were written.

There is a strong current in feminist criticism that rejects contemporary theoretical approaches, like those of Freud or Lacan, for example, on the grounds of their implicitly masculine bias. The next move is then to adopt alternative theories or even bypass theory altogether by way of a direct appeal to experience or a specifically feminine understanding of the world. The essays reprinted here have taken what I believe to be a more difficult path. While questioning the tendency of each of these given theoretical approaches to avoid the complexity of sexual difference or elide the difficulties specific to feminine sexuality, they have nonetheless done so by critically returning to and extending those approaches. To take just one example, several of the essays reprinted here address the claim of psychoanalytic film theory (following Roland Barthes's analyses of bourgeois narrative form in *S/Z*) that classical film narrative perpetually restages the Oedipal drama solely from the masculine side, following the hero through his difficult separation from the mother to eventual identification with paternal authority. In showing that classical film narrative is, in fact, more ambiguous and irresolute than the Oedipal model that film theory has proposed, these essays, in pursuit of a more complex account of sexual difference for *both* sexes, return to and reread psychoanalysis. They do so through a reconsideration of such crucial psychoanalytic concepts as identification, fantasy, object relations, voyeurism, fetishism, and the imaginary.

To put it bluntly, none of these essays belongs to what could be called the "what if" school of feminist criticism: What if women had an Electra complex to complement the male's Oedipal complex? What if the crucial psychical relation were not to the phallus as a symbolic organ but to the real of the mother's body? What if there were no such thing as penis envy but, rather, "womb envy"? What if the male spectator's relation to the screen were determined solely by an innate fear or hatred of the woman's superior sexuality? Or, most commonly: What if we could hold on to the notion of the unconscious and dreamwork, and just forget about castration and the Oedipus complex? These "what if's" are no more than the signs marking the well-worn dissident paths of a reductive biologism, sociologism, or mysticism of the feminine; a kind of thinking, not solely confined to feminism, which sidesteps or dismisses years of reasoning and debate on the problematic status of these "alternatives." The essays in this volume have rejected such alternatives inasmuch as they represent merely another version of the easily accepted (because narcissistically desired) or the already known (the comfort of repeating the same), choosing instead to engage directly the arguments of contemporary film theory. The reader will thus find throughout the volume a feminist development of film theory that initially takes that body of work on its own terms, but then proceeds to question and often radically renovate not only its ideas about the spectator, the filmic apparatus, enunciation, point of view, and narrative form, but also filmic pleasure and belief.

An introduction to a collection of feminist literary theory would be obliged to describe the obstacles faced by feminists confronting the long and established history of literature and its criticism. Film theory, however, has had a much shorter history, and is thus less "institutionalized." It is true that established ways of writing about film became dominant early in its history— auterism, the "great man" theory of technological development, the master-piece tradition, the film as read through the taste and sensibilities of the critic. But contemporary film theory, as represented by theorists like Christian Metz, Raymond Bellour, Roland Barthes, Jean-Louis Baudry, Thierry Kuntzel, and Stephen Heath, has been notable for an anti-establishment iconoclasm and theoretical force that matches that of feminist film criticism. Thus, while the articles in this collection criticize or revamp many of the premises of recent film theory, it is striking to see how often their interests and conclusions nonetheless coincide. For example, Raymond Bellour and Stephen Heath's textual analyses of classical film (referred to throughout the volume) demonstrate that the narrative and symbolic problem of establishing the difference between the sexes is the primary motivating force of the classical Hollywood film. Sexual difference, for them, is a force in relation to which all filmic structures, whether the relation of one shot to the next, or the overall dramatic organization of the film, must be seen.[1] So too these male theorists have sometimes responded directly to the feminist critiques of their work, thus establishing an exchange of ideas that has been beneficial on all sides. Many of the terms of this debate are addressed explicitly in Janet Bergstrom's interview with Raymond Bellour in this volume.

In what follows I want to outline the main issues raised in each of the articles in the volume, not because the articles cannot speak for themselves, but to provide an overall sense of how they have been part of a continuing dialogue both with and within film theory.

While the essays cannot be neatly assigned their places in a linear history of "feminist film theory," several connections and influences do stand out. The later essays are so indebted to the early work of Pam Cook, Claire Johnston, and Laura Mulvey that they are as much a response to them as they are a dialogue with film theory itself. Reading these articles written in the mid-1970s evokes a strong sense of the excitement generated by the enthusiastic British reception of French theory, particularly that of Louis Althusser and Jacques Lacan. In retrospect, the convergence of film and feminism with a new and forceful reading, on the one hand, of ideological determinations, and, on the other, of the Freudian emphasis on the relation of sexuality to language and image, could not have been more fortuitous, or its effects more productive. As a result, feminists discovered in film a seemingly perfect object for study. Cinema, as a sort of microcosm, provided a model for the construction of subject positions in ideology, while its highly Oedipalized narratives lent themselves to a reading of the unconscious mechanisms of sexual difference in our culture. So too the fact that the compass of film extends from the forms of mass culture to those of the avant-garde, allowed feminist theorists to examine the question of audience and reception in all of its complexity.

That feminist film theory has made such a significant contribution to feminist theory in general (as well as feminist literary and art theory) is no doubt due to the productivity of that convergence.

What, then, were some of those groundbreaking issues raised in the early British work? In "The Place of Woman in the Cinema of Raoul Walsh," Pam Cook and Claire Johnston announced their aim to lay the foundations of a feminist film criticism. They proposed to apply the theories of Jacques Lacan to film, in part because they saw in his work a way of avoiding the kind of crude psychoanalytic reading limited to detecting "symptoms" or discovering sexual symbolism. Cook and Johnston also felt that a Lacanian analysis of film opened the way for a joint articulation of the psychical and the social, especially in the light of Lacan's debt to Lévi-Strauss's structural anthropology. They took as their example *The Revolt of Mamie Stover* because, like several of Walsh's films, its story concerns the social and sexual problems of an individual woman. At first sight the film seems to depict an exceptionally powerful heroine, a barroom hostess who goes into business to amass a fortune for herself. Cook and Johnston argue that if one analyzes the Jane Russell character not as a "symbol" but in terms of her overall narrative funtioning in the film, Mamie Stover can be seen to be the subject of the fiction only insofar as she agrees to be its object. The film is not, in fact, about Mamie Stover, nor about feminine sexuality, which, they insist, is entirely repressed in the film. On the contrary, they suggest that the narrative positions Mamie as a structuring absence in the film (she even describes herself as a "have-not"), one of those structuring absences—lacks—which Lacan argues is necessary for the continuance of desire. She is the cause of desire, as well as its object, but she cannot be its subject; or, in Lévi-Strauss's terms, the woman is no more than an "empty sign" exchanged by men.[2] In addition to offering a more complex account of the function of women in classical cinema as a basis for a feminist film theory, Cook and Johnston also aimed at making positive prescriptions for a feminist counter-cinema. How could such a negative analysis of the role of woman in Hollywood film lead to such positive prescriptions? The authors take up the *Cahiers du Cinéma* method of "symptomatic" reading to show that while feminine sexuality in the classical film is repressed, this repression creates internal conflicts in the film which cause it to fissure and split open, thus revealing its ideological contradictions. Feminists working toward a counter-cinema were encouraged first to learn the lessons of this ideological de-naturalization of woman in the Hollywood cinema in order to dismantle the system from within.

Cook and Johnston next set out to demonstrate how Dorothy Arzner's films are, in fact, concerned with "dismantling the system from within" ("Approaching the Work of Dorothy Arzner" and "Dorothy Arzner: Critical Approaches"). To further their claim that the contradictions of a rigidly constraining patriarchal definition of woman are bound to irrupt in the film, they turned to one of the few women who had worked within the Hollywood system. What happens, they ask, when a woman director attempts to locate and convey the "discourse of a woman" in a representational form which is "entirely male"? The discourse of the woman in Arzner films like *Christopher Strong* (1933) or *Dance Girl Dance* (1940) gives the filmic system its structural coherence, "while at the same time rendering the dominant discourse of the male fragmented and incoherent." They point to devices in Arzner's films that ironically subvert patriarchal values, devices such as the deliberate use of feminine stereotypes, a Russian Formalist-like "making-strange" (in Arzner's case, of "male" values such as ownership), and an emphasis on female sexuality as transgressive (Johnston), or more Brechtian devices of distantiation like the use of tableaux or "pregnant moments" (Cook). Again, their aim is not only to clarify the role of the woman in classical film, but also to pinpoint strategies for feminist filmmaking.

Among the many issues raised by Cook and Johnston's work, two in particular were to become central to feminist theorizing about film. First, their attempt to find ruptures, gaps, contradictions, and other points of resistance in the apparently seamless patriarchal fabric of the classical film. As we shall see, the task of isolating "ruptures" in the classical text often proved more difficult than their work suggested. Furthermore, to define those textual disturbances as instances of a femininity rubbing against the patriarchal grain of the film was an increasingly problematic exercise. How could feminists account for the disruptive effects of femininity in the classical film without falling back on an essentialist notion of "femininity" or "Woman" as an eternal and *naturally* subversive element? There is no feminist advantage in positing either a historically unchanging feminine essence or a monolithic patriarchal repression of that essence. The very idea of an essence is ahistorical and asocial, and suggests a set of traits not amenable to change, while the "repression" thesis fosters the belief that, once liberated from patriarchal constraints, femininity would finally assume its unadulterated and naturally given forms. A second and related issue directs us to filmmaking itself. Claire Johnston's work stands as a notable exception to the wholesale repudiation of Hollywood and its forms by feminist film theorists in the 1970s. Not only did she urge feminist filmmakers to study Hollywood as a negative example, she also stressed, in a more positive vein, the need to incorporate into feminist films Hollywood's mechanisms of pleasure. As she stated in her influential and widely cited 1973 *Screen* pamphlet, *Notes on Women's Cinema* (London: SEFT), "In order to counter our objectification in the cinema, our collective fantasies must be released: women's cinema must embody the working through of desire: such an objective demands the use of the entertainment film" (p. 31). Subsequent feminist writing about film, however, while it set itself the task of describing in great detail the nature of those pleasures provided by the "entertainment" film, did so only to demonstrate their limits and to encourage feminist filmmakers to adopt avant-garde or experimental approaches that were distinctly anti-Hollywood. Like the issue of femininity as a disturbance in the classical film, the question of feminist film's relation to Hollywood will recur throughout the essays in this volume, although never perhaps so forcefully and pragmatically stated as in Johnston's early work.

In fact, discussions of avant-garde film and analyses of Hollywood cinema are interwoven throughout this collection, often within a single article. Some feminist critics feel strongly that feminist analyses of classical film are doomed to be no more than academic exercises, or mere applications of theories derived from masculine interests and modes of thinking. Such critics would place a greater value on the discussion of documentary, activist, independent, or experimental work that more directly addresses and articulates the concerns of women. In the essays included in this volume, however, a case is made for both kinds of work. "Reading against the grain" of classical film (and its theory) is a necessary complement to the attention given more experimental or "independent" work that attempts not only to thwart the conventional representation of women in film but to convey the interests and concerns of women. Even if one believes that the only lesson feminists can learn from Hollywood is a negative one (how not to make films that depend on voyeuristic responses and a sadistic subjection of the woman to male fantasy), a working knowledge of the mechanisms of pleasure and modes of power of this dominant institution would seem to be indispensable. Such knowledge could be equally important to feminist filmmakers who do not entirely reject the forms of Hollywood, in the belief that the kinds of identification and pleasure associated with popular forms should not be overlooked in the attempt to make films with a wider appeal.

It was Laura Mulvey's now famous 1975 essay "Visual Pleasure and Narrative Cinema" that provided the theoretical grounds for the rejection of Hollywood and its pleasures: "Women, whose image has continually been stolen and used . . . cannot view the decline of traditional film form with anything . . . more than sentimental regret." Militating against the conventional voyeurism and sadism of the male spectator's relation to the woman on the screen, Mulvey calls for a cinema of "dialectics and passionate detachment," which will destroy that spectator's satisfaction, pleasure and privilege. "Visual Pleasure and Narrative Cinema" thus offered the first feminist consideration of the play and conflict of psychical forces at work between the spectator and the screen. Because film can control the dimension of time through editing and narrative, as well as the dimension of space through changes in editing and camera distance, cinematic codes create a gaze, a world, and an object which in turn produces "an illusion cut to the measure of desire." But the image of the woman on the screen, while erotic, constantly threatens to reveal the fact of castration through the exposure of her own lack of a penis. The representation of woman as signifier of castration thus induces in the spectator's unconscious the mechanisms of voyeurism and fetishism (scopophilia, disavowal) as a defense against that threat. If all of this is true, Mulvey suggests, then feminists have no choice but to reject the forms of classical cinema inasmuch as they are constructed on the basis of a male fantasy entirely detrimental to women, one which inevitably makes the woman a passive recipient of the aggressive male look.

Mulvey herself was to return to the issues raised in "Visual Pleasure and Narrative Cinema" in an article published six years later, "Afterthoughts on 'Visual Pleasure and Narrative Cinema' inspired by *Duel in the Sun*." Asked many times since the publication of her influential essay why she had referred to the spectator as "he," she replies by insisting that her original interest lay in the relationship of the image of the woman on the screen to the tendency of classical Hollywood film to "masculinize" the spectator, regardless of the actual sex of the person watching the film. However, the persistent question addressed to her, "what about the woman in the audience?" and her own interest in films—especially melodrama—in which the woman is the "subject" of the film in both senses of the term, convinced her that her emphasis on the masculinity of the spectator might have closed off some lines of questioning. Mulvey's response came in the wake of an increasing number of close studies of films, such as those of Mary Ann Doane on the "woman's films" of the 1940s (*Caught, Rebecca*), in which the implied spectator is not male. It also followed a new theoretical line of inquiry into the presumed masculinity of the spectator in articles like Janet Bergstrom's "Enunciation and Sexual Difference." Mulvey now concludes that the film does provide or construct a place for the female spectator, but that it is an awkward or difficult one: she is a sort of transvestite, forced to assume another role in order to "read" the image.

Just as "Visual Pleasure and Narrative Cinema" has been frequently revisited by both Mulvey herself and other writers who have questioned or supplemented certain of its conclusions,[3] so too the seminal work of Cook and Johnston demanded serious critical reconsideration. The first direct discussion of their work came several years after its appearance, in a pair of articles written in 1979 by Janet Bergstrom ("Rereading the Work of Claire Johnston") and Jacquelyn Suter ("Feminine Discourse in *Christopher Strong*"). Bergstrom examined Claire Johnston's theoretical approach as it had been consistently expressed in her articles over a number of years, while Suter offered a reading of a Dorothy Arzner film that challenged several of Cook and Johnston's ideas about feminine subversion of the Hollywood film.

While acknowledging that Johnston's *Notes on Women's Cinema* had laid the groundwork for many important areas of research, Bergstrom argued that it was essential for feminist film theory to reconsider the way in which Johnston had too readily assumed the coherence of concepts like feminine specificity, woman's desire, pleasure or entertainment in film, enunciation and discourse in film. She also argues that it is only through offering highly interpretive readings of isolated moments that Johnston is able to support her thesis about "ruptures" in the dominant cinema's patriarchal discourse. Although Johnston had argued for an emphasis on the specifically filmic means of representation, Bergstrom maintains that she does not in fact pay sufficient attention to the complex work of signification in the film, nor to the fact that the meaning of any given moment in the narrative is largely determined by its relationship to the entire discursive structure of the film. Above all, she says, Johnston disregards persuasive evidence from the textual analysis of classical films that ruptures or gaps are generated only in order to be ultimately covered over by the work of the film itself. Not only is this rupturing activity characteristic of the classical text, it is in large part a precondition of the pleasure it provides.

While Bergstrom draws attention to the need to examine fully the complexities of filmic enunciation, Jacquelyn Suter gives us a sketch of what might be gained from such attention in her reading of "feminine discourse" in *Christopher Strong*. Suter chooses to focus her discussion on a film by Dorothy Arzner because of the privileged place given her work by Cook and Johnston, inasmuch as it was seen to exemplify not only a transgression of the patriarchal discourse of film but also "the working through of [woman's] desire." In contrast to Cook and Johnston, Suter believes that femininity *does* exist in the film: far from being repressed, it plays a major role in structuring the filmic discourse. The strength of Suter's essay is that it demonstrates the difficulties encountered in trying to diagnose what feminine discourse *is* in the film and how it is enunciated. For example, all of the characters in *Christopher Strong*, male and female, speak a patriarchal discourse, defined in the film as a rigid adherence to the values of bourgeois monogamy, no matter what the price for the woman. At the same time, however, a feminine point of view on patriarchal dominance is clearly articulated, as the women frequently speak out against its rules and contradictions. In fact, the women in the film, especially Cynthia, the courageous and independently-minded aviator who falls in love with the happily married Chris, come to represent the contradictions of patriarchy, or as Suter puts it, "the feminine discourse enunciates the very problematic that the narrative must resolve." For the narrative to resolve itself on the side of monogamy, however, that value must first be challenged, then countered, and ultimately effaced. Thus Cynthia *must* express her desire because it has a crucial narrative function: it is only through the love he returns to Cynthia that Chris can understand and approve of his daughter's love for the man she intends to marry against his wishes. And it is only through Chris's transgressive affair with Cynthia that he and his wife are able to reaffirm their monogomous devotion to each other. Needless to say, it is only "logical" that Cynthia is conveniently eliminated at the end of the film by way of her suicide, under the cover of an attempt to set a world altitude record.

Suter's essay complicates the question of "the working through of [woman's] desire"[4] in classical film by showing that the preeminent desire here is not the woman's desire, but the film's desire to resolve itself, both formally and in terms of the issue of monogamy. This claim is quite close to the conclusion reached by Raymond Bellour in his textual analyses of Hitchcock's films (cited by Suter): the female character's desire, far from being repressed in the film, pervades the classical text and is crucial to that text's logic of enunciation. Such a thesis is clearly very pessimistic in that it forecloses any notion of a "progressive" classical film, progressive, that is, in terms of depicting a woman as the subject of desire. The problem for feminist film theory then lies in recognizing the power of the classical film to incorporate contradiction or rupture, insofar as these are *required* for its own narrative ends, while still refusing to see this institutional power as monolithic and therefore impervious to resistance. Several of the essays that I will discuss shortly (Bergstrom, Rose, Doane, Copjec) confront the apparently total determinism of the cinematic institution with the feminist need to argue for the possibility of resistance or change within that institution and its aesthetic forms.

Elizabeth Cowie's two-part essay on *Coma* ("The Popular Film as a Progressive Text") also speaks to the potential progressiveness of the Hollywood film. Like Cook, Johnston, and Suter, she chooses to discuss a film whose protagonist, Dr. Susan Wheeler, is a strong, independent woman, and asks whether *Coma* differs from the usual Hollywood product because it has such a protagonist. The interest of this article lies in the way it ranges widely over issues of narrative, genre, and identification, starting from an analysis of the way in which the critical/journalistic establishment received the film. Cowie finds a remarkable continuity of method between the trade and daily paper reviews of *Coma* and those published in film magazines. She shows that all of these reviews proceed by way of highly selective (and ultimately superficial) content readings: the film is "about" a strong, independent woman. She goes on to demonstrate, however, that this image of Susan Wheeler is ambiguously constructed. Although Wheeler exhibits intelligence and single-mindedness in investigating a series of mysterious deaths in her hospital, she does not in fact discover the answer (she even fails to recognize who the villain is) and in the end has to be rescued by her boyfriend as she is about to be killed. Cowie argues that this and other observations invite us to consider that the reviewers are responding to the "image" of the woman rather than to the film-as-process; that is, they are able to understand both Susan Wheeler and the film as "progressive" only insofar as they ignore the narrative strategies as a whole. For, like Cynthia's desire in *Christopher Strong*, Susan Wheeler's independent spirit functions only to help achieve a certain narrative strategy; in the film's generic shift from detective story (in which Wheeler is the intrepid investigator) to suspense thriller (in which she is the helpless victim), it is her initial independence which ultimately makes her the victim of the events she is investigating. To show that Susan Wheeler, as a character, is "strong," while as an active agent within the narrative she is "weak," is to put into question any notion of her role as a progressive one.

In the same vein, Cowie offers a useful criticism of the use of "recuperation" as a critical term by feminists. It is not that Hollywood has recuperated "our" progressive image of a strong, independent women (there is no such single, pre-given image, but many, variously contested, ideas about what a modern, feminist woman would be), it is rather that the images and meanings *produced* by the film "can be judged inadequate and unacceptable to the feminist political project."

Cowie then goes on to take up the difficult issue of identification, and this leads her to question two of the major models of cinematic identification, those of Laura Mulvey and Christian Metz, respectively. Just as she has presented a concise overview of narrative theory in order to bring a more sophisticated understanding of character and genre to the discussion of sexual difference in *Coma*, she now surveys theories of filmic point of view with the aim of providing a newer and more complex account of identification. For Cowie, "identification" is a problem of narrative. The viewer is implicated in the film, as it were, through what he or she can see and know of the action, a seeing and knowing that sometimes coincides with the vision and knowledge of the characters and sometimes not—to great effect in the machinations of suspense and horror. *Coma*'s mid-film genre shift—from, initially, a detective film in which knowledge is shared equally by protagonist and spectator, to a suspense thriller in which the spectator knows slightly more than the now victimized heroine—is crucial to the setting up of positions of identification. What is new in the way Cowie describes the various shifts of identification in the film is her theoretical insistence that *the gender of the character does not necessarily determine the viewer's identification*; as she succinctly puts it, "it doesn't matter here that it is a man or a woman." Cowie thus rejects a simple notion of identification as an appropriation of identity ("I wish to be her or him"), in which the viewer "identifies" with the image or the character as a sexed role.

But there is a second way in which Cowie transforms our understanding of identification, and here she takes on both Mulvey and Metz, for whom identification seems to be no more than a kind of molding or assimilation of the spectator to an ideology or at least a set of ideas. Their account of identification assumes that the viewer "loses" herself or himself in the process of viewing; the viewer identifies not with an image or character but an ideological content. Cowie argues that when film theorists—feminist or otherwise—have turned to psychoanalysis, and Lacan in particular, for an account of how the spectator is constituted as a subject for and by the film, they have often depicted that spectator as possessing a look that is already given, one that is already male. This is certainly the case with Mulvey, but Metz too seems to assume as much in his definition of the primary cinematic look as "oneself seeing oneself." In contrast, Cowie's model of identification involves a continual construction of looks, ceaselessly varied through the organization of the narrative and the work of narration. The value of such a model is that it leaves open the question of the production of sexual difference in the film rather than assuming in advance the sexuality of the character or spectator.[5]

If Cowie delineates a more complex picture of identification, it is because she is able to draw upon the semiological studies of narrative and point of view in the 1970s, and her essay provides an exceptionally detailed introduction to those studies. Similarly, in "Enunciation and Sexual Difference," Janet Bergstrom begins by offering a useful survey of the methods and aims of "textual analysis," as seen in the work of Roland Barthes and developed in film by Raymond Bellour, in order to demonstrate how filmic textual processes affect identification, especially in its relation to sexual difference. She then takes up Bellour's conclusion that each textual level of the film is characterized by a fundamental dissymmetry linked to the difference between the sexes. With the code of point of view, for example, Bellour argues that even when a woman appears to possess a privileged vision (as in the Bodega Bay sequence of *The Birds* where Melanie's immoderate desire is translated into precociousness of vision), one finds instead an intricately structured subversion of that privilege, in which the privilege is ultimately reassigned to the men in the film (including Hitchcock) as well as the men in the audience. Bellour points out that the woman's desire, as manifested in her look, must be given an initial emphasis *in order* for it to be appropriated by the male character or spectator. Bergstrom sees in Bellour's formulation an advance over Mulvey's model of identification in its stress on the desire "which speaks in [the woman's] look," rather than on her body as a scopic object or fetish. Showing how the woman participates in the logic of desire which structures the film helps to counter an idea of the woman as a merely passive recipient of the aggressive male look, thus bringing "identification" more in line with Freud's account of the complexity of the process.

Although Bergstrom credits Bellour with attempting to describe the difference between masculine and feminine identification (as Mulvey does not do), she finds his account to be somewhat over-simplified, at least in psychoanalytic terms. In her interview with him, Bellour says that he believes the woman spectator identifies entirely along the lines of her own masochism (Hollywood has so little to offer her otherwise), or according to a short-lived sadism exercised against the masculine subject, which is bound to backfire on her. Bergstrom demurs, holding our for "a play of identifications in classical film [that] allows for more possibilities than that." In "Enunciation and Sexual Difference," she goes on to describe this freer play of identifications by giving an example from one of Bellour's most favoured theoretical objects, *Psycho*. In his analyses, she says, Bellour seems to conceive of masculinity and femininity as oppositions, despite his insistence on the constant oscillation of the spectator between object choice and identification (similar to the active and passive scopophilia Mulvey describes). However, to posit such an oscillation depends on a belief in a theory of bisexual response, but neither Bellour nor Mulvey follow out the implications of this important Freudian idea even though the films they analyse often blur sexual categories or boundaries in a way that invites this kind of consideration. Thus in *Psycho*:

> Wouldn't Norman's scenario have to read something like this? When he meets Marion, it is as the son to an available woman. When he watches her in the shower, Norman is the son watching the mother (Marion), imagining himself as the mother's lover ("the imaginary and ungraspable relation of the primal scene"). When Norman, impersonating his mother, kills Marion, it is as the mother killing a rival for her son's affection. . . . Each shift necessitates corresponding changes in the imaginary identifications of the other characters in the scenario.

Bergstrom concludes by pointing out that such an oscillation of identification across sexual categories is not unique to psychosis (Norman's affliction), but is inherent in the very structure of fantasy, a suggestive idea that will be explored in detail in later essays in this collection.

In one of the first feminist critiques of semiological and psychoanalytic film theory, "Paranoia and the Film System" Jacqueline Rose had already examined the question of the presumed sexual dissymmetry in classical film's point of view system. In this important study of *The Birds*, written in part as a reply to Bellour's own article on the film, Rose wanted to suggest that textual theorists had too hastily assimilated the structure of classical film to an orthodox psychoanalytic description of the male's negotiation of the Oedipus complex, in other words, his "integration into the Symbolic through a successful Oedipal trajectory." When Rose points to Melanie Daniels's catatonic state at the end of *The Birds*, she does so in order to say something about the place of the woman in the Hitchcockian system, but also to emphasize the way contemporary film theory has understood and described that place. While agreeing with Bellour that *North by Northwest* (another film he had studied) exhibits perfectly the ideal Oedipal scenario for the male character, Rose objects to extending this same analysis to a film like *The Birds* in which the Oedipal narrative closure is not as clearly achieved as in the former film, and in which that closure depends on relegating the woman either to catatonia or infantile speechlessness. In Bellour's version—that is, in his answer to the question "Why do the birds attack Bodega Bay/Melanie?"—he argues that the birds, as representatives of the men in the film, and ultimately its director (as a figurative stand-in for all men in the culture), attack Melanie as a punishment for her sexual aggressiveness (bringing the love birds to Bodega Bay as part of a flirtation with Mitch). In Rose's reading of the film, however, the birds "emanate" from an inherent instability in the film's own system which releases an "aggressivity" that focuses around the woman, one that finally cannot be contained by the film. This systematic instability allows Mitch to "successfully" resolve his Oedipal task only at the cost of Melanie's sanity and sexuality.

Where does this aggressivity come from? For Rose, it originates in the point of view structure of the film, particularly in the system of shot/reverse-shots whose ubiquity in the film is a Hitchcockian signature. As we have seen, Bellour describes Melanie's motorboat trip out and back across Bodega Bay in order to show how her look appears to predominate, but is actually circumscribed and contained by the looks of the male characters (and Hitch-cock's, and the male spectator's). What seems to be symmetry is actually dissymmetry: women look only in order to be looked at while looking. But Rose adds another element to the shot/reverse-shot structure of Mitch and Melanie's specular reciprocity. She reminds us that the Lacanian description of the mirror-phase not only accounts for this kind of structure but also characterizes it as paranoid and aggressive. Because it is a specular image, cause and effect are reversible (the gull attacks Melanie because she brought the love birds to Bodega Bay), while the reciprocity of the structure provides for mutual aggression (the attacking birds are associated with *both* Mitch and Melanie). The birds then are not representatives of Mitch and the other men in the film but the *sign* of the aggressivity released by the filmic reproduction of the Imaginary in the shot/reverse-shot system. Rose argues that the aggressivity focuses around the woman because of her privileged relation to the Imaginary deriving from the strength of the pre-Oedipal bond between the mother and the girl.

An important point being made here, and one vital to subsequent feminist work, is that the "disruption" of the text is not the result of a feminine essence rubbing against the patriarchal grain of the film, but rather the conflation of two separate elements: a contradiction or lack in the textual system of the film itself (the aggressivity released by the miming of the Imaginary in the shot/reverse-shot structure) and the traits of the female character (Melanie's sexual forwardness). The significance of Rose's argument is that the woman *comes to represent* (through the textual work of the film) both the difficulty of sexual difference *and* the problems of cinema as a representational form. This question of how and why the woman in the film comes to bear such a heavy representational burden will constitute the focus of several later feminist readings of classical film.

Rose's complaint against Bellour's reading of *The Birds* is twofold. On the one hand, she questions his application of the psychoanalytic model to classical film—*The Birds* does not represent a smooth, Oedipal outcome for the man. On the other hand, she questions the psychoanalytic model itself, or rather Bellour's understanding of that model. His is not only a wishfulfilling version of psychoanalysis—one that assumes the possibility of a stable sexual identity, and thus a real "resolution" for the Oedipal male subject—but also a use of psychoanalysis that neglects the difficulties specific to feminine sexuality (for example, the greater strength of the girl's pre-Oedipal bond to the mother), and thus to related difficulties within the film (Melanie's final infantilization).

In a later article on *Psycho* ("Psychosis, Neurosis, Perversion"),[6] Bellour took the opportunity to reply to Rose, presenting his case in even stronger terms. He agrees that the reciprocity of looks in the alternation of shot/ reverse-shots evokes the "structure of the cinematographic apparatus, and thereby of the primitive apparatus it imitates, namely the mirror wherein the subject structures himself, through a mode of narcissistic identification of which aggressivity is an indelible component." However, he goes on to say that this imaginary structure can only be understood within the system in which it occurs, that is, Hitchcock's films in particular, or classical American cinema in general. In this system the aggressive element can never be separated from "the inflection it receives from sexual difference, and in the attribution of this difference to the signifier that governs it. In other words, it is directed from the man towards the woman, and that difference which appears due to woman is nothing but the mirror-effect of the narcissistic doubling that makes possible the constitution of the male subject through the woman's body" (pp. 118–9). To support his argument that cinema reduces femininity to the narcissistic mirroring of masculinity, Bellour takes up Luce Irigaray's similar observation about psychoanalysis, that it always collapses sexual difference into one, masculine sexuality. He therefore concludes that, in the American cinema, "the woman occupies a central place only to the extent that it's a place assigned to her by the logic of masculine desire."

Although Bellour's arguments are highly persuasive in their attention to textual evidence, feminist theorists nonetheless have a strong interest in maintaining that the classical narrative system is neither perfect nor infallible in its repression of the woman's desire. But this wish on their part, which is understandable, confronts them with a serious rhetorical obstacle. If feminist critics are to insist that the male privilege in classical film cannot be as totalizing as the textual theorists have contended, then they must meet head-on the warning that Freud in his "Dostoyevsky's knife" footnote in "Female Sexuality" issued to the defenders of women's interests: it is an argument that cuts both ways. That is, if feminists maintain that there is some masculine interest or prejudice at stake in the theoretical "fact" that female sexuality in the classical film serves only to mirror or be subsumed by that of the male, then opponents can say that this feminist objection is a natural one, that it has no basis other than an instinctive feminine refusal of a view that is unflattering to them. But it should be clear by now that there is more than wishful thinking at work behind the feminist counter-arguments on this issue. Feminists, for example, can point to the psychoanalytic thesis that all perfectly totalizing systems are basically defensive, aimed at denying or disavowing the knowledge of sexual difference and the threat of castration which it implies. As we shall see, Joan Copjec has presented a forceful reading of film theory exactly along these lines. Another approach, one put forward by Mary Ann Doane,[7] uses Michel Foucault's idea about repression to argue that there is no such thing as a perfectly repressive mechanism (for example, classical film or the filmic apparatus). If power is defined as a network of power *relations*, those relations are ceaselessly being contested. Femininity, as a position produced within those power relations, thus carries its own productive and positive charge; it can never be merely or simply repressed. Yet another approach to describing the "instability" of the classical system can be seen in Stephen Heath's important article which demonstrates the basic principles of textual analysis, "Film and System: Terms of Analysis."[8] While this essay adds considerably to the argument that classical film (the example here is *Touch of Evil*) aims toward achieving "homeostasis" through the resolution of all sexual and textual contradiction, Heath prefers to characterize this tendency as an illusionistic effect of the filmic economy rather than a fact of its textual organization. Following Barthes, he shows that there is always an excess that escapes the narrative system. This loss, moreover, is fundamental to that system because any attempt to recover it newly instigates and sustains the movement or narrative progress of the film.

The common problem posed by these essays, whether explicitly or implicitly, is that of acknowledging the determinism of the classical system and its seemingly perfect fit with the mechanisms of male fantasy, while recognizing where that system or those mechanisms necessarily founder. Again, this raises the question of how this can be done without falling back on an essentialist notion of feminity as the natural spoke in the wheels.

Mary Ann Doane's work presents a highly original critique of the theoretical assumption that classical film narrative, if not the entire cinematic apparatus, is geared toward male fascination and pleasure ("*Caught* and *Rebecca*: The Inscription of Femininity as Absence"). She takes as her counter-examples films like *Caught* and *Rebecca* that were made by the studios in the 1940s specifically for a female audience, in order to show that the standard theoretical model cannot fully account for films deliberately constructed for a female spectator. If Hollywood narratives, she asks, are analyzed simply as "compensatory structures designed to defend the male psyche against the threat offered by the image of the woman," and if classical cinema's appeal to male voyeurism or fetishism is infinite, then how are these "women's films" able to construct a position of female spectatorship (and how, theoretically, are we to make an argument for it)? Doane's approach differs from the feminist analyses of Hollywood film discussed above insofar as it is the first to examine systematically the spectator as an empirical subject: how does filmic identification function for *women*? Up to this point the theoretical emphasis has been either on the classical film's tendency to "masculinize" the spectator (Mulvey, Bellour) or the spectator's oscillation across a range of identificatory positions not determined in advance by the spectator's actual gender (Bergstrom, Cowie). Bergstrom had pointed out that Bellour is one of the few theorists to assume a difference in men's and women's responses to film, but the role he assigns the female spectator is a particularly bleak one, entirely circumscribed by her masochism in relation to the events occuring on the screen. Doane goes much further than Bellour in offering a detailed description of the specular and narrative possibilities for the female spectator, but it is significant that her conclusions are even more pessimistic than his.

Because Doane agrees with theorists like Mulvey and Bellour that the classical film is constructed with a male spectator in mind, and that in the Hollywood cinema, the "male protagonists [act] as relays in a complex process used to insure the ego-fortification of the male spectator," she stresses the classical film's difficulty in constructing a subject position based on female subjectivity and desire. Such a subject position is, in fact, so equivocal that the classical film becomes "hysterical." She goes on to qualify this characterization, however, by acknowledging the tendency of the woman's film to "disintegrate"—thus privileging the metaphor of paranoia as a more appropriate one to describe the symptomatic activity of films of this genre. Why do the films tend to disintegrate? Because they have been constructed to be the mirror image of the films described by Mulvey in which the centered spectator possesses a desiring look, a look that controls (or appears to control) the images and events taking place on the screen. But it is only through the most convoluted means that a woman can take up such a position. Citing Julia Kristeva's description of the double or triple twists of female homosexuality, Doane compares it to the position of the female spectator of these films: "I am looking, as a man would, for a woman"; or else, "I submit myself, as if I were a man who thought he was a woman, to a woman who thinks she is a man." Why is female looking so problematic in these films? When the woman looks, she, like the male spectator more typically, is given an objectified image of a woman to look at. In Ophul's *Caught* as well as in Hitchcock's *Rebecca*, the heroine is seen looking at idealized images of women in a fashion magazine. The narcissism in the film-text echoes the narcissistic relation of the female character to the screen. Unlike the male spectator, however, she cannot fetishize the image: lacking any distance from it, she has no choice but to become it. The woman in the film, like the woman in the audience, can look only at herself (or versions of herself). This desire to look is quickly transformed into a desire to be looked at. Significantly, though, the desire to be looked at is itself transformed into a paranoid fear of being looked at. This fear is strikingly presented in both *Caught* and *Rebecca* in two projection-room scenes in which the woman is confronted with the apparatus of the cinema, the apparatus which controls her image as well as her access to other images. It is almost as if the films are compelled to act out the difficulty or impossibility of constructing a position for a woman spectator.

Not only does Doane try to account for feminine identification in film, she also attempts to link the problem of the woman's sexual identity to that of her class position. Contributing to the paranoia that pervades the plots and point of view systems of these films is the horror and paranoia induced by the threat of crossing class boundaries, or mixing classes by marriage ("Model Nabs Millionaire!" is a headline in *Caught*).

Doane's conclusions about feminine identification in classical film sustain the pessimistic view that Hollywood's effects are relentlessly deterministic with respect to the woman's desire. As we have seen, her own analyses of the role of the female character as well as the female spectator are no more "positive" than those of the male theorists. Perhaps for this reason, in a later article included in this volume, "Woman's Stake: Filming the Female Body" she states her concern about the consequences of a kind of theoretical activity (presumably including her own) which inevitably leads to the conclusion that the woman is incapable of an autonomous representation or symbolization. Because contemporary film theory, feminist or otherwise, has so persuasively argued that classical film as well as the cinematic apparatus itself (apparatus as both "institution" and "technology") are implicated in a fantasy of sexual difference that privileges masculinity, it is increasingly difficult to imagine making films in which the woman's relation to desire and language might be figured differently. Doane fears that the strength of the feminist dedication to "deconstructing" every aspect of classical film and the cinematic apparatus will lead to a practice that defines itself only negatively. In attempting to demystify the "natural" feminine body or divest it of its patriarchally-imposed meanings, feminists risk eliminating any consideration of the feminine body. She cites the work of the experimental filmmaker, Peter Gidal, as an example of where this one-dimension extremist logic can lead: he refuses to include in his films any representation of a woman on the grounds that the perception of that image is too culturally rooted in an idea of her essential, biological difference. Doane believes that anti-essentialist feminists arrived at this theoretical dead-end by adhering too strictly to the psychoanalytic claim that there is only one libido, that this libido works in relation to lack, and that the symbolic representation of this lack is the phallus. The further claim is that sexuality is inextricable from discourse, and that a fundamental condition for entry into the world of language and the realm of the symbolic is a break in an initial plenitude. (Representation can only take place when something is missing.) Therefore, because a woman does not have a penis, the embodiment of the phallus and the signifier of lack, she cannot represent such a break to herself, and, theoretically, has no access to signification, to discourse. But as Doane says, "we know that women speak." To describe how it is that women speak, she argues that we must have a theory that rethinks the relation of language to the body. (She is concerned to point out, however, the advantage of retaining the psychoanalytic idea of the body as *fiction*: the fantasmatic body rather than a putatively natural one.)

Doane finds a more acceptable account of the relation of language to the body in Jean Laplanche's recently renovated version of the Freudian concept of anaclisis, which describes how the drives, which are sexual, emerge by "leaning" or "propping" themselves on the nonsexual or presexual instinct of self-preservation (the fantasmatic and eroticized breast, for example, is a displacement from the milk it gives to satisfy hunger). Although I will not attempt here to summarize Laplanche's very complex reformulation of anaclisis, it is important to understand how this model interests Doane. Rejecting what she sees as the psychoanalytic relegation of women to silence and the inability to represent, she takes up the theoretical cause of anaclisis to "provide the woman with an autonomous symbolic representation," that is, to try to account not only for the fact that women speak, but to describe *how* it is that they speak. In the same vein she takes up the work of Luce Irigaray, who because of her modeling of language on the shapes and forms of the female body, is one of the anti-essentialists' most frequent targets. Doane's brief defense of Irigaray invites comparison with the much longer and equally sympathetic consideration given her work by Meaghan Morris.[9] Morris describes Irigaray's work as a *rhetoric*, an attempt to invent a new imaginary of the body which would allow women to speak the difference of their bodies and sexualities which has been suppressed by the discourses of philosophy, psychoanalysis, and the social sciences. Although Irigaray's "This Sex Which Is Not One" is often described as an attempt to make women's language mimic the form of the female sex, Morris insists that Irigaray's famous image of the two lips (two labia) is not presented "as a form discovered in nature which is appropriate to an existing female language" (pp. 87–88) but is rather a polemically constructed metaphor, one which would be *productive* rather than *mimetic*.

Doane recognizes the risk taken by theories which attempt to define or construct a feminine specificity ("not essence") because patriarchy, after all, has ceaselessly constructed its own metaphors of the feminine body. She believes, however, that this risk must be taken in order to give a theoretical account of the feminine body and to articulate a new syntax of this body for film. Following Kristeva in her claim that it is possible to generate a discourse only by first positing a body, Doane goes on to discuss several experimental films made by women that attempt just such a theoretical elaboration of the woman's body, films that "'lean' on the body in order to formulate the woman's different relation to speech, to language." She argues that films like *Thriller, Jeanne Dielman, Riddles of the Sphinx* and *The Story of Anna O.* radically refigure the terms of the female body.

In an essay whose rhetorical force matches the complexity of its argument, Joan Copjec also insists that film theory has excluded or failed to theorize the body, specifically the woman's body. In *"India Song/Son nom de Venise dans Calcutta désert*: The Compulsion to Repeat," she offers one of the most sustained feminist critiques of a widely accepted film theoretical model—the "filmic apparatus." Suggestively comparing French film theory with American speech act theory, she demonstrates their common failings, in particular their inability to deal with anything that falls outside their carefully constructed systems. Copjec gives credit to Metz, Baudry, and Bellour for turning film theory away from the investigation of film as a reproduction of reality to one which construes film as an event that produces a subject. She argues, nevertheless, that this important theoretical exclusion of the "profilmic" and the new emphasis on film as enunciative system tended to eliminate any consideration of the woman in that system. She compares the shift in film theory from an emphasis on film as reproduction to film as event with a similar move in linguistic theory from an attention to the linguistic object to an investigation of the speech event. In speech act theory the "performative" utterance perfectly exemplifies how speech functions as action or event. Saying "I do" in the context of a wedding ceremony is both a statement and the accomplishment of an action. The question of context is important here because a performative is an utterance whose meaning depends upon its being intentionally, appropriately, and consistently repeated. The example also shows that an utterance cannot be considered true or false, "because it can only be true, that is, according to the laws of logic, identical with itself." Copjec sees a strikingly similar emphasis on identity and sameness in the apparatus theories, theories equally marked, she says, by a "compulsion to repeat." Baudry, for example, describes cinema as an apparatus which returns the subject to an earlier, infantile state in which satisfaction can be hallucinated. For Metz, the cinema is a true institution (apparatus in a larger sense) because, like all institutions, it takes charge of the mechanisms of its own reproduction: the cinematic apparatus gives us not only films but also the very desire to go to the cinema. And at the level of narrative-as-apparatus, Bellour argues that the classical narrative system resolves its contradictions through differentially repeating them, in what he calls the "repetition-resolution effect." In all of these versions of the apparatus theory, the repetition of the same is fully understood in a psychoanalytic sense. But Copjec points out that the psychoanalytic definition of repetition favored by these theorists, repetition as mastery or as a path to satisfaction, is one forcefully rejected by Freud in his later writings. In "Beyond the Pleasure Principle" psychoanalysis moved beyond its early understanding of repetition as restitution or reproduction of a lost object. As Freud observed of his nephew's fort/da game, mastery of the mother's absence is secondary to the primary feat of replaying the loss itself, of "returning to the ever-open gap introduced by the absence," an activity that situates itself beyond the pleasure principle in its suggestion that pleasure is not always a priority in the unconscious. The problem with the apparatus theories then lies in the assumption that the apparatus actually satisfies the subject's demand, that the apparatus always successfully accomplishes what it aims to do. (Copjec adds that a further problem with this theoretical position is that it anthropomorphizes the apparatus by ascribing to it an *intention*.) Copjec is one of the few feminists writing about film to cite the work of Derrida, and here she introduces his reading of Freudian repetition ("Freud and the Scene of Writing") to show that the apparatus is most flawed in its emphasis on the sufficiency of the subject, thereby losing the sense of radical insufficiency given it by the later Freud. Simply put, there is no room in this perfectly functioning homeostatic system for a *difference*. The apparatus theories work well to describe the structures of point of view, voyeurism, exhibitionism, and identification, as long as those structures are, repeatedly, male, but cannot account for that difference, the woman, the body, or that which is outside.

Like Doane, Copjec argues that it is not the body, but a *relation* to the body, that must be introduced into film theory. She too argues that the extreme anti-essentialist position, in which soma and psyche run parallel, excludes such a relation to the body. Again citing Derrida, she argues that it is important to understand representation not as a matter of either language or the body alone but of the "otherness" of each to the other. In a companion article, "The Anxiety of the Influencing Machine,"[10] written shortly after "The Compulsion to Repeat" but not reprinted here, Copjec further comments on the tendency of the apparatus theories to close themselves off to difference. She suggests that the theory of the suture, introduced into film theory from psychoanalysis, which sees subjects as a linguistic construction, can counter this tendency inasmuch as representation is seen as an effect of a displacement, a deviation which entails an irretrievable loss. All subjects, male and female, are produced in language. "Language," however, is not seen as a monolithic structure, patriarchal or otherwise, but as a set of particular discourses inscribing the categories of sexual difference. As Copjec takes up these terms, masculinity and femininity are ensembles of multiple effects rather than unified opposing fields. Unlike Doane, however, who urged that the model of anaclisis, or "propping" on the body, be adopted as a substitute for the relation to the phallus in order to describe the specificity of feminine sexuality, Copjec argues that the concept of castration should not be discarded because it "allows the analysis of the radical *constitution* of difference" (p. 58).

In a move typical of the essays in this collection, Copjec chooses to elaborate her argument in a discussion of an experimental film made by a woman. To counter what she sees as the tendency toward repetition and closure in both classical film and the theories of classical film, she offers a reading of Marguerite Duras's "remake" of *India Song, Son nom de Venise dans Calcutta désert*, a film that exposes the workings of the repetition compulsion. Duras's "remake" (a repetition *par excellence*) consists of the soundtrack of *India Song* played over images of the deserted ruin of the former set. The only "action" in the film is that which occurs in the viewer's fantasmatic reconstruction of *India Song*, an *India Song* now marked by loss and death in the absence of an anchoring referent for the voices heard on the soundtrack. The film is concerned with repetition, then, but only in relation to the "otherness" equally inscribed there. For Copjec, this resistance to closure in both *India Song* and its "remake" is best seen in the way the voices are not tethered to the images and in the way the mirror, a central element of the decor, not only reflects but becomes an active agent, even a transgressor. As a result, *Son nom de Venise . . .* is not a "film of illusionary effects, but of the lost causes of repetition."

This same impulse to take up a film that both elucidates and questions the way film theory has drawn upon psychoanalytic ideas had already led Elisabeth Lyon to the work of Marguerite Duras. In "The Cinema of Lol V. Stein," *India Song* is presented as a film which "proposes to us a reading of psychoanalytic theory." Lyon insists, however, that neither the film nor her reading of it is intended as a "corrective" to psychoanalysis; rather, the film "takes up and interrogate[s] within the terms of psychoanalytic theory . . . the question of desire." But if her reading of the film is not intended as a corrective, it is at least an extension of psychoanalysis inasmuch as the film accomplishes something that psychoanalytical film theory claims that women cannot do: represent the lack that is the precondition of all symbolic activity. Nonetheless (again to cite Doane's words), "we know that women speak," and in *India Song* what is spoken or represented is precisely the woman's relation to lack. The film's deployment of off-screen voices and their ambivalent and impossible desiring relation to the inaccessible image of Anne-Marie Stretter—a woman who, the film tells us, is already dead—stages a representation that is fundamentally about loss and distance. In enacting a fantasy of loss and distance, then, the film also enacts a fantasy of desire, a desire that cannot be satisfied, and is ultimately a desire for an unsatisfied desire. As "the mise en scène of this impossibility," *India Song* thus leaves open the question of desire, and of a feminine position in relation to it, refusing, in contrast to classical film, to "answer" that question with an assured definition of both masculine and feminine desire, and of desire itself.

Like several of the essays here, "The Cinema of Lol V. Stein" chooses to introduce the issue of the body and of feminine desire through a discussion of the structure of fantasy. This choice represents a deliberate shift from the model of voyeurism and fetishism which dominated both film theory and earlier feminist analyses of film. In that work, voyeurism was almost always taken up in terms of the active male look onto the passive and receptive woman's body. Fetishism was seen in terms of the scenario described by Freud in which the little boy looks at his mother's body and, notwithstanding his perception that she has no penis, avows that it is there nonetheless. The structure of fantasy, however, is far more complex and flexible in its disposition of masculine and feminine roles, active and passive drives. In Freud's analysis of a beating fantasy reported to him primarily by female patients, "A Child Is Being Beaten,"[11] the emphasis is on the multiple and successive identificatory positions taken up by the host of the fantasy. The progressive stages of the fantasy are revealed by the patient only slowly and reluctantly. At first she simply reports having a fantasy that "a child is being beaten." Next she says that it appears that "my father is beating the child," then "behind" that scenario is a more masochistic one consisting of "I am being beaten by my father." Finally, she reveals that "I am probably looking on." As Freud puts it, the situation of being beaten, "which was originally simple and monotonous" ["a child is being beaten"] may go through the most complicated alternations and elaborations" (p. 186). During the three stages of this fantasy, then, the woman identifies, respectively with the adult doing the beating, the child being beaten, and with herself as a spectator viewing the beating. She can thus be both subject or object, or identify with the entire scene itself. As a model for understanding identification in relation to sexual difference, the feminist interest in this structure of fantasy lies in the fact that such a model does not dictate in advance what "masculine" or "feminine" identification would be or how an actual spectator might take up any of the possible positions. Several new questions can be raised by acknowledging the complexity of the process of identification for both men and women. What, for example, would feminine voyeurism or fetishism be? What is the role of masochism in the male spectator's relation to the film? Do we have any examples of such identificatory configurations in classical or experimental film? Such questions will doubtless receive a great deal of attention in the near future.

What are other future areas of work or interest for the kind of feminist film theory represented in this volume? In a very brief and necessarily suggestive way, I would like to mention two. First, there is the recent attempt to historicize or contextualize the major working concepts of contemporary film theory, such as the apparatus, enunciation, the cinematic subject, sexual difference, and the imaginary and symbolic orders. An early indication of this historicizing impulse can be seen in this volume in Mary Ann Doane's work on the female spectator of the woman's films of the 1940s. The second area of interest is popular culture. Because of the increasing effects the media have on our daily lives in shaping our ideas of what constitutes the social, the personal, and the political, there is a new sense of urgency among feminists to understand how those everyday effects bear on the unconscious and social construction of femininity. The ideas and methods developed by feminist film theory over the last decade—as seen in these pages—have begun to make a unique and forceful contribution to the study of the forms of mass culture. It is not, of course, a matter of "applying" film theory to the analysis of television or advertising, for example, since a great deal of valuable theoretical work has already been done in the field of popular culture studies. The aim would rather be to supplement the study of mass culture with the feminist understanding of identification, subjectivity, and sexual difference illuminated by the essays in this volume.

As this manuscript was going to press the news came of Claire Johnston's tragic death. I hope that *Feminism and Film Theory* can serve as a fitting memorial to the intelligence and political verve Claire brought to all her projects. To understand just how precious her work has been to feminist writing on film, one has only to read through the essays collected here, both her own essays and those of others who have built upon her work, and then ask: "Where would we have been without her?" Sadly, we are without her now.

Notes

1.   The most important of these textual analyses include Raymond Bellour's "*Les Oiseaux*: analyse d'une séquence," *Cahiers du Cinéma* no. 219 (1969); translated as "*The Birds*: Analysis of a Sequence," available in mimeographed form from The British Film Institute, Educational Advisory Service; "Le Blocage symbolique" (on *North by Northwest*), *Psychanalyse et Cinéma*, special issue of *Communications* no. 23 (1975); "Hitchcock, the Enunciator" (on *Marnie*), *Camera Obscura* no. 2 (Fall 1977); "Psychosis, Neurosis, Perversion" (on *Psycho*), *Camera Obscura* no. 3–4 (Summer 1979); and Stephen Heath's "Film and System: Terms of Analysis," Part I, *Screen* 16, no. 1 (Spring 1975); Part II, *Screen* 16, no. 2 (Summer 1975).

2.   There has been a great deal of feminist discussion and critique of the idea of woman as an "empty" sign exchanged by men. See, for example, Elizabeth Cowie, "Woman as Sign," *m/f* no. 1 (1978).

3.   For one important rethinking of Mulvey's model of identification, see "The Difficulty of Difference," D. N. Rodowick, *Wide Angle 5*, no. 1 (1982).

4.   Claire Johnston, "Women's Cinema as Counter-Cinema," in *Notes on Women's Cinema*, *Screen* Pamphlet 2 (London: SEFT, 1973).

5.   For another important feminist critique of Metz's use of psychoanalytic concepts like "the imaginary," and "identification," see Jacqueline Rose, "The Imaginary," in *Sexuality in the Field of Vision* (London: Verso, 1986), pp. 194–97.

6.   See note 1 for reference.

7. Mary Ann Doane, "Film and the Masquerade—Theorising the Female Spectator," *Screen* 23, nos. 3–4 (Sept.–Oct. 1982): 29.

8. See note 1 for reference.

9. Meaghan Morris, "A-Mazing Grace: Notes on Mary Daly's Poetics," *Intervention* 16.

10. Joan Copjec, "The Anxiety of the Influencing Machine," *October* 23 (Winter 1982).

11. Sigmund Freud, "'A Child Is Being Beaten': A Contribution to the Study of the Origin of Sexual Perversions," *The Standard Edition of the Complete Psychological Works of Sigmund Freud*, vol. 17, ed. and trans. James Strachey (London: The Hogarth Press, 1958), pp. 179–204.

1

The Place of Woman in the Cinema of Raoul Walsh

Pam Cook and Claire Johnston

The following analysis of the place of women in some of Raoul Walsh's films relies on concepts borrowed from the psychoanalyst Jacques Lacan, whose work constitutes a radical re-reading of Freud. The basis of that reading is the insight that Freud thought his theory of the unconscious in terms of a conceptual apparatus which he forged in the face of pre-Saussurian linguistics, anticipating the discoveries of modern linguistics. Lacan therefore proceeds to a re-reading of Freud's theory of the light of concepts produced by and for structural linguistics. This obviously involves the rejection of the vast bulk of post-Freudian psycho-analysis. Now that it has become clear that Freud conceived the unconscious as being structured like a language, any decipherment of the discourse of the unconscious must abandon all the unfortunately widespread misconceptions regarding the reading—i.e., selection—of "symptoms" and of the kind of sexual "symbolism" propagated by Jung.

> J. Lacan distinguishes the *Symbolic* from the *Imaginary* and the *Real*. The Imaginary relationship with the other occurs in a dual situation which is primarily narcissistic. Aggressiveness and identification with the image of the other predominate at this stage. The *Symbolic* element is one that intervenes to break up an Imaginary relationship from which there is no way out. The child meets the "third element" upon birth; he enters a world ordered by a culture, law, and language, and is enveloped in that Symbolic order. Finally, Lacan distinguishes the *Other*, the locus from which the code emanates, from the Imaginary *other*. (M. Mannoni, *The Child, his 'Illness' and the Others*, London, 1970, p. 23n)

The Other, as the locus of the Law (e.g., the law of the prohibition of incest), as the Word (i.e., the signifier as unit of the code) is the "Name-of-the-Father" around which the Symbolic order is constructed. The child, or indeed, any human being, as a subject of desire is constituted from the place of the Other: his "I" is a signifier in someone else's discourse and he has to find out how and where "I" fits into the social universe he discovers.

It has often been argued that there are a number of films directed by Raoul Walsh which appear to present women as strong and independent characters. The authors of the following essay take issue with this type of reading and attempt to demonstrate that women (e.g., Mamie Stover) in fact function as a signifier in a circuit of exchange where the values exchanged have been fixed by/in a patriarchal culture. Although Lévi-Strauss pointed out that real women, as producers of signs, could never be reduced to the status of mere tokens of exchange, i.e. to mere signs, the authors argue that, in films, the use of images of women and the way their "I" is constituted in Walshian texts play a subtle game of duplicity: in the tradition of classic cinema and 19th-century realism, the characters are presented as "autonomous individuals"; but the construction of the discourse contradicts this convention by reducing these "real" women to images and tokens functioning in a circuit of signs the values of which have been determined by and for men. In this way, the authors are attempting to help lay the foundations of a feminist film criticism as well as producing an analysis of a number of films directed by Walsh.

Between 1956 and 1957 Raoul Walsh made three films which center around the social, cultural and sexual definition of women. At first sight, the role of woman within these films appears a "positive" one; they display a great independence of spirit, and contrast sharply with the apparent "weakness" of the male protagonists. The first film in this cycle depicts a woman occupying the central function in the narrative; the Jane Russell vehicle, *The Revolt of Mamie Stover*, tells the story of a bar-room hostess's attempts to buck the system and acquire wealth and social status within patriarchy. *The King and Four Queens*, made the same year, depicts five women who hide out in a burnt-out ghost town to guard hidden gold. *Band of Angels*, made the following year, tells the story of a Southern heiress who suddenly finds herself sold into slavery at the time of the American Civil War. Walsh prefigured the problematic of the independent woman before this period, most notably in a series of films he made in the 1940s, some of which starred the actress Ida Lupino, who later became one of the few women film-makers to work in Hollywood: *They Drive by Night*, *High Sierra* and *The Man I Love*. However, undoubtedly the most useful films for providing a reference point for this cycle are *Manpower* (1941) and *The Bowery* (1933); in these films, Walsh celebrates the ethic of the all-male group, and outlines the role which women are designated to play within it. Walsh depicts the male hero as being trapped and pinned down by some hidden event in his past. In order to become the Subject of Desire he must test the Law through transgression. To gain self-knowledge and to give meaning to memories of the past, he is impelled towards the primal scene and to the acceptance of a symbolic castration. For the male hero the female protagonist becomes an agent within the text of the film whereby his hidden secret can be brought to light for it is in woman that his "lack" is located. She represents at one and the same time the distant memory of maternal plenitude and the fetishized object of his phantasy of castration—a phallic replacement and thus a threat. In *Manpower* Walsh depicts an all-male universe verging on infantilism—the camaraderie of the fire-fighters from the "Ministry of Power and Light." Sexual relationships and female sexuality are repressed within the film, and Marlene Dietrich is depicted as only having an existence within the discourse of men: she is "spoken," she does not speak. As an object of exchange between men, a sign oscillating between the images of prostitute and mother-figure, she represents the means by which men express their relationships with each other, the means through which they come to understand themselves and each other. *The Bowery* presents a similar all-male society, this time based totally on internal all-male rivalry; within this highly ritualized system the women ("the skirts") assume the function of symbols of this rivalry. Whatever the "positive" attributes assigned to them through characterization, woman as sign remains a function, a token of exchange in this patriarchal order. Paul Willemen in his article on *Pursued* describes the role of the female protagonist Teresa Wright/Thorley as the "specular image" of the male protagonist Robert Mitchum/Jeb: she is the place where he deposits his words in a desire to "know" himself through her.

In her book *Psychoanalysis and Feminism* Juliet Mitchell, citing Lévi-Strauss, characterizes a system where women are objects for exchange as essentially a communications system.

> The act of exchange holds a society together; the rules of kinship (like those of language to which they are near-allied) are the society. Whatever the nature of the society—patriarchal, matrilineal, patrilineal, etc.—it is always men who exchange women. Women thus become the equivalent of a sign which is being communicated.

In Walsh's oeuvre, woman is not only a sign in a system of exchange, but an empty sign. (The major exception in this respect is Mamie Stover, who seeks to transform her status as object for exchange precisely by compounding a highly articulated, fetishized image for herself.) The male protagonist's castration fears, his search for self-knowledge all converge on woman: it is in her that he is finally faced with the recognition of "lack." Woman is therefore the locus of emptiness: she is a sign which is defined negatively: something that is missing which must be located so that the narcissistic aim of the male protagonist can be achieved. The narrative structure of *Band of Angels* is particularly interesting in the light of this model. The first half of the story is concerned with events in Manty/Yvonne de Carlo's life which reduce her from the position of a lady to that of a slave to be auctioned in the slave market. Almost exactly half way through the story—at the "center" of the film—Clark Gable appears and takes possession of her: from that moment the unfolding of his "dark secret" takes precedence. It becomes clear that Manty/Yvonne de Carlo's story was merely a device to bring into play the background (the slave trade, crumbling Southern capitalism) against which the "real" drama is to take place. Manty/Yvonne de Carlo is created in Clark Gable's image: half black and half white, she signifies the lost secret which must be found in order to resolve the relationship between Clark Gable and Sidney Poitier—the "naturalization" of the slave trade.

One of the most interesting aspects of this *mise-en-scène* of exchange in which woman as sign is located is the way Walsh relates it directly and explicitly to the circulation of money within the text of the film. Marx states that under capitalism the exchange value of commodities is their inherent monetary property and that in turn money achieves a social existence quite apart from all commodities and their natural mode of existence. The circulation of money and its abstraction as a sign in a system of exchange serves as a mirror image for woman as sign in a system of exchange. However, in Walsh's universe, women do not have access to the circulation of money: Mamie Stover's attempt to gain access to it takes place at a time of national emergency, the bombing of Pearl Harbor, when all the men are away fighting—it is described as "theft." As a system, the circulation of money embodies phallic power and the right of possession; it is a system by which women are controlled. In *Band of Angels* Manty/Yvonne de Carlo is reduced to a chattel and exchanged for money on the slave market; she is exchanged for money because of her father's "dark secret" and because of his debt. In *The King and Four Queens* the women guard the gold but they cannot gain access to it directly. Its phallic power lies hidden in the grave of a dead husband, surrounded by sterility and devastation. Clark Gable gains access to it by asserting his right of possession by means of tossing a gold coin in the air and shooting a bullet through the middle of it, a trick which the absent males of the family all knew: the mark of the right of possession. The ticket system in *The Revolt of Mamie Stover* takes the analogy between money and women one stage further: men buy tickets at "The Bungalow" and at the same time they buy an image of woman. It is the symbolic expression of the right men have to control women within their imaginary system. This link between money and phallic power assumes its most striking image in Walsh's oeuvre when Jane Russell/Mamie, having accumulated considerable savings as a bar hostess in Pearl Harbor, declares her love for Richard Egan/Jimmy by asking

The Revolt of Mamie Stover (Raoul Walsh, 1956)

him if she can place these savings in his safety deposit box at the bank: "there's nothing closer between friends than money." Recognizing the significance of such a proposition, he refuses.

The Revolt of Mamie Stover is the only one of these films in which the female protagonist represents the central organizing principle of the text. As the adventuress *par excellence* she is impelled to test and transgress the Law in the same way that all Walsh's heroes do: she would seem to function at first sight in a similar way to her male counterpart, the adventurer, within the narrative structure. But as the film reveals, her relationship to the Law is radically different. Her drive is not to test and transgress the Law as a means towards understanding a hidden secret within her past, but to transgress the forms of representation governing the classic cinema itself, which imprison her forever within an image. As the credits of the film appear on the screen, Jane Russell looks into the camera with defiance, before turning her back on America and walking off to a new life in Pearl Harbor. This look, itself a transgression of one of the classic rules of cinematography (i.e., "don't look into the camera"), serves as a reference point for what is to follow. Asserting herself as the subject rather than the object of desire, this look into the camera represents a reaching out beyond the diegetic space of the film and the myths of representation which entrap her. The central contradiction of her situation is that she can only attempt to assert herself as subject through the exploitation of a fetishized image of woman to be exchanged within the circulation of money; her independence and her desire for social and economic status all hinge on this objectification. The forms of representation generated by the classic cinema—the myths of woman as pin-up, vamp, "Mississippi Cinderella"—are the only means by which she can achieve the objective of becoming the subject rather than the object of desire. The futility of this enterprise is highlighted at the end of the film when she returns once more to America in a similar sequence of shots; this time she no longer looks towards the camera, but remains trapped within the diegetic space which the film has allotted to her.

The film opens with a long-shot of a neon-lit city at night. Red letters appear on the screen telling us the time and place: SAN FRANCISCO 1941. *The Revolt of Mamie Stover* was made in 1956—the story is therefore set within the living memory/history of the spectator. This title is the first indication that the film will reactivate the memory of an anxiogenic situation: the traumatic moment of the attack on Pearl Harbor and the entry of the United States into the Second World War. Simultaneously, on the sound band, sleazy night-club music swells up (clip-joints, predatory prostitution, female sexuality exchanged for money at a time when the country, its male population and its financial resources are about to be put at risk). A police car (one of the many representations of the Law in the film), its siren wailing insistently over the music (a further indication of imminent danger), drives fast onto a dockside where a ship is waiting. As it draws up alongside the ship, a female figure carrying a coat and a small suitcase gets out of the car and appears to turn back to look at the city from which she has obviously been expelled in a hurry. Jane Russell then looks straight into the camera (see the preceding page).

Up to this point the text has been multiply coded to signify danger/threat. The threat is closely associated with sexuality—besides the music, the red letters on the screen indicate red for danger and red for sex. Paul Willemen has pointed out that the "look" in *Pursued* is a threatening object: the *Cahiers du Cinéma* analysis of *Young Mr. Lincoln* also delineates Henry Fonda/ Lincoln's "castrating stare" as having the same threatening significance. Besides this threatening "look" Jane Russell has other dangerous connotations: qualities of aggression, of preying on the male to attain her own ends. Her "look"—repeated many times during the film, directed towards men, and explicitly described at one point as "come hither"—doubly marks her as signifier of threat. In the absence of the male, the female might "take his place": at the moment of Jane Russell's "look" at the camera, the spectator is directly confronted with the image of that threat. The fact that this image has been expelled from a previous situation is also important. Jane Russell actually represents the repudiated idea: she *is* that idea. Thus the threat is simultaneously recognized and recuperated: the female cannot "take the place" of the male; she can only be "in his place"—his mirror image—the "you" which is the "I" in another place.

This moment of dual fascination between the spectator and Jane Russell is broken by the intervention of a third organizing principle representing the narrative, as the titles in red letters "Jane Russell Richard Egan" appear over the female figure. The title has the effect of immediately distancing the spectator: it reminds him of the symbolic role of the narrative by locating Jane Russell as an imaginary figure. In psychoanalytic terms the concept "imaginary" is more complex than the word would immediately seem to imply. It is a concept central to the Lacanian formulation of the "mirror stage" in which the "other" is apprehended as the "other which is me," i.e., my mirror image. In the imaginary relationship the other is seen in terms of resemblance to oneself. As an imaginary figure in the text of the film Jane Russell's "masculine" attributes are emphasized: square jaw, broad shoulders, narrow hips, swinging, almost swashbuckling walk—"phallic" attributes which are echoed and re-echoed in the text; for example, in her aggressive language— she tells a wolf-whistling soldier to "go mend your rifle, soldier"; when Richard Egan/Jimmy fights Michael Pate/Atkins at the Country Club she shouts "give him one for me, Jimmy." The girls at "The Bungalow" hail her as "Abe Lincoln Stover." Jane Russell/Mamie is the imaginary *counterpart* of the absent spectator and the absent subject of the text: the mirror image they have mutually constructed and in whom both images converge and overlap.

Again, borrowing from Lacan, the function of the "Symbolic" is to intervene in the imaginary situation and to integrate the subject into the Symbolic Order (which is ultimately the Law, the Name of the Father). The narrative of *The Revolt of Mamie Stover*, in that it presents a particular model of the world historically, culturally and ideologically overdetermined, could be said to perform a symbolic function for the absent spectator. The anxiety-generating displacement—Jane Russell/Mamie—appears to threaten the narrative at certain points. For example, after having promised to marry Richard Egan/Jimmy, give up her job at "The Bungalow" and become "exclusively his," and having taken his ring in a symbolic exchange which is "almost like the real thing" and "makes it legal," Jane Russell/Mamie leaves her man at the army camp and returns to "The Bungalow" to resign. However, she is persuaded by Agnes Moorehead/Bertha Parchman to continue working there, now that Michael Pate/Atkins has gone (been expelled), for a bigger share of the profits and more power. Richard Egan/Jimmy is absent, so he won't know. His absence is important: it recalls another sequence earlier in the narrative which shows in a quick succession of shots Richard Egan/Jimmy and the army away at war while Jane Russell/Mamie is at the same moment buying up all the available property on the island, becoming "Sto-Mame Company Incorporated" with Uncle Sam as her biggest tenant. Jane Russell/Mamie makes her biggest strides in the absence of men: she threatens to take over the power of exchange. By promising to marry and give it all up, she is reintegrated into an order where she no longer represents that threat. Richard Egan/Jimmy can be seen as the representative of the absent spectator and absent subject of the discourse in this structure: they are mutual constructors of the text—he is a writer who is constantly trying to write Jane Russell/Mamie's story for her. When Jane Russell/Mamie goes back to work at "The Bungalow" she in effect negates his image of her in favor of an image which suggests destruction and purging—"Flaming Mamie"—and becomes again a threatening displacement, reproduced and enlarged 7 foot high. When Richard Egan/Jimmy is confronted with this threatening image at the army camp, when a soldier shows him a photograph of her, a bomb drops and he is wounded. In the face of this renewed threat he returns to "The Bungalow" and in his final speech to Jane Russell/Mamie repudiates her as his imaginary counterpart. The narcissistic fascination with her is ended; he realizes he can no longer control her image.

The symbolic level of the narrative in maintaining its order in the face of a threat is reasserted in the final sequence where the policeman at the dockside re-echoes Richard Egan/Jimmy's words of rejection: "Nothing's changed, Mamie. You aren't welcome here." Jane Russell/Mamie replies that she is going home to Leesburg, Mississippi (this is what Richard Egan/Jimmy was always telling her she must do). When the policeman remarks that she does not seem to have done too well, she replies: "If I told you I had made a fortune and given it all away, would you believe me?" When he says "No," she replies "I thought so." This exchange contains a final assertion that the protagonist cannot write her own story: she is a signifier, an object of exchange in a play of desire between the absent subject and object of the discourse. She remains "spoken": she does not speak. The final rhetorical question seals her defeat.

On the plane of the image, the symbolic order is maintained by an incessant production, within the text, of images for and of Jane Russell/ Mamie from which she is unable to escape, and with which she complies through a *mise-en-scène* of exchange. In order to become the subject of desire, she is compelled to be the object of desire, and the images she "chooses" remain locked within the myths of representation governed by patriarchy. This *mise-en-scène* of exchange is initiated by her expulson by the police at the dockside—the image of predatory whore is established. This image is elaborated during the next scene when the ship's steward tells Richard Egan/Jimmy about her reputation as sexual predator ("she ain't no lady"). Mamie interrupts the conversation, and realizing that Richard Egan/Jimmy as a scriptwriter in Hollywood is interested in her, she suggests he should write and buy her story—the hard-luck story of a "Mississippi Cinderella." Growing emotional involvement with him leads her to reject the idea of being "written" in favor of "writing" her own story, and to seek out an image more consistent with the wealthy "hilltop" milieu of which Richard Egan/Jimmy is part, epitomized by Jimmy's girlfriend ("Miss Hilltop"). Jane Russell/Mamie asks Richard Egan/Jimmy to "dress her up and teach her how to behave"; he refuses. Their relationship from then on is characterized as one of transgression: they "dance without tickets" at the country club, away from the "four don'ts" of "The Bungalow." For her image as a performer and hostess at "The Bungalow" Jane Russell/Mamie has dyed her hair red and has assumed the name of "Flaming Mamie" ("Mamie's not beer or whisky, she's champagne only"). The image of "Flaming Mamie" is at one and the same time an assertion and a negation of female sexuality; sexually arousing ("Fellas who try to resist should hire a psychiatrist" intones the song) but at the same time the locus of sexual taboo ("Keep the eyes on the hands" she says in another number—they tell the story). It is at "The Bungalow" that the ticket system formalizes this *mise-en-scène* of exchange; men literally buy an image for a predetermined period of time. (It is this concept of exchange of images which Jane Russell/Mamie finally discards when she throws the ticket away as she leaves the boat at the end of the film.) Reduced once again to the image of a common prostitute when they go dancing at the country club and having decided to stay at "The Bungalow" in spite of Richard Egan/Jimmy, she finally assumes the iconography of the pin-up, with the "come hither" look; an image emptied of all personality or individuality; an image based on the effects of pure gesture. This image was prefigured in an extraordinary sequence at the beach when Jane Russell/Mamie jumps up from the sand where she has been sitting with Richard Egan/Jimmy in order to take a swim. As she does so, she turns back to look at him and her image becomes frozen into the vacant grin of a bathing suit advertisement. Talking about money, Jane Russell/Mamie describes herself at one point as a "have not"; this recurrent imbrication of images, the telling of story within a story which the film generates through a *mise-en-scène* of exchange, serves to repress the idea of female sexuality and to encase Jane Russell/Mamie within the symbolic order, the Law of the Father.

Walsh criticism to date has been dominated by the notion of "personality"; like the American adventurer *par excellence* he so often depicts, Walsh, as one of the oldest pioneers, has come to be regarded as of the essence of what is called "classic" Hollywood cinema—a cinema characterized traditionally by its linearity, its transparency: in short, the effect of "non-writing." Andrew Sarris has even gone so far as to say of him: "only the most virile director can effectively project a feminine vulnerability in his characters." This notion of authorship has been criticized by Stephen Heath in the following terms: "the function of the author (the effect of the idea of authorship) is a function of unity; the use of the notion of the author involves the organization of the film . . . and in so doing, it avoids—this is indeed its function—the thinking of the articulation of the film text in relation to ideology." A view of Walsh as the originating consciousness of the Walsh oeuvre is, therefore, an ideological concept. To attribute such qualities as "virility" to Walsh is to foreclose the recognition of Walsh as subject within ideology. This feminist reading of the Walsh ouevre rejects any approach which would attempt to delineate the role of women in terms of the influence of ideology or sociology, as such an approach is merely a strategy to supplement auteur analysis. We have attempted to provide a reading of the Walsh oeuvre which takes as its starting point Walsh as a subject within ideology and, ultimately, the laws of the human order. What concerns us specifically is the delineation of the ideology of patriarchy—by which we mean the Law of the Father—within the text of the film. As Lévi-Strauss has indicated: "The emergence of symbolic thought must have required that women, like works, should be things that were exchanged." The tasks for feminist criticism must therefore consist of a process of de-naturalization: a questioning of the unity of the text; of seeing it as a contradictory interplay of different codes; of tracing its "structuring absences" and its relationship to the universal problem of symbolic castration. It is in this sense that a feminist strategy for the cinema must be understood. Only when such work has been done can a foundation for a feminist counter-cinema be established. Woman as signifier of woman under patriarchy is totally absent in most image-producing systems, but particularly in Hollywood where image-making and the fetishistic position of the spectator are highly developed. This is indeed why a study of "woman" within the

Hollywood system is of great interest. A study of "woman" within Walsh's oeuvre, in particular, reveals "woman" as the locus of a dilemma for the patriarchal human order, as a locus of contradictions. *Cahiers du Cinéma* in an editorial described such texts in the following terms: "an internal criticism is taking place which cracks the film apart at the seams. If one reads the film obliquely, looking for symptoms, if one looks beyond its apparent coherence one can see that it is riddled with cracks; it is splitting under an internal tension which is simply not there in an ideologically innocuous film. The ideology thus becomes subordinate to the text. It no longer has an independent existence; it is presented by the film." The function of "woman" in Walsh as the locus of "lack," as an empty sign to be filled, the absent center of a phallocentric universe marks the first step towards the de-naturalization of woman in the Hollywood cinema. In a frenzied imbrication of images (*The Revolt of Mamie Stover*) the Phallus is restored; but in this distanciation the first notes of the "swan-song of the immortal nature of patriarchal culture" (Juliet Mitchell) can be heard.

2

Dorothy Arzner: Critical Strategies

Claire Johnston

The last few years have witnessed a radical re-assessment of the role women have played in the cinema which would be impossible to imagine outside the context of a feminist politics. From the outset, the Women's Movement has assumed without question the importance of mobilizing the media for the women's struggle, at the same time subjecting them to a process of interrogation. This re-assessment[1] has involved both a taking stock of the role women have played as a creative force in the cinema, and an examination of the whole problem of woman as spectacle. An important departure was the growth of women's film festivals in various parts of the world with the aim of providing a historical perspective to the problem of women and cinema and of opening up for the first time possibilities for serious study of an area of cinema totally neglected by orthodox film historians and film theorists.

It is in this context and as a follow-up to the extensive season of women's films held at the National Film Theatre in 1973 that the present season of films by Dorothy Arzner and this accompanying pamphlet must be seen. Working in Hollywood in the 20s, 30s and early 40s, Dorothy Arzner was virtually the only woman at that time able to build up a coherent body of work within the Holywood system. However, very little is as yet known of her work as a whole, and apart from some explorations undertaken by two American film critics writing in the small film magazines,[2] Karyn Kay and Gerald Peary (whose rare interview with Arzner is reprinted here), nothing substantial has been written about her career as a director. In Andrew Sarris's polemical classic *The American Cinema* she remains a nonentity in a "ladies' auxiliary" mentioned as an afterthought to his all-male pantheon. Orthodox film historians, on the other hand, have concentrated on her career as an editor for such directors as James Cruze (see Kevin Brownlow, *The Parade's*

Gone By and Lewis Jacobs, *The Rise of the American Film*), or else have cited her as a directorial curiosity specializing in that esoteric commodity "feminine psychology" (see David Robinson, *Hollywood in the Twenties*).

It is therefore the intention of this pamphlet to suggest some approaches to Dorothy Arzner's work as a Hollywood director and to indicate in what way her films are relevant for feminists today. In so doing feminist film critics are not attempting to establish Arzner as some cult figure in a pantheon of Hollywood directors nor, indeed, in a pantheon of women directors. To see analyses of work by women directors in these terms is to misunderstand the crucial issues which the study of a woman director in the Hollywood system inevitably raises for feminist film criticism. In the first place, there is the question of film history itself. Why do feminist film critics place considerable emphasis on the role women have played, however marginal, in film history? Quite clearly women in the film industry have remained until recently "unspoken," repressed by film history. But do feminist film critics simply want to introduce women into film history? To answer this question, it is necessary to examine the ideology which has dominated film history up to now. Film historians (as J. L. Comolli's critique in *Cahiers du Cinéma*[3] makes clear) have until very recently confined themselves to the accumulation of "facts" and the construction of chronologies. From these, they have attempted by a process of induction to derive an interpretation of historical events closely linked to liberal notions of "progress" and "development." The historicism and pseudo-objectivism of this approach leaves little room for theory of any kind. Indeed, it is commonly believed that the pursuit of theory must inevitably be at the expense of "facts." Merely to introduce women into the dominant notion of film history, as yet another series of "facts" to be assimilated into the existing notions of chronology, would quite clearly be sterile and regressive. "History" is not some abstract "thing" which bestows significance on past events in retrospect. Only an attempt to situate Arzner's work in a theoretical way would allow us to comprehend her real contribution to film history. Women and film can only become meaningful in terms of a theory, in the attempt to create a structure in which films such as Arzner's can be examined in retrospect. This is not, however, to ignore the political importance of asserting the real role women have played in the history of the cinema. As the French philosopher Michel Foucault has indicated,[4] the need for oppressed peoples to write their own histories cannot be overstressed. Memory, an understanding of the struggles of the past, and a sense of one's own history constitute a vital dynamic in any struggle. The role of women in film history, then, inevitably raises questions about the nature of film history as such, and it is for this reason that this pamphlet has approached Dorothy Arzner's work from the point of view of feminist politics and film theory, as prerequisite research before any attempt at an insertion into film history can be undertaken.

The second issue raised by Dorothy Arzner's work which arises out of the problems outlined above is discussed in some detail in Pam Cook's essay "Approaching the Work of Dorothy Arzner." To understand the real achievement of her work, it is necessary to locate it within the constraints imposed by the Hollywood studio system and in relation to the patriarchal ideology of Hollywood cinema. In this context we employ "ideology" in the sense that the Marxist philosopher Louis Althusser uses the term.[5] Ideology is a system of representations: "images, myths, ideas or concepts." Ideology in this sense is not concerned with beliefs which people consciously hold; in fact, as Althusser emphasizes, "it is profoundly unconscious," representing itself as at once transparent, "natural" and universal to the viewer. In her article Pam Cook stresses the point that the system of representations generated by classic Hollywood cinema fixes the spectator in a specific, closed relationship to it, obliterating for the spectator the possibility of experiencing contradiction. She then proceeds to analyze the ways in which Dorothy Arzner's films, through a displacement of identification, through discontinuity and a process of play, succeed in generating a set of contradictions so that a denaturalization of patriarchal ideology is effected and the fixed relationship of the spectator is disturbed. However, this argument is based on the premise that classic Hollywood cinema locks the spectator in a fixed position. Undoubtedly the cinema, as a popular art which implies a viewing situation analogous in many respects to voyeurism (a position exploited by directors such as Hitchcock), encourages a fetishistic reading (see p. 47). Obviously the question of woman as spectacle is also linked closely to the voyeuristic position of the spectator.

Yet the fetishistic reading is not the only possible reading of a "progressive" classic film text. In recent years there has been an increased interest in the different strategies of reading which some "progressive" classic Hollywood films appear to require by virtue of the contradictions which can be found in such films between the specific hierarchy of interrelated discourses[6] which each film text comprises and the discourse of the dominant ideology (which in this case is the ideology of patriarchy). Attention has been drawn to a whole group of classic Hollywood films (for example those of Sirk and Ford) which generate within themselves an interal criticism of the dominant ideology. (For further definition of this group of films, see "Cinema/Ideology/Criticism" by Comolli and Narboni, translated in *Screen*, vol. 12, no. 1 [Spring 1971].) This internal criticism facilitates a process of denaturalization; behind the film's apparent coherence there exists an "internal tension" so that the ideology no longer has an independent existence but is "presented" by the film. The pressure of this tension cracks open the surface of the film; instead of its ideology being simply assumed and therefore virtually invisible, it is revealed and made explicit. It is in these terms that I would like to discuss the work of Dorothy Arzner: as a group of "progressive" classic film texts which de-naturalize the workings of patriarchal ideology. My approach differs from that of Pam Cook to the extent that I do not consider Arzner's work in terms of revolutionary strategies such as notions of "pregnant moment" and "tableaux," but in terms of dislocations and contradictions between the discourses which the film text comprises and that of the ideology of patriarchal culture within which the film is placed.

The Arzner Oeuvre

In general, the woman in Arzner's films determines her own identity through transgression and desire[7] in a search for an independent existence beyond and outside the discourse of the male. Unlike most other Hollywood directors who pose "positive" and "independent" female protagonists (Walsh,[8] Fuller, Cukor and Hawks, for example), in Arzner's work the discourse of the woman, or rather her attempt to locate it and make it heard, is what gives the system of the text its structural coherence, while at the same time rendering the dominant discourse of the male fragmented and incoherent. The central female protagonists react against and thus transgress the male discourse which entraps them. The form of transgression will depend on the nature of the particular discourse within which they have been caught. These women do not sweep aside the existing order and found a new, female order of language. Rather, they assert their own discourse in the face of the male one by breaking it up, subverting it, and, in a sense, rewriting it. It is this form of rewriting which then becomes the structuring principle of the text, the particular nature of the rewriting depending on what is being rewritten.

In *Christopher Strong* we are presented with the epitome of this desire for transgression in the character of Cynthia Darrington, world champion aviatrix ("I want to do it because I want to do it"). Cynthia achieves her project through role-reversal: by an over-identification with the male universe, flying planes, breaking records, and living and competing in a male world. ("I want to break records, I want to train hard.") *Wild Party* depicts a situation in which desire and transgression are articulated through an unswerving loyalty to the all-female group, the "hard-boiled maidens" who arrange nightly raids on local speakeasies and men's colleges. In *First Comes Courage* it is Nicole's perilous masquerade as a counter-espionage agent, living the life of a social outcast in extreme danger because of her marriage to a German commandant, which defines the articulation of desire and transgression. In *Craig's Wife* the project assumes pathological proportions. Harriet Craig's masochistic and obsessional relationship with her house and domesticity drives her to sacrifice everything and everyone for material security, order and cleanliness. Her obsessional desire involves expelling any acknowledgment of the value of family ties, while at the same time she guards with passion the physical integrity of her home. *Nana*, adapted from Zola's novel, follows the same basic preoccupations with the possibility of desire and transgression under patriarchy. Nana is a sexual adventuress who, by becoming the object of desire for men, seeks instead to become the *subject* of desire by exploiting the place in patriarchy assigned to her through the achievement of wealth and social influence. *Merrily We Go To Hell* and *Honor Among Lovers*, in the tradition of sophisticated social comedy of the thirties (*e.g.* Ernst Lubitsch) generate a play on the central motifs of sex and money, and it is within this discourse that the re-structuring intervention of the woman's discourse must be placed. In *Honor Among Lovers* Julia articulates her desire for transgression by rejecting Jerry, her wealthy playboy boss, precisely because, as he says "there's nothing you want that I can't give you," and marries a man without money who gambles everything on the stockmarket. In so doing she destroys the possibility of running Jerry's business, albeit as his secretary (at one point Julia describes hell as a place where women have to "remain private secretaries through all eternity"), though this is presented as infinitely preferable to a marriage which makes her feel "unhappy" and "afraid" and finally leads to bankruptcy and betrayal. In *Merrily We Go To Hell* the position is reversed. It is the woman, Joan, who is rich, and it is her father's refusal to relinquish her, and his offer of money to Gerry (the alcoholic news reporter and writer) not to marry his daughter, which forms the framework in which she will articulate her desire for transgression.

Undoubtedly *Dance, Girl, Dance* offers the most complex and far-reaching examination of the discourse of woman in relation to the other discourses in the text, in that it poses two central figures: Bubbles, the burlesque queen, and Judy, the aspiring ballet dancer, and it is only in this film that Arzner examines the question of woman as spectacle in patriarchy. Also, here, desire and transgression are articulated through a systematic presentation of opposites. Bubbles's desire to please, to exploit her sexuality for success and money, to "get her man," is contrasted with Judy's desire for self-expression, for work and the achievement of physical grace, and for acknowledgment within the terms of bourgeois culture. *Dance, Girl, Dance* also employs an additional element, the self-conscious use of sterotyping; Bubbles as the archetypal vamp and Judy as her naïve and innocent straight girl generate within the text of the film an internal criticism of it and of the function woman has within the narrative. The mythic qualities of this primitive iconography become, in effect, a shorthand for an ideological tradition in order to provide a critique of it, generating a series of reverberations which serve to de-naturalize the ideology of patriarchy in operation. In most Arzner films, however, this crude stereotyping occurs only in minor characters (*e.g.*, Claire Hempstead in *Merrily We Go To Hell* and the Ginger Rogers character in *Honor Among Lovers*) and does not derive from the discourse of the woman, but, rather is a facet of the discourse of the male.

In the Arzner oeuvre, then, the dominant discourse, situated as it is within the constraints of classic Hollywood cinema and the rules of verismilitude we associate with it—that is, the discourse of the male—is not privileged in any way, nor does it provide us with the knowledge to judge the truth of the discourses within the film as a whole. Structural coherence is provided by the discourse of the woman, and it is this which calls into question the dominant discourse and the nature of patriarchy into which it locks; dislocating it, deforming it in the sense that the Russian Formalist Shklovsky uses the term "*ostranenie*," the device of *making-strange*. In his essay "Art as a Device"[9] Shklovsky describes the device in relation to Tolstoy's story *Kholstomer*, where the entire story is related by a horse describing its reactions to the notion of "belonging" to a man, thus viewing property relations from an entirely new perspective; the unfamiliar making us pause and look anew at objects which have always appeared perfectly "natural" up to this moment. Such a device of *making-strange* would seem to be the key strategy by means of which the discourse of the woman subverts and dislocates the dominant discourse of the man and patriarchal ideology in general.

In Arzner's films it is the universe of the male which invites scrutiny, which is rendered strange. In this way, the discourse of the male can no longer function as the dominant one, the one which speaks the truth of the secondary discourses in the film. It is only the discourse of the woman, and her desire for transgression, which provides the principle of coherence and generates knowledge, and it is in woman that Arzner locates the possibility of truth within the film text. It is also for this reason that the narrative appears disjointed and fragmented; the conventions of plot and development are quite fully in evidence, but the work of the woman's discourse renders the narrative strange, subverting and dislocating it at the level of meaning. *Craig's Wife* offers a sustained example of this strategy. Here, the rituals of housework and the obsession with order acquire, as the film progresses, a definite validity, and it is evidence of people living and breathing in the house which is rendered strange. The marks of a trunk having been pulled along the floor or someone having sat on a bed acquire a sinister meaning within the text of the film. Another example is the character of Doris Blake in *Honor Among Lovers* who is likened by her millionaire boy-friend, always depicted shrouded in a massive fur coat, to an animal: "she's dumb but nice" . . . "I'm breaking her in." The marriage sequence in *Merrily We Go To Hell* in which a corkscrew, a token of Gerry's inebriated past and an omen for the future, is hurriedly used as a wedding ring works in a similar fashion. The entire relationship between Jimmie Harris and his estranged wife Elinor in *Dance, Girl, Dance* is another example of this device in operation, as is the love-making scene in *Christopher Strong* in which at the moment of sexual consummation, Strong gently and tenderly exhorts Cynthia to give up flying. Only at one point in Arzner's work, as far as I am aware, is a decisive *break* effected between the dominant discourse and the discourse of the woman—in the momentous scene in *Dance, Girl, Dance* where Judy, in a fit of anger, turns on her audience and tells them how she sees them. This return of scrutiny in what is assumed within the film to be a one-way process, a spectacle to be consumed by men, constitutes a direct assault on the audience *within* the film and the audience *of* the film, directly challenging the entire notion of spectacle as such. This break, a *tour-de-force* in terms of Arzner's work, is nevertheless directly recuperated by the enthusiastic applause which follows, and the discourse of the woman, although it appears momentarily supreme, is returned to the arena of the spectacle.

The drive towards resolution of the narrative and closure of the dominant discourse in the classic Hollywood film traditionally involves the "happy ending" or its inversion, both embodying the notion of unification, the completion of the man by the woman and the myth of sexual complementariness. In Arzner's work there is a systematic refusal of such a unification. The subversion of the dominant discourse continues, even though the woman fails to impose her desire upon it. The discourse of the woman is not eliminated, and the endings of Arzner's films, whether "happy" or "tragic" in the conventional sense, mark, in the final analysis, the triumph of the discourse of woman in surviving at all. *Dance, Girl, Dance* shows Judy exchanging the humiliation of the spectacle for the defeat of the final embrace with Steve Adams, the patriarchal presence which has haunted her throughout the film ("silly child, you've had your own way long enough"). As she turns to the camera, her face obscured by a large floppy hat, Judy, half crying, half laughing, exclaims "when I think how simple things could have been, I just have to laugh." This irony marks her defeat and final engulfment, but at the same time it is the final mark of subversion of the discourse of the male. *Merrily We Go To Hell* offers a similar strategy of subversion within the "happy ending," but it takes a different form. Having lost her baby in childbirth Joan takes the recalcitrant Gerry in her arms and murmurs "my baby"; this ironic, even pathological, gesture of substituting the lover for the dead child facilitates the "happy ending," but this regression also represents the mark of Joan's desire on the final images of the film text. This type of "happy ending" is consistent with Douglas Sirk's remark[10] about his own "happy endings"—"it makes the aporia more transparent."

The "tragic" type of ending employed frequently by Arzner represents a similar refusal of unification and closure and a resolution instead to play out the discourse of the woman to the bitter end. In *Christopher Strong* it manifests itself in final suicide on a solo flight, as Cynthia watches her past life and the impossible contradictions between her career and her lover flash before her eyes as her plane hurtles to the ground. For Nana the decision to

Craig's Wife (Dorothy Arzner, 1936)

take her own life in the face of impossible constraints placed on her by her lovers and their codes of gallantry is expressed as a sense of relief, as almost pleasurable: "I was born all wrong" . . . "I'm glad I'm going." The final lonely image of Harriet Craig surrounded by her immaculate, empty home implies that the narrative has been resolved, the solitary, emphatically artificial tear in her eye suggesting a sense of irony: convention demands that the tear be there, but its artificiality underlines the contradictions of her pyrrhic victory. This final image of isolation is paralleled in *First Comes Courage* where Nicole rejects her lover to continue her masquerade to the end, a solitary figure on a burning hill. In all these cases, the discourse of the woman fails to triumph *over* the male discourse and the patriarchal ideology, but its very survival in the form of irony is in itself a kind of triumph, a victory against being expelled or erased: the continued insistence of the woman's discourse is a triumph over non-existence.

In this essay I have not attempted to trace in detail the ways in which the strategies of dislocation, subversion and contradiction operate within the texts of individual films, though a close analysis is quite clearly a necessity at some point. Such an analysis would involve the tracing of these dislocations and contradictions within the film text through which meaning is produced: a process which has a resemblance to the examination of permanent traces left upon the "Mystic Writing-Pad" described by Freud,[11] although in this case the traces are not linked directly to memory. In this essay I have attempted to situate the system of strategies which Arzner employs within her work as a whole, and have indicated that it would be incorrect to look at her work simply as a coherent structure of themes and motifs, in the *auteurist* manner. Rather, it should be seen in terms of a re-writing process. In this process the discourse of the woman is the principal structuring element which re-writes the dominant discourse of the film text together with the patriarchal ideology into which it locks. Arzner's strategies at this level cannot in any sense be seen as revolutionary ones for feminism. Her position in classic Hollywood cinema in many aspects can be paralleled to Lenin's assessment of Tolstoy's position in Soviet literature. Both are progressive artists who hold a specific and important position in history precisely because they open up an area of contradiction in the text, but at the same time they are unable radically to change these contradictions. For this reason, it is particularly important that films such as those of Arzner should be studied by feminists involved in developing a feminist counter-cinema. Her films pose the problem for all of us: is it possible to sweep aside the existing forms of discourse in order to found a new form of language? The French semiologist Roland Barthes has suggested that all stories are based on the structure of the Oedipus myth.[12] How, then, is it possible to produce feminist art which is not based on such a structure and the repression of the feminine which underpins it? In posing the question in the way she does, and through the working out of her own solution as a process of re-writing, Dorothy Arzner has made one of the most important contributions to the development of a feminist counter-cinema.

Notes

1. See the magazine *Women and Film*, and *Notes on Women's Cinema*, a *Screen* pamphlet, SEFT, 1973.

2. Articles and interview in *Cinema* (USA), Fall, 1974; "Dorothy Arzner's *Dance, Girl, Dance*" in *The Velvet Light Trap*, Fall 1973.

3. "Technique and Ideology," *Cahiers du Cinéma*, Nos. 229, 230, 231, 233, 235, 241.

4. "Entretien avec Michel Foucault," *Cahiers du Cinéma*, Nos. 251–52.

5. Louis Althusser, *For Marx*, Allen Lane, London, 1969.

6. I use "discourse" to refer to a particular level of "speech" within a film attributable to a source (or more precisely a "subject"—not to be confused with a character in the film—and thus answers the question "Who is speaking here?"). It derives from the manner in which the textual system of the film operates. Thus within a film there may be a variety of discourses, each having a different perspective on the action; though in classic Hollywood cinema, a male discourse is almost invariably dominant.

7. The notions of desire and transgression used here do not coincide with the conventional ones, but derive from psychoanalytic usage. Readers are referred to *The Language of Psychoanalysis* by J. Laplanche and J.-B. Pontalis, Hogarth Press, London, 1973.

8. "The Place of Women in the Cinema of Raoul Walsh" by Pam Cook and Claire Johnston, in *Raoul Walsh*, ed. Phil Hardy, Edinburgh Film Festival, 1974.

9. *Théorie de la Littérature*, ed. Tzvetan Todorov, Editions du Seuil, Paris, 1965.

10. Jon Halliday, *Sirk on Sirk*, Cinema One, London, 1971.

11. "Note on the Mystic-Writing Pad," by Sigmund Freud, in *Collected Papers* Vol. 5, Hogarth Press, 1950.

12. Roland Barthes, *Le Plaisir du Texte*, Editions du Seuil, Paris, 1973.

3

Approaching the Work of Dorothy Arzner

Pam Cook

The films of Dorothy Arzner provide us with an opportunity to investigate a range of film texts made within a production system already in the late 20s and early 30s highly articulated in terms of the dominant ideology of classic Hollywood cinema. There is no doubt that Arzner made complex and interesting films of great relevance to women now in our struggle for our own culture; but the point is not to claim for her a place in a pantheon of "best Hollywood directors," since the positing of any such pantheon would ignore the complexity of the relationship between ideology and the production of film texts. In looking again at some of Arzner's films, then, we are looking at a body of work produced within the constraints of a studio system heavily determined by economic and ideological factors (*Nana*, in spite of the potential interest of the story, remains little more than a vehicle for Anna Sten, Goldwyn's protégée and hoped-for box office answer to Dietrich and Garbo, relentlessly photographed in soft-focus by Gregg Toland). Our object will be to define some strategies for a critique of patriarchal ideology[1] in general.

To approach the films in this way is not to try to elevate them to the status of masterpieces, nor simply to regard them as objects worthy of study, but instead to see them as texts (complex products demanding an active reading in terms of the contradictions at work in them), which are produced within a system of representation which tries to fix the spectator in a specific closed relationship to the film. Thus we are attempting to take from Arzner's films some ideas which will open out the problem of the place of women within that system.

Stephen Heath in an article on Brecht remarks:

Classic film is finally less a question of *mise-en-scène* than of *mise-en-place*, and anything that disturbs that place, that position, the fictions of myself and my "Reality" can only be theoretical, the theatralization of representation in its forms: film theater, critical cinema, a cinema of crisis and contradiction. ("Lessons from Brecht," *Screen*, Vol. 15, No. 2 [Summer 1974].

In the history of classic cinema this *"mise-en-place"* has been articulated in response to the demands of patriarchal ideology, with specific consequences for the place of women in representation; for in this structure the place of woman is defined as the locus of "lack," an empty space which must be filled in the working through of man's desire to find his own place in society.[2] The use of female stereotypes, modfied only slightly to meet the demands of changing fashion, has contributed to the propagation of myths of women which relate primarily to the desires of men. The role of women in the film narrative can be seen to perform a similar function: to bring into play the desire of the male protagonists. While there is no doubt that there are progressive elements in many Hollywood films (for example, those of Sirk or Ford) which posit the idea of female desire, nevertheless ultimately these films operate a closure on the possibilities of the working through of this desire (*i.e.*, of articulating and satisfying desire through phantasy). The films of Dorothy Arzner are important in that they foreground precisely this problem of the desire of women caught in a system of representation which allows them at most the opportunity of playing on the specific demands that the system makes on them.

This concept of play permeates every level of the texts: irony operates through the dialogue, sound(s), music, through a play on image, stereotype and gesture, and through complex patterns of parallels and reversals in the overall organization of the scenes. Perhaps the most exemplary film in this sense is *Dance, Girl, Dance* which has often been acclaimed by feminist critics as a work of major importance. However, it would be a mistake to read the film in "positive" terms as representing the progress of its heroine to "maturity" or "self-awareness." The value of the film lies not in its creation of a culture-heroine with whom we can finally and fully identify, but in the ways in which it *displaces* identification with the characters and focuses our attention on the problematic position they occupy in their world. A positive reading of the film would imply a conclusion which would be a final closure of the film's contradictions; but this ignores the complexity of the film's structure of reversals. When Judy O'Brien finally turns on her audience in fury and in her long speech fixes them in relation to *her* critical look at them it does indeed have the force of a "pregnant moment" (see p. 52). The place of the audience *in* the film and the audience *of* the film is disturbed, creating a break between them and the ideology of woman as spectacle, object of their desire. The shock-force of the moment is emphasized by the embarrassment of the audience in the film, and the silence which follows the speech. However, in another masterly reversal, the moment is upended as the enthusiastic clapping of the woman in the audience (Steve Adams's secretary, whose relationship to her boss is depicted in the film as, ironically, one of friendly but almost complete oppression of her by him) escalates into a standing ovation, thus re-locating Judy's speech *as* a performance. The cat-fight between Judy and Bubbles which follows almost immediately takes place on the stage to the accompaniment of music from the burlesque orchestra which resembles the music used for *Tom and Jerry* cartoons. This has the double force of condensing the girls' conflict of desires, and by presenting that conflict as sexually exciting for the cheering, cat-calling audience, calls into question the processes by which women's desires are presented as a spectacle for consumption. In this way our identification with Judy's inspiring words is displaced into an awareness of the continuing process of contradictions at work in the struggle with ideology.

Similarly in the court-room sequence which follows, Judy in the dock speaks with confidence and self-assurance about herself and her relationship to the other people in the film, much to the admiration of her audience and the fair-minded and liberal judge. However, we next see Judy at Steve Adams's dance academy where she finally discovers his identity and the real reason for his pursuit of her—her ability as a dancer. Even as Judy tries to assert her independence in the conversation with Steve which ends the film, the ground is pulled from under her

> STEVE: *The Judge and I decided* you were in no mood to take favors.
> JUDY: I'm still in no mood . . .
> STEVE: Now listen to me *you silly child.* You've had *your own way* long
>   enough—now you're going to listen to me . . .
> STEVE: (to the dancing instructor): She was born with more than any dancer
>   we've got and she knows less. *It's our job to teach her all we know.* (My
>   italics)

> Judy's moment of triumphant independence becomes a thing of the
> past as she collapses into Steve's arms *in tears.*

> JUDY: When I think how easy it might have been I could laugh.
> STEVE: Go ahead and laugh, Judy O'Brien.

In this final ironic reversal Judy "gets what she wants" at the expense of any pretensions to "independence" she had. Again, by displacing our expectations of identification with Judy's positive qualities into a recognition of the weakness of her position within male-dominated culture, the film's ending opens up the contradictions inherent in that position (our position) thus encouraging us as spectators to recognize the all-important problematic of the difficulties of the working through of female desire under patriarchy.

Without doubt *Dance, Girl, Dance* provides the clearest example, by its play on stereotypes and reversals, of ironic method, especially as it fore-

Dance, Girl, Dance (Dorothy Arzner, 1940)

grounds the contradiction between women's desire for self-expression and culture, and the cultural processes which articulate a place for woman as spectacle. However, further examples of Arzner's concern with playing with formal elements to conceptualize women's position in ideology can be found in another earlier film. *Merrily We Go To Hell*, made in 1932, displays the seeds of the method which is so rigorously and economically articulated in *Dance, Girl, Dance* in 1940. This is not to suggest that we can formulate a coherent and exhaustive method to apply to all Arzner's films. What follows is a tentative enquiry into some of the ways in which this early post-silent comedy treats the problem of the relationship of the spectator to the forms whereby classic cinema represents the place of woman.

Merrily We Go To Hell tells the story of an insecure young heiress, Joan Prentice (Sylvia Sidney), whose stern and upright father owns a food-processing business, and who falls in love with a penniless journalist and would-be playwright, Gerry Corbett (Fredric March), who drinks heavily to forget his failure and his broken affair with a successful actress. Joan decides to marry Gerry, in spite of her father's resistance to the idea on the grounds of Gerry's unreliability. Gerry agrees to the marriage despite his fears that his continuing obsession with Claire, the actress, will prevent him from making a go of it.

Meaning is created in the film through the play of oppositions: the "strength" of Joan's father is contrasted with Gerry's "weakness" and inability to control his own actions. Similarly Joan's lack of confidence about her identity contrasts sharply with Claire's self-possession and ability to control her "audience" through a highly articulated image of female sexuality. The conflict of desires between the four protagonists provides the motivation for what happens in the film, but the progress of the narrative and the final reconciliation of Joan and Gerry is complicated on several levels.

The Narrative

The structure of the narrative is episodic: there is no smooth flow from one scene to another, and each scene demands to be read in itself for the meanings it creates. In this way we are constantly distanced from a desire to follow the "destiny" of the characters in any transparent or linear fashion. Rather we are led in a series of uneven "events" to question the "inevitable Truth"[3] of the narrative and to look at the situations in which the protagonists find themselves. By 1932 the codes of suspense were well established in Hollywood cinema. Intercutting of sequences and shots to provide an illusion of simultaneous action had been extensively used in the silent cinema not only to create comedy but also in psychological/social drama, where identification with the central character and the final *dénouement* of the story were essential to the representation of Truth. It is significant therefore that Arzner's film presents its story in a succession of tableaux, where the organization of meanings within each scene takes precedence over the smooth forward-flow of a narrative which would give an impression of Reality. An example from the film might be the opening scene.

The film opens with an image of Fredric March (Gerry) alone in the half-darkness crouched behind a barricade of whisky bottles from which position he is drunkenly and only half-aloud enacting an imaginary battle with the "horrible people" at the "horrible party" he is attending. The camera draws back to show us that he has withdrawn to a balcony from which he can see the party—through a brightly-lit window. A couple dancing move into view through the window and seem to begin an argument. Gerry shows an interest in the scene, and we are taken in closer to find Sylvia Sidney (Joan) struggling violently with the sexual advances of a very large, very drunk man. She breaks away and rushes out onto the balcony, unaware of Gerry's presence or the fact that he has been watching with interest and amusement.

In these first few seconds notions of watcher/watched, fear of and inability to cope with sexual demands, innocence, flight and withdrawal are quickly established. The rest of the scene takes place almost entirely on the balcony and is concerned with depicting the nature of the relationship between Gerry and Joan and Joan's place within it. Joan describes herself as "stupid" and a "nobody," but when she tells Gerry her name he immediately connects her with "Prentice Products" and points out a neon advertising sign on the sky-line, thus placing *her* as a product. In the face of her self-negation he emphasizes her class status (courtesy of her father), her "niceness" ("I think you're *swell*) and her need to give (the "gingerbread and *crème-de-menthe*" song links Joan's wealth with her quality of mothering sexuality). Gerry creates Joan's "image" for her.

Joan's escort intervenes to take her home, and in spite of her obvious pleasure in Gerry's company she leaves passively to get her coat. Gerry, after a small quarrel with Joan's friend, becomes involved in more drinking with his own friends, and when Joan comes out onto the balcony again to say goodbye we are given a subjective shot in which Gerry's vision is totally blurred—he can't see her at all, and when he asks who she is, she replies "Oh, nobody." From this description it can be seen that the scene is circular in structure, and that although we are given certain expectations as to what might happen next (Joan asks Gerry to tea the next day) it is rather the processes at work in the relationship between Gerry and Joan that occupy our attention, through the use of irony on the level of dialogue and image.

The next scene, showing Joan at home with her father, does not follow on easily from the first, but sets out to show a different situation: the relationship between Joan and her father in which she is depicted as child-like and over-indulged. In the first scene it is Gerry who occupies this child-like position vis-à-vis Joan. Thus by means of parallels which are also contrasts the film sets up tensions on the formal level which act as distancing mechanisms to create new meanings.

Narrative interruptions

The film uses basically two forms of narrative interruption: the "gag" and the "pregnant moment." Both can operate at the level of a small section of a scene, or incorporate a whole scene, but they both serve to introduce elements of discontinuity into the narrative.

Gags

An example of the short gag comes at the end of the wedding scene when Gerry places the metal corkscrew on Joan's hand instead of the ring. As she opens her hand the screw is pointing inwards, towards the soft palm of the hand. She laughs, but the vicious connotations of that image create a shock-effect on the level of the meaning of their relationship and her place in it.

A long gag is used in the scene where Gerry first arrives at Joan's house, late for his tea appointment. He meets Joan's father at the door and after their initial curt encounter follows Mr. Prentice into the house, practically running to keep up with the long, stern strides of the older man. Left alone, Gerry becomes interested in a picture on the far wall and has to make his way across the highly polished floor by stepping on his handkerchief so he won't lose his balance. Joans finds him there, they sit down to talk, and Gerry extends the gag as they get up to leave by expressing his insecurity again in terms of always having been used to "places with sawdust on the floor." The gag does nothing to further the flow of the narrative, rather it arrests it, along with any expectations we may have of the future happiness of the two protagonists.

Dance, Girl, Dance makes use of the gag as a strategy of intervention at the level of the place of the spectator in relation to the film spectacle. The burlesque show sequence plays the position of the film-audience against that of the audience in the film to produce a shift in meaning. We see Bubbles performing a mock striptease. From the position of the burlesque audience we watch as the wind-machine threatens to tear off all her clothes, and she hides behind a tree on the stage. The excitement of the burlesque audience is intense as Bubbles's clothes come flying onto the empty stage. The film-audience is suddenly given a privileged shot of Bubbles behind the tree, fully clothed, while the burlesque audience can still be heard whistling and shouting. In that moment our position as spectators of the spectacle is shifted, the mechanism of the fantasy structure within which Bubbles and her burlesque audience are operating is made explicit, and we are made to take a distance on our own place within the ideology of illusionism as it constructs the fictions of our Reality for us.

Pregnant moments

The force of the pregnant moment is that it works against the complex unity of the text by opening up the whole area of representation to the question of desire and its articulation. In Merrily We Go To Hell we see Joan at her engagement party waiting for Gerry to arrive before she announces their forthcoming marriage. The party is well under way, except for the marked absence of Gerry. Joan's father comes to the top of the stairs, the camera behind him as he dominates the party below. Cut to Joan dancing with her friend Gregg. They are chatting and move towards a large mirror on the far side of the room from the stairs and dance before it for a moment before Joan suddenly becomes aware of the "image" of her father on the stairs, looking at her, reflected in the mirror. She stands for some seconds gazing at her own reflection in the mirror and the "image" of her father in the background before she moves across the room to talk to him. She seems fascinated, held in a fixed relation to the "image" in the mirror, and as we are faced with that image of fascination we are aware of a tension between desire and the patriarchal Law.

Narrative reversals

It has already been pointed out by Karyn Kay and Gerald Peary[4] that the narrative structure of Dance, Girl, Dance comprises a system of repetition and reversal, and the scenes quoted above describing the reversals which follow Judy O'Brien's speech to the burlesque audience are a good example of this method. In *Merrily We Go To Hell* we can detect a similar structure of repetition/reversal based on the oppositions rejection/pursuit and flight/reconciliation. This form of reversal is another way of disturbing the linear flow of the narrative: we are pulled backwards and forwards in a play between memory and anticipation which defeats any final closure of contradictions.

In *Merrily We Go To Hell* this system is important to the central problematic: in the absence of any code of action of her own, Joan is forced to emulate the actions of others. This point is forcibly made in the scene immediately following the mirror-image sequence described above. Joan's father complains irritably about Gerry's absence, because he "can't stand for her to be humiliated." Joan is called outside, where she finds Gerry in a taxi lying in a fetal position, in a drunken stupor. She becomes very upset and repeats her father's words:"He can't do this to me". . . "I can't stand the humiliation." She takes her car and drives wildly into the night in an attempt to escape the intolerable pressure of contradictory demands from her father and Gerry. As she is "torn," so the mechanisms which attempt to fix her place are pulled apart.

The scene of final reconciliation between Gerry and Joan is an example of the use of ironic reversal to open up contradictions rather than present a closure in which the destiny of the characters is sealed and given as a fixed Truth. Joan is in hospital after the death of her baby. In the darkness of the hospital room she mistakes Gerry at first for her father. Then as he kneels to put his head on her breast and declares his love for her, she puts her arms around him and murmurs "Gerry, my baby, my baby" as the film ends. The image of reconciliation, unity, plenitude is shot through with connotations of death, loss and absence. The entire text of the film is cracked open as the workings of ideology in the construction of female desires is exposed.

Play with stereotypes

The use of stereotypes in classic Hollywood cinema is generally recognized as serving a double function. As Panofsky has suggested the use of a limited set of signs based on genre conventions in early cinema was intended to help the audience read the narration of the film more easily. They were given a set of fixed recognition points so that they felt comfortable in relation to the film. However, as cinema developed, we can see from the fact that male stereotypes changed much more rapidly than female stereotypes that the use of stereotypes has a specific ideological function: to represent man as inside history, and woman as eternal and unchanging, outside history. It is this representation of myths of women as a-historical that Arzner's films seek to question. By demonstrating that the fixed female stereotypes are actually a focus on contradictions for women her films cause reverberations within sexist ideology which disturb our place within it. As the myths are disengaged from ideology, the transparency of the myths is destroyed and they are recognized as constructs within representation.

Dance, Girl, Dance uses the standard stereotypes of Vamp/Straight Girl to demonstrate the operation of myth at every level of the film. Judy's position as stooge in Bubbles's act is only the logical extreme of her problem throughout the film: caught in her "image" of a "nice girl with class" she is also stooge in her relationships with the rest of the girls in Madame Basilova's dancing troupe, and in her relationship with Jimmie, and finally with Steve Adams. Because the burlesque show is a logical extreme it is the point at which we can most clearly see the mechanisms of ideology at work. Bubbles controls her audience by offering them an "image" of female sexuality which operates on the level of fantasy—an "image" which parodies myths of women as child-like yet sexually provocative and sophisticated through the use of song and gesture. Judy's box-office value as a stooge is to stimulate the demand for Bubbles's brand of "oomph." The function of her performance is to increase the desire of the burlesque audience by postponing satisfaction of that desire, through her presentation of herself as spiritual, sexually innocent, dedicated to an art which transcends sexuality. By showing that both these "images" fulfill specific demands for the burlesque audience, the film causes us to question the function of Judy's dream of dancing the "Morning Star" ballet, which is only the other side of the coin of her burlesque performance. Judy's desires are totally compatible with the laws of sexist ideology, for as the "Urban Ballet" sequence clearly shows (its structure is parallel, in reverse, to the burlesque show) myths of the innocence of women, whether idealized and spiritual or sexually provocative, exist at all levels of representation. By demonstrating the specific place of these myths within male-dominated culture Arzner's film de-naturalizes them.

Judy O'Brien's problem with her "nice-girl image," her contradictory desire to please others and yet fulfill her own dream, has a precedent in the form of Joan's struggle in *Merrily We Go To Hell*. This film also uses the Vamp/Straight Girl stereotypes to point up contradictions on the level of ideology, and Joan also has her "moment of truth" when she confronts Gerry with his obsession with Claire's "image" as she is about to leave him. The problematic of the "nice-girl image" is presented as a problem on the level of the working through of desire. The role of the "nice-girl" is to suppress her own desires in favor of those of the male. Yet Arzner's "nice-girls" are shown as having desires which conflict with those of the male, at the same time as they desire to please the male. It is at this point of tension between desire and ideology of the problematic of women as subject of desire that the myth breaks down, for the "nice-girl" is impelled by her contradictory desires to explore the possibilities open to her on the level of the "image," only to find that those possibilities are limited by factors which are outside her control.

It is on the level of the "image" that *Merrily We Go To Hell* explores this problem. When Joan describes herself as a "nobody" to Gerry when they first meet, she is in effect offering him an empty page on which he may write his own description of her, which he proceeds to do by placing her first as her father's daughter (a child), then as a provider of loving support (the "ginger-bread and *crème-de-menthe*" song), then as a "nice-girl" ("I think you're swell"). All apsects of this "image" are brought into play during the film— Gerry refers to Joan more than once as "the finest of Prentice Products," and his repetition of "I think you're swell" continues until it is finally emptied of all significance except its ideological function (in the scene where Joan leaves him) of maintaining the image for himself after it has clearly been discarded by Joan. On the visual level Joan as a "nice-girl" appears gift-wrapped in her wedding gown as the ideal of innocence (the place of the corkscrew gag in puncturing this image has already been noted). Joan the housewife dresses plainly and does the darning while her husband struggles creatively with his typewriter, summing up ironically his view of marriage: "Mrs. Gerry Corbett, you're Mrs. Simon Legree."[5] (As Gerry characterizes himself as a slave in relation to his wife, the shot of Joan's hands darning his sock denies us the possibility of accepting his description of her as "Mrs. Simon Legree," *i.e.*, a slave driver; by use of this irony the contradictions of the "image" which Gerry gives Joan, contradictions which make the marriage a problem for her, are made explicit.) Again, Joan the cook is found in the kitchen dressed in a shapeless apron, apparently happy in her supportive role (the counterpart to this is Vi's bitter speech about her own failure as a wife). However, when Joan is confronted by an elegant and sophisticated Claire at the office of Gerry's agent, her own place begins to seem threatened; her "image" becomes problematic.

Joan's problem with her place *vis-à-vis* Gerry's relationship with Claire is also formulated at the level of the "image." After the second meeting between Joan and Gerry when he confesses his unhappy love-affair, Gerry is shown talking to a photograph of Claire which depicts her as sexually provocative: "I've met a girl who's just the opposite of your lovely fleshy self." The same photograph of Claire appears later in the newspaper, which causes the fight between Gerry and the gossip-columnist over his motives for marrying Joan. In Gerry's play Claire represents a sexually experienced woman who can manipulate the demands of male ideology to make men do what she wants. Claire is public property, and it is in the tension between the place of woman as public and private property than Joan is caught. Faced with this contradiction and the prospect of losing Gerry, Joan abandons her "nice-girl image" for that of the sophisticated and promiscuous wife, public property, a "new identity" which is posed as problematic precisely because it is presented *as* an "image" *articulated* in response to the demands of male ideology.

The scene which perhaps most clearly emphasizes a preoccupation with the function of the image in "holding representation at a distance" is the scene in which Gerry and Claire enact a mock love-scene in front of imaginary film cameras as Joan looks on. Gerry and Claire are framed in the doorway as they kiss, their enthusiastic audience of friends applauding. We see the "scene" at first from behind Joan, and watch with her as the mock-kiss becomes "real" and the mock-directors are forced to shout "Cut!" As Gerry and Claire become aware of Joan's presence they look towards her and in a reverse shot we now see Joan (from behind Gerry) framed in the doorway in her turn, transformed into the "image" of an embittered, frustrated woman. This reversal, by implicating us in the pleasure/pain aspect of our voyeuristic relationship to the film, nevertheless holds off identification by reminding us that we are engaged in a process of fabricating images. This intervention prevents us from accepting the film on any level as Reality. *Merrily We Go To Hell,* by operating a process of montage of interventions, asserts the text as a process of dialectical play between image and narrative, and by implicating us in that process *as* spectators calls into question the forms of cinematographic representation through which ideology attempts to fix our place for us. From this concern in Arzner's films with the potential displacement-effect of the friction of image and diegesis,[6] and the montage of interventions of ironic reversals and narrative interruptions, we can learn much about the possibility of our own intervention as feminist critics and film-makers in patriarchal ideology.

Notes

1. Patriarchal ideology refers to the patriarchal laws which govern our society and which produce contradictions (see Juliet Mitchell, *Psychoanalysis and Feminism*, Allen Lane, 1974).

2. Heath bases his model of representation in the cinema on the Freudian structure of the fetish. I am suggesting that in this structure the place of woman (who is seen to be lacking the male penis, and endowed with the "saving substitute") is fixed as the locus of the problem both of the recognition of the threat of castration, and of the disavowal of that threat (thus she is "the empty space which must be filled"). Heath claims that his model applies to all classic cinema. My reading of *Merrily We Go To Hell* suggests that Arzner's film offers a critique of this structure by means of a displacement of meanings which seeks to transform this "fixed place" of the spectator. (For further discussion of this question, see "The Place of Woman in the Cinema of Raoul Walsh" by Pam Cook and Claire Johnston.)

3. The use of capitals is intended here and elsewhere in this article to indicate that concepts such as truth or reality are specifically constructed, not natural "givens" with universal validity.

4. "*Dance, Girl, Dance,*" by Karyn Kay and Gerald Peary, in *Velvet Light Trap* No. 10 (Fall 1973), p. 26.

5. A character from *Uncle Tom's Cabin*.

6. The self-contained fictional world of the film.

4

Visual Pleasure and Narrative Cinema

Laura Mulvey

I Introduction

A. A Political Use of Psychoanalysis

This paper intends to use psychoanalysis to discover where and how the fascination of film is reinforced by pre-existing patterns of fascination already at work within the individual subject and the social formations that have moulded him. It takes as starting point the way film reflects, reveals and even plays on the straight, socially established interpretation of sexual difference which controls images, erotic ways of looking and spectacle. It is helpful to understand what the cinema has been, how its magic has worked in the past, while attempting a theory and a practice which will challenge this cinema of the past. Psychoanalytic theory is thus appropriated here as a political weapon, demonstrating the way the unconscious of patriarchal society has structured film form.

The paradox of phallocentrism in all its manifestations is that it depends on the image of the castrated woman to give order and meaning to its world. An idea of woman stands as lynch pin to the system: it is her lack that produces the phallus as a symbolic presence, it is her desire to make good the lack that the phallus signifies. Recent writing in *Screen* about psychoanalysis and the cinema has not sufficiently brought out the importance of the representation of the female form in a symbolic order in which, in the last resort, it speaks castration and nothing else. To summarize briefly: the function of woman in forming the patriarchal unconscious is two-fold, she first symbolizes the castration threat by her real absence of a penis and second thereby raises her child into the symbolic. Once this has been achieved, her meaning in the process is at an end, it does not last into the world of law and language except as a memory which oscillates between memory of maternal plenitude and memory of lack. Both are posited on nature (or on anatomy in Freud's famous phrase). Woman's desire is subjected to her image as bearer of the bleeding wound, she can exist only in relation to castration and cannot transcend it. She turns her child into the signifier of her own desire to possess a penis (the condition, she imagines, of entry into the symbolic). Either she must gracefully give way to the word, the Name of the Father and the Law, or else struggle to keep her child down with her in the half-light of the imaginary. Woman then stands in patriachal culture as signifier for the male other, bound by a symbolic order in which man can live out his fantasies and obsessions through linguistic command by imposing them on the silent image of woman still tied to her place as bearer of meaning, not maker of meaning.

There is an obvious interest in this analysis for feminists, a beauty in its exact rendering of the frustration experienced under the phallocentric order. It gets us nearer to the roots of our oppression, it brings an articulation of the problem closer, it faces us with the ultimate challenge: how to fight the unconscious structured like a language (formed critically at the moment of arrival of language) while still caught within the language of the patriarchy. There is no way in which we can produce an alternative out of the blue, but we can begin to make a break by examining patriarchy with the tools it provides, of which psychoanalysis is not the only but an important one. We are still separated by a great gap from important issues for the female unconscious which are scarcely relevant to phallocentric theory: the sexing of the female infant and her relationship to the symbolic, the sexually mature woman as non-mother, maternity outside the signification of the phallus, the vagina. . . . But, at this point, psychoanalytic theory as it now stands can at least advance our understanding of the status quo, of the patriarchal order in which we are caught.

B.   *Destruction of Pleasure as a Radical Weapon*

As an advanced representation system, the cinema poses questions of the ways the unconscious (formed by the dominant order) structures ways of seeing and pleasure in looking. Cinema has changed over the last few decades. It is no longer the monolithic system based on large capital investment exemplified at its best by Hollywood in the 1930s, 1940s and 1950s. Technological advances (16 mm, etc.) have changed the economic conditions of cinematic production, which can now be artisanal as well as capitalist. Thus it has been possible for an alternative cinema to develop. However self-conscious and ironic Hollywood managed to be, it always restricted itself to a formal mise-en-scène reflecting the dominant ideological concept of the cinema. The alternative cinema provides a space for a cinema to be born which is radical in both a political and an aesthetic sense and challenges the basic assumptions of the mainstream film. This is not to reject the latter moralistically, but to highlight the ways in which its formal preoccupations reflect the psychical obsessions of the society which produced it, and, further, to stress that the alternative cinema must start specifically by reacting against these obsessions and assumptions. A politically and aesthetically avant-garde cinema is now possible, but it can still only exist as a counterpoint.

The magic of the Hollywood style at its best (and of all the cinema which fell within its sphere of influence) arose, not exclusively, but in one important aspect, from its skilled and satisfying manipulation of visual pleasure. Unchallenged, mainstream film coded the erotic into the language of the dominant patriarchal order. In the highly developed Hollywood cinema it was only through these codes that the alienated subject, torn in his imaginary memory by a sense of loss, by the terror of potential lack in fantasy, came near to finding a glimpse of satisfaction: through its formal beauty and its play on his own formative obsessions. This article will discuss the interweaving of that erotic pleasure in film, its meaning, and in particular the central place of the image of woman. It is said that analyzing pleasure, or beauty, destroys it. That is the intention of this article. The satisfaction and reinforcement of the ego that represent the high point of film history hitherto must be attacked. Not in favor of a reconstructed new pleasure, which cannot exist in the abstract, nor of intellectualized unpleasure, but to make way for a total negation of the ease and plenitude of the narrative fiction film. The alternative is the thrill that comes from leaving the past behind without rejecting it, transcending outworn or oppressive forms, or daring to break with normal pleasurable expectations in order to conceive a new language of desire.

II Pleasure in Looking/Fascination with the Human Form

A. The cinema offers a number of possible pleasures. One is scopophilia. There are circumstances in which looking itself is a source of pleasure, just as, in the reverse formation, there is pleasure in being looked at. Originally, in his *Three Essays on Sexuality*, Freud isolated scopophilia as one of the component instincts of sexuality which exist as drives quite independently of the erotogenic zones. At this point he associated scopophilia with taking other people as objects, subjecting them to a controlling and curious gaze. His particular examples center around the voyeuristic activities of children, their desire to see and make sure of the private and the forbidden (curiosity about other people's genital and bodily functions, about the presence or absence of the penis, and, retrospectively, about the primal scene). In this analysis scopophilia is essentially active. (Later, in *Instincts and Their Vicissitudes*, Freud developed his theory of scopophilia further, attaching it initially to pre-genital auto-eroticism, after which the pleasure of the look is transferred to others by analogy. There is a close working here of the relationship between the active instinct and its further development in a narcissistic form.) Although the instinct is modified by other factors, in particular the constitution of the ego, it continues to exist as the erotic basis for pleasure in looking at another person as object. At the extreme, it can become fixated into a perversion, producing obsessive voyeurs and Peeping Toms, whose only sexual satisfaction can come from watching, in an active controlling sense, an objectified other.

At first glance, the cinema would seem to be remote from the undercover world of the surreptitious observation of an unknowing and unwilling victim. What is seen of the screen is so manifestly shown. But the mass of mainstream film, and the conventions within which it has consciously evolved, portray a hermetically sealed world which unwinds magically, indifferent to the presence of the audience, producing for them a sense of separation and playing on their voyeuristic phantasy. Moreover, the extreme contrast between the darkness in the auditorium (which also isolates the spectators from one another) and the brilliance of the shifting patterns of light and shade on the screen helps to promote the illusion of voyeuristic separation. Although the film is really being shown, is there to be seen, conditions of screening and narrative conventions give the spectator an illusion of looking in on a private world. Among other things, the position of the spectators in the cinema is blantantly one of repression of their exhibitionism and projection of the repressed desire on to the performer.

B.   The cinema satisfies a primordial wish for pleasurable looking, but it also goes further, developing scopophilia in its narcissistic aspect. The conventions of mainstream film focus attention on the human form. Scale, space, stories are all anthropomorphic. Here, curiosity and the wish to look intermingle with a fascination with likeness and recognition: the human face, the human body, the relationship between the human form and its surroundings, the visible presence of the person in the world. Jacques Lacan has described how the moment when a child recognizes its own image in the mirror is crucial for the constitution of the ego. Several aspects of this analysis are relevant here. The mirror phase occurs at a time when the child's physical ambitions outstrip his motor capacity, with the result that his recognition of himself is joyous in that he imagines his mirror image to be more complete, more perfect than he experiences his own body. Recognition is thus overlaid with mis-recognition: the image recognized is conceived as the reflected body of the self, but its misrecognition as superior projects this body outside itself as an ideal ego, the alienated subject, which, re-introjected as an ego ideal, gives rise to the future generation of identification with others. This mirror-moment predates language for the child.

Important for this article is the fact that it is an image that constitutes the matrix of the imaginary, of recognition/misrecognition and identification, and hence of the first articulation of the "I," of subjectivity. This is a moment when an older fascination with looking (at the mother's face, for an obvious example) collides with the initial inklings of self-awareness. Hence it is the birth of the long love affair/despair between image and self-image which has found such intensity of expression in film and such joyous recognition in the cinema audience. Quite apart from the extraneous similarities between screen and mirror (the framing of the human form in its surroundings, for instance), the cinema has structures of fascination strong enough to allow temporary loss of ego while simultaneously reinforcing the ego. The sense of forgetting the world as the ego has subsequently come to perceive it (I forgot who I am and where I was) is nostalgically reminiscent of that pre-subjective moment of image recognition. At the same time the cinema has distinguished itself in the production of ego ideals as expressed in particular in the star system, the stars centering both screen presence and screen story as they act out a complex process of likeness and difference (the glamorous impersonates the ordinary).

C.   Sections II. A and B have set out two contradictory aspects of the pleasurable structures of looking in the conventional cinematic situation. The first, scopophilic, arises from pleasure in using another person as an object of sexual stimulation through sight. The second, developed through narcissism and the constitution of the ego, comes from identification with the image seen. Thus, in film terms, one implies a separation of the erotic identity of the subject from the object on the screen (active scopophilia), the other demands identification of the ego with the object on the screen through the spectator's fascination with and recognition of his like. The first is a function of the sexual instincts, the second of ego libido. This dichotomy was crucial for Freud. Although he saw the two as interacting and overlaying each other, the tension between instinctual drives and self-preservation continues to be a dramatic polarization in terms of pleasure. Both are formative structures, mechanisms not meaning. In themselves they have no signification, they have to be attached to an idealization. Both pursue aims in indifference to perceptual reality, creating the imagized, eroticized concept of the world that forms the perception of the subject and makes a mockery of empirical objectivity.

During its history, the cinema seems to have evolved a particular illusion of reality in which this contradiction between libido and ego has found a beautifully complementary fantasy world. In *reality* the fantasy world of the screen is subject to the law which produces it. Sexual instincts and identification processes have a meaning within the symbolic order which articulates desire. Desire, born with language, allows the possibility of transcending the instinctual and the imaginary, but its point of reference continually returns to the traumatic moment of its birth: the castration complex. Hence the look, pleasurable in form, can be threatening in content, and it is woman as representation/image that crystallizes this paradox.

III   Woman as Image, Man as Bearer of the Look

A.   In a world ordered by sexual imbalance, pleasure in looking has been split between active/male and passive/female. The determining male gaze projects its phantasy on to the female figure which is styled accordingly. In their traditional exhibitionist role women are simultaneously looked at and displayed, with their appearance coded for strong visual and erotic impact so that they can be said to connote *to-be-looked-at-ness*. Woman displayed as sexual object is the leit-motif of erotic spectacle: from pin-ups to strip-tease, from Ziegfeld to Busby Berkeley, she holds the look, plays to and signifies male desire. Mainstream film neatly combined spectacle and narrative. (Note, however, how in the musical song-and-dance numbers break the flow of the diegesis.) The presence of woman is an indispensable element of spectacle in normal narrative film, yet her visual presence tends to work against the development of a story line, to freeze the flow of action in moments of erotic contemplation. This alien presence then has to be integrated into cohesion with the narrative. As Budd Boetticher has put it:

> What counts is what the heroine provokes, or rather what she represents. She is the one, or rather the love or fear she inspires in the hero, or else the concern he feels for her, who makes him act the way he does. In herself the woman has not the slightest importance.

(A recent tendency in narrative film has been to dispense with this problem altogether; hence the development of what Molly Haskell has called the "buddy movie," in which the active homosexual eroticism of the central male figures can carry the story without distraction.) Traditionally, the woman displayed has functioned on two levels: as erotic object for the characters within the screen story, and as erotic object for the spectator within the auditorium, with a shifting tension between the looks on either side of the screen. For instance, the device of the show-girl allows the two looks to be unified technically without any apparent break in the diegesis. A woman performs within the narrative, the gaze of the spectator and that of the male characters in the film are neatly combined without breaking narrative verisimilitude. For a moment the sexual impact of the performing woman takes the film into a no-man's-land outside its own time and space. Thus Marilyn Monroe's first appearance in *The River of No Return* and Lauren Bacall's songs in *To Have and Have Not*. Similarly, conventional close-ups of legs (Dietrich, for instance) or a face (Garbo) integrate into the narrative a different mode of eroticism. One part of a fragmented body destroys the

Renaissance space, the illusion of depth demanded by the narrative, it gives flatness, the quality of a cut-out or icon rather than verisimilitude to the screen.

B.   An active/passive heterosexual division of labor has similarly controlled narrative structure. According to the principles of the ruling ideology and the physical structures that back it up, the male figure cannot bear the burden of sexual objectification. Man is reluctant to gaze at his exhibitionist like. Hence the split between spectacle and narrative supports the man's role as the active one of forwarding the story, making things happen. The man controls the film phantasy and also emerges as the representative of power in a further sense: as the bearer of the look of the spectator, transferring it behind the screen to neutralize the extra-diegetic tendencies represented by woman as spectacle. This is made possible through the processes set in motion by structuring the film around a main controlling figure with whom the spectator can identify. As the spectator identifies with the main male[1] protagonist, he projects his look on to that of his like, his screen surrogate, so that the power of the male protagonist as he controls events coincides with the active power of the erotic look, both giving a satisfying sense of omnipotence. A male movie star's glamorous characteristics are thus not those of the erotic object of the gaze, but those of the more perfect, more complete, more powerful ideal ego conceived in the original moment of recognition in front of the mirror. The character in the story can make things happen and control events better than the subject/spectator, just as the image in the mirror was more in control of motor coordination. In contrast to woman as icon, the active male figure (the ego ideal of the identification process) demands a three-dimensional space corresponding to that of the mirror-recognition in which the alienated subject internalized his own representation of this imaginary existence. He is a figure in a landscape. Here the function of film is to reproduce as accurately as possible the so-called natural conditions of human perception. Camera technology (as exemplified by deep focus in particular) and camera movements (determined by the action of the protagonist), combined with invisible editing (demanded by realism) all tend to blur the limits of screen space. The male protagonist is free to command the stage, a stage of spatial illusion in which he articulates the look and creates the action.

C.1   Sections III. A and B have set out a tension between a mode of representation of woman in film and conventions surrounding the diegesis. Each is associated with a look: that of the spectator in direct scopophilic contact with the female form displayed for his enjoyment (connoting male phantasy) and that of the spectator fascinated with the image of his like set in an illusion of natural space, and through him gaining control and possession of the woman within the diegesis. (This tension and the shift from one pole to the other can structure a single text. Thus both in *Only Angels Have Wings* and in *To Have and Have Not*, the film opens with the woman as object of the combined gaze of spectator and all the male protagonists in the film. She is isolated, glamorous, on display, sexualized. But as the narrative progresses she falls in love with the main male protagonist and becomes his property, losing her outward glamorous characteristics, her generalized sexuality, her show-girl connotations; her eroticism is subjected to the male star alone. By means of identification with him, through participation in his power, the spectator can indirectly possess her too.)

But in psychoanalytic terms, the female figure poses a deeper problem. She also connotes something that the look continually circles around but disavows: her lack of a penis, implying a threat of castration and hence unpleasure. Ultimately, the meaning of woman is sexual difference, the absence of the penis as visually ascertainable, the material evidence on which is based the castration complex essential for the organization of entrance to the symbolic order and the law of the father. Thus the woman as icon, displayed for the gaze and enjoyment of men, the active controllers of the look, always threatens to evoke the anxiety it originally signified. The male unconscious has two avenues of escape from this castration anxiety: preoccupation with the re-enactment of the original trauma (investigating the woman, demystifying her mystery), counterbalanced by the devaluation, punishment or saving of the guilty object (an avenue typified by the concerns of the *film noir*); or else complete disavowal of castration by the substitution of a fetish object or turning the represented figure itself into a fetish so that it becomes reassuring rather than dangerous (hence overvaluation, the cult of the female star). This second avenue, fetishistic scopophilia, builds up the physical beauty of the object, transforming it into something satisfying in itself. The first avenue, voyeurism, on the contrary, has associations with sadism: pleasure lies in ascertaining guilt (immediately associated with castration), asserting control, and subjecting the guilty person through punishment or forgiveness. This sadistic side fits well with narrative. Sadism demands a story, depends on making something happen, forcing a change in another person, a battle of will and strength, victory/defeat, all occuring in a linear time with a beginning and an end. Fetishistic scopophilia, on the other hand, can exist outside linear time as the erotic instinct is focused on the look alone. These contradictions and ambiguities can be illustrated more simply by using works by Hitchcock and Sternberg, both of whom take the look almost as the content of subject matter of many of their films. Hitchcock is the more complex, as he uses both mechanisms. Sternberg's work, on the other hand, provides many pure examples of fetishistic scopophilia.

C.2   It is well known that Sternberg once said he would welcome his films being projected upside down so that story and character involvement would not interfere with the spectator's undiluted appreciation of the screen image. This statement is revealing but ingenuous. Ingenuous in that his films do demand that the figure of the woman (Dietrich, in the cycle of films with her, as the ultimate example) should be identifiable. But revealing in that it emphasizes the fact that for him the pictorial space enclosed by the frame is paramount rather than narrative or identification processes. While Hitchcock goes into the investigative side of voyeurism, Sternberg produces the ultimate fetish, taking it to the point where the powerful look of the male protagonist (characteristic of traditional narrative film) is broken in favor of the image in direct erotic rapport with the spectator. The beauty of the woman as object and the screen space coalesce; she is no longer the bearer of guilt but a perfect product, whose body, stylized and fragmented by close-ups, is the content of the film and the direct recipient of the spectator's look. Sternberg plays down the illusion of screen depth; his screen tends to be one-dimensional, as light and shade, lace, steam, foliage, net, streamers, etc., reduce the visual field. There is little or no mediation of the look through the eyes of the main male protagonist. On the contrary, shadowy presences like La Bessière in *Morocco* act as surrogates for the director, detached as they are from audience identification. Despite Sternberg's insistence that his stories are irrelevant, it is significant that they are concerned with situation, not suspense, and cyclical rather than linear time, while plot complications revolve around misunderstanding rather than conflict. The most important absence is that of the controlling male gaze within the screen scene. The high point of emotional drama in the most typical Dietrich films, her supreme moments of erotic meaning, take place in the absence of the man she loves in the fiction. There are other witnesses, other spectators watching her on the screen, their gaze is one with, not standing in for, that of the audience. At the end of *Morocco*, Tom Brown has already disappeared into the desert when Amy Jolly kicks off her gold sandals and walks after him. At the end of *Dishonored*, Kranau is indifferent to the fate of Magda. In both cases, the erotic impact, sanctified by death, is displayed as a spectacle for the audience. The male hero misunderstands and, above all, does not see.

In Hitchcock, by contrast, the male hero does see precisely what the audience sees. However, in the films I shall discuss here, he takes fascination with an image through scopophilic eroticism as the subject of the film. Moreover, in these cases the hero portrays the contradictions and tensions experienced by the spectator. In *Vertigo* in particular, but also in *Marnie* and *Rear Window*, the look is central to the plot, oscillating between voyeurism and fetishistic fascination. As a twist, a further manipulation of the normal viewing process which in some sense reveals it, Hitchcock uses the process of identification normally associated with ideological correctness and the recognition of established morality and shows up its perverted side. Hitchcock has never concealed his interest in voyeurism, cinematic and non-cinematic. His heroes are exemplary of the symbolic order and the law—a policeman (*Vertigo*), a dominant male possessing money and power (*Marnie*)—but their erotic drives lead them into compromised situations. The power to subject another person to the will sadistically or to the gaze voyeuristically is turned on to the woman as the object of both. Power is backed by a certainty of legal right and the established guilt of the woman (evoking castration, psychoanalytically speaking). True perversion is barely concealed under a shallow mask of ideological correctness—the man is on the right side of the law, the woman on the wrong. Hitchcock's skillful use of identification processes and liberal use of subjective camera from the point of view of the male protagonist draw the spectators deeply into his position, making them share his uneasy gaze. The audience is absorbed into a voyeuristic situation within the screen scene and diegesis which parodies his own in the cinema. In his analysis of *Rear Window*, Douchet takes the film as a metaphor for the cinema. Jeffries is the audience, the events in the apartment block opposite correspond to the screen. As he watches, an erotic dimension is added to his look, a central image to the drama. His girl-friend Lisa had been of little sexual interest to him, more or less a drag, so long as she remained on the spectator side. When she crosses the barrier between his room and the block opposite, their relationship is re-born erotically. He does not merely watch her through his lens, as a distant meaningful image, he also sees her as a guilty intruder exposed by a dangerous man threatening her with punishment, and thus finally saves her. Lisa's exhibitionism has already been established by her obsessive interest in dress and style, in being a passive image of visual perfection; Jeffries's voyeurism and activity have also been established through his work as a photo-journalist, a maker of stories and captor of images. However, his enforced inactivity, binding him to his seat as a specta-tor, puts him squarely in the phantasy position of the cinema audience.

In *Vertigo*, subjective camera predominates. Apart from one flash-back from Judy's point of view, the narrative is woven around what Scottie sees or fails to see. The audience follows the growth of his erotic obsession and subsequent despair precisely from his point of view. Scottie's voyeurism is blatant: he falls in love with a woman he follows and spies on without speaking to. Its sadistic side is equally blatant: he has chosen (and freely chosen, for he had been a successful lawyer) to be a policeman, with all the attendant possibilities of pursuit and investigation. As a result, he follows, watches and falls in love with a perfect image of female beauty and mystery. Once he actually confronts her, his erotic drive is to break her down and force her to tell by persistent cross-questioning. Then, in the second part of the film, he re-enacts his obsessive involvement with the image he loved to watch secretly. He reconstructs Judy as Madeleine, forces her to conform in every detail to the actual physical appearance of his fetish. Her exhibitionism, her masochism, make her an ideal passive counterpart to Scottie's active sadistic voyeurism. She knows her part is to perform, and only by playing it through and then replaying it can she keep Scottie's erotic interest. But in the repeti-tion he does break her down and succeeds in exposing her guilt. His curiosity wins through and she is punished. In *Vertigo*, erotic involvement with the look is disorientating: the spectator's fascination is turned against him as the narrative carries him through and entwines him with the processes that he is himself exercising. The Hitchcock hero here is firmly placed within the symbolic order, in narrative terms. He has all the attributes of the patriarchal super-ego. Hence the spectator, lulled into a false sense of security by the apparent legality of his surrogate, sees through his look and finds himself exposed as complicit, caught in the moral ambiguity of looking. Far from being simply an aside on the perversion of the police, *Vertigo* focuses on the implications of the active/looking, passive/looked-at split in terms of sexual difference and the power of the male symbolic encapsulated in the hero. Marnie, too, performs for Mark Rutland's gaze and masquerades as the perfect to-be-looked-at image. He, too, is on the side of the law until, drawn in by obsession with her guilt, her secret, he longs to see her in the act of committing a crime, make her confess and thus save her. So he, too, becomes complicit as he acts out the implications of his power. He controls money and words, he can have his cake and eat it.

III   Summary

The psychoanalytic background that has been discussed in this article is relevant to the pleasure and unpleasure offered by traditional narrative film. The scopophilic instinct (pleasure in looking at another person as an erotic object), and, in contradistinction, ego libido (forming identification processes) act as formations, mechanisms, which this cinema has played on. The image of woman as (passive) raw material for the (active) gaze of man takes the argument a step further into the structure of representation, adding a further layer demanded by the ideology of the patriarchal order as it is worked out in its favorite cinematic form—illusionistic narrative film. The argument returns again to the psychoanalytic background in that woman as representation signifies castration, inducing voyeuristic or fetishistic mechanisms to circumvent her threat. None of these interacting layers is intrinsic to film, but it is only in the film form that they can reach a perfect and beautiful contradiction, thanks to the possibility in the cinema of shifting the emphasis of the look. It is the place of the look that defines cinema, the possibility of varying it and exposing it. This is what makes cinema quite different in its voyeuristic potential from, say, strip-tease, theater, shows, etc. Going far beyond highlighting a woman's to-be-looked-at-ness, cinema builds the way she is to be looked at into the spectacle itself. Playing on the tension between film as controlling the dimension of time (editing, narrative) and film as controlling the dimension of space (changes in distance, editing), cinematic codes create a gaze, a world, and an object, thereby producing an illusion cut to the measure of desire. It is these cinematic codes and their relationship to formative external structures that must be broken down before mainstream film and the pleasure it provides can be challenged.

To begin with (as an ending), the voyeuristic-scopophilic look that is a crucial part of traditional filmic pleasure can itself be broken down. There are three different looks associated with cinema: that of the camera as it records the pro-filmic event, that of the audience as it watches the final product, and that of the characters at each other within the screen illusion. The conventions of narrative film deny the first two and subordinate them to the third, the conscious aim being always to eliminate intrusive camera presence and prevent a distancing awareness in the audience. Without these two absences (the material existence of the recording process, the critical reading of the spectator), fictional drama cannot achieve reality, obviousness and truth. Nevertheless, as this article has argued, the structure of looking in narrative fiction film contains a contradiction in its own premises: the female image as a castration threat constantly endangers the unity of the diegesis and bursts through the world of illusion as an intrusive, static, one-dimensional fetish. Thus the two looks materially present in time and space are obsessively subordinated to the neurotic needs of the male ego. The camera becomes the mechanism for producing an illusion of Renaissance space, flowing movements compatible with the human eye, an ideology of representation that revolves around the perception of the subject; the camera's look is disavowed in order to create a convincing world in which the spectator's surrogate can perform with verisimilitude. Simultaneously, the look of the audience is denied an intrinsic force: as soon as fetishistic representation of the female image threatens to break the spell of illusion, and the erotic image on the screen appears directly (without mediation) to the spectator, the fact of fetishization, concealing as it does castration fear, freezes the look, fixates the spectator and prevents him from achieving any distance from the image in front of him.

This complex interaction of looks is specific to film. The first blow against the monolithic accumulation of traditional film conventions (already undertaken by radical film-makers) is to free the look of the camera into its materiality in time and space and the look of the audience into dialectics, passionate detachment. There is no doubt that this destroys the satisfaction, pleasure and privilege of the "invisible guest," and highlights how film has depended on voyeuristic active/passive mechanisms. Women, whose image has continually been stolen and used for this end, cannot view the decline of the traditional film form with anything much more than sentimental regret.

Notes

1.   There are films with a woman as main protagonist, of course. To analyze this phenomenon seriously here would take me too far afield. Pam Cook and Claire Johnston's study of *The Revolt of Mamie Stover* in Phil Hardy, ed., *Raoul Walsh*, Edinburgh 1974, shows in a striking case how the strength of this female protagonist is more apparent than real.

5

Afterthoughts on "Visual Pleasure and Narrative Cinema" inspired by *Duel in the Sun*

Laura Mulvey

So many times over the years since my article "Visual Pleasure and Narrative Cinema," was published in *Screen*, I have been asked why I only used the *male* third person singular to stand in for the spectator. At the time, I was interested in the relationship between the image of woman on the screen and the "masculinization" of the spectator position, regardless of the actual sex (or possible deviance) of any real live movie-goer. In-built patterns of pleasure and identification impose masculinity as "point of view," a point of view which is also manifest in the general use of the masculine third person. However, the persistent question "what about the women in the audience?" and my own love of Hollywood melodrama (equally shelved as an issue in "Visual Pleasure") combined to convince me that, however ironically it had been intended originally, the male third person closed off avenues of inquiry that should be followed up. Finally, *Duel in the Sun* and its heroine's crisis of sexual identity brought both areas together.

I still stand by my "Visual Pleasure" argument, but would now like to pursue the other two lines of thought. First (the "women in the audience" issue), whether the female spectator is carried along, as it were by the scruff of the text, or whether her pleasure can be more deep-rooted and complex. Second (the "melodrama" issue), how the text and its attendant identifications are affected by a *female* character occupying the center of the narrative arena. So far as the first issue is concerned, it is always possible that the female spectator may find herself so out of key with the pleasure on offer, with its "masculinization," that the spell of fascination is broken. On the other hand, she may not. She may find herself secretly, unconsciously almost, enjoying the freedom of action and control over the diegetic world that identification with a hero provides. It is *this* female spectator that I want to consider here. So far as the second issue is concerned, I want to limit the area under consideration in a similar manner. Rather than discussing melodrama in general, I am concentrating on films in which a woman central protagonist is shown to be unable to achieve a stable sexual identity, torn between the deep blue sea of passive femininity and the devil of regressive masculinity.

There is an overlap between the two areas, between the unacknowledged dilemma faced in the auditorium and the dramatic double-bind up there on the screen. Generally it is dangerous to elide these two separate worlds. In this case, the emotions of those women accepting "masculinization" while watching action movies with a male hero are illuminated by the emotions of a heroine of a melodrama whose resistance to a "correct" feminine position is the crucial issue at stake. Her oscillation, her inability to achieve stable sexual identity, is echoed by the woman spectator's masculine "point of view." Both create a sense of the difficulty of sexual difference in cinema that is missing in the undifferentiated spectator of "Visual Pleasure." The unstable, oscillating difference is thrown into relief by Freud's theory of femininity.

The female spectator's pleasure

Freud and femininity

For Freud, femininity is complicated by the fact that it emerges out of a crucial period of parallel development between the sexes; a period he sees as masculine, or phallic, for both boys and girls. The terms he uses to conceive of femininity are the same as those he has mapped out for the male, causing certain problems of language and boundaries to expression. These problems reflect, very accurately, the actual position of women in patriarchal society (suppressed, for instance, under the generalized male third person singular). One term gives rise to a second as its complementary opposite, the male to the female, in that order. Some quotations:

> In females, too, the striving to be masculine is ego—syntonic at a certain period—namely in the phallic phase, before the development of femininity sets in. But it then succumbs to the momentous process of repression, as so often has been shown, that determines the fortunes of a woman's femininity.[1]

> I will only emphasize here that the development of femininity remains exposed to disturbances by the residual phenomena of the early masculine period. Regressions to the pre-Oedipus phase very frequently occur; in the course of some women's lives there is a repeated alternation between periods in which femininity and masculinity gain the upper hand.[2]

"Femininity":

We have called the motive force of sexual life "the libido." Sexual life is dominated by the polarity of masculine–feminine; thus the notion suggests itself of considering the relation of the libido to this antithesis. It would not be surprising if it were to turn out that each sexuality had its own special libido appropriated to it, so that one sort of libido would pursue the aims of a masculine sexual life and another sort those of a feminine one. But nothing of the kind is true. There is only one libido, which serves both the masculine and the feminine functions. To it itself we cannot assign any sex; if, following the conventional equation of activity and masculinity, we are inclined to describe it as masculine, we must not forget that it also covers trends with a passive aim. Nevertheless, the juxtaposition "feminine libido" is without any justification. Furthermore, it is our impression that more constraint has been applied to the libido when it is pressed into the service of the feminine function, and that—to speak teleogically—Nature takes less careful account of its [that function's] demands than in the case of masculinity. And the reason for this may lie—thinking once again teleologically—in the fact that the accomplishment of the aim of biology has been entrusted to the aggressiveness of men and has been made to some extent independent of women's consent.[3]

One particular point of interest in this passage is Freud's shift from the use of active/masculine as *metaphor* for the function of libido to an invocation of Nature and biology that appears to leave the metaphoric usage behind. There are two problems here: Freud introduces the use of the word *masculine* as "conventional," apparently simply following an established social–linguistic practice (but which, once again, confirms the masculine "point of view"); however, secondly, and constituting a greater intellectual stumbling block, the feminine cannot be conceptualized as different, but rather only as *opposition* (passivity) in an antinomic sense, or as *similarity* (the phallic phase). This is not to suggest that a hidden, as yet undiscovered femininity exists (as perhaps implied by Freud's use of the word "Nature") but that its structural relationship to masculinity under patriarchy cannot be defined or determined within the terms offered. This shifting process, this definition in terms of opposition or similarity, leaves women also shifting between the metaphoric opposition "active" and "passive." The correct road, *femininity*, leads to increasing repression of "the active" (the "phallic phase" in Freud's terms). In this sense Hollywood genre films structured around masculine pleasure, offering an identification with the *active* point of view, allow a woman spectator to rediscover that lost aspect of her sexual identity, the never fully repressed bed-rock of feminine neurosis.

Narrative grammar and trans-sex identification

The "convention" cited by Freud (active/masculine) structures most popular narratives, whether film, folk-tale or myth (as I argued in "Visual Pleasure"), where his metaphoric usage is acted out literally in the story. Andromeda stays tied to the rock, a victim, in danger, until Perseus slays the monster and saves her. It is not my aim, here, to debate on the rights and wrongs of this narrative division of labour or to demand positive heroines, but rather to point out that the "grammar" of the story places the reader, listener or spectator *with* the hero. The woman spectator in the cinema can make use of an age-old cultural tradition adapting her to this convention, which eases a transition out of her own sex into another. In "Visual Pleasure" my argument was axed around a desire to identify a pleasure that was specific to cinema, that is the eroticism and cultural conventions surrounding the look. Now, on the contrary, I would rather emphasize the way that popular cinema inherited traditions of story-telling that are common to other forms of folk and mass culture, with attendant fascinations other than those of the look.

Freud points out that "masculinity" is, at one stage, ego-syntonic for a woman. Leaving aside, for the moment, problems posed by his use of words, his general remarks on stories and day-dreams provide another angle of approach, this time giving a cultural rather than psychoanalytic insight into the dilemma. He emphasizes the relationship between the ego and the narrative concept of the hero:

> It is the true heroic feeling, which one of our best writers has expressed in the inimitable phrase, "Nothing can happen to me!" It seems, however, that through this revealing characteristic of invulnerability we can immediately recognize His Majesty the Ego, the hero of every day-dream and every story.[4]

Although a boy might know quite well that it is most *unlikely* that he will go out into the world, make his fortune through prowess or the assistance of helpers, and marry a princess, the stories describe the male phantasy of ambition, reflecting something of an experience and expectation of dominance (the active). For a girl, on the other hand, the cultural and social overlap is more confusing. Freud's argument that a young girl's day-dreams concentrate on the erotic ignores his own position on her early masculinity and the active day-dreams necessarily associated with this phase. In fact, all too often, the erotic function of the woman is represented by the passive, the waiting (Andromeda again), acting above all as a formal closure to the narrative structure. Three elements can thus be drawn together: Freud's concept of "masculinity" in women, the identification triggered by the logic of a narrative grammar, and the ego's desire to phantasize itself in a certain, active, manner. All three suggest that, as desire is given cultural materiality in a text, for women (from childhood onwards) trans-sex identification is a *habit* that very easily becomes *second Nature*. However, this Nature does not sit easily and shifts restlessly in its borrowed transvestite clothes.

A heroine causes a generic shift

The Western and Oedipal personifications

Using a concept of character function based on V. Propp's *Morphology of the Folk-tale*, I want to argue for a chain of links and shifts in narrative pattern, showing up the changing function of "woman." The Western (allowing, of course, for as many deviances as one cares to enumerate) bears a residual imprint of the primitive narrative structure analyzed by Vladimir Propp in folk-tales. Also, in the hero's traditional invulnerability, the Western ties in closely with Freud's remarks on day-dreaming. (As I am interested primarily in character function and narrative pattern, not in genre definition, many issues about the Western as such are being summarily side-stepped.) For present purposes, the Western genre provides a crucial node in a series of transformations that *comment* on the function of "woman" (as opposed to "man") as a narrative signifier and sexual difference as personification of "active" or "passive" elements in a story.

In the Proppian tale, an important aspect of narrative closure is "marriage," a function characterized by "princess" or equivalent. This is the only function that is sex-specific, and thus essentially relates to the sex of the hero and his marriageability. This function is very commonly reproduced in the Western, where, once again "marriage" makes a crucial contribution to narrative closure. However, in the Western the function's presence has also come to allow a complication in the form of its opposite, "not marriage." Thus, while the social integration represented by marriage is an essential aspect of the folk-tale, in the Western it can be accepted . . . or not. A hero can gain in stature by refusing the princess and remaining alone (Randolph Scott in the Ranown series of movies). As the resolution of the Proppian tale can be seen to represent the resolution of the Oedipus complex (integration into the symbolic), the rejection of marriage personifies a nostalgic celebration of phallic, narcissistic omnipotence. Just as Freud's comments on the "phallic" phase in girls seemed to belong in limbo, without a place in the chronology of sexual development, so, too, does this male phenomenon seem to belong to a phase of play and phantasy difficult to integrate exactly into the Oedipal trajectory.

The tension between two points of attraction, the symbolic (social integration and marriage) and nostalgic narcissism, generates a common splitting of the Western hero into two, something unknown in the Proppian tale. Here two functions emerge, one celebrating integration into society through marriage, the *other* celebrating resistance to social demands and responsibilities, above all those of marriage and the family, the sphere represented by woman. A story such as *The Man Who Shot Liberty Valance* juxtaposes these two points of attraction, and spectator phantasy can have its cake and eat it too. This particular tension between the doubled hero also brings out the underlying signficance of the drama, its relation to the symbolic, with unusual clarity. A folk-tale story revolves around conflict between hero and villain. The flashback narration in *Liberty Valance* seems to follow these lines at first. The narrative is generated by an act of villainy (Liberty rampages, dragon-like, around the countryside). However, the development of the story acquires a complication. The issue at stake is no longer how the villain will be defeated, but how the villain's defeat will be inscribed into history, whether the *upholder* of law as a symbolic system (Ranse) will be seen to be victorious or the *personification* of law in a more primitive manifestation (Tom), closer to the good or the right. *Liberty Valance*, as it uses flashback structure, also brings out the poignancy of this tension. The "present-tense" story is precipitated by a funeral, so that the story is shot through with nostalgia and sense of loss. Ranse Stoddart mourns Tom Doniphon.

This narrative structure is based on an opposition between two irreconcilables. The two paths cannot cross. On one side there is an encapsulation of power, and phallic attributes, in an individual who has to bow himself out of the way of history. On the other, an individual impotence rewarded by political and financial power, which, *in the long run*, in fact becomes history. Here the function "marriage" is as crucial as it is in the folk-tale. It plays the same part in creating narrative resolution, but it is even more important in that "marriage is an integral attribute of the upholder of the law. In this sense Hallie's choice between the two men is pre-determined. Hallie equals princess equals Oedipal resolution rewarded, equals repression of narcissistic sexuality in marriage.

Woman as signifier of sexuality

In a Western working within these conventions, the function "marriage" sublimates the erotic into a final, closing, social ritual. This ritual is, of course, sex-specific, and the main rationale for any female presence in this strand of the genre. This neat *narrative* function restates the propensity for "woman" to signify "the erotic" already familiar from *visual* representation (as, for instance, argued in "Visual Pleasure"). Now I want to discuss the way in which introducing a woman as central to a story shifts its meanings, producing another kind of narrative discourse. *Duel in the Sun* provides the opportunity for this. While the film remains visibly a "Western," the generic space seems to shift. The landscape of action, although present, is not the dramatic core of the film's story, rather it is the interior drama of a girl caught between two conflicting desires. The conflicting desires, first of all, correspond closely with Freud's argument about female sexuality quoted above, that is: an oscillation between "passive" femininity and regressive "masculinity." Thus, the symbolic equation, woman equals sexuality, still persists, but now rather than being an image or a narrative function, the equation opens out a

Duel in the Sun (King Vidor, 1947)

narrative area previously suppressed or repressed. She is no longer the signifier of sexuality (function "marriage") in the "Western" type of story. Now the female presence as center allows the story to be actually, *overtly*, about sexuality: it becomes a melodrama. It is as though the narrational lens had zoomed in and opened up the neat function "marriage" ("and they lived happily . . .") to ask "what next?" and to focus on the figure of the princess, waiting in the wings for her one moment of importance, to ask "what does *she* want?" Here we find the generic terrain for melodrama, in its woman-oriented strand. The second question ("what does *she* want?") takes on greater significance when the hero function is split, as described above in the case of *Liberty Valance*, where the heroine's choice puts the seal of married grace on the upholder of the Law. *Duel in the Sun* opens up this question.

In *Duel in the Sun* the iconographical attributes of the two male (oppositional) characters, Lewt and Jesse, conform very closely to those of Ranse and

Tom in *Liberty Valance*. But now the opposition between Ranse and Tom (which represents an abstract and allegorical conflict over Law and history) is given a completely different twist of meaning. As Pearl is at the center of the story, caught between the two men, their alternative attributes acquire meaning *from* her, and represent different sides of her desire and aspiration. They personify the split in *Pearl*, not a split in the concept of *hero*, as argued previously for *Liberty Valance*.

However, from a psychoanalytic point of view, a strikingly similar pattern emerges, Jesse (attributes: book, dark suit, legal skills, love of learning and culture, destined to be Governor of the State, money, and so on) signposts the "correct" path for Pearl, towards learning a passive sexuality, learning to "be a lady," above all sublimation into a concept of the feminine that is socially viable. Lewt (attributes: guns, horses, skill with horses, Western get-up, contempt for culture, destined to die an outlaw, personal strength and personal power) offers sexual passion, not based on maturity but on a regressive, boy/girl mixture of rivalry and play. With Lewt, Pearl can be a tomboy (riding, swimming, shooting). Thus the Oedipal dimension persists, but now illuminates the sexual ambivalence it represents for femininity.

In the last resort, there is no more room for Pearl in Lewt's world of misogynist machismo than there is room for her desires as Jesse's potential fiancée. The film consists of a series of oscillations in her sexual identity, between alternative paths of development, between different desperations. Whereas the regressive phallic male hero (Tom in *Liberty Valance*) had a place (albeit a doomed one) that was stable and meaningful, Pearl is unable to settle or find a "femininity" in which she and the male world can meet. In this sense, although the male characters personify Pearl's dilemma, it is their terms that make and finally break her. Once again, however, the narrative drama dooms the phallic, regressive resistance to the symbolic. Lewt, Pearl's masculine side, drops out of the social order. Pearl's masculinity gives her the "wherewithal" to achieve heroism and kill the villain. The lovers shoot each other and die in each other's arms. Perhaps, in *Duel*, the erotic relationship between Pearl and Lewt also exposes a dyadic interdependence between hero and villain in the primitive tale, now threatened by the splitting of the hero with the coming of the Law.

In *Duel in the Sun*, Pearl's inability to become a "lady" is highlighted by the fact that the perfect lady appears, like a phantasmagoria of Pearl's failed aspiration, as Jesse's perfect future wife. Pearl recognizes her and her rights over Jesse, and sees that she represents the "correct" road. In an earlier film by King Vidor, *Stella Dallas* (1937), narrative and iconographic structures similar to those outlined above make the dramatic meaning of the film *although it is not a Western*. Stella, as central character, is flanked on each side by a male personification of her instability, her inability to accept correct, married "femininity" on the one hand, or find a place in a macho world on

The Man Who Shot Liberty Valance (John Ford, 1962)

Stella Dallas (King Vidor, 1937)

the other. Her husband, Stephen, demonstrates all the attributes associated with Jesse, with no problems of generic shift. Ed Munn, representing Stella's regressive "masculine" side, is considerably emasculated by the loss of Western accoutrements and its terrain of violence. (The fact that Stella is a mother, and that her relationship to her child constitutes the central drama, undermines a possible sexual relationship with Ed.) He does retain residual traces of Western iconography. His attributes are mapped through associations with horses and betting, the racing scene. However, more importantly, his relationship with Stella is regressive, based on "having fun," most explicitly in the episode in which they spread itching powder among the respectable occupants of a train carriage. In *Stella Dallas*, too, a perfect wife appears for Stephen, representing the "correct" femininity that Stella rejects (very similar to Helen, Jesse's fiancée in *Duel in the Sun*).

I have been trying to suggest a series of transformations in narrative pattern that illuminate, but also show shifts in, Oedipal nostalgia. The "personifications" and their iconographical attributes do not relate to parental figures or reactivate an actual Oedipal moment. On the contrary, they represent an internal oscillation of desire, which lies dormant, waiting to be "pleasured" in stories of this kind. Perhaps the fascination of the classic Western, in particular, lies in its rather raw touching on this nerve. However, for the female spectator the situation is more complicated and goes beyond simple mourning for a lost phantasy of omnipotence. The masculine identification, in its phallic aspect, reactivates for her a phantasy of "action" that correct femininity demands should be repressed. The phantasy "action" finds expression through a metaphor of masculinity. Both in the language used by Freud and in the male personifications of desire flanking the female protagonist in the melodrama, this metaphor acts as a straitjacket, becoming itself an indicator, a litmus paper, of the problem inevitably activated by any attempt to represent the feminine in patriarchal society. The memory of the "masculine" phase has its own romantic attraction, a last-ditch resistance, in which the power of masculinity can be used as postponement against the power of patriarchy. Thus Freud's comments illuminate both the position of the female spectator and the image of oscillation represented by Pearl and Stella.

> In the course of some women's lives there is a repeated alternation between periods in which femininity and masculinity gain the upper hand.

> The phallic phase . . . but it then succumbs to the momentous process of repression as has so often been shown, that determines the fortunes of women's femininity.

I have argued that Pearl's position in *Duel in the Sun* is similar to that of the female spectator as she temporarily accepts "masculinization" in memory of her "active" phase. Rather than dramatizing the success of masculine identification, Pearl brings out its sadness. Her "tomboy" pleasures, her sexuality, are not accepted by Lewt, except in death. So, too, is the female spectator's phantasy of masculinization at cross-purposes with itself, restless in its transvestite clothes.

Notes

1.   Sigmund Freud, *Femininity*, vol. 22 of *The Complete Psychological Works, Standard Edition* (London, 1951).

2.   Sigmund Freud, *Analysis Terminable and Interminable*, vol. 23 of *The Complete Psychological Works, Standard Edition* (London, 1951).

3.   Sigmund Freud, *Femininity*, vol. 22 of *The Complete Psychological Works*.

4.   Sigmund Freud, *Creative Writers and Day-Dreaming*, vol. 9 of *The Complete Psychological Works, Standard Edition* (London, 1951).

6

Rereading the Work of Claire Johnston

Janet Bergstrom

There is an argument running throughout Claire Johnston's work which has to do with the relationship of the "progressive classical film" and a potential feminist counter-cinema. It is striking, on rereading this series of articles today—the five major essays and/or pamphlets published year by year since 1973, when *Notes on Women's Cinema* came out[1]—how little the basic argument has changed, both as it outlines the goals and methods of feminist film criticism and the parameters of a feminist film practice. We have decided to review this work now because, important as its influence has obviously been, there hasn't yet been any direct discussion of the central argument as such. As a result, a number of basic problems with its elaboration have gone unexamined, and have, moreover, been replicated in various articles based on Johnston's work. To an extent, our interest stems from a review of our own critical development: for the first issue of *Camera Obscura* we borrowed certain critical assumptions and procedures from these articles which we now find inadequate.

Before going any further, what is meant by the "progressive classical film?" The term is borrowed, as Johnston notes, from a *Cahiers du Cinéma* editorial which was published by Comolli and Narboni in October 1969 called "Cinema/Ideology/Criticism."[2] In it they outline a theoretical base for *Cahiers*' critical work directed toward an analysis of different relations between films and ideology. Seven types of films are differentiated in these terms. After the explicit content, the main criterion is whether or not the films challenge the traditional "depiction of reality," meaning the conventional means of cinematic representation. The first group includes the majority of films, which are "imbued through and through with the dominant ideology in pure and unadulterated form and give no indication that their makers were even aware of the fact." The opposite type is the film which attacks its "ideological assimilation" explicitly in its content, and which also attacks the traditional means of representation. A third type is the film with explicitly political content, but traditional form (Costa-Gavras's Z). A fourth is the film whose content is "not explicitly political, but in some way becomes so through the criticism practiced on it through its form." (*The Bellboy, Persona*). Then there is cinéma verité, divided between those films which do and do not challenge the dominant "methods of depiction." And there is also the category which concerns us now, which includes:

> films which seem at first sight to belong firmly within the ideology and to be completely under its sway, but which turn out to be so only in an ambiguous way. For though they start from a non-progressive standpoint, ranging from the frankly reactionary through the conciliatory to the mildly critical, they have been worked upon, and work, in such a real way that there is a noticeable gap, a dislocation, between the starting point and the finished product. . . . An internal criticism is taking place which cracks the film apart at the seams. If one reads the film obliquely, looking for symptoms, if one looks beyond its apparent formal coherence, one can see that it is riddled with cracks: it is splitting under an internal tension which is simply not there in an ideologically innocuous film. The ideology becomes subordinate to the text. It no longer has an independent existence. It is *presented* by the film. This is the case with many Hollywood films, for example, which, while being completely integrated in the system and the ideology, end up by partially dismantling the system from within.

The *Cahiers* collective analysis of *Young Mr. Lincoln* in 1970 was carried out on the assumption that it was this kind of progressive text, as was their analysis of *Morocco* later in the same year.[3]

This section of the *Cahiers* editorial is quoted at length in two of Johnston's articles, and Johnston follows its main lines closely, adding, however, a difference in emphasis: within this category, it is those films which present the working of patriarchal ideology which will be of interest to feminist film critics. Johnston's argument, then, has to do with the relationship between this "progressive classical film" and a feminist counter-cinema. It will be called here, for convenience, the rupture thesis because it is about "entertainment" films in which the feminine "voice," by formal means, breaks through (ruptures) the patriarchal discourse. It is equally about the lessons to be learned from these examples for feminist filmmaking.

As presented most fully and clearly in *Notes on Women's Cinema*, Johnston's thesis goes roughly as follows. The cinéma verité approach to feminist filmmaking, as well as the sociological approach to feminist film criticism—this describes the predominant modes of feminist film activity when the pamphlet came out in 1973—are rejected on the grounds that they have restricted their interest to women as subject matter and, taken in by realism, they fail to understand how the representation of woman functions within it. "Any revolutionary strategy must challenge the depiction of reality; it is not enough to discuss the oppression of women within the text of the film; the language of the cinema/the depiction of reality must also be interrogated so that a break between ideology and text is effected" (p. 29). One of the most polemical aspects of Johnston's article is that, not only does it reject what had been made specifically as feminist films by political collectives, but, ignoring also a Godardian type of interrogation of the ways meaning is produced in cinema, it takes as a model a particular kind of "entertainment film." (*Women and Film*, in contrast, had at this time rejected further work on Hollywood film on the grounds that it was endlessly reduplicating positions of women subjected to male fantasies.) The important reason given for this choice of a model within Hollywood cinema, from the standpoint of feminist theory, is that "women's cinema must embody the working through of desire." Because of the importance of this objective, Johnston maintains that the barriers which political filmmaking had thrown up between itself and the entertainment film—*either* political *or* entertainment—should come down, and aspects of each should be combined. Such a suggestion was another polemical move on Johnston's part, since most political filmmakers then saw pleasure or entertainment as part of the bourgeois dominant cinema, and they intended to break completely with this model.

The argument continues: feminist film critics should study the progressive classical film insofar as it exposes sexist ideology by investigating how signifying systems function there and, more specifically, how woman and the woman's desire figure there. This knowledge could be used as the basis for feminist filmmaking. To this end, Johnston suggests looking first at "films made by women within the Hollywood system which attempted by formal means to bring about a dislocation between sexist ideology and the text of the film" (p. 29). Dorothy Arzner's and Ida Lupino's films are proposed as progressive, and Nelly Kaplan's films are taken as examples of entertainment films made outside Hollywood which show the "working through of the woman's desire." The notion of a woman as fetish, functioning to mask and thereby ensure the repression of sexual difference (the sexual distinction becomes male/non-male instead of male/female) is introduced here, following the *Cahiers* reading of *Morocco*, as one direction in which work on signifying systems could proceed, and it will be developed in the subsequent essays which will work with, successively, concepts of ideology, textuality, enunciation, and suture in attempts to specify the placement of the subject by and through textual and symbolic systems.

In Johnston and Pam Cook's essay "The Place of Woman in the Cinema of Raoul Walsh" (1974), it is the way woman functions as empty sign, as the "lack," that is presented by the text. In "Femininity and the Masquerade" (1975), Johnston suggests that Tourneur, by foregrounding the repression of femininity in *Anne of the Indies*, exposes the mechanism of the fetish. In the introduction to the Arzner pamphlet (1975), Johnston quotes much of the *Cahiers* position directly and says that she will discuss Arzner's films in the same terms, "as a group of 'progressive' classic film texts which de-naturalize the working of patriarchal ideology." In her essay which follows, she says that "in Arzner's work the discourse of the woman, or rather her attempt to locate it, and make it heard, is what gives the system of the text its structural coherence, while at the same time rendering the dominant discourse of the male fragmented and incoherent." Pam Cook, in her companion essay, also argues in terms of the rupture thesis in language very close to that of *Cahiers*: "The entire text of the film [*Dance, Girl, Dance*] is cracked open as the workings of ideology in the contruction of female desires is exposed" (p. 15). And in Johnston's extremely condensed essay on suture in the *Edinburgh '76 Magazine*, she argues that *Jeanne Dielman*, by refusing to present us with the security of the reverse shot, opens up an eruption of the semiotic (which in this essay seems to be equated with the drives as well as the "feminine"), and that the rupture here threatens the fragmentation of the Symbolic order itself through the over-inscription of the repression of sexual difference. In these essays, the rupture thesis has been put forward first in terms of Surrealism (Nelly Kaplan and shocking the audience into awareness), then Russian Formalism and strange-making, de-naturalization, distanciation, and the eruption of the semiotic.

In retrospect, *Notes on Women's Cinema* clearly laid the groundwork for many important areas of research—through an insistence on a theoretical rather than a sociological approach to feminist filmmaking and criticism, a recognition of the importance of feminist criticism and theory *for* feminist filmmaking, an emphasis on the importance of an understanding of how the representation of women operates in classical narrative film, rather than in the casual and wholesale dismissal of Hollywood films from consideration, the connections made between language, discourse and the working through of the woman's desire, the introduction of topics within feminist theory such as woman-as-sign, the relationship between woman, representation and fetishism, the rejection of the idealistic notion that a political film had to reject pleasure—all this pointed ahead to the present moment, even if, now, it is necessary to go back to try to be precise and explicit about concepts that were then taken as self-evident: feminine specificity, woman's desire, pleasure or entertainment in film, enunciation and discourse in film.

There are a number of problems with the rupture thesis which go along with the assumption that there is a category of entertainment films which "exhibit a contradiction between ideology and text." Leaving aside the apparently reified way in which ideology is being used, most of the problems that we want to point out come from a lack of attention to the film-text as such in Johnston's (and Cook's) arguments. Not only does she not provide us with any textual analyses which could demonstrate the "working through" of the woman's desire or the woman's discourse in terms of a film's systems, whether for a section or on the level of the narrative as a whole, but the signifying material of film is almost entirely neglected, and this means film in its processes of producing meaning. Johnston's criticism of the sociologial critics was that they didn't take account of film's specificity, of film as a signifying system. But in fact, one finds very little attention to the signifier in these articles. Her arguments operate almost exclusively on the level of the narrative signifieds, these signifieds being equivalent here to highly interpreted narrative events.

For example, in her essay on Arzner, Johnston wants to show that the "tragic" endings of many Arzner films represent a "refusal of unification and closure [characteristic of the "dominant discourse in the classical Hollywood film"] and a resolution instead to play out the discourse of the woman to the bitter end" (p. 7).

> In *Christopher Strong* it manifests itself in final suicide on a solo flight, as Cynthia watches her past life and the impossible contradictions between her career and her lover flash before her eyes as her plane hurtles to the ground. For Nana the decision to take her own life in the face of impossible constraints placed on her by her lovers and their codes of gallantry is expressed as a sense of relief, as almost pleasurable: "I was born all wrong" . . . "I'm glad I'm going." The final lonely image of Harriet Craig surrounded by her immaculate, empty home implies that the narrative has been resolved, the solitary, emphatically artificial tear in her eye suggesting a sense of irony: convention demands that the tear be there, but its artificiality underlines the contradictions of her pyrrhic victory. . . . In all these cases, the discourse of the woman fails to triumph *over* the male discourse and the patriarchal ideology, but its very survival in the form of irony is in itself a kind of triumph, a victory against being expelled or erased: the continued insistence of the woman's discourse is a triumph over nonexistence.

That these narrative descriptions are highly interpreted is easy to see. Further, the irony which Johnston sees operating in these Arzner endings is stated as if it is part of a factual account of the narrative. It is assumed that these endings will be understood as ironic by everyone, and that this irony will work, for all spectators, in the woman's favor.

The problem, beyond presenting interpretations as if they were objective descriptions, is with certain implicit assumptions about the classical film. If one takes the view that there is a basic level of narrative information which is given out moment by moment in a film—let's say a level of narrative denotation—then, in theory, one would be able to point to any given moment (which would, of course, include numerous visual representations) and summarize its narrative "content." But these moments only take on their meanings from their value relative to the rest of the narrative; they figure, textually, in many discursive chains within the filmic system, none of which permit them to furnish an easy, univocal significance. It is a much simpler, and falsifying, model of meaning in film which takes interpreted narrative elements for "narrative signifiers" than models closer to Freud's which recognize the kinds of processes which overdetermine, as well as repress, significance. The tear in Harriet Craig's eye may well "mean" what is suggested in this essay. But, for one thing, that "meaning" may be cancelled out or overdetermined or made equivocal by other narrative interests, and, for another, we have no evidence or argument on the level of textual processes to back up the interpretation. We are being asked to believe a simple assertion.

The ruptures in the films Johnston discusses are based on key moments in a film which are stated, as in these examples, very briefly and are virtually never presented in any contextual complexity. Although Johnston refers to Stephen Heath's analysis of *Touch of Evil*[4] at the beginning of her article on *Anne of the Indies*, his article serves to demonstrate what, at the very least, presents a major paradox for what she is arguing—that is, the seemingly unlimited capacity for classical narrative film to create gaps, fissures, ruptures, generated most of all by its difficulty in containing sexual difference, only to recover them ultimately and to efface the memory, or at least the paths, of this heterogeneity. It is just this rupturing activity that is said to be characteristic of the classical text, and which, moreover, is thought to be the condition of a large part of its pleasure.

Near the end of the Arzner article, Johnston herself acknowledges the need for close analysis of these films: "In this essay I have not attempted to trace in detail the ways in which the strategies of dislocation, subversion and contradiction operate within the texts of individual films, though a close analysis is quite clearly a necessity at some point" (p. 7). However the way it is put, and the fact that she hasn't yet given us any, suggests that the usefulness of close analysis would be limited to a verification of her theses.

Jacquelyn Suter's analysis of *Christopher Strong* however (in this volume) shows the contrary of the victory of the woman's discourse in at least this film of Arzner's. The analysis begins from the question: what is woman's discourse and who speaks it in *Christopher Strong*, where the woman (Cynthia Darrington) is explicitly presented as both the subject and the object of desire. For the purpose of her paper and following up on Johnston's own terms, Suter attempts to mark when Cynthia may be said to represent feminine discourse (when she acts in her own interests—as subject of her own desire) and when she falls into place as object of the interests Christopher Strong represents, particularly family unity. (Discourse is taken here to mean the logic of actions as well as words.)

Although Cynthia, an aviatrix, appears to be an exceptionally daring and individual woman, acting in her own interests, on the structural level, far from being the independent figure she seems to be during much of the film, she serves a specific and crucial narrative function which undercuts her apparent strength. The film involves two couples, each threatened when one partner takes a lover. One of the couples is Christopher Strong and his wife; the lover is Cynthia. The other is Strong's daughter, Monica, who takes a lover, and her fiancé, who will become her husband. Structurally, Cynthia serves a mediating function between the partners and eventually reestablishes the unity of both couples, enabling Christopher's daughter to marry, and he and his wife to maintain their marriage. Cynthia's role is crucial to the resolution of the narrative, but this solution of the narrative's problems makes her unnecessary, and she is disposed of in her final, suicidal flight.

This analysis is important in the way it demonstrates the need to take the narrative movement as a whole into consideration rather than arguing, as Johnston consistently does, for the importance of one element, or even of elements chosen from throughout the narrative if they are still taken as moments, as points of rupture.

> Throughout the film, a pattern can be discerned: when Cynthia is concerned with aviation, she functions for herself alone. But when she involves herself with the Strong family, she functions for them as a mediator. This final flight collapses both types of functioning into one: her aviation is utilized as a vehicle of mediation. The fact that Cynthia chooses to remove herself through an activity uniquely her own expresses the conflict between acting out her own desires and acting out the desires of others. The superimposition sequence is a visual/aural signifier of Cynthia caught within this paradox.
>
> The above examples illustrate the impossibility within this film text for woman to exercise herself as subject outside the patriarchal order. When her voice is not undermined on the micro level, it is recuperated on the macro level by narrative constraints. *Christopher Strong* would seem to be structured around the containment of feminine discourse and all that this implies regarding the repression of feminine desire. ("Feminine Discourse in *Christopher Strong*," pp. 98–99)

The point in quoting this is not to voice a disagreement about the significance of particular actions or moments in *Christopher Strong*, but to show, again, some of the problems in the way Johnston's arguments are proposed.

The other side of arguing in terms of key moments which indicate a rupture in the film-text is the problem of predicting or prescribing the audience response to these moments. The basic notion of the position of the spectator/subject with respect to this "progressive" text has not changed perceptibly in Johnston's articles over the years, nor has the conception of the necessarily determining action of the ruptures in that text on the spectator, that is, the way it is claimed that, through them "ideology is revealed and made explicit" to the viewer. For example, in "The Place of Women in the Cinema of Raoul Walsh," Johnston and Cook say (having commented that the title credits of *The Revolt of Mamie Stover* are shown over the image of

Jane Russell's body), "The title has the effect of immediately distancing the spectator: it reminds him of the symbolic role of the narrative by locating Jane Russell as an imaginary figure" (p. 31). Describing the tear in Harriet Craig's eye as ironic would be another example, or Johnston's confident reading of the end of *Dance, Girl, Dance*: "This irony [referring to Judy's final words, 'when I think how simple things could have been, I just have to laugh'] marks her defeat and final engulfment, but at the same time it is the final mark of subversion of the discourse of the male" (p. 7).

The problems one can get into trying to assign specific reactions or reflexive thoughts to the spectator at specific moments in a film are well known to *Camera Obscura* from experience. In the article on *Deux Fois* in *Camera Obscura/1*, we described the operation of deconstruction devices in terms very similar to Johnston's. We were, however, finally convinced that our basic assumptions about audience response were unrealistic after giving a presentation in San Francisco on the Straub/Huillet film *Introduction to Arnold Schoenberg's "Accompaniment to a Cinematographic Scene."* When we attempted to explain how, to take one example, the black leader separating some sections of the film functioned to distance the spectator, how viewing and understanding this film was necessarily different from the processes of identification, fascination, etc. going on when one watched a linear, transparent, illusionistic Hollywood film, members of our audience simply disagreed with us, and continued to disagree with us every time we told them how they were supposed to have reacted to a given moment in the film or a given strategy. There were those who maintained, moreover, that they could enjoy the Schoenberg film as if it were a Hollywood film.

Besides experiences such as this one, it was the work on textual analysis of classical film—and the work of Bellour, Heath and Kuntzel has been very important for us here—which convinced us that we were operating from too simplistic a view of how Hollywood (narrative-representational) film functions, and especially of the endlessly varied ways in which the *effect* of linearity and transparency can be achieved—a global effect which is felt, most of all, *after* the film—over what apparent obstacles, and with what finesse in luring and moving the spectator, through gaps, enigmas, excesses as part of the narrative pleasure. Thierry Kuntzel's "The Film Work, 2"[5] which is a demonstration of how the textual system of *The Most Dangerous Game* functions and, as well, a demonstration of specific processes of meaning production at work in the classical film such as condensation and displacement, is a very good example, methodologically, of the ways in which overdetermination of meaning, redundancy across different levels of meaning, figuration across different matters of expression, make sure that certain meanings are clear, even if they are not fully conscious. And all of Bellour's work goes to establish how redundancy is endlessly reinscribed both on the formal and narrative levels of the film.[6] One can specify the parameters of audience reaction/placement more convincingly, even if not an exact meaning at an exact moment, through these kind of analyses which operate in terms of signifying chains, as does psychoanalysis, than by arguing in terms of isolated moments.

Finally, it wasn't necessary for Johnston to restrict her analysis of the entertainment film to the progressive classical text, as if a feminist counter-cinema could learn its most valuable lessons from imitating, even negatively, the classical cinema of rupture (if that category is anyway still acceptable). Textual analyses of the most classical of films—*North by Northwest, Psycho, Marnie, The Birds, Gigi, Touch of Evil, The Most Dangerous Game*—have shown consistently how women function in different but equally crucial ways to insure narrative, to position the enunciation. These analyses are also the most advanced we have on investigating how enunciation and the logical consistency of the film—how it makes sense; who is addressing whom—are organized via the spectator. Those of us who want to investigate the open question of how feminine discourse, feminine desire, may organize filmic enunciation, how feminine discourse might constitute textual logic differently, can best, perhaps, begin here.

Notes

1.   Claire Johnston, ed. *Notes on Women's Cinema*, BFI pamphlet, 1973. "Women's Cinema as Counter-Cinema," "Introduction to Nelly Kaplan"; Pam Cook and C. Johnston, "The Place of Woman in the Cinema of Raoul Walsh," Edinburgh pamphlet on Raoul Walsh, 1974; C. Johnston, "Femininity and the Masquerade: *Anne of the Indies*, Edinburgh pamphlet on Jacques Tourneur, 1975; C. Johnston, ed. *The Work of Dorothy Arzner*, BFI pamphlet, 1975. "Dorothy Arzner: Critical Strategies," C. Johnston. "Approaching the Work of Dorothy Arzner," P. Cook; C. Johnston, "Towards a Feminist Film Practice: Some Theses," *Edinburgh 76 Magazine*, 1976.

2.   Jean-Louis Comolli and Jean Narboni, "Cinema/Ideology/Criticism," *Cahiers du Cinéma*, October 1969; translated in *Screen*, 12, no. 1 (Spring 1971); reprinted in *Screen Reader* no. 1 (1977) and in *Movies and Methods*, Bill Nichols, ed. (University of California Press: 1976).

3.   *Cahiers* collective text on *Young Mr. Lincoln*, *Cahiers du Cinéma*, 1970; translated in *Screen*, 13, no. 3 (Autumn 1972); reprinted in *Screen Reader* no. 1 and in *Movies and Methods*. *Cahiers* collective text on *Morocco*, *Cahiers du Cinéma*, 1970.

4.   Stephen Heath, "Film and System: Terms of Analysis," part 1, *Screen*, 16, no. 1 (Spring 1975); part II, *Screen*, 16, no. 2 (Summer 1975).

5.   Thierry Kuntzel, "Le Travail du Film, II," *Communications*, no. 23 (1975); translated as "The Film-Work, 2," *Camera Obscura* no. 5 (Spring 1980).

6.   Of Raymond Bellour's articles, see especially "*Les Oiseaux:* analyse d'une séquence," *Cahiers du Cinéma* no. 219 (1969); translated as "*The Birds*: Analysis of a Sequence" (available in mimeographed form from the British Film Institute, Educational Advisory Service; "L'evidence at le code," *Cinéma: théories, lectures*, special film issue of *Revue d'Esthétique* (1973); translated as "The Obvious and the Code," *Screen*, vol. 15, no. 4 (Winter 1974–75) (on *The Big Sleep*); "Le blocage symbolique," *Psychanalyse et Cinéma*, special issue of *Communications*, no. 23 (1975) (on *North by Northwest*); "To Segment, To Analyze," *Quarterly Review of Film Studies*, vol. 1, no. 3 (August 1976) (on *Gigi*; published under imperfect conditions: the notes are missing and the journal did not review the translation); "Hitchcock, the Enunciator," *Camera Obscura*, no. 2 (Fall 1977) (on *Marnie*); "Psychose, nevrose, perversion," *Ça* (1979). Translated as "Psychosis, Neurosis, Perversion," *Camera Obscura*, no. 3–4 (1979) (on *Psycho*).

7

Feminine Discourse in *Christopher Strong*

Jacquelyn Suter

Feminine discourse: What is it? Who speaks it? How is it spoken? First, by discourse, I shall mean an ideological position from which a subject "speaks" (acts/interacts) within the social order. Delineating parameters for what might constitute the feminine in cinematic representation may best be approached by examining how discourses present themselves in a given film text. Dorothy Arzner's *Christopher Strong* (1933) presents an exceptional site at which examination of patriarchal and feminine discourses may begin, for this film explicitly offers the problematic of female desire within a patriarchal order.

The Patriarchal Discourse

As text, *Christopher Strong* attempts to pass itself off as "realist" by maximizing the modes of connection between sign and referent. The most prominent of these modes is a meta-discourse (the narrative structure) which produces effects of sequentiality and unmediated conflation between fictive constructs (characters) and real people. The result of such binding between sign and referent is a text which proclaims unproblematical coherence: "The writing disappears behind the logic of what is written, as if the writing were not there, as if the text was not text, but an unwritten, effaced by an unproduced, natural reality."[1] In *Christopher Strong*, the patriarchal discourse is structured by elements which attempt to produce the effect of coherence (the mode of expression called "realist") and, in this way, is allowed a position of authority in the film. Thus the meta-discourse, the narrative structure itself, is the primary mode of patriarchal expression which attempts to repress the feminine voice and to eradicate all expression of difference that is undefined in relation to this superior discourse.

A short description of the diegesis at this point will facilitate further discussion: Cynthia Darrington (Katherine Hepburn), an aviatrix, falls in love with a married man, Christopher Strong (Colin Clive). Simultaneously, Chris's daughter Monica is in love with a married man, Harry Rawlinson. Harry finally obtains a divorce, and he and Monica marry. Meanwhile, Cynthia and Chris continue their love affair, and Chris's wife Elaine patiently awaits the end of marital disruption. Cynthia becomes pregnant but does not tell Chris because he would then be forced to marry her out of duty—not out of love as she desires. The hopelessness of their situation compels Cynthia to commit suicide by crashing her plane. Because it is thought that the crash is a result of an accident while attempting to break the world altitude record, she is valorized as brave and courageous at the film's end. After Cynthia's death, Chris and his wife Elaine are reunited.

This description, like the narrative itself, foregrounds the relationship between Cynthia and Chris and relegates to a sub-plot the relationship between Harry and Monica. However, a close analysis reveals that what could be conventionally referred to as a sub-plot actually functions to work through the problematic that the narrative has set for itself: the existence of a multiple sexual relationship within a social order founded upon monogamy. Initially, Monica and Harry are ostensibly engaged in multiple sexual relationships which, for further discussion, will be called a relationship of plurality. Chris and Elaine have a marriage that is strictly monogamous. Cynthia is that character which disrupts monogamy between Chris and Elaine while, simultaneously, moving Monica and Harry toward monogamy. Cynthia, then, oscillates among the four characters and functions as a mediator between the values of multiple sexual relationships (plurality) and strict monogamy. Cynthia's narrative presence sets the fiction in motion by provoking conflict, and her figure mediates that same conflict towards its ultimate resolution. A chart will enable us to see the narrative movement.

Cynthia/Chris apart
Monica/Harry in plurality
Elaine/Chris together

C/C together
M/H in serialization
E/C apart

C/C apart
M/H in monogamy
E/C together

At the beginning of the film, Cynthia/Chris and Elaine/Chris are in opposite relation to each other, and Monica/Harry are in plurality. As the narrative progresses, however, Monica/Harry move toward monogamy only at the expense of a reversal in relationship among Cynthia/Chris/Elaine. Elaine/Chris function in a position of estrangement so that Cynthia/Chris can function in a position of transgression which, by the paradox of the story, furthers Monica/Harry toward monogamy. By the end of the film, Cynthia/ Chris and Elaine/Chris are in the same relationship to each other as in the beginning, while Monica/Harry are the only couple to have made a permanent change. The circularity of position of Cynthia/Chris and Elaine/Chris and the concomitant change in position of Monica/Harry encourage the spectator to accept monogamy as the preferred ethic. The preference of monogamy over any other ethic offered in the film is the knowledge gained through this narration. By the process of closure and resolution toward the "truth," the narrative discourse asserts itself as dominant. Thus, patriarchal ideology is spoken by the structure of events, the narrative discourse. *What* is spoken is the valorization of monogamy.

How the patriarchal discourse speaks requires investigation into the film's structure of address: the specific ways in which the spectator-subject is positioned with respect to the discursive chains. Stephen Heath in "Notes on Suture" (*Screen*, Winter 1977/78) explores the various modes of subject address, and finds one of them to be a redefinition of spatial disposition within each shot. The following description of a suture in *Christopher Strong* illustrates how the spectator-subject is solicited for the patriarchal position at a crucial moment in the narrative.

Chris is brought to a party as an *objet trouvé* in a treasure hunt, the requirement of which is to find a man "who has been married for over five years, never been unfaithful to his wife, and is not ashamed to admit it." At the moment when he attests to his unique morality by saying "I think that the devotion to one's country, one's home, and the one woman is the very root of man's happiness in life," the camera movement implicates the spectator in the following manner: Chris is in long-shot with the party guests gathered around him, and when he begins speaking, he explicitly addresses them. However, as he continues to speak, the camera tracks in to a medium close-up of him while, simultaneously, excluding the party guests (diegetic audience) from the frame. Before the reframing of the filmic space had removed the diegetic audience, the larger scale of the shot functioned to disperse identification into a more contextual situation: the spectator could identify with both Chris and the party guests simultaneously, or (put another way) the spectator could identify with Chris through the diegetic audience who are positioned as spectators with respect to him. However, when the reframing eliminates the diegetic audience, the contextual situation is diminished so that the spectator identification is displaced onto and intensified upon Chris at a point in the narrative where monogamy is initially established.

Although Heath properly cautions against reducing the concept of suture to a shot/reverse shot structure (the Oudart/Dayan formulation), this type of subject address remains a most forceful one for situating the spectator within the filmic signifying system. Let us, then, examine a second example from *Christopher Strong* which utilizes this form of address to engage the spectator for the patriarchal discourse.

Toward the end of the film when Cynthia has functioned as both paternal and maternal surrogate in order to reconcile Chris and Elaine to Monica's marriage, Elaine confronts Cynthia in a series of six shots which convey the superiority of monogamy. In this series, Elaine's words, in effect, acknowledge that the transgression between her husband and Cynthia enabled Chris to understand the desire for union between two people in love. Now that Monica and Harry are married and expecting a child, Cynthia is no longer needed. Elaine gives Cynthia "a mother's sincerest thanks" for her part in bringing the couple into the familial. It is at this crucial point in the narrative in which Cynthia is being informed of the joys of matrimony (which her efforts promoted and from which she is excluded) that a shot/reverse shot structure occurs that places the spectator in the place of Elaine and in the place of Cynthia for three shots each. While each maintains equality in the codes of camera distance, movement, and angle, Elaine is privileged in another code in each of the three shots in which Cynthia dominates in the image. The first shot of Cynthia is the shortest in duration of all the six. The second shot in which Cynthia is in the image, Elaine's voice occupies part of the soundtrack. And in the third shot, Cynthia is absent from the phonetic track altogether, averting her eyes from Elaine. Over and above the fact that Elaine is privileged in the six shots by several codes, the importance of this particular series is that the shot/reverse shot structure occurs at a point in the narrative where the spectator is positioned in the place of Elaine, who speaks the patriarchal discourse, and in the place of Cynthia, who receives it— finally, in silence. Even though the spectator is positioned with respect to two different characters, the shot/reverse shot structure speaks univocally—the difference being that the spectator identifies now with the speaker-who-delivers, then with the listener-who-receives the patriarchal voice.

From the above examples, we can see that the patriarchal discourse speaks from all areas of the film text. On the macro level, the narrative discourse is organized toward resolution of the problematic between multiple and single relationships. The role of the female protagonist is constructed to facilitate the narrative movement toward monogamy by functioning as the agent which provokes that movement. By this process, the desire of woman is pressed into the service of narrative logic. In subsequent sections of this essay, we shall return to specific examples of the occlusion of feminine desire by narrative constraints. In demonstrating how the patriarchal discourse speaks on the micro level, it becomes clear that specific codes must be read through

Christopher Strong (Dorothy Arzner, 1933)

and across the cinematic discourse as a whole in order to understand how any one code functions at any given point.[2] And finally, in answering the question *who* speaks the patriarchal discourse, it is self-evident that patriarchy is spoken by both sexes. By the end of *Christopher Strong*, all major characters support this discourse.

The Feminine Discourse

If the patriarchal discourse is so highly organized that it is spoken from the superior position of the narrative discourse itself, and if by film's end it has conscripted all characters to speak with its voice, can we locate a feminine discourse at all? The feminine voice is indeed present and definable, having an organization of its own which is interwoven with/into the patriarchal. If we understand the feminine discourse in this manner, one is prevented from seeing it as solely a strategy of intervention into the patriarchal discourse. Thus, the feminine, as well as the patriarchal, structures the film text. But in saying this, we shall examine several sequences which illustrate how the feminine structure does not dominate the text. Precisely because the feminine discourse is a part of the narrative structure and not ec-centric to it, it is liable to eventual usurpation by the meta-discourse.

One of the ways that the feminine voice affirms itself is to call into question the dominant assumptions of patriarchy. One of these instances occurs when Monica has had a brief sexual encounter with another man (Carlo) and when Harry learns of it, he refuses to marry her. Monica's first reaction is to threaten suicide unless Cynthia agrees to mediate between her and Harry. In venting her anger about the situation, Monica says "if father had been half as careful about Carlo as he was about Harry, it wouldn't have happened." Monica is charging her father with a breach of one of his patriarchal duties: to protect the women in his charge from violation.

It seems that Monica has written a suicide letter to her father, one which "would hurt him terribly if he read it." Although the content is never made clear, it is reasonable to assume that Monica's letter confronts Chris directly with patriarchal irresponsibility. Now that Monica decides not to kill herself, because she has faith in Cynthia's mediatory efforts, she does not want to charge her father with negligence. Consequently, she asks Cynthia to phone her father to request that he not read her letter. The conflict between the obligation, yet irreproachability, of the patriarch is enunciated when Cynthia asks Monica to phone him herself. Monica replies, "I couldn't talk to him now—I wouldn't make any sense." The importance of this reply is that the conflict between patriarchal obligation and irreproachability is displaced from a direct confrontation into a character trait—Monica's senselessness.

In this verbal exchange, senselessness is opposed to reason; feminine opposed to masculine; daughter opposed to the Law of the Father. Woman has lost her voice. The feminine is not expected to speak and, when attempted, is not expected to be coherent. Up to the point of Monica's declaration of "senselessness," she had been articulating her situation with perfect clarity to Cynthia. However, when Cynthia presents the idea of confrontation with Chris, Monica lapses into incoherence. If Monica were to phone her father, it is not that she wouldn't make *any* sense—she would make *too much* sense. The narrative will not, cannot, allow the conflict to be resolved directly because, in its unmasked form, it is unresolvable within the parameters of patriarchy.

Jacques Derrida's work permits insight into analysis of feminine discourse, seeking, as it does, to expose the hierarchization of dichotomies within the Western metaphysical tradition. In Western thought, dualities such as Essence/Appearance, Truth/Error, Masculine/Feminine are not accorded equality, but rather one term attains preeminence over the other, relegating it to secondary status. This process results in the suppressed term being interpreted only in terms of the primary one and not defined in a context of difference. Thus, the feminine is defined in *relation* to the masculine—defined as non-male. In our example, the problematic of feminine desire under patriarchy, which Monica articulates to Cynthia, is silenced when set in relation to her father, to the representative of the Law. The feminine voice (here, the literal masking of the figural) cannot speak within the hierarchical relation.[3]

The choice of this instance in *Christopher Strong* as an example of assertion of feminine voice is not without problems. The importance lies not so much in the failure of Monica to confront and challenge patriarchal authority, but rather in the moment when Cynthia poses the question to Monica: "Why don't you call him yourself?" What may seem to be an innocuous utterance actually posits the problematic heretofore discussed in all its contradictions. However, Monica is not free to answer the question, "I will." Narrative constraints demand that she refuse the challenge ("senselessness" being only one of the many fictive reasons that could have been chosen to silence her) because the logic of the narrative requires that Monica eventually and thoroughly accept the very values at issue now. But still, Cynthia's question speaks from an ideological position which articulates the contradictions inherent in the patriarchal duty of protection of women. The resolution of the contradiction between the obligation yet irreproachability of the patriarchal posture is one aspect of the rationale of the narrative pattern. The narrative must resolve the problematic because the two attributes are the twin pillars of patriarchal power and, as such, must be accepted as cohesive. Cynthia, as enunciator of the narrative contradiction, establishes the text itself as a system which functions by and for contradiction. This example epitomizes the paradox of a feminine discourse within a patriarchal meta-discursive structure: the woman may indeed enunciate patriarchal contradiction, but this enunciation is required so that the narrative movement may resolve it and, thus, efface it as problematical.

Another term of organization of the feminine discourse juxtaposes elements within a shot to create ironic commentary upon the patriarchal. Toward the end of the film, after Cynthia has died in her plane crash, a single shot of a newspaper is constructed as follows. A close-up of a news item headline reads:

> Lady Cynthia Darrington
> Honored Today
> Unveil Monument to Englishwoman
> Who Died Breaking Altitude Record

A swish pan, down and to the right, focuses in close-up upon another item:

> . . . Buckingham Palace
> _____
>
> Sir Christopher and Lady
> Strong are sailing next week
> on the 'Olympic' for America
> _____
>
> Fall From Tower Bridge

Roland Barthes's essay "Structure of the *Fait-Divers*"[4] provides a basis for interpreting this shot. Barthes differentiates between a news item proper and a *fait-divers* (a journalistic "filler"). The headline regarding Cynthia is a news item because its content is sufficiently important to refer it to events outside of itself—it is defined in relation to knowledge anterior to the present event. In this case, Cynthia is a world-renowned aviatrix whose death most probably made world-wide headlines before this particular article appeared. Thus, we might say that this article has duration, has a history. Structurally, it is a headline with a following story which, in contrast to the *fait-divers*, signifies its importance and underscores its durational aspect. On the other hand, a *fait-divers* is defined by its immanence: all that one needs to know about it is contained within itself. It is without duration, a closed structure. In this shot, the notice of the Strong's departure is accentuated as a filler by being sandwiched between fragments of what appear to be other fillers. The formal construction of this notice signifies unimportance—unorganized dissemination of news. Furthermore, the fact that Cynthia's news item and the Strong's filler are spatially connected by a swish pan delineates the structural contradiction between them, emphasizing the importance of the one and the frivolity of the other. Further irony manifests itself by the fact that the boat "Olympic" nourished Chris and Cynthia's transgressive love affair at an earlier time. Thus, the discordancy on the level of the narrative signified between the juxtaposed news items generates a powerful commentary upon the sacrifices required to keep patriarchy intact.

However, as in the prior example, the feminine discourse emerging here from irony is not free from potential recuperation by the patriarchal. The juxtaposed items, metaphoric substitutions for death and reunion, "rhyme" with the narrative logic. Just as the swish pan generates movement from one metaphor to the next, the narrative discourse presses toward resolution by elimination of a character who, in turn, effects reunion of others. In this manner, death and reunion on the micro level of the shot mirror the chain of the discourse—the referential and discursive levels reinforcing each other in a bind of univocality.

In *Christopher Strong*, the angles are predominantly frontal, the scale is mostly medium range, the camera is static in most shots, and there is a relatively small amount of shot/reverse shot structures. It has been noted that this kind of visual configuration often possesses the potential to disrupt the effect of narrative homogeneity (see especially, Stephen Heath, "Narrative Space," *Screen*, Autumn 1976). But in the case of a film like *Christopher Strong* which does not utilize the tableau-like structure as a consistent organizing principle, isolated disruption of spatial parameters cannot, by themselves, be said to work for a feminine expression. Even though the spectator is not positioned in these shots to look at a character through the mediated eyes of a fictive other, the frontal, static shot in *Christopher Strong* has a definite drawback as a mode of address functioning for feminine discourse. The spectator's ability in the tableau-like shot to view characters in relation to each other is the primary method utilized to represent Cynthia visually as mediator, as one who functions for others. Through a frontal camera position, Cynthia is perfectly framed several times between Monica and Harry and once between Chris and Elaine: the two couples who her narrative function demands that she ultimately bring/restore to monogamy.

Occlusion of the Feminine Discourse

The previous section demonstrated how *Christopher Strong* contains a feminine discourse, even though the patriarchal eventually usurps it. However, the importance is that the feminine *does* exist and, most importantly, poses the question of an incoherent text in which the feminine discourse enunciates the very problematic that the narrative must resolve. In this section, I want to focus specifically upon three examples that illustrate the (re)pression of feminine desire into the service of narrative logic, the primary mode of patriarchal expression in this film.

When Chris and Cynthia initially consummate their love, a single-shot sequence consists of a close-up of a woman's hand leaning against what appears to be a bedside table with a lamp and clock atop. It is assumed to be nighttime because the clock reads 3:20, and the disembodied hand switches the lamp on at the beginning of the shot. The voices of Chris and Cynthia whisper off-screen. Over and above the fact that this moment actualizes Cynthia's sexuality with Chris, this encounter is her very first realization of sexual desire at all. The importance of her desire on the level of the narrative signified is in ironic inversion to the paucity of narrative signifiers. Four items fill the frame, only one of which can be considered a signifier for Cynthia— her hand. At the moment in the film when feminine sexual desire is at its zenith, the subject of that desire is off-screen. Moreover, the *object* of *her* desire, Chris, is also off-screen. The metonymic hand within the frame is all that represents woman as the subject of desire. Furthermore, this moment is the only one in the film in which off-screen space prevails in importance over on-screen space. This shot functions to structurally elide all explicit signifiers of sexuality. A double relay of desire is enacted here: 1) Christian Metz in "The Imaginary Signifier" (*Screen*, Summer 1975) locates the cinematic signifier on the side of the imaginary because in the cinema "the activity of perception in it is real (the cinema is not a fantasy), but the perceived is not really the object, it is its shade . . ." (p. 48). Thus, the cinematic signifier combines simultaneously a dialectic between presence and absence. The spectator-subject is present in and for an image the codes of which mark in full detail only its place as absent. 2) Diegetically, the spectator's expectation of (a "looking for") the fulfillment of sexual desire on the part of the characters never occurs within the only space that it can be seen: in-frame. Similar to the working of the cinematic signifier, a dialectic functions between what is present and what is absent. In both cases, there is a gap between the function of the eye and the purpose of the gaze. Jacques Lacan designates this site as that which gives rise to desire on the level of the scopic drive: what one wants to see and looks for is not there.[5] The desired object is "elsewhere"—cinematically, in an irrecoverable pro-filmic event and, in this particular shot, diegetically off-screen.[6]

In addition to the importance of this shot for feminine desire, it is also illustrative of the way in which narrative logic inducts that same desire into its own service. Consummation between Chris and Cynthia violates Chris's ethic of monogamy, but without this transgression he would be unable to understand the passionate love that makes Monica and Harry want to marry. Hence, transgression serves a positive function in the narrative by bringing Monica and Harry into monogamy. The consummation is symbolically one of the most outstanding of Cynthia's mediatory acts. If it were not for *her* desire for sexual union with Chris, he would lack the awareness necessary to permit Monica's and Harry's sexual union. Thus, consummation and transgression collude: what should have been an expression of Cynthia as the subject of desire actually functions to make her the object of desire—the desire of the narrative for resolution. The importance of the consummation sequence cannot be overemphasized. Woman is the locus of the paradox of desire: the wish for absolute fulfillment, yet the need always to remain just this side of completion in order for desire to survive as desire. The diegesis re-enacts the paradox: Cynthia functions both to create monogamy and to threaten it. At the nexus of psychical and diegetic desire, the viewer is positioned in the cinematic discourse by a shot configuration that parallels desire on the level of the signifier: the frame terminates the seen/scene for the spectator-subject.

A second example of feminine occlusion occurs when Cynthia decides to commit suicide by crashing her plane under the guise of an accident while attempting to break the current altitude record. While in flight, a sequence begins which consists of an extreme close-up of the altimeter face over which is superimposed important moments between her and Chris. The final superimposition is a close-up of a newspaper photo of Chris wearing a stern demeanor. The voice heard over the superimposition repeats the word "duty"—an insistent signifier reminding her that her mediatory function is not yet over. Her death is the final mediation for the Strong family because it removes the last obstacle (herself) between Chris and Elaine. Cynthia's death brings the narrative to resolution.

Throughout the film, a pattern can be discerned: when Cynthia is concerned with aviation, she functions for herself alone. But when she involves herself with the Strong family, she functions for them as a mediator. This final flight collapses both types of functioning into one: her aviation is utilized as a vehicle of mediation. The fact that Cynthia chooses to remove herself through an activity uniquely her own expresses the conflict between acting out her own desires and acting out the desires of others. The superimposition sequence is a visual/aural signifier of Cynthia caught within this paradox.

The above two examples illustrate the impossibility within this film text for woman to exercise herself as subject outside the patriarchal order. When her voice is not undermined on the micro level, it is recuperated on the macro level by narrative constraints. *Christopher Strong* would seem to be structured around the containment of feminine discourse and all that this implies regarding repression of feminine desire.

The final sequence of the film not only effaces the feminine voice by recuperation but also obliterates all textual contradiction by presenting two shots which close the narrative discourse in a flourish of mythical homogeneity. The first is a long-shot of a monument representing an idealized, androgynous figure with outstretched wings surrounded by lush foliage in an idyllic milieu. An old woman sits on a bench in the left foreground, bespeaking "eternal vigilance." Also, an old couple playing a hand organ walk across frame in the foreground, functioning as the only element within the shot anchoring it naratively to the rest of the film. They appeared in the beginning of the film as Monica rushed from the treasure hunt party to look for the unique man—her father. Witnesses then to the search for the ideal man, they are now witnesses to the death of the ideal woman. The mise-en-scène of this shot signifies Cynthia's apotheosis. The vivacious, reckless aviatrix who accomplished real feats is here immortalized into an ahistorical, androgynous symbol within the universal pantheon of "those who dare." Cynthia has been fetishized: her threat circumvented by her transformation into legend. Represented as an objet d'art lacking sexual differentiation, she now permits scrutiny and adoration without fear. However, the price for this safety from the recognition of sexual difference is a near-break in spatio-temporal orientation within the narrative. The strongly codified mythicality of the mise-en-scène provides no clue to the location nor to the fictive time of this idealized site. Total disorientation is subverted, however, because the old couple link this shot to the diegesis in general. The link is weak, but it prevents a complete break with the diegesis. Its advantage lies in revealing a gap that requires narrative fill, pointing towards a space/place of textual vulnerability.

The second shot in this sequence, a close-up of a plaque on the monument in the previous shot reads:

In Memory
of
Lady Cynthia Darrington
whose life and death
were a source of inspiration
and courage to all

Rhetorically, the wording of the inscription reintroduces Cynthia's motto ("courage conquers death") in a distorted way. First, the word "courage" on the plaque is the predicate, not the subject of the sentence as in the motto. In reversing the subject-predicate order of the motto, the condensed inscription reads: "death [is] . . . courage." In short, the meaning of the plaque valorizes Cynthia's courage to die, not to live as does her motto. The banal, aphoristic wording of the inscription departicularizes the motto's original terseness, draining it of meaning.

In these two shots, Cynthia's historicity is removed; her force as a particular individual is denuded. In *Mythologies*, Barthes contends that one of the functions of myth is to empty reality of history and replace it with "Nature." The dialectical role that Cynthia performed in the text has been diluted by these shots into a harmonious display of essences. In this manner, woman—atomized, reconstituted, and dispersed across the smooth field of this final sequence—caps the ideology of patriarchy spoken by the narrative discourse. Cynthia, silenced as speaker of the feminine, is transformed into legend to speak the myth of patriarchy: monogamy is the only viable ethic, worthy enough to give one's life to preserve.

This essay has attempted to delineate the parameters within which a feminine discourse may be thought by a close (but necessarily selected) examination of a single film text. What I should like to do now in these concluding remarks is to pose problematics about potential modes of feminine expression and to indicate some directions that seem productive.

In "Visual Pleasure and Narrative Cinema" (*Screen*, Autumn 1975, Chapter 4 in this book), Laura Mulvey explains how conventional active/passive heterosexual division of labour both dictates narrative structure and spatial configuration. The male protagonist advances the narrative through his activities and does so in an illusionistic space allowing his actions to be read as "natural." In *Christopher Strong*, however, we have a role reversal: the woman is the active member in terms of life-style in general and career in particular. Even though I have described how her character (that accretion of fictive traits—strong, independent, reckless—called "Cynthia" increasingly functions to work through a dilemma of patriarchy, it should also be noted that she is never constructed as, what Mulvey calls, a "static, one-dimensional fetish." Cynthia's images are never produced so that "the beauty of the woman as object and the screen space coalesce." Because of the predominantly frontal angles and distanced scale, she, as well as the male, functions within a definable milieu. In a case such as this, *either* sex speaking from a three-dimensional spatial configuration presents the problem of "realism": the utilization of cinematic strategies to produce the effect of the spectator-subject as an excluded observer, rather than as a part, of the discursive chain. Moreover, it is important for Cynthia's narrative function that she *not* be spatially configured one-dimensionally: the construction of the effects of "reality" is required for her to command spatial authority in order to correspond to an imaginary relation of totality and coherence (for the sake of the narrative as a production of meanings within a symbolic system attempting to constantly re-play the imaginary experience of unity). Hence, if feminine discourse gains from a non-iconic shot structure (as Mulvey defines it) by enjoining a "place" from which to speak with authority (like the active male protagonist), *how* that place is cinematically constructed is of paramount importance, and how the woman diegetically *functions* within that place is equally crucial.

Mulvey also contends that dislaying the woman as pure erotic spectacle for the spectator (fetishistic scopophilia) tends to impede narration by breaking the verismilitude required for spatial (thus narrative) coherence. Since in *Christopher Strong* much of the feminine discourse is recuperated by narrative logic, it would seem that any construct which has the potential to intercede in that linear/spatial movement would be advantageous. However, the problematic of this strategy has been explicitly articulated in the analysis of Jackie Raynal's *Deux Fois* (*Camera Obscura* 1, 1976). In short, in order for Raynal to interrogate cinematic voyeurism, she has to offer her own body as a fetish. Similarly, in Mulvey's example of Sternberg's photographing of Dietrich, the price of minimizing narrativity is the fragmented body of woman. With respect to the advantages to be accrued for feminine expression by the fetishistic representation of woman, two points are worth considering. First, how much of a difference would isolated iconic shots of woman make in a narrative so powerfully organized toward univocal closure as, say, *Christopher Strong*?[7] And, secondly, if the fetishized image of woman conceals the fact of castration from the unmediated look of the spectator and prevents distantiation from that image, thus constituting a situation of disavowal of sexual difference, that situation simply reduplicates the precise problem that should be one of the challenges of a feminine discourse. It would seem that utilizing shots which promote a false coherence would be in contradistinction to what a feminine expression would desire to achieve: an intervention into patriarchal order by generating a text which foregrounds contradiction and by positioning the spectator in such a way that throws into question his/her voyeuristic relation to the image.[8]

Undoubtedly, the fact that we can locate certain formal transgressions in a film advances our knowledge of what might constitute a feminine discourse. But we should also be aware that isolated interruptions do not necessarily deconstruct the narrative discourse in any significant way. It seems that a systematic rethinking of the entire terms of narrative logic, a reformulation of its elements into an order different from what has come to be known as the classic text, may allow the feminine to express itself more forcefully.

Chantal Akerman's *Jeanne Dielman, 23 Quai du Commerce, 1080 Bruxelles* provides an example of what this reformulation might consist. In this film, instead of isolated interventions into a classic text, we have a systematic reordering of certain crucial elements upon which the classic text depends, and a recognition of other elements which the classic text chooses invariably to ignore. Conventionally, a text depends upon a hierarchy of images to sustain two major narrative codes—the hermeneutic and proairetic. That is to say that it depends upon movement towards a dénouement, and its economy dictates that no events be extraneous to this purpose. Akerman, in showing a woman's daily routine in all its banality, breaks with convention because these images do not necessarily function to advance the narrative (although they can be read that way). Akerman says that she found a plot *because* she wanted to show certain gestures in women's lives that are customarily left out of films.[9] One importance of this unorthodox procedure in approaching the *idea* of narrative construction is that the characters are not subservient to a plot. Each character's action may be viewed as a Brechtian social *gestus* through which we read an entire social situation, an ideology. In *Jeanne Dielman*, narrative logic constructed in this manner, refusing linear development and emphasizing character gesture, allows the possibility for the woman's discourse to be figured differently.

In this essay, I am not the least of those who have referred to *Jeanne Dielman* as presenting certain positive directions for feminine expression. There is a danger, however, in elevating any one film to the status of "the first masterpiece in the feminine in the history of the cinema" as Louis Marcorelles put it.[10] *Jeanne Dielman* can certainly bear further analysis in terms of feminine discourse and, equally important, further examination of our relation to it as film theorists. In all events, analysis of what constitutes feminine discourse may best be served by continuous examination of how the feminine is figured in specific film texts, thus avoiding the pitfall of isolating certain formal structures as *inherently* more conducive to feminine expression than others. In taking *Christopher Strong* as my object of analysis, I have attempted to elucidate precisely some of those dangers, to reveal the complexity of the feminine voice, and to articulate the difficulty of its expression within a patriarchal symbolic order.

Notes

1. Sam Rohdie, "Notes from a Pedant," *Quarterly Review of Film Studies*, 1, No. 2 (May 1976), p. 156. Rohdie is very helpful in articulating the theoretical issues involved in writing about what has come to be known as the "classic realist text." Rohdie contends that the issue is how to write "about" the text without, at the same time, being categorical and nominal. My own discourse, this text entitled "Feminine Discourse in *Christopher Strong*," I offer as an example of the difficulty in finding a solution to Rohdie's cautionary remarks against the halting the heterogeneity of the text in the critical act: "to name its plural and thereby to close it" (p. 160).

2.   Nick Browne asserts that "if a discourse carries a certain impression of reality it is an effect not exactly of the image, but rather of the way the image is placed by the narrative or argument" (p. 36). "The Spectator-in-the-Text: The Rhetoric of *Stagecoach*," *Film Quarterly*, 29, No. 2 (1975/76). In the main, I agree with Browne. However, I would maintain that whatever "impression of reality" a discourse constructs is a *simultaneous* effect of the structure of the image, its particular functioning in the narrative, and the spectator-screen relationship as constituting positionality for a subject.

3.   I am indebted to Shoshana Felman's excellent discussion of similar problems in "Woman and Madness: The Critical Phallacy," *Diacritics*, 5, No. 4 (1975).

4.   Roland Barthes, *Critical Essays*, trans. Richard Howard (Evanston: Northwestern Univ. Press, 1972), pp. 185–195.

5.   Elaboration of the Lacanian formulation of desire on the level of the scopic drive may be found in the section "Du regard comme objet petit a" in *Le Séminaire de Jacques Lacan, Livre XI: Les quatre concepts fondamentaux de la psychanalyse* (Paris: Editions du Seuil, 1973). The English translation of this section is in *The Four Fundamental Concepts of Psycho-Analysis*, trans. Alan Sheridan (New York: Norton, 1978), pp. 67–119.

6.   Metz in "The Imaginary Signifier" comments upon the frame as a censorship mechanism: "the point is to gamble simultaneously on the excitation of desire and its retention" (*Screen*, Summer 1975, p. 74).

7.   Is it even so clearly defined that all of the Sternberg/Dietrich films work against linearity by privileging situation over suspense, plot misunderstanding rather than conflict? And further, how can we separate so assuredly "situation" and "suspense" when talking about narrativity? Surely, "misunderstanding" will involve "conflict" within the plot at some level of narration.

8.   Paul Willemen in "Voyeurism, the Look and Dwoskin" (*Afterimage* 6, Summer 1976) explores the ways in which the films of Steve Dwoskin attempt to interrogate voyeurism by turning the scopic drive back onto the spectator-subject, thereby forcing the viewer "to confront the considerable sadistic components present in his/her act of looking and by implication, confront the castration fears provoked by the investigation of the naked female form in the diegesis" (p. 47). It is obvious that in acknowledging the spectator-subject as one who is looked at, and not only one who looks, Dwoskin's work has not freed itself from the paradox that operates in *Deux Fois*: the most forceful displacement of voyeuristic pleasure is *necessarily* carried out upon the object which embodies what is most at stake in the voyeuristic situation—the body of woman.

9.   Akerman's comment about her work is from an interview with Camera Obscura (November, 1976), excerpts of which may be found in *Camera Obscura/2*, 1977, pp. 118–121.

10.   "Certainement le premier chef-d'oeuvre au féminin de l'histoire du cinéma," *Le Monde* (Jan. 22, 1976).

8

The Popular Film as a Progressive Text— a Discussion of *Coma*—Part 1

Elizabeth Cowie

Coma is the title of a film released in Britain at the end of 1978. A mainstream American film, gaining general distribution (it has gone to most of the local cinemas in this country); it was a big box-office hit, especially in the USA; it was produced by MGM with well-known stars—Genevieve Bujold, Michael Douglas and Richard Widmark, on a comfortable if not blockbuster budget. A commercial film like so many others; part of a system which feminists have accused and attacked as exploitative and oppressive to women. But is *Coma* different just because it has a female protagonist[1] and just because Dr. Susan Wheeler is an independent, "strong" woman?

How has Hollywood managed to produce if not a wholly acceptable, at least a more possible, positive representation of women? What does it mean to see in *Coma* a progressive film or position for women? How far *is* the film different? And how far, in any case, does it impinge on dominant conceptions of women?

The Difference of *Coma*

The question is, of course, somewhat disingenuous. The terms of the question of difference are not those of one film compared to another, of a statistical comparison of the number of heroines or areas of titilating flesh. The question is asked exactly in terms of the subjective, obvious, commonsense notion

I would like to acknowledge the help of Manuel Alvarado, whose provocative comments on *Coma* have contributed to the development of this article.

of film, as the question of how does the film *appear* different? Reviews from national and trade journals and newspapers have been used here to give an "answer," not because they represent "public opinion"—though they may—but because they are organized responses to the film. While they are personal responses (their importance as opinion, of taste, on cinema), they are also a representation of the film to the public and a placing of it for another audience, for the readers of that journal or newspaper. Thus there will also be an emphasis within many reviews on the genre of the film (a basis for selection by film-goers), on its stars, its story and so on, as well as evaluation, since such reviews are themselves part of the institution cinema in their construction of an audience for film.

Most obviously, reviewers comment on the "difference" of Genevieve Bujold as protagonist. John Pym writes in *Sight and Sound*, "the casting against type of Genevieve Bujold as the austerely coiffed surgeon with the feminist wiles and slightly grating Canadian accent, adds an authority which the other name players palpably fail to supply . . . The burden of the plot falls on Bujold's shoulders, and the film's success depends on the fact that not only can she run with its absurdities, she can also so assuredly take us with her." More simply, the *Sunday People* said, "she does a Paul Newman-type strenuous detective act, climbing ventilation shafts and crawling along ducts with an escape on the roof of a speeding ambulance for afters . . . It is a good gimmick, despite a stunt-woman almost certainly somewhere in the hospital setting . . ." (Why "despite"?—stunt-men commonly replace male stars, though not for the most "macho" actors, e.g. Burt Reynolds, and why demand action and violence to be "real" when the film is not?) Edward Buscombe, writing for *Tribune*, takes this issue of difference even further: "So what's progressive about that? Well, Dr. Wheeler is a woman . . . and what's refreshing in a mainstream Hollywood movie is the way the character of Dr. Wheeler (played by Genevieve Bujold) works against the stereotype. Far from breaking down when she hears of the death of her friend, Wheeler's response is an icy determination to get to the truth. While all around her men are scoffing and telling her not to be silly, she is the only one with the nerve and intelligence to uncover what's happening. The film also subverts stereotypes in the casting . . . It would have been all too easy to cast a heavyweight in the central role and thereby load the dice. No one expects Anne Bancroft, Vanessa Redgrave or Jane Fonda to break down and cry for help. But with the frail and delicate Bujold in the part, the point is effectively made that to be strong and resourceful women don't have to imitate men." (The simplification of the issue of steratyping is a problem; does Jane Fonda ever imitate men?) Alan Brien makes a similar point: "Throughout almost any other thriller in the Perils-of-Pauline style, the threatened female would turn to some male for protection. But the most original twist arrives when Dr. B, looking like an adrenalin-high, fighting-feminist Judy Garland, launches her own counter-offensive" (*Sunday Times*).

If Edward Buscombe is right in seeing a subversion of stereotype in *Coma*, then reviews should exhibit a difficulty in dealing with the film, unless they took account of this. The Alan Brien review clearly does the latter. Yet many of the press reviews make no comment on the gender of the protagonist (some making no mention at all, for example David Robinson in *The Times*), but are simply descriptive, such as Margaret Forwood in *The Sun*: "Genevieve Bujold stars as the young surgeon who believes there is something nasty going on in the operating theater." The *Hollywood Reporter* simply welcomed the film saying "If nothing else, MGM's *Coma* reminds us just how long it has been since we saw a good mystery thriller on the big screen," making no special mention of the gender of the detective.

An implicit comment appears, perhaps, in reviews such as that in the *Evening News*: "Like trim and pretty Dr. Susan Wheeler, we begin to smell a rat as patients keep unaccountably dying in *Coma* . . . A plucky little bantam fighter for the truth . . ." The praising recognition is couched in adjectives appropriate for women (and boys). Or Genevieve Bujold's role is played down in favor of a witty report on the film, as in Derek Malcolm's review in *The Guardian*: "Genevieve Bujold is a young medic at the hospital with a suspicious intern lover, who gets sufficiently muffed when her best friend dies after the botched abortion to ask kindly Chief of Staff Richard Widmark to check through his records." The account is inaccurate and the film trivialized, but popular mainstream film often is; perhaps *Guardian* readers are not thought to go to films like *Coma*, and the review is therefore used as an entertaining balance to the serious-minded responses to more "significant" films. The *News of the World* review seems to work in a similar way, but it's inaccuracy is now bizarre: "A gruesome little thriller set in a hospital where patients arrive with minor illnesses and leave in coffins. Michael Douglas plays a doctor who wants to know what's going on. So, too, does his mistress, Genevieve Bujold. Both have some hair-raising moments with Richard Widmark lurking sinisterly in the background. A super shocker."

In the reviews which take up the issue of the "difference" of the female protagonist in *Coma*, there is an emphasis on the character and role of Dr. Susan Wheeler as different. Thus Margaret Bilbow, writing for the trade journal *Screen International* says "The rarity of having a woman as the plucky investigator makes a welcome change of identification for female viewers; what men lose from the absence of punch-ups they gain from coming over all-protective. Genevieve Bujold's Susan is a well-rounded characterization, intelligent, courageous but never unfeminine in the butch superwoman or invincible sexpot styles of telly heroines. Her vulnerability is played down by director Michael Crichton; it is all the more telling when he reminds us that tights and shoes with heels are not the best thing to wear when scrambling about on ladders." The audience for this review will be exhibitors rather than film-goers, hence the comments on identification and the possible points of appeal to both men and women. But the review also clearly marks the way in which the role of Susan Wheeler does not fit existing stereotypes of role-reversal, with the suggestion that instead it is *realistic*; the film does not simply exploit the stereotype of female vulnerability, nor make the character unfeminine. Hence the importance of the shoes and tights—(re)used in the film as a typical (stereotyped) sign of female vulnerability inasmuch as it points to (is a vivid reminder of) the encumberances of conventional women's clothing, the marks of the feminine. Edward Buscombe makes a similar comment, but takes it further: "*Coma* is no tract, though it manages to make points about stereotyping without hitting the audience over the head— probably the more successful tactic if you're trying to reach a popular audience. For example, in the course of finding out exactly how the comas are being induced, Wheeler has to crawl up a ventilation shaft in the bowels of the hospital. Edging up a ladder she then has to make a jump across to a ledge. In order to get a better grip with her feet she takes off her tights, thus literally shedding the trappings of femininity . . . What's additionally admirable is that the director resists the temptation to titillate the men in the audience by poking the camera up the lady's skirt." Would that shoes and tights were the only such trappings, and does it matter that we do not see, since the camera affords us the position of view in its angled shots below her on the ladder— the place if not the sight of the voyeur? Alan Brien comments more accurately, "Alone she climbs up inside the ventilation ducts, a bizarre blend of vertigo and libido with the voyeuristic camera watching from below as she discards her panty-hose to make a long-legged leap."

Margaret Hinxman in the *Daily Mail* takes up the point about the realism of the character: "Another intriguing aspect of the film is that Genevieve Bujold emerges as a real, complicated person; not just a frightened lady caught in a trap. She is scratchy, unreasonable and intractable. She wears hardly any make-up and her hair is obviously in need of the next shampoo and set. There is a kind of stubborn fanaticism about everything she says and does. It is a superbly constructed performance which stiffens the backbone of what has to be the best thriller of 1978." The plausibility of the character is also emphasized by Brien: "these are only a few of the daring, athletic improbabilities we are conditioned to find commonplace when our star is Burt Reynolds or Paul Newman, but still likely to strain credulity when she is called Genevieve Bujold. Crichton defuses such sexist prejudices partly by the speed, dash and bravura of his story-telling, partly by the creation of a prickly, likeable, contemporary liberated woman." The reviewer in *The Sunday Mirror* reached the opposite conclusion however: "Genevieve Bujold as Dr. Wheeler, tries to get to the bottom of the mystery. In the process she makes life hell for the rest of the staff. Her lover, Dr. Bellows, doesn't believe her theories . . . Miss Bujold is so tedious and hysterical that I don't blame Doc Bellows for disbelieving her . . ."

The issue of the "difference" of *Coma* is also the issue involved in the question of its progressive representation of women, the point made by Edward Buscombe in his discussion of subversive stereotyping. Penny Hollow, writing for *Spare Rib*, takes this further, though she recognizes that there are problems with the film: "parts of it are very plausible and very frightening . . . [but] I was so busy applauding Genevieve Bujold I forgot to be cowardly. She storms through the film undaunted and unstoppable, at last providing me with the heroine for which I've been searching . . . Most of all she *does* things. Berger's remarks that "men act—women appear" doesn't apply to Bujold. She chucks fire extinguishers about, overturns security guards and escapes from the house of horrors without hanging around a man's neck . . . But the film isn't a simple role reversal; macho female battling single-handed against authority and a terror such as the world has never known before. Bujold may be able to keep her white suit in immaculate condition even when crawling around the innards of the hospital, but the rest of the time she is very human. It's both refreshing and touching to realize, for example, that Bujold isn't risking her life for her country or mankind, but for a woman, a friend she cares deeply about. She has fights with her lover and walks out in frustration because of his sexism. Her vulnerability and fear when she is followed in the street will ring bells in all too many women's minds . . . I do have vague misgivings about the ending: if *Coma* had been the conventional Hollywood melodrama, who would have rescued the hero? . . . Despite these doubts, my initial response still stands; any film which features a woman in a role of such strength deserves a visit. Enjoy *Coma* for Bujold's acting and the stupefied silence in the audience when they realize she's going it alone."

What is emphasized in many of the reviews, therefore, is the kind of character and role of Susan Wheeler; not unfeminine, but independent, a woman to identify with in the place of "hero." Majorie Bilbow's point of a "welcome change of identification" seems to suggest, however, that she assumes women normally identify with the male hero, but she has no reverse expectation of men, offering instead an alternative structure of pleasure and identification for them—"coming over all-protective." It is on the basis of the kind of hero *Coma* has that a progressive and feminist claim is made. Clearly the film's story is not about the lives of women, about a women's issue or of the position of women in society. Yet the role of Susan Wheeler is the kind of representation which many would like to see more of. But what does it mean to extrapolate one character, even if she is the protagonist, from the film as a whole? How is the "positive" character of Susan constituted and articulated within the film? These questions are posed in a context where the film is not a "feminist film" and indeed the producers make no such claim (though it can be seen as part of a new Hollywood genre of "independent women" films); but where its treatment of its female protagonist has been seen as progressive, although also as finally recuperated.

I want to take up the issue of *Coma*'s potential progressiveness and final recuperation since either conclusion seems to me to misconstrue the work of the film. I will argue that the dichotomy itself is false since it demands a fragmentation of the film into its elements and this denies the productivity of the film, both across the film as such, and in its insertion into structures and discourses of distribution and exhibition, and also film reviewing and even theoretical writing. Such a denial allows the "contents" of the film to be pitted one against the other in a totting up of points in a snakes and ladders game where the ostensibly conventional ending (Susan is rescued by Mark Bellows) recuperates the image of Susan earlier in the film, and we have to go back to start.

For the problem of this kind of argument is the basis on which the selection and evaluation of the elements is to be made. To make any evaluation of these selected elements as such they must be presumed to have already existing, fixed and determinate meanings, which can be set one against the other. This can be seen in looking at the kinds of elements picked out in the reviews, which can always be balanced by other elements in the film. The progressive elements are seen exclusively in the role and character of Dr. Susan Wheeler as a "strong woman," based first and foremost on the fact that she is the protagonist of the film, not simply because the action centers on her, but also in the way the action is initiated and carried out by her. She is the active agent, instigating the investigation and the series of events of the film, a contrast to the usual passive roles of women (Penny Hollow's point), even to the point of physical danger which she successfully overcomes through her own resourcefulness and cunning. Secondly, there is the character of Susan, intelligent, successful (resident surgeon), tough, capable (treating patients, her investigation), resourceful, caring (her affection for Nancy, her kindness to the small boy patient), warm and loving (the weekend away with Mark), but also independent and self-respecting (the argument with Mark), demanding equality (her "scratchiness") and human, self-questioning (the scene with the psychiatrist). Ordinary, in the sense of visual presentation, her unelaborate and slightly unkempt hairstyle, the lack of make-up, and the "low-key" style of dress—white hospital skirt and coat, casual slacks and shirts etc. There is also the element of moral rectitude in Susan—her role is one of searching after the truth, and she rejects the power-politics of the hospital engaged in by Mark and Dr. Harris.

A corollary to these points, however, is that the film also shows Susan's independence as a problem; she is taken to be either a hysterical woman, neurotic, or just a trouble-maker, by the other characters. Nevertheless her suspicions and her investigation prove all too well-founded and she is vindicated. The emphasis on these elements, in the character and role of Susan Wheeler, obscures the way in which, through choosing another list of elements, the film could be argued as totally conventional in its representation of women. First of all, Susan Wheeler is the only example in the film of a "positive" image of women; there are very few other female characters; all her colleagues are male, and her investigations lead her exclusively to encounters with other men—the pathologists, the anaesthetists, the computer operator, the maintenance man—until she arrives at the Jefferson Institute and the other key villain, who is a woman. And while Susan is presented as an "ordinary" though attractive woman, her best friend Nancy Greenly is, and in contrast, glamorously beautiful. Furthermore, we are first introduced to Nancy in close-up as the camera picks her out from amongst the dancing class, which Susan is also attending—pretty women in leotards, relaxing and exercising in a conventionally feminine way, dancing—titillating and voyeuristic. An alternative might have been to show a game of squash, or the narrative function of the meeting of Susan and Nancy with its discussion of Nancy's abortion could have been fulfilled by meeting in a bar, as male characters might have done. Not only does the scene afford a display of women's bodies, but it positively maintains a stereotype of the beautiful woman in Nancy Greenly; thus Susan is seen as the exception, even by the film. Equally, while the film does not present any explicit sex scenes, it does offer here for the viewers' pleasure the spectacle of the woman's body, as it did at the beginning of the film for example, when Susan is taking a shower, we view her through the glass screen, moving sensuously under the water, from a position which first frames Mark in profile close-up to the camera, and then over his shoulder, his point-of-view. Or later when Susan has woken suddenly from a nightmare, she goes over to the window of her hotel room and the camera shows a reverse shot of her standing naked, seen through the window.

The image of Susan Wheeler as a "strong woman" is itself, it could be argued, ambiguously constructed. She breaks down in tears during the second interview with Dr. Harris, and responds with helpless frustration, futilely beating the roof of her car, when it fails to start, then later, having dealt with a would-be assassin by covering him with cadavers, she collapses in hysterical crying when she arrives at Mark's flat. Yet earlier, after discovering the horribly-burnt body of the maintenance man, she calmly sets about finding for herself the gas lines, and then obtains illegal access to Dr. George's records. The idyllic weekend away at the beach, too, not only offers romantic images of love but also a conventional couple. Mark active, Susan passive—for example when he chases her on the beach and catches her in his arms. Perhaps the most important problem for a progressive reading based on "elements" is simply that, although Susan is the investigator, she doesn't discover "the answer"; she fails to realize, or even consider, Dr. George *Harris* as the villain. Thus though she is in a position of knowledge in the film, normally denied women, she still doesn't "know," to her cost.

The question remains, then, of what can be said of *Coma*, in terms of its elements. On balance, is the film progressive? Or only so in parts? Are these then recuperated by the final scene of Susan's rescue by Mark, and the held hands as she is taken away on the stretcher? To assess in terms of elements is simply to end up with value judgments outside of the specific practice of film; it becomes an issue not of film analysis but political "guesswork." Moreover it is the *image* which is accorded a progressive quality rather than the film, thus the film-as-process is denied, it is reduced to stasis, the moment of the image. For instance, is the question of the image of Susan as progressive and positive posed *within* the film or in relation to cultural values within the Women's Movement which are then brought to bear on the film? It is the former which I believe should be addressed, in relation to the operations of the film itself, thus opening up the ways in which film works as a discursive practice constituting "images" of women, definitions in circulation; though precisely neither in isolation, nor arbitrarily. This raises a challenge to the notion of progressive which is implied if the question is posed in the latter terms above, which rely on a given fixed content which can be evaluated through a "master" discourse, here feminism. For the film cannot be read as progressive in relation to definitions constituted outside the film, either alternative or dominant, which exist as contents given form, a representation, within the film. Since the political terrain of the Women's Movement is the constitution of these definitions and their reconstruction within different determinants, it is absurd to make recourse to fixed contents behind those definitions, demanding a replacement of content, of the real or true image/ woman's body for the false, distorted, dispossessed one.

Similarly, and as a corollary, the argument of the recuperation of "our" images, of progressive images, by dominant and opposed forces, also falls.[2] Here there is an appeal to the image as in some sense an object, *a* content, which can be held by either camp, but whose specific use by one will have different effects on the other. Thus, given the current position of women, it is assumed that the images produced by women on behalf of feminism will always be appropriated by dominant interests and turned against us. Recuperation always implies that a potentially progressive content or meaning has been inserted or taken up into another context where it "loses" that meaning. The notion correctly emphasizes the circulation of images and meanings, but at the same time denies the moments of productivity in that circulation, of possible redefinition, by the Women's Movement as well as, inevitably, by the image industry. The issue of images should be one or production, not hoarding.

An example here would be the quotation of the image of a "liberated" woman in the "Virginia Slims" advertising campaign, which has been referred to by feminists as typical of the recuperation of positive images of women by reactionary forces—the advertising group, the tobacco company. The thesis is that the struggle by women for equality and liberation is both signaled by the advert, and divested of its political import. This is argued both on a crude level—if it's good for them (the cigarette company, advertisers), then it must be bad for us; and on a more elaborated level in relation to theories of manipulation of her image. In the "Virginia Slims" case, the advert makes an appeal as part of its written text to the issue of women's liberation: "We've come a long, long way," which is used together with images to signify this progress through a contrast—a woman being squeezed into a Victorian corset as against the freedom of a parachutist's-type jump-suit—and a notion of liberation is produced not in terms of women as workers, or our position as mothers, but in terms of other commodities—leisure activities, cars, clothes, and, of course, cigarettes. The question of change for women is represented as fashion (the connotative level of the images, their glossiness, the beautiful women, the color, sense of texture, etc.), as individual and as achieved. In other words *a* meaning of "women's liberation" is produced within the advert, which draws on, as one connotative context, the demands for liberation raised by the Women's Movement, but it neither simply uses "images of" the Women's Movement nor does it deny any notion of liberation, though it does project its notion of liberation as one associated with a particular consumer position. It cannot seek to take back or deny the meaning as already inherent in the notion of liberation, since there is no one meaning.

In relation to the image therefore, there is no need to claim any kind of necessary conspiracy on the part of either advertising firms or capitalist companies such as cigarette manufacturers to control women by taking "our" positive images and turning them against us. That images produced by the Women's Movement will enter circulation as "quotable" is inevitable, but the problem of recuperation is a red herring. The specificity of images, the idea that images have forms of construction and production of meaning, acts against a notion of the simple control or manipulation of these forms by such interests.

In a similar way, film is also a site of the production of meaning; this is not to suggest that a film is always already complete in its meaning, which is given or produced once and for all, a literally discrete production, but to indicate the film as a site of specific intersection—in its actual production, the film-making, and subsequently in its consumption—of other discursive practices, and inserted into specific institutions—of the distribution and exhibition of film, for example, but also of film reviewing, film theory. In this sense a film is not "progressive" as a given effect of its content but as the result of its insertion within particular institutions and discourses. Nevertheless the terms of judgment of "progressiveness" are constituted outside the film, within political discourse, and hence themselves also not simply given. Heeding this last point, I want to look at *Coma* in relation to the arguments for a positive, progressive reading of the film, but now looking at the specific production of the film, the project or work of the film as a whole. I emphasize narrative over and above other filmic operations as it seems most pertinent to the questions I want to address to *Coma*. In the following, I am concerned to put forward the basis for a tentative textual analysis of the film. To look, in fact, at what *is* happening in *Coma*. This is undertaken in two ways: first, by looking at the nature and determinants of the narrative structure in *Coma*; and secondly, as a consequence, to consider the effects of these determinants, and the particular construction this produced, for Susan Wheeler's place within the narrative, and for the viewer's place in relation to both the narrative and to Susan. This second series of considerations will be discussed in Part 2.

The Story and its Narration

To start with, how to grasp the story of *Coma*? I've used the term "narrative structure," which marks a concern with the way a film works, comes together as a system of meaning, though narrative is only one part of filmic articulation.[3] This kind of concern emerges in the work of the Russian formalist critics on literature, and in Vladimir Propp's analyses of Russian folktales, and is continued, for example, in the work of Claude Lévi-Strauss on myths. The presumption is that the "content" of the narrative, whether poem, story, folktale or myth, is crucially dependent on the form through which it is constructed; the form is thus not a simple expression of an already-existing content, but a system of representation through which a "content" is constituted. Considered in this way the distinctions form and content must themselves disappear in favor of analytic categories through which a narrative can be understood to come into being in its process of narration. What is being separated here, then, is not the story from its forms of representation as though the story might be told any number of ways, but the story as referring to the representation as such, the tale recounted, a telling, which can be summarized into its actions and events, their logic, and the characters so implicated. Story, as it were, marks the possibility of a tale, which is only produced in its telling. The poverty of a story's synopsis bears witness to the importance of narration within the story, but whose logic and description always escapes such summary, such reduction to *a* "content." To shift from the poverty of synopsis to a "full" description would be to re-tell the tale, to construct a new narration, and hence a new narrative, an/other story. This is seen when a novel is used as the basis for a film (*Coma*, too, is taken from a novel); the form of the narration of the novel cannot be transposed to the film, which must be stripped down to a mediate form, the film script, on which a shooting script can be constructed, and then the filming itself.

What I am interested in here is not simply the possibility of narrativity, but the way in which certain narrative strategies have implications for mean-

ing within the film. How meaning has been constructed through the operations of the narrative devices, the process of narration, so that those operations, devices, necessarily have effects for the meaning constructed. Rather
than part of the means of articulation of meaning, literally its representation,
they can be seen as involved in the constitution of meaning, its coming into
being.

Meaning is an effect, a production of the text, but it is not thereby simply
an end sum: "meaning is not 'at the end' of the narrative, it runs across it; just
as conspicuous as the purloined letter [a reference to Poe's short story],
meaning eludes all unilateral investigation" (Barthes, *Image-Music-Text*, p.
87). Thus "To understand a narrative is not merely to follow the unfolding of
the story, it is also to recognize its construction in "storeys," to project the
horizontal concatentations of the narrative "thread" on to an implicitly
vertical axis; to read (to listen to) [to watch] a narrative is not merely to move
from one word to the next, it is also to move from one level to the next" (*ibid*).

Film is a system of meaning and like other systems constitutes a discursive practice. What is implied however in considering a *narrative discourse*?
Discourse can here be taken at its simplest as the organization of utterances:
"A discourse is a long 'sentence' (the units of which are not necessarily
sentences)" (*ibid*, p. 83). While typically utterances have the form of language, this is not necessarily the case, and thus film too can be considered as
discourse without thereby limiting analysis to the verbal or linguistic within
film. To designate the discourse "narrative" is presumably to specify a
sub-division or even genre within discourse in terms of literary analysis[4]. This
seems to be the result of "commonsense" rather than formal analysis, for
instance Genette writes: "in common practice, the most obvious and the most
central usage, *narrative* designates the narrative statement, the oral or written
discourse which relates an event, or a series of events"—in other words,
stories (p. 38)[5]. But a large number of diverse texts are involved in relating
events—from police evidence in a court of law, a pathologist's report on the
events of death, etc., which we would not normally consider "stories." More
importantly, the forms of narrative structure which Genette goes on to
discuss do appear in discourses which he would exclude from narrative—he
cites Spinoza's *Ethics* for example. While indeed no event is there recounted,
enigmas, as philosophical problems, are set up, and a structure of resolution
played out—the "philosophy" itself.

Narrativity it would now seem is, in a sense, integral to discourse.
Nevertheless it is necessary to retain a notion of "narrative" as something
more specific, to deal with those discourses in which narrativity as such
constitutes the meaning of the text. Thus it is necessary to differentiate the
statement whose meaning exists in its narrative operations, for example the
detective story, from one which while having the form of narrative, has its
meaning constituted in its insertion within a series of further discourses, again

taking the example of the police statement to a court of law. However, the distinction is not one between "true" stories and "untrue" stories or fiction. Rather it is the different constitution of the relationship of the "reader" to the knowledge of the discourse. In this more limited sense, narrative is the representation of the relationship to knowledge where the problem of knowledge in relation to events is set up wholly by and within the text, and thus the *text* will resolve the problem, give the answer. It does not matter whether the knowledge is "real" or not, past or present. As a result, for example, the documentary film does not cease to be narrative film by virtue of the truth of its statement or images; the classic documentary in fact is heavily "recounted," often with a voice over—the story of coal, or the story of truants, etc., and its status as discourse is constituted not as part of negotiations between union and management in the coal industry, not between school and parents over truancy, but within cinema and television as discursive institutions.

Narrative discourse is distinguished therefore not so much by its ontology, its essential qualities, but in being a form of representation which provides its own determining conditions of reading, of meaningfulness. What is involved in the relation of representation can be seen for example in the Western film, which can be understood as an allegory of American politics, the American way of life, but which is read as a Western (albeit allegorical) and not as politics. More often a film or novel makes reference, is situated within, significant political or social events, and in narrativizing these within its own system, separates them from the discursive practice, the political or social determinants, which constituted their meaning as political or social; they may signify politics within the film, but this as such cannot constitute the film as political.

The Possibility of Knowledge and the Determination of the Enigma in Narrative[6]

Narrative discourse always offers a relation, and knowledge may well also be provided but is never the heart of the matter, of the narrative. What is important therefore is not "what" but "how" and narrative can now be seen as a potentially progressive form in constituting knowledge and the relation to that knowledge (e.g. passive, active, determined or open), rather than being an arena of defined knowledge, or its reflection, pitting one knowledge against another, the determinants of each lying outside the film. In other words this is the question of the relation between the knowledge constituted in the text in comparison with a knowledge from elsewhere.

The most explicit example of the narrative defined in terms of strategies around the representation of knowledge is the case of the detective novel, where the narrative consists in the relations of knowledge, and ignorance, of the detection, rather than in the solution of by whom and why X was murdered etc. Thus so many detective stories end by bringing together the elements of detection in an explanation of the process of the crime, while the narrative proper, the 150 odd pages prior, have been the story of the detection and not of the crime. The detection is indeed our relation to the knowledge of the crime, a knowledge finally given as it were apart from the narration of the novel.

Detective *films* provide a number of complications on this strategy, most seriously because there is a double structure of narration—visual and verbal, with the visual having a convention (cinematically) of "truth" whereas the verbal is sometimes true, sometimes false. The device of the final explanation is also only partially effective in a film since it deals with only one level of the presentation of the enigma or mystery; it resolves the state of knowledge within the film but it cannot resolve the level of knowledge given the viewer in *seeing* the actions and events portrayed. In the novel the detective can explain the murder to the other characters *and* to the reader in one process, but in the film the detective can explain only to the other characters within the film, and the level of cinematic narration will not be resolved through this. For example, in *Double Indemnity*, (although this is not a detective film proper) Walter Neff has come to the end of his story, which is the "story" of the film, recounted by him into a dictaphone machine, but told to the audience through the convention of flashback, and now the film will finish *its* story, the story of the relationship of Neff to Keyes, the claims man with the "little man" inside him who always tells him when a claim is sour, and against whom Neff had sought to pull off the perfect con—the double indemnity life insurance policy which would actually be murder—ostensibly for the woman he loves (they kill her husband). But the film's ending is of Keyes arriving at the office as Neff finishes his story and it closes with a repetition of earlier scenes where Neff would strike a match with one hand to light Keyes's cigar, commenting "I love you too," but this time Keyes lights a cigarette for Neff, now slumped to the floor, prevented from fleeing by his bullet wound, and repeats "I love you too."

Thus the project of the detective novel or thriller becomes displaced within film from the detection proper to the process as such, and hence to the characters, situations, motives, relations.

The Detective

Marjorie Bilbow in her review of *Coma* says, "It is not the who and the why that makes the story an entertaining mixture of suspense and black humor but the macabre how of Susan's investigations." *Coma* is thus not exactly a classic detective story of "whodunnit," which has been loosely defined as "works which may or may not include a classical detective, but whose narrative is organized around the movement towards a final revelation which rationally attributes criminal culpability to at least one among a group of more or less equally treated characters" (Derry, p. 111). The detective narrative must play fair with its readers, or audience, and allow them to make a calculated guess as to the solution. Introducing the murderer on the last page is not "fair," so the "clues" must be present but disguised in a number of ways. While *Coma* has a detective—Dr. Susan Wheeler—there is no suspect; or rather, she suspects a number of characters, *all* of whom act suspiciously in relation to her investigation (Dr. George, the Chief of Anaesthesia, in particular, is picked out by the camera a number of times, staring "suspiciously" at Susan). However no clue is offered beyond the hostility and lack of help from certain characters, until the "revelation" at the Jefferson Institute of "George" as the head of the conspiracy. But it is in fact only another clue—George refers not to the Chief of Anaesthesia but to the first name of Dr. Harris. Harris however has been unsuspected within the film, and by Susan, though possibly not by the audience.

In any case the film does not start with a criminal act; the enigma is not one of murder initially and hence of who did it, but the problem of how normal, healthy patients undergoing minor surgery, are becoming comatose following the operation. It is initially, therefore, a problem of medical knowledge and part of the project of the investigation will be the reconstitution of the problem as a criminal act. Susan Wheeler has to show that the comas *are* all unlawful deaths; the film however, despite the abundance of corpses, cadavers and moribund bodies, lacks evidence in terms of a body defined as murder victim. Of course the audience will presume that murder and sinister intent have been involved all along, reinforced by prior publicity of the film in terms of "someone is getting away with murder," but the initial detection within the film is the *establishment* of this possibility.

It would be quite typical, too, within a detective film for the protagonist to suspect sinister underpinnings, where other characters deny it (the suicide or accident which is really murder) though usually they are fortunate enough to have a body. However in *Coma* this is not quite the case either since Susan commences her role as detective not in order to reveal, to prove, but to understand *how*, "I just want to understand" she says, which narratively is given as her response to grief over the condition of her best friend Nancy. As a result this places Susan in a position where she, as it were, doesn't know what she is doing—the knowledge she seeks is not the one she can or will obtain. She is given a pre-eminently masculine trait, the desire for knowledge, but she is seeking a medical knowledge to understand a criminal act and hence is doubly ignorant of what she seeks to understand though her attempt to discover the truth of the first will bring about the exposure of the second. Since she effectively reveals the crime through her attempts to solve a "medical" mystery, her investigation is therefore literally a spectacle,[7] and her position as detective/protagonist in possession of knowledge clearly qualified.

A similar process can be seen in Hitchcock's *North by Northwest* where the hero Thornhill (Cary Grant) is forced to find a man called Kaplan who in fact does not exist but is a cover for a female agent. He too, like Susan, has the wrong question, or quest but in this film the "blindness" of Thornhill is presented as comic, which is narratively extended in the character of Thornhill through his relationship with his mother. In *North by Northwest* Thornhill is forced to take on the role of detective, seeking knowledge, but is never in the position of detective, is never knowledgeable, or rather never has true knowledge in the film until the end.[8]

Coma uses this same narrative device but covertly. Susan appears to be a place of knowledge, agent of the discovery of knowledge, but she is consistently displaced from this position, this time not by comedy but by a denial and dismissal of the knowledge she asserts and seeks, i.e. that the coma cases are suspicious at all. The ending where she does not perform the final decisive act, is thus simply a culmination of this displacement rather than a contradiction of her role as protagonist; it is not a cop-out but the logical conclusion. The moment Susan has "true" knowledge, that Dr. George Harris is the villain, she is "returned" to the role of woman as victim, literally prostrate on the operating table (see also here the still of her being undressed by nurses, and its uncanny similarity to the pose in the earlier shot with Mark, the later image appearing as an "echo" of the earlier one as part of the same order of being held in place).

For the detective story, however, the position of the detective as knowledgeable is crucial. The detective will always know more than any other character, and also more than the audience or reader, though he will not know the whole truth of the enigma or else the film or novel, as a process of "unraveling" the truth, would be manifestly a fabrication (in *The Big Sleep*, for example, this can be seen in the way that Humphrey Bogart, as Marlowe, always seems to know already what has happened or is going to happen). This problem of the detective knowing, or at least knowing more, is extremely difficult for narration, leading to devices like the figure of Dr. Watson in the *Sherlock Holmes* stories, who relates the narrative of detection and therefore speaks from a position of ignorance ostensibly equivalent to that of the reader, while being able to point to and reveal the knowledge of Holmes.

In addition the detective story needs to relate the tale of the detection in a way which will hold the interest of the reader or audience in "how" rather than simply "who" (the how of detection rather than the crime), since otherwise the reader will simply go to the end of the book to learn the answer, or the film will be made pointless if the audience have already "found out" the answer. While the narrative is predicated on a question and its answer, its existence lies in the telling of the tale—but a telling which must be effaced since the telling is always a *delay*, a rhetorical device which if "seen" will expose the contrivance and hence disrupt that "suspension of disbelief in favor of knowing" which is central to narrative. The problem arises most severely for the detective narrative because it is formed on such a simple enigma, of who perpetrated the criminal act.

To return to *Coma*: Susan is clearly never in command of more knowledge than the viewer. On the contrary, the viewer at times has knowledge unknown to her, the conversation between Harris and the psychiatrist is an important example. Nor can she be said to have greater knowledge of the enigma than the other characters, since they don't even recognize one; and certain characters withhold knowledge—the charts of patients etc. Finally, she gives away knowledge to other characters in the course of the film—to Mark and to Dr. Harris. This is important since the role of detective as possessor of superior knowledge is central to the detective format.

I have been concerned to look at *Coma* as a detective narrative because it is within that genre that Susan Wheeler can have the role of protagonist as dominant initiator and principal agent of the action and hence narrative in the film—an important point for feminist interest in the film. While Susan *appears* to have that role inasmuch as she sets in motion a train of events as a result of her investigations—though the links are not immediately clear— and she actively pursues her investigation, which involves strenuous physical effort and danger, a would-be assassin (male) whom she effectively disposes of beneath a pile of frozen cadavers, yet, like Thornhill in *North by Northwest*, she does so *blindly*, and she is denied the definitive action, the capture of the villain (which is achieved by Mark but shown by the arrival of policemen at the operating theater). She doesn't really know, but nevertheless acts; the Jefferson Institute seems important in her investigation, for example, as simply a link between coma cases rather than as part of any general hypothesis she is formulating. And despite the clue we already have, that another link between the cases is that all of them have been tissue-typed, Susan doesn't seem to be anticipating what she will find at the Institute.

The Conspiracy of *Coma*

If Susan is not a true detective in *Coma*, then what is the status of her investigation, and of her as investigator? It is not a question of discovering the "real" detective within the film, but of recognizing the absence of such an agent. Yet a mystery is posed, and solved, within *Coma*, and the problem is how this comes about. In fact there is a shift from mystery to suspense; that is, the issue of knowledge in the film moves from one of "answer" to one of "what will happen." The interest is now no longer in detection and solution, but in how the characters will act, and hence in *re*solution. Suspense here is thus the "waiting to know."

This shift is not, however, simply fortuitous—that there just isn't a detective—since in *Coma* Susan is clearly offered as one; thus *Coma* seeks to operate through the conventions of both the detective and the suspense genre, the shift between them being effected through the narrative's construction of an enigma of both a mystery and a *threat*.[9] This is not simply to refer to the danger inherent in tackling the mystery but to suggest that the protagonist within suspense never narratively has the "upper hand," but is always a potential victim to the mystery under investigation. This I will argue later is integral to suspense in a number of ways, but first I want to consider the shift in *Coma* from a detective story to a suspense thriller and how this is brought about in the narrative.

As noted already, one of the problems within the film is that while the investigation is central, its object has to be asserted and then justified in the process of the investigation. Susan's response to her best friend's coma following a straightforward operation is to try to understand why it happened. She establishes the issue of coma for herself and then asserts it as a general problem, since she cannot understand Nancy's condition from within the (medical) knowledge she has. Checking all the cases of unexplained coma at the hospital over the past year, she discovers that the rate for these cases is far higher than could be statistically expected. The basis on which she is trying to make sense of Nancy's condition thus shifts from the purely individual to one of the enigma of unexplained coma cases in general. However her investigation is never recognized within the film, in the sense of being either authorized or reasonable. The hospital authorities reject the need for her investigation—all apsects of the coma cases have already been covered and therefore its implication must be one of negligence on the part of the hospital and staff. Hence it is also viewed with hostility and there is an attempt to stop her—the reprimands from Dr. Harris, the argument with Dr. George, the enforced visit to the psychiatrist.

Such an "opposition of disbelief" is seen in many films, where the hero must do battle against bureaucracy as well as with the "real" villain, but these difficulties or "trials" put before the protagonist operate as simple forms of delay in the narrative. This is not quite the case in *Coma*. First of all Susan's investigation is not directed towards a suspected third party, but at the hospital itself; since she doesn't initially recognize the criminal nature of the cause behind the coma cases, hospital malpractice and cover-up must be assumed to be involved (though the film never reveals Susan's suppositions on this), therefore the hospital management's response is logical and expected, in fact quite "reasonable." Secondly, not only her investigation, but Susan herself is set up by the hospital as unreasonable—the opposition to her investigation becoming an opposition to her. The status of the investigation, therefore, while central is also highly problematic. The film at this point could simply be a psychological drama about the "problems" of Susan Wheeler, the personal difficulties of a woman doctor in an all-male world.

This means that the status of Susan as protagonist is crucial, for both she and the investigation must seem plausible, her suspicions well-founded and reasonable, and the investigation therefore necessary and justified. Two factors inter-relate in confirming Susan's credibility as protagonist: first of all there is audience expectation, created through cinema advertising, prior publicity and reviews, that *Coma* is not a psychological drama, and that a conspiracy will soon be made apparent. The problem of the coma cases immediately fits as the "sinister mystery," so that the audience will accept all along that the investigation is justified, and see its questioning in the film as a narrative twist. Secondly, this expectation will confirm Susan Wheeler as the investigator inasmuch as she has already been offered within the film for identification as the protagonist. This can be seen in the film in a number of ways: the film opens on Susan driving to the hospital, her place of work, which is a conventional way of introducing the chief character. The following scenes at the hospital, of Susan taking a conference on a patient, in the operating theater etc., present her as a doctor in charge, authoritative, in possession of knowledge. After the row with Mark, we see Susan in her flat, the narrative thus following Susan rather than Mark, confirming the bias of the opening shots. In addition Susan is presented as having a number of positive traits which encourage identification with her as protagonist: she holds a position of moral rectitude in her rejection of the hospital politics and careerism expressed by Mark, or the political wheeling and dealing of Dr. Harris. Her care and concern for patients is contrasted to the general theme in the film of the typical de-personalized care given in hospitals, of doctors' insensitivity—while the surgeon operating on Nancy Greenly says "I just want to get this mother off the table." Susan is later shown giving lollipops to a small boy patient (he in fact needs a kidney transplant, a typical example of the narrative over-determination in *Coma*).

What then of the narrative twist, of the "opposition of disbelief" to her investigation within the hospital? I want to argue that this is more than just a narrative twist, that it is a crucial narrative strategy which in effect sets up a kind of second, "false" conspiracy within *Coma* onto which the real conspiracy and threat are displaced for much of the film. What makes this second conspiracy possible are the very features which provided the basis for a feminist reading of the film, that is, the construction of Susan as a *strong independent woman* prepared to think and act on her own. As such she is shown as continually "difficult" in the film in relation to other characters. This is set up in the row with Mark at the beginning of the film which both establishes Susan's strength and independence, securing the credibility of her investigation and of subsequent "heroic" scenes, *and* sets her up as a difficult woman, a problem as a woman. As she walks out of his flat she says "I just want some respect" but Mark replies "You don't want a relationship, you run away from it. You don't want a lover, you want a goddam wife." Against the reasonableness of her demands for Mark to "help out" is set his accusation that she can't handle her femininity, can't cope with a relationship. Her independence is identified with "her problem" in their relationship and thus also portrayed as a weakness—she is also vulnerable—and this theme is continued in the next scene where she arrives at her own flat (strikingly tidy and peaceful in comparison with Mark's) as the phone is ringing, which she finally answers, too late; the caller has hung up. Poignant, the "too late" evoking a sense of loss, we assume the call was from Mark. Suggesting that, yes, she does want him really. Expelling an image of Susan as totally domineering, it also reinforces the theme of her vulnerability. This theme recurs subsequently, always related to her position as a woman: for instance she herself repeats Mark's accusation to the psychiatrist; and earlier, in insisting on pursuing the investigation she says to Mark "You think that just because I'm a woman I'm going to be upset. I just want to understand. I wish you'd stop treating me as if there was something wrong with me." Dr. Harris, too, says "I can protect you 'cos you're good. And a woman"; and Susan says again to him that people seem to think there's something wrong with her, and not that the problem is the cases of coma.

Susan is quite right. Her independence, as it is constructed in the film, is played on within it in commonsense sexist terms: if she is so independent then there must be something wrong with her. Which is also a way in which her investigation is denied in the film by the other characters. This takes the form of a kind of male conspiracy, of a collective male prejudice against the idea that a woman could be right—that if a woman is saying something disagreeable she must be neurotic. The "opposition of disbelief" sets her up as overwrought and upset at her best friend's condition, as unreasonable and paranoid—"shown" by the way she does not react as a woman should, but yet *over*-reacting, as a woman would. Harris comments after their second interview "Women. Christ," and the psychiatrist's report is that she's "rather paranoid and upset." This locks into the exploitation of the connotations of

Harris: "Take the weekend off, Sue."
Susan Wheeler: "I'm so embarrassed . . ."
Harris: "Don't be. Our emotions are what make us human."

Harris: "Women—Christ."

the independent woman, the idea that she's a problem to those around her, i.e. to men. A sense of conspiracy builds up and is developed, for example, in the scene where Mark is exhorted by the Chief Resident (whose job he hopes, and is encouraged to believe, he will get) to "Do something about her," though Mark can only repeat that "she likes to do things her own way." Importantly, these scenes are unknown to Susan; the audience has a privileged position of knowledge: of an apparent conspiracy to control her, to stop her investigation, on the basis that she is really simply paranoid.

The scene in which Susan is apparently followed by a suspicious-looking man (who later proves to be the hired killer) culminates this narrative strategy. Following the frustrations of that day, she leaves to go home and finds that her car won't start. It's too much and she collapses in rage and frustration, uselessly beating the roof of the car with her fists, her aggression ineffectual and defeatist, the position of victim, the violence emphasizing her lack of control, her "feminine" position. The scene is shot to encourage our cinematic identification with her position, alternating close and medium-long shots of Susan, from a position to the side of her, with only a few reverse shots close-up from the other side of the car. We see her turn around and notice something, and only then are we given a full reverse shot which reveals a man

standing in shadows opposite her. Susan hurries to the subway and as the train pulls away we turn with her to see the face of the same man, left standing on the platform. The scene suggests that Susan suspects this man tampered with her car, is following her; we are led to identify with her projection of threat from this man although such a reading is not yet narratively supported but could simply be further evidence of Susan's paranoid and hence unfounded fears. Thus the scene both introduces the first mark of the "true" conspiracy and completes the construction of Susan as paranoid: she goes to see Mark who reassures her that her car is always breaking down, and then "proves" the absurdity of her theories of carbon monoxide poisoning as the cause of the coma cases by checking the operating room's equipment.

They then go away for the weekend (as Dr. Harris suggested), for Susan to "recover"; where the narrative requires it Susan is weak and "feminine," against character. The idyllic weekend extends this, with images of the classic romantic couple and the portrayal of love and tenderness within conventional male/active, female/passive roles. Susan has been put back in place. This sequence is, though, a false resolution, a hiatus, which seems narratively unnecessary (and unfortunate in terms of a progressive reading of the film). But it does serve to complete the "male conspiracy," and to hold a tension about whether it really is "all over." An opposition is set up between the safety of this sequence where Susan is "normal" and the scenes where she is actively pursuing her investigation—the end of the film repeating this structure with Susan's rescue by Mark, the last shots showing her prostrate on the stretcher, her hand held by Mark, ceasing to be "independent" once the narrative ends.

The weekend does have one important function in advancing the investigation: passing the Jefferson Institute, Susan makes Mark stop the car and she goes in to have a look, the camera revealing very well the ominous architecture of the building. She is met by a woman who informs her that "there is no staff" and that "I am in charge," telling Susan that she must visit during official times. Here, where Susan will find the real conspiracy (it is a long-term care hospital for brain-damaged patients to which all the coma cases have been transferred, and is the locale for the auction of "spare parts") she finds another woman; this balances her as protagonist, setting the two up as adversaries. But even more it avoids rupturing the "male conspiracy" by not presenting at this point a man as bearer of the real conspiracy, but a woman instead. (Susan's assailant cannot stand for the conspiracy itself, since he is simply an agent rather than a locus for the conspiracy. Her ability to deal with him, but not with the true locus, Harris, is important.)

My argument has been, therefore, that suspense is created within the film around a second, "false" conspiracy, while the true one is elsewhere; it is not in fact Dr. George, despite the clues foisted on us when the camera picks him out, staring at Susan in the coffee-room, or in the lift before her final meeting with Harris; nor is it Mark, whose suspicious phone-call when she arrives at his flat after discovering the gas line and disposing of the assassin, was actually to her mother. There is excitement around Susan's successful engagements with the "enemy" but anxiety that she has not dealt with the main enemy. This has a number of consequences. It produces a certain confusion in the ending since the "false" conspiracy is not resolved, but disappears with the emergence and resolution of the "real" conspiracy, located in the figure of Dr. Harris who can now become the sole bearer of the "false" conspiracy as well. *In addition, the basis for a feminist appropriation of Susan Wheeler's role as a strong woman is radically changed since to extrapolate just this element from the narrative now becomes a willful denial of the film's work.* It is not a question of recuperation, however, since it is impossible to make any such separation of a progressive content from the narrative strategy as a whole; not only is it not a story "about" an independent woman, but that independence itself is the mode of constructing her as victim. What is interesting in *Coma* is not any element of progressivity nor its supposed recuperation of such an element, but the way in which the "independence" of Susan Wheeler is constructed in order to fulfill a certain narrative strategy through which a different kind of suspense and tension (the holding off of the solution through a "false" conspiracy) can be created than with a male role— commercially a "good gimmick" with the added bonus that it is "socially relevant." The political evaluation of the film must be affected by this understanding of its filmic process in terms of the production and circulation of images and meanings. Thus the problem, politically, of *Coma* is not that it recuperates its progressive meaning (or any other) but that the meaning and image produced within it can be judged inadequate and unacceptable to the feminist political project.

It has been argued that the "false" conspiracy is only possible because the protagonist is a woman and that this strategy is crucial to the effectivity of the narrative as suspense. *Coma* can now be considered in relation to its specific production within this narrative strategy, and the consequent implications for the construction of its representation of a woman protagonist. To do this it is necessary to relate the "false" conspiracy to the narrative production of suspense itself. However to reconsider *Coma* as a suspense thriller is to reorganize the assumptions of knowledge in the film; Susan Wheeler will then become victim to the events she seeks to engage with—the film becomes about how little she knows rather than how much. As a character she is "strong" but as an actant within the narrative she is "weak." And this is a narrative strategy across the film as a whole rather than in "moments" of suspense. Certain other questions will also be taken up: that of the relation of the spectator to the protagonist in the suspense film, of the forms of identification in play and how the *gender* of the protagonist might be implicated as a factor in the position of the spectator in relation to the film.

Discussion of *Coma*—Part 2

The Suspense Thriller

The "suspense thriller" is broader than the detective thriller, and it easily accommodates the elements of horror (the operation, the autopsy, the cadavers, the strung-up bodies at the Jefferson Institute), the melodrama of the lovers' relationship and the issue of medical ethics (spare-part surgery) which the film also contains, as amplifications of the context, narrative embellishments rather than digressions. However it is not merely a question of how well the various elements of the film "fit" a generic sub-category, for a suspense thriller involves very different relations of identification and viewing. First, the audience will tend to have *greater* knowledge than any of the characters in certain sequences or across the whole film. Secondly, the audience is implicated within the film quite differently, or rather, more extremely. The latter issue of spectator position and identification will be taken up more extensively later in relation to the place of the subject within the cinematic look and the structure of paranoia.

Suspense, as a form of narrative, is always a problem of knowledge. Where the detective or mystery thriller is an unfolding, unraveling of the enigma through clues and deduction in which the reader/viewer is underprivileged in relation to narrative actants, in the suspense thriller there is a continual holding back, interruptions in the pursuit of the resolution of the enigma by the characters, and a privileged position of the reader/viewer in relation to the elements of danger and often to the enigma as well. Both strategies are effectively forms of *delay*, which, as Barthes has argued, is indeed central to all narratives: "To narrate (in the classic fashion) is to raise the question as if it were a subject which one delays predicating; and when the predicate (truth) arrives, the sentence, the narrative, are over, the world is adjectivized (after we had feared it would not be)" (*S/Z* p. 79).

The operations of the unfolding of the enigma Barthes designated as the hermeneutic code—the "Voice of Truth"—because it is the code through which we will know, but whose operations within the text must always be putting off of knowledge, else the story will end. It has a contradictory role therefore; it is the mode by which the answers will be given, and it is the mode whereby the answer is withheld in favor of continued narration, the story as the period of delay between the setting of the enigma and the solution. Thus the hermeneutic codes structure the enigma according to the expectation and desire for its resolution in terms of both enabling and delaying the solution.

In his earlier essay on the structure of narrative Barthes (1966) had also emphasized this function as part of the form of narrative as a system; he called it distortion (or distending), the holding apart of the elements which will give the solution, and the space thus created is then "filled up" with the narrating. Instead of a chronological or natural time, another, "logical" time is created with very little connection with real time, held together in the logic of narrating. For example, in literature, the character holds out his hand to shake that of another character and between the beginning of the gesture and its completion might be inserted paragraphs of description, responses, thoughts on the context of the handshake, the appearance of the other character, the position of the character in relation to others in the narrative etc. In film, the camera might cut between a shot over the shoulder of the first character, to a reverse shot of that character, (shot/reverse-shot), or to the point-of-view of another character, or no character's position; or a cut-away could be made, to a photograph (of that character), or an object, or to other events elsewhere (cross-cutting). Barthes goes on to argue that

> "suspense" is clearly only a privileged—or "exacerbated"— form of distortion: on the one hand, by keeping a sequence open (through emphatic procedures of delay and renewal), it reinforces the contact with the reader [viewer], has a manifestly phatic function; while on the other, it offers the threat of an uncompleted sequence, of an open paradigm (if, as we believe, every sequence has two poles), that is to say, of a logical disturbance, it being this disturbance which is consumed with anxiety and pleasure (all the more so because it is always made right in the end). "Suspense," there, is a game with structure, designed to endanger and glorify it, constituting a veritable "thrilling" of intelligibility: by representing order (and no longer series) in its fragility, "suspense" accomplishes the very idea of language: what seems most pathetic is also the most intellectual—"suspense" grips you in the "mind," not in the "guts."
> (*Image-Music-Text*, p. 119)

Here, and in the earlier quotation, Barthes is associating narrative-as-delay with the structure of language; of the sentence, as always a question of the subject and predicate; and as order. In a sense the story redoubles on the structure of language, rather than merely using it as means to express its content. But in addition, and related to the issues of language, narrative-as-delay opens up expectation, creates a structure which, in putting off the answer, determines the expectation for that answer, producing the demand for an answer and thus opening onto desire. Narrative-as-delay is therefore always a question of position in relation to a knowledge (the answer, the "truth"). In suspense this delay is not only "exacerbated," but the way in which it is effected is such that a different form of relation to knowledge is brought about. Hitchcock points to the way that suspense is not produced through a simple "not knowing," it is not just a delay in coming to know, but always depends on the fact that *something* is known, and it is the form of this lack of full knowledge which is the basis of suspense:

> We are now having a very innocent little chat. Let us suppose that there is a bomb underneath this table between us. Nothing happens, and then all of a sudden, "Boom!" There is an explosion. The public is *surprised*, but prior to this surprise, it has been an absolutely ordinary scene, of no special consequence. Now, let us take a *suspense* situation. The bomb is underneath the table and the public *knows* it, probably because they have seen the anarchist place it there. The public is *aware* that the bomb is going to explode at one o'clock and there is a clock in the decor. The public can see that it is a quarter to one. In these conditions the same innocuous conversation becomes fascinating because the public is participating in the scene. The audience is longing to warn the characters on the screen. (pp. 58–59)

Here the audience is offered a partial knowledge, that there is a bomb and the suspense is the delay in knowing whether it will explode, whether the characters will act/or gain knowledge to prevent the explosion, or what. Our knowledge is effectively "useless" since though we know something could happen, we can neither act to prevent its occurrence, nor find out the answer sooner than the film narrates it to us. Our place and relationship is literally constructed by the narrating. The delay itself is effected by the narration, the cutaway shots to the bomb beneath the table, the innocuous clock, the innocent conversation presented as shot/reverse-shot, "the logical disturbance" which Barthes speaks of. The difference, the dissonance, thus created has the effect of redoubling anxiety, since not only is there a threat, but it is unknown to the characters. And the audience is impelled into the scene in its concern on behalf of the characters, yet its place, or position, is *outside* the scene, is never only that of the characters (we see the bomb beneath the table, an "impossible" shot).

The audience sees the "full" scene whose "meaning" emotionally implicates them, but precisely whose seeing places them outside the film. Thus it is not simply that the viewer knows more than the characters, it is not a twist on the detective story in which, for once, the viewer has more clues than the detective, but that the relation to that knowledge which is produced in its narration is different. We don't necessarily know the whole of the enigma but we are already given what the character must find out, indeed often "endure," and the form of the gap between the two knowledges produces suspense. This is clear in the following quote from Hitchcock, in which the suspense is surely the effect of the knowledge-structure:

> To my way of thinking, mystery is seldom suspenseful. In a whodunnit, for instance, there is no suspense, but a sort of intellectual puzzle. The whodunnit

generates the kind of curiosity that is void of emotion, and emotion is an essential ingredient of suspense . . . fear depends upon the intensity of the public identification with the person who is in danger . . . A curious person goes into somebody else's room and begins to search through the drawers. Now, you show the person who lives in that room coming up the stairs. Then you go back to the person who is searching, and the public feels like warning him, "Be careful, watch out. Someone is coming up the stairs." Therefore, even if the snooper is not a likeable character, the audience will still feel anxiety for him. (pp. 58–59)

Suspense or narrative delay is typically a *local* operation of the narrative system, existing within a sequence or segment of narration. In many of his films however, Hitchcock seems to create whole series of scenes structured in terms of this sense of suspense, so that it thereby constitutes the overall narrative form in the film rather than being just one "element." This has important consequences. As already noted, the "hero" is displaced as site of knowledge though he or she never ceases to be the protagonist—provoking and taking action within the narrative. However a different structure of identification/implication within the narrative is established with the abandonment of the illusion that we are finding out along with/in competition with the detective and we are thrust into the insecurity of not-yet knowing (all) but worse off than the character since we know something. Thus "having knowledge" in the suspense film is not simply part of the pleasure of "finding out," indeed it is associated with the thrill of *un*pleasure, and hence it is not commensurable across types of narrative. This marks the radical divergence possible within a general strategy of delay, and shows the importance of the narrative's construction of the positions of protagonist and viewer/reader vis-à-vis the knowledge itself. The character of protagonist in suspense becomes, in a way, the victim of the narrative—acting blindly in comparison with the audience's knowledge.

It is as a structure of suspense that the "false" conspiracy (the construction of Susan Wheeler as paranoid) discussed earlier is produced, but now understood not only in terms of an anxiety on the part of the spectator but more importantly as the production of a privileged knowledge for the viewer and different position of "view" of identification, than that within the detective strategy.

It could be asked at this point whether there is any general connection between the production of the protagonist as victim in suspense and the fact that the central character in *Coma* is a woman. But obviously suspense is not gender specific—it is as protagonist not as woman that Susan is thus "victim." If it is argued that the position of protagonist in suspense is nevertheless "feminine" irrelevant of her or his actual sex, then the production of this position and its nature as "feminine" would also have to be explored. The strategy of suspense is simply a tactic of delay within the *narrative* and its predication on the personal problems of the protagonist is merely typical of other strategies of delay in films—e.g. the sub-plot of the hero's marriage/relationship on the rocks because of his job as policeman/detective. Perhaps it is in the ending of the film, however, that Susan Wheeler as woman is finally "put back in place"? But it is within the *suspense* strategy that Susan is "out of place" as the difficult, independent woman, and by the end of the film this strategy has disappeared. In any case, despite being drugged by Harris (the drugging of the hero was a typical plot device in 1940s thrillers) and being prepared for a deadly appendectomy, she ingeniously pages Mark by setting off his buzzer and he, now finally alerted to the danger, leaves to deal with the poisonous gas-lines, following the description that Susan had earlier given him.

It is not now a question, however, of replacing the weighing up of images of women in *Coma* with that of narrative construction, pitting one strategy against another in order to assess its positivity for women. First, these constructions are not discrete strategies but operate across the whole film, separated out only in analysis. Second, Susan's character is not then independent of these constructions, to be assessed as if she were a real person, but remains a function of the narrative and its constraints and demands in the narration of the enigma of the coma cases.

What then of identification? Identification, I will argue is the position of the spectator as it is constructed through the codes of narration which "play" out the story of the film. By codes of narration I am referring to all those means by which the film's story is presented, by which the "meaning" of the film is produced and conveyed, narration referring to the way in which the story comes to be told. Involved here therefore are all the elements of lighting (long dark shadows versus bright sunlight for example), decor and staging, including casting, make-up, actors' gestures and positions and movements in frame, as well as camera angle, height, distance, framing, focus etc. It also includes editing. "Codes" marks the way in which these means to meaning are systematized within the film, ceasing to be arbitrary elements and coming together as a systematic structuring within the film. The "detective" and the "suspense" elements in *Coma* represent two different narrative strategies, operating in different sequences of the film, which employ differing systems of narration and importantly, as a result, producing differing placings of the spectator in relation to the actions and characters constructed. In the "detective" sequences these differences were set up in terms of a relation to knowledge: the detective knowing more than the spectator, whose access to knowledge will be through the detective; in suspense the spectator has access to knowledge additionally to that of the protagonist.

In the system of the film Susan is most positively represented in the moments of her role as detective. These are marked by her determined and effective action in investigating the coma cases, dispatching her attacker, and escaping from the Jefferson Institute. However the structure of detection is set up through particular strategies of filmic narration. Narratively Susan is the source of action—when she finds the maintenance man dead she pursues the investigation, following the gas-lines he had mentioned and exploring the ventilation shaft. Similarly she initiates action in the sequence where she goes to Dr. George's offices to check the records, and responds with effective action when she is disturbed and then pursued by a hired killer. This is emphasized by the way in which the camera consistently offers us Susan's point-of-view (POV)[10] within the action, showing us Susan intercut with what she sees but without at this point introducing the alternative position of her attacker. Susan is presented as dominant as actor, appearing in charge of the action because we only see it from her position, her viewpoint or in the place of her viewpoint. This filmic strategy (a combination of camera position, the organization of action, and subsequent editing in which shots are cut up and alternated) pulls the spectator into identification with the place and source of action—Susan Wheeler. And the character is attributed through these devices a power to act, to take charge of the situation, within the scene. Our expectation is that she will deal with her attacker, will escape from the Jefferson Institute, since no alternative possibility is created by any alternative position of view of the action; for example where she is pursued by the killer the action is dominantly presented from Susan's point-of-view. When a shot which can be taken as the killer's POV is finally shown, as he follows her, we have always already seen her one step ahead or at any rate we never know more than Susan when we view from his point-of-view. "Knowledge" is on the side of Susan, for when we return to Susan's point-of-view she is always

already in charge of the events, taking action, so that when the killer searches the cold-storeroom full of cadavers where Susan is hiding she is already in position to act—pulling the row of cadavers down on top of him and making her escape. In the scenes of her escape from the Institute, when we no longer have Susan's point-of-view, we then become less knowledgeable in relation to the action and events than Susan (the spectator-position typical of the classic detective narrative), so that when she is pursued into a room on the second floor of the Institute and the camera follows her attackers into it, showing the broken window, with the guard's comments that she won't get far, we are not yet aware that she has ingeniously hidden herself above them in the ceiling cavity.

It could be argued that, inasmuch as identification is thus constructed, through Susan's POV, it is thereby a "positive" image, a "positive" protagon- ist, and a woman. But "positive" here no longer as a term of social evaluation, for in what way could a "negative protagonist" be constructed by the system of narration? This positive image of a woman is the effect of the narrative action and filmic narration at this point; gender per se is not determining. However the protagonist is a woman and to that extent the "image" or form of identification and reading the film encourages at this point is atypical in combining this mode of narration and gender designation. While the argu- ment has shifted emphasis from identification as content and placed it in terms of narrative strategy, it is important to note that this does not exist across the whole film—precisely within the suspense strategy a different form of filmic narration is adopted. Nor is it conditional upon Susan Wheeler as a *woman*—which would presumably be in terms of her specific feminine qualities—but on the character-function of the investigator, who is given as a woman within other, earlier constructions in the film. Thus the believability of Susan as heroic protagonist is at no time dependent on the establishing of her as possessing special powers of strength etc., but on the contrary she is presented as unexceptionally feminine, with her small, slight image, used in other films precisely in its fragility.

From Identification to Paranoia

The question, then, of the structures of identification, of position, produced through the strategy of suspense? What is important is not the mere posses- sion by the audience of more knowledge than the protagonist but the rela- tionship to this knowledge and its unfolding. In his discussion of suspense Hitchcock emphasizes that he wants the audience to *care* about his charac- ters, and speaks of the importance of "the intensity of the public identifica- tion with the person who is in danger." But this is achieved only by breaking up that identification, refusing any simple identity of character and spectator point-of-view within the action. The spectator is *engaged on behalf* of but not in the position of the character—a very dangerous place. Instead of viewing the action from the place of the protagonist with POV shots alternating with non-subjective shots, in suspense the camera strategy will effect an undermining of the protagonist's POV and thus her or his dominance over the action, so that the scene will be equally or even predominantly viewed from *another* position.

The major sequence of the suspense strategy in *Coma* is the scene discussed earlier, where Susan leaves the hospital to go home, upset and demoralized following a harrowing meeting with Harris. Narratively Susan is not initiating or in charge of the action that follows, and will eventually respond by trying to flee. Susan emerges from the building and walks down the steps to her car, parked almost directly in front. The camera affords us this view from a position to the left of the building and to the side but in front of the car. Susan gets into the car, but it won't start and she finally gets out and, remaining on the driver's side, turns and begins to hit the car on its roof, so that she now faces the hospital building and away from the road. Throughout this action the camera cuts between its original long-shot position to the side-left and a full close-up of Susan's face from the front. These camera positions are alternated for a number of shots. Objectively, we observe Susan's hysterical loss of control from long-shot; but the alternation with close-ups pulls us into an identification with her response of frustration and helplessness. This develops through the powerful mirror-identification possible with the close-up here since it is not narratively motivated as another character's viewpoint. The long-shot/close-up alternation presents Susan's subjective responses and experience.

However the structure of shots offers only a partial position of identification since it lacks Susan's POV; we never view the situation from Susan's position, although we are enabled to *interpret* it from her position through the view afforded by the close-up. In addition an anticipation is set up—not only of what will happen next but of how, or from where, with whose look, we will see it. We lack a look within the scene, of Susan's or another character's look. The anticipation becomes anxious expectation; because the question remains, who is in control of this view? Whose view is it?—since the general narrative system of *Coma* has consistently worked through shot/reverse-shot and establishing or long-shot, which has been the structure of the preceding sequence in Harris's office, alternating between Harris seen from or near to Susan's position, and the reverse, Susan seen from or near Dr. Harris's position, and medium-long shots from neither character's place, showing either both Susan and Harris—he gives her his handkerchief to wipe her eyes; or one character only, the latter giving the audience a "privileged" view over the characters. Thus the beginning of the scene with Susan's car is incomplete in terms of the expectations created by the already-established narrative system of organized camera position and editing shots. The narrative expectation of "what will happen next" is exacerbated or doubled-over in the filmic narration. Anxiety in the anticipation arises in the lack of signified, of meaning, to the narration at this point, which only the intervention of something else, or another look, another character, can break and resolve. On the other hand such a "view," or signified, is already implicit in its lack, we are aware of its absence, an absence which thus structures our viewing—held to the inescapable two-look structure of camera/our look and Susan's look seen by us but not seeing us. The "sinister quality" or anxiety is an effect of this structure; the doubling structure of the two looks offers an imaginary relationship of look, Lacan's mirror identification pulling us as spectators into an imaginary totality, an "imaginary" fullness of view and knowledge. I emphasize that it is the *structure*, not a particular content, which is at issue here. But this apparent structure of full knowledge is, as I have argued, clearly not so—narratively we don't yet know what the scene "means" in terms of the overall narrative, nor is it clear what is going to happen or why this scene is happening. Moreover, as Jacqueline Rose has argued, this structure of apparent plenitude is always already broken up insofar as the structure of looks is reversible—being seen from the place where I look—thus containing a potential splitting in its constitution. And it is this potential reversibility, of looking and being looked at, which Lacan defines as the paranoic alienation of the ego, leading Jacqueline Rose to argue that "paranoia could be said to be latent to the structure of cinematic specularity in itself, in that it represents the radical alterity of signification (the subject spoken from elsewhere)" (p. 89).[11]

Thus, at another level, the anxiety of suspense, its effectivity as an "exacerbated form of delay" (Barthes) lies in its drawing into play the paranoia of specularity latent in all cinema through a narrational structure of camera looks in which the third look is kept absent. Narratively, there clearly will be another look, which will be provided by Susan; but first the camera shows Susan looking, as she turns round and sees something behind her and to her left but *not* in the place of the camera. We are *then* given a point-of-view reverse shot, showing a man standing in shadows across the road. The place to which Susan looks is clearly represented as one of threat—since it is precisely the reverse place of her own look, and hence also of ours as spectators. Meaning now is in place, we understand that this man has been watching her for some time, perhaps has tampered with her car, and may be a potential threat. This meaning has clearly been constructed through the form of representation—Susan is shown as victim, in the play of events she is not in control of, and this emerges as a result of Susan's look which draws the man into the narrative scene, as a (potential) aggressor and source of events.

The scene, however, contains a further element of suspense beyond the structure just described. For what is involved in this scene is not only or primarily the revelation of part of the real conspiracy, but it also continues the narrative construction of Susan as paranoid—the "false" conspiracy—and thus unjustified in her assumption of threat from this man. This is possible because the position of Susan as place of narrative truth and knowledge has been undermined by earlier scenes emphasizing her paranoia (the psychiatrist's report for example), that is, her "false" interpretation of events and reality in the film. The suspense then exists first of all in our concern on behalf of Susan, that is, from her position of paranoia, and secondly because, through our privileged knowledge, we have even more reason than she to be justifiably "paranoid."

What has emerged through this discussion of suspense is a notion of identification in relation to characters not in terms of her or his character traits, the "I wish to be her or him" identification where there is an appropriation of identity. Rather it is the position of the character, as actant, a locus within the narrative or activity—of both doing and being done to—which is presented as a position of view and hence knowledge, in which we locate ourselves and thus identify with. And this is a production of the form of narration. Thus we are "involved" with, identify with, care about (even if only for a moment) characters we may not like, nor necessarily wish to be like, but whose position and place within the narrative we adopt—and this against sexual difference, as it were. That is, the gender of the character is not a necessary determinant of identification; it doesn't matter here that it is a man or a woman.

However such identifications are intermittent. The narration pulls us into the place, the point-of-view, of characters, but equally offers another view, other characters, or in contrast, the camera's "objective" look, unmotivated as a character's view. Yet this last "look" is not simply a neutral observer's position, since it exists within a series, a total system of views. First of all, this system is not arbitrarily constructed but will consistently privilege certain views in certain ways—thus Susan's controlling look as active protagonist, which she loses as victim to suspense. Secondly, the shifting "views" offered the spectator are not discrete, so that in shot/reverse-shot, once this system is established within a scene, a view from one character-position will always imply the reverse view possible and hence another position. Thus no position of view is unitary within the film system but is always undercut by a possible other "view." The camera's "objective" view, while implying nonidentification thus confirms the previously held position of identification and grounds continuing identification—for example through close-ups of a character preceding a cut to the character's POV. Our identification, which is apparently displaced, is simply re-inforced in the presentation of a *loss* of identification of position. The "objective" camera look is therefore never properly objective, the spectator as neutral observer evaluating the scene, but is always an impassioned spectator—Hitchcock's "caring public" caught in the play of the narrative and the structure of identification. And the "privileged knowledge" possible to the spectator through this objective look intensifies any structure of identification established while placing the spectator out-of-place in relation to a character's position, an out-of-placeness which provokes an anxiety (the look which is returned) which is incorporated narratively in suspense.

Identification insofar as the narrative in its narration takes hold of us puts us as spectators in play in the narrative world of the film. The question remains however, of sexual difference in this structure of identification. This in several ways. First, it is raised in the demand for a positive content to images of women, in order to enable a politically progressive identification by women with these images. But this positive content has always been thought of as the conferring of "positive" attributes on women (activity, independence, aggressive roles). These are not themselves gender-specific and the question remains of the construction and specificity of gender. A further difficulty is involved in the unproblematic assumption of identification as the assimilation of viewer to image/character as sexed role, in terms of a model for identity: stars, for example, as cultural heroes or heroines. But, as I have argued, in film at least, identification implies more than a mere assimilation of, or modeling on, the persona of the character on the part of the spectator, as a content taken up or rejected.

Second, another view has taken identification as the central political issue, insofar as it assimilates the viewer to its particular system of meaning. While the latter is clearly important, "identification" here is held to be the means for simply forming or molding opinion, reproducing existing sets of ideas, ideologies, and this is taken to be the political stake in relation to film, by both right and left as well as by feminists with the question of control of films, television etc. thus becoming central. What is assumed is that the viewer "loses" her or himself in the process of viewing—"ideology" working against the viewer's wishes or best interests in appropriating her or him to pleasure—in Bogart, Eastwood or Genevieve Bujold.[12]

Is not the notion of identification with a simple content retained here? In the rejection of ideology as a simple content, sheer signified, within the film, certain film theorists have looked at psychoanalysis in order to describe the process by which the spectator is implicated within the film, through the construction of the spectator as subject for the film. This construction is predicated on Lacan's theorization of the construction of the subject. Human subjectivity is constructed through a series of identifications, a positioning of self and others. Within psychoanalysis this identification is founded through the look—the child's look into the mirror at its own reflection, which is later organized in the entry into the symbolic through the intervention of a third term—the phallus or Name-of-the-Father; this structure sets up a privileging of the look (the look as *objet petit a*) on the one hand, and on the other hand, through the theory of the Oedipal complex and the threat of castration, it is given a determining content—woman as representing lack and castration and thereby affirming its (the phallus) presence elsewhere, in the man.[13] The issue of sexual difference in cinema is introduced as an already given, the look in cinema being constructed as the male gaze.[14] The subject constructed in cinema, for film, thus appears always to be a masculine viewing subject within this theory.

I have sought to problematize the way in which cinema is thought in relation to the look, insofar as I argue that there is no single or dominant "view" or look in cinema (either the male gaze or Metz's identifying with oneself seeing), but a continual construction of looks, with a constant production of spectator-position and thus subject. It is the structure of the look in cinema which is important, in the taking up of a position of looking rather than the locating a content to that look. Thus identification in cinema is a question of continually shifting construction of subject position across the determinants of the film system—the organization of narrative and narration. To consider the subject-in-process in this way within the film system, produced through the *structure* of identification rather than predicated on a particular content is to now keep open the question, and problem, of the production of sexual difference within cinema.

Notes

1. The term "protagonist," indicating the chief actor, character or combatant, is used here in preference to "heroine" to describe Genevieve Bujold's role as Dr. Susan Wheeler in order to emphasize the narrative function of the hero; the "heroine" is not normally the female equivalent of "hero."

2. Rosalind Coward has discussed this problem in terms of incorporation in relation to sexual liberation "where some truly liberatory force which has no relation whatsoever with capitalism is re-absorbed back into the existing capitalist forms"; her critique of this notion has been drawn on in the development of the following argument.

3. For example, against the hegemony of narrative, structuralist/materialist film-makers such as Malcolm Le Grice and Peter Gidal have argued that their films are non-narrative, that they definitively break with traditional definitions of narrative. For discussion of this see *Structural Film Anthology*, ed Peter Gidal, and "The Avant-Garde and Its Imaginary" by Constance Penley. More importantly for my arguments in this article, the notion of specularity within cinema is not obviously given by narrative alone, but is as much a part of what has been called the "machine of cinema." The question of the "look of the spectator" which is suggested here is taken up in more detail in part 2 (cf. Stephen Heath, "Narrative Space").

4. "Discourse" is here used to indicate 1. The film as a system of meaning, taken as a unit, the individual "work"—film as a system of utterances. 2. It is also used within analyses of narratives to distinguish the story from its telling, its *narration*, thus following E. Benveniste's distinction between *histoire* and *discours*, where "discourse" is always marked by the presence of a subject of the enunciation, a "person" who tells the tale—the narrator/author, and thus specifying a mode of address; see also T. Todorov "Categories of the Literary Narrative" and G. Genette, note 5 below. 3. A further, and different use of "discourse" is made by M. Foucault, referring to "a group of statements in so far as they belong to the same discursive formation . . . it

is made up of a limited number of statements for which a group of conditions of existence can be defined" (p. 117). Statements here are no longer the simple utterance of narration but are constituted "in so far as they can be assigned particular modalities of existence," "thus . . . clinical discourse, economic discourse, the discourse of history, psychiatric discourse" (p. 107) and also, I would argue, cinematic discourse, within which "the film" is the level of statement. Cinematic discourse is not, however, identical with the institution of cinema. The importance of this second shift in the use of "discourse" is that it places the production of discourse, of statements, within determinant conditions which exist on a broader level than the individual: "the individual subject is thus displaced across the range of discourses in which he or she participates" MacCabe, p. 30.

5. A variety of concepts have been produced for the structural analysis of narratives, including those by Propp, Bremond, and Greimas, as well as Todorov, Genette and Barthes. A number of orders of distinction are typically set up, indicating the way in which the "meaning" of the narrative is a complex of levels. Genette distinguishes the story as the events or content; the narrative as such—the signifier, statement or text itself; and finally, narration, the act which produces the narrative (p. 38); Todorov uses two levels: story comprising a logic of actions and a "syntax" of characters; and discourse comprising the modes of the narrative. Barthes adds his own typology: functions; actions; and narration.

6. Apposite to the possibility of knowledge and the constitution of the enigma in *Coma*, and to the issue of gender there, is the following child's riddle: "A man was driving his son to school when they were involved in a car accident. The father is killed and the child badly injured. Arriving at the hospital he is taken to the operating theater, whereupon the surgeon seeing the child, cries out "my son, my son." What is their relationship?

7. The issue of spectacle, of the look within the film, will be taken up in the second part of this article in relation to the place of the spectator within the structure of suspense as paranoia. Here I am referring to the concern with *display* in the film, the display of bodies, the revelation and framing of characters through glass doors, windows, characters seemingly discovered for us by the camera as it cuts to a new shot. There is also the spectacle of the revelation of the conspiracy, we *see* Susan discover how the comas are produced in patients, we follow her through the innards of the hospital as she traces the gas line; in particular we see her discover the real nature of the Jefferson Institute as she *watches* the removal of organs from a patient *after* we, but not Susan, have seen the head nurse conduct an auction of "spare parts."

8. Thornhill's place as one of knowledge is explicitly undermined at the beginning of the film, to be "refound" at the end. For a discussion of this oedipal journey *see* Raymond Bellour, "Le Blocage Symbolique" and Kari Hanet's summary of this article.

9. The film is full of half-completed narrative strategies—the "horror" of the hospital setting, the autopsy and cadavers etc., the melodrama of the two lovers, the theme of medical ethics in relation to definitions of death and "spare-part surgery."

10. The point-of-view shot is elaborated by Edward Branigan in his article "Formal Permutations of the Point-of-view Shot" (*Screen* vol. 16 no. 3 1975), as "a shot in which the camera assumes the position of a subject in order to show us what the subject sees. More precisely, the POV shot is composed of five elements usually distributed in *two* shots." This is organized as shot A, 1, the establishment of a point in space; 2, the establishment of an off-camera object by glance from the point. There is then 3, a transition between shots A and B which will involve temporal continuity. Shot B is then the reverse view of A, in which element 4 is the location of the camera at the point or very close to the point in space defined be element one above; 5, the object of element two, the source of glance, is revealed. See also Stephen Heath's article "Narrative Space," *Screen* vol. 17 no. 3 1976, which includes a discussion of point-of-view shots in relation to the construction of narrative space.

11. Jacqueline Rose addresses the shot/reverse-shot structure in her article "Paranoia and the Film System" which discusses Hitchcock's *The Birds* (*Screen* vol. 17 no. 4 1976 and Chapter 10 of this book). Where she identifies this cinematic code with a production of paranoia insofar as she argues that this process "mimes the dialectic of the imaginary relation, while demonstrating: that this relation is reversible (it is this which Lacan defines as the paranoiac alienation of the ego); that the subversion of the imaginary polarization is not only a function of the fact that the subject is looked at from the point of its own projection, but that the look can in itself be externalized" (p. 92). She locates in the shot/reverse-shot structure the aggressivity of the imaginary dialectic since its presentation of two "looks" mimes that within the imaginary dialectic and it also reveals its potential reversal inasmuch as the camera must alternate between the positions of each look, and further it thus exposes the presence of a third look (undermining the imaginary dialectic), of the camera in neither position which "cancels the observer's centrality and subjects the observer and the observed to a gaze whose signified is attack." She indicates that her use of paranoia is in terms of the aggressivity of the imaginary dialectic and that "It is clear that, taken in this sense, the structure of paranoia is not sexually differentiated but refers to the reversibility of an ego-structure which is restricted to two terms." This article together with Jacqueline Rose's extended discussion of Lacan's concept of the Imaginary in relation to film and psychoanalysis ("The Imaginary," to be published in a collection edited by Colin MacCabe, Macmillan) have been extremely helpful in developing my arguments on *Coma*.

12. Naome Gilburt's article "To Be Our Own Muse: The Dialectics of a Culture Heroine" in *Notes on Women's Cinema*, ed. Claire Johnston is an example of the concern with roles and positive identification; Siegfried Kracauer's *From Caligari to Hitler* (Princeton University Press 1947) is an example of the second concern with an ideological subsumption of the spectator by the film. In relation to the concern with the construction of the spectator's position, see in particular the special numbers of *Screen* on Brecht, vol. 15 no. 2 and vol. 16 no. 4, for example Stephen Heath's "Lessons From Brecht" in vol. 15 no. 2.

13. On the Mirror Phase see Jacques Lacan, *Ecrits, A Selection*, "The mirror stage as formative of the function of the I as revealed in psychoanalytic experience": "We have only to understand the mirror stage *as an identification*, in the full sense that analysis gives to the term: namely, the transformation that takes place in the subject when he assumes an image . . ." (p. 2). Lacan later develops the concept of the look in his discussion "Of the Gaze as *Objet petit à*" in *The Four Fundamental Concepts of Psycho-Analysis* Penguin 1979.

14. For a discussion of psychoanalysis and cinema, and in particular the structure of identification and look, see Christian Metz, "The Imaginary Signifier," in *Screen* vol. 16 no. 2 1975. His position on the imaginary relation within cinema is taken up and challenged in Jacqueline Rose's article "The Imaginary" mentioned in note 11 above. Stephen Heath addresses the issue of psychoanalytic concept of the look in cinema in relation to sexual difference in his article "Difference" (*Screen* vol. 19 no. 3 1978), raising but not answering the question "Is it possible for a woman to take place in a film without representing male desire?" (p. 96).

References

Roland Barthes, "Introduction to the Structural Analysis of Narratives" (1966) *Image-Music-Text* trans. S. Heath Fontana 1977

S/Z trans. R. Miller Jonathan Cape 1975

Raymond Bellour, "Le Blocage Symbolique" in *Communications* 23

E. Benveniste, *Problems of General Linguistics* University of Miami Press 1971

C. Bremond, *Logique du récit* Paris 1973

Rosalind Coward, " 'Sexual Liberation' and the family" *m/f* no. 1 1978

Charles Derry, "Towards a Categorization of Film Narrative" in *Film Reader* no. 2 1977 Northwestern University Illinois

M. Foucault, *The Archaeology of Knowledge* Tavistock 1974

G. Genette, "Narrative Discourse (Introduction)" in *Film Reader* no. 2 1977

Peter Gidal, ed., *Structural Film Anthology* British Film Institute 1976

A. J. Greimas, *Sémantique structurale* Paris 1966

Kari Hanet, "Bellour on *North by Northwest*" *Edinburgh '76 Magazine*

Stephen Heath, "Narrative Space" *Screen* v. 17 n. 3 1976

Alfred Hitchcock, interviewed by François Truffaut in *Hitchcock*, Simon and Schuster 1967

Malcolm Le Grice, *Abstract Film and Beyond*, Studio Vista 1977

C. Lévi-Strauss, *Structural Anthropology* Penguin 1968

Colin MacCabe, "The discursive and the ideological in film—notes on conditions of political intervention" *Screen* v. 19 n. 4 1978

Constance Penley, "The Avant-Garde and Its Imaginary" *Camera Obscura* 1977 Berkeley California

V. Propp, *Morphology of the Folktale* University of Texas Press Austin London 1968

T. Todorov, "Categories of the Literary Narrative" *Film Reader* no. 2 1977

9

Paranoia and the Film System

Jacqueline Rose

If the image content has been projected onto the P[erception] end, its libidinal cathexis must first have been removed from it. Then it has the character of a perception. In paranoia, the libido is withdrawn from the object: a reversal of this is *grief*, in which the object is withdrawn from the libido. (Freud: "A Few Theoretical Remarks on Paranoia," Sigmund Freud/C. G. Jung: *Letters*, p. 39).

The aggressive tendency appears as fundamental in certain series of significant states of personality, the paranoid and paranoiac psychoses (Lacan "L'Agressivité en psychanalyse," *Ecrits*, p. 110).

This paper emerges from the need to query a semiotic practice which assimilates its own systematicity to an institutionalized psychoanalytic exigency—integration into the Symbolic through a successful Oedipal trajectory. That dissatisfaction with this practice should focus on a film (Hitchcock's *The Birds*) in which the woman is both cause and object of the aggressivity which drives the narrative to a point at which its resolution is coincident with her "catatonia" is not incidental to the query. The woman takes up the place of the delusion whose progressive real-ization is charted by the film (in the final sequence, Melanie Daniels fights off (sees) birds which are not there). Since her assignment to this place is the price of the narrative closure as well as the symptom of its subversion, it is from here, properly, that the query can be posed.

The question of hallucination raises a number of issues:

the pertinence of the topographical concept of regression and that of paranoid projection for a metapsychology of film;

paranoia as the aggressive corollary of the narcissistic structure of the

---

This article was first presented as a paper at the "Psychoanalysis and the Cinema" event at the Edinburgh International Film Festival 1976. That paper has here been modified slightly in response to criticisms and comments at the event, for which I am grateful. Discussion of major problems and future avenues I have restricted to a final Comment.

ego-function: here, considered not in relation to hallucination, but in terms of the imaginary dialectic which is the point of resistance to symbolization;

the relationship of the latter as *structure* (inversion and reflexion) to certain specific codes of the filmic substance of expression which may indicate, interior to the film system, the necessity of its own dissolution.

Regression and Projection: Development of the Concept and Problems

Freud introduced the groundwork for the concept of regression in the 1895 *Project for a Scientific Psychology (Standard Edition of the Complete Psychological Works of Sigmund Freud*, London 1953–74, Volume 1) in relation to the infant's wishful activation of a mnemic image during a state of urgency. The infant cathects the mnemic trace of the desired object as perception. Later on, writing of the hallucinatory nature of dream-cathexes, Freud adduced the evidence of primary memory as explanation of this formal characteristic of the dream: "We might revert to the nature of the primary process and point out that the primary memory of a perception is always a hallucination" (ibid, p. 339). The perceptual nature of primary memory can therefore be related to the dream form, but its content (the hallucinatory cathexis of the desired object) is inferred from the latent content of the dream itself: "That this [dreams as wish-fulfillments] is their nature, is, however, very easily shown. It is precisely from this that I am inclined to infer that *primary wishful cathexis, too, was of a hallucinatory nature*" (ibid, p. 340).

In Chapter VII of *The Interpretation of Dreams (Standard Edition*, Vol. V), Freud uses the concept of regression to explain the transformation of dream thoughts into sensory images. Since the lowering of censorship in sleep is sufficient to explain only the conscious emergence of a previously repressed thought content but not its form, there must be a regression through the psychic apparatus which carries the content back to its primary status as perception. Freud insists that the concept is purely descriptive and not explanatory; regression explains the formal transformation, but it has not in itself been explained. The question remains as to what causes the retrogressive movement, and also why the thought travels past the mnemic image to the hallucinatory revival of the perception. To this question Freud replies that the displacement of psychic intensities proper to the primary process makes possible the complete reversion to the perceptual system, but he emphasizes that this does not constitute an explanation of the phenomena. His reply to the first question—that regression is caused by the loss of motility during sleep—is immediately contradicted by the appearance of hallucinatory phenomena during waking life:

> My explanation of hallucination in hysteria and paranoia and of visions in mentally normal subjects is that they are in fact regressions—that is, thoughts transformed into images—but that the only thoughts that undergo this trans-

formation are intimately linked with memories that have been suppressed or remain unconscious (p. 544).

The relationship between regression and paranoia is, however, problematic. Freud seems to identify them in this quotation, but six years later, in his correspondence with Jung (Sigmund Freud/Carl Gustav Jung: *Letters*, Princeton N.J. 1974), Freud gives some of his most specific statements on the mechanism of paranoiac delusion. Their disagreement centers on the definition of ego-libido, crucial for the later consideration of paranoia in its relation to narcissism. Freud describes paranoia as the outward projection of a rejected idea—the content of a desire—which reappears as perceived reality, against which repression manifests itself anew as opposition. Withdrawal of the cathexis is the precondition of the perceptual registration of the image. Hostility to the object is the endogenous perception of this withdrawal. The clinical picture of paranoia corresponds to the secondary defensive struggle when the libido returns to the object: "With a reversal to unpleasure [the libido] clings to the perceptions into which the object has been transformed . . . The libidinal cathexis heightens the images that have become perceptions, transforming them into hallucinations" (*Letters*, p. 40). Gradually all the repressed libido transforms itself into conviction in the perceptual image of the projected object: "Delusion is a libido-inspired belief in reality" (ibid). Paranoia can be distinguished from amentic and hysterical hallucination on a number of counts. Firstly, in the case of the latter, the image of the desired object is over-cathected with libido and transformed directly into perception via hallucination; secondly, there is no reversal of value. In paranoia, there is first a reduction of libido cathexis; the intensification of the hallucination through a return of suppressed libido is secondary. Furthermore, contradicting his earlier statement in *The Interpretation of Dreams*, Freud states that in paranoia there is little regression: the idea appears as a word through audition and not as a visual image. But, he concludes, "I still fail to understand the undoubtedly secondary visual hallucinations; they look like secondary regressions" (ibid, p. 48). In "A Case of Chronic Paranoia" (1896, *Standard Edition*, Vol. III, pp. 174–85), Freud's female patient experienced first a sense of general hostility from the external world, then the conviction of being watched, and finally visual hallucinations and voices. The auditory and visual hallucinations were simultaneous; between them they make up the sensory strata of the paranoiac phenomenon.[1]

Freud therefore disengages the concept of regression from paranoia, but if the topographical definition is suspended (and this only partially, cf above), the temporal definition is central to his description. The withdrawn libido which has been removed from the image of the object returns to the ego and becomes auto-erotic; return to auto-eroticism could be seen as a coalescence of the two forms of temporal libidinal regression—return both to an earlier object and to an earlier mode of functioning. Aggrandisement of the ego (Schreber) is the narcissistic corollary of the constitution of a hostile object world. Note that in this position, Schreber's identification is with the place of a woman.

Lacan throws the aggressivity of paranoid psychosis back to the ontology of the ego-function. By doing so, he gives a structural grounding to Melanie Klein's description of the paranoid position in the early ego-formation of the child. Aggressivity is attendant on the narcissistic relation and the structures of misrecognition which characterize the formation of the ego:

> This form will in effect be crystallized in the conflictual tension internal to the subject, which determines its desire for the object of desire of the other: it is here that the primordial concourse is precipitated into an aggressive rivalry, and it is from this that the triad of the other, the ego and the object is born ("L'Aggressivité en psychanalyse," *Ecrits*, Paris 1966, p. 113).

Paranoia is latent to the reversibility of the ego's self-alienation. Furthermore, since the projective alienation of the subject's own image is the precondition for the identification of an object world, all systems of objectification can be related to the structure of paranoia. Aggressivity is latent to the system, but it will also be discharged where the stability of the system is threatened. The imaginary dialectic is the inter-subjective equivalent of the narcissism subtending ego-formation; it is the point of resistance to symbolization and the disavowal of difference.

Paranoia has therefore been referred multiply:

to the basic ontology of the ego-function;

to the systematicity of discourse;

and, as a clinical manifestation, to a delusional reconstruction of the real.[2]

Hallucination and the Film

Suspension of motility on the part of the spectator allows for a partial identification of the film process with the dream, countered by the greater elaboration of the film system and by the fact that the image perceived as real constitutes a concrete perceptual content in the cinema (the images and sounds of the film itself—see Christian Metz, "Le Film de fiction et son spectateur," *Communications*, n. 23, 1975, pp. 108–35). The counter-flux to a full regression is therefore provided by the film itself. On the other hand, the spectator's identification of the film substance with a fictional world constituted as real partly upholds the pertinence of a comparison with regressive hallucination. With this difference: the hallucination of the dream process obeys the dictates of the pleasure principle and consists of a wishful cathexis of the object. The film "can please or displease." Identification of the film with the oneiric process stalls, therefore, not on the mechanism of hallucination but on its associated affect. The horror film could be said to insert itself into the space of this disjunction, producing images to *excite* displeasure (always associated with the visualization/audition of a repressed content), so that it is the reversal of affect which precisely allows the recognition of the repressed image-content in the real. The mechanism comes close to that of paranoia, and it is the specificity of *The Birds* to internalize this mechanism into the narrative content of the film.

At the same time, paranoia could be said to be latent to the structure of cinematic specularity in itself, in that it represents the radical alterity of signification (the subject is spoken from elsewhere). To suggest this is to challenge the idea of the spectator's subsumption into an imaginary totality and to point to the potential splitting of that totality within the moment of its constitution. For the woman, the alterity of signification is the locus from which she is spoken as excluded and also from which she is *taken* as picture— the image representing the moment of freezing of her sexuality (cf Freud: "A Case of Paranoia Running Counter to the Psycho-analytic Theory of the Disease," op cit).

In *The Birds*, the woman is object and cause of the attack. On the level of narrative, she moves from one form of persecution (Melanie Daniels is known because she is talked and written about—"She's in all the columns, Mitch") to another (she is accused of bringing the birds to Bodega Bay), so that the attack of the birds becomes the cause of persecution. And again in terms of the positions of identification into which the spectator is drawn. At two points, the spectator is induced into her place. At the point of accusation, the object of the accuser's look is the camera itself. When the birds attack Melanie Daniels in the attic (the final attack), a rapid shot holds on a bird, its mouth open, flying into the camera. With a reversal exemplary of the fundamental paradox of identification, Melanie's hallucination in the final sequence is to fight off non-existent birds in the place of the camera previously identified with herself.[3] The identification of Melanie Daniels and the place of the spectator are split into the two terms of an aggressive polarization, implying retrospectively that the aggressivity of the birds is reversible and self-directed.

By internalizing the mechanism of paranoia into the film, *The Birds* releases an aggressivity which finally cannot be contained within the terms of a resolution (see below). But this subversion can be read into the conventions of the cinematic institution itself in a way which indicates the very instability of that institution: the constant lapses of a system which would construct itself according to a rhetoric. Taking another film which belongs in the same cinematic context and which has been the object of detailed analysis, and then a segment of *The Birds*, it is clear that this aggressivity undercuts the stability of one of the dominant framing devices of classical Hollywood cinema.

Paranoia and the Film System

In the crop-dusting sequence of *North by Northwest*, the hero, who has gone to meet the non-existent character with whom he has been mistakenly identi-fied, is attacked out of the sky. A detailed break-down of the segment (Raymond Bellour: "Le Blocage symbolique," *Communications* 23, 1975; cf also Kari Hanet: "Bellour on *North by Northwest*, *Edinburgh '76 Magazine*) has revealed its structuration according to a partially sustained series of oppositions between the subject and the object of his vision. This series is unstable, manifesting a constant tendency toward its own disequilibrium, the points of its rupture being precisely the points of attack. On the level of content only, the source of the attack is referred across the segment into the body of the narrative, and a paradigm of means of locomotion is established whose multiple effectivity can be read from the systems of repetition and duplication which it drives and in which it is caught throughout the film. Each system which can be identified in the film text is overdetermined in its relation to the minutest segmental component or unit of the film; the plurality of the system, its fragmentation into a multiplicity of mutually referring units is the condition of its organization into a narrative, based on a constant (eternal) return or repetition which determines the possibility of its resolution. The system is fragmented but omnipotent, indicating the submission of desire to the dictates of the law, Oedipus as the terminal zone and mover of repetition.

The micro-system, which constantly doubles back and folds over the terms of its own production, duplicates the process of repetition and resolu-tion which characterizes the global system of the film text, to which it thus relates in defiance of its apparent autonomy or closure. In this way the codes specific to the cinematic substance of expression, which seem to escape the impress of the diegesis, are nonetheless bound to it.

But [the convergent effect of symbolization] is still inscribed and propagated in [the filmic system's] smallest signifying units through the movement of repetition-resolution in which they are perpetually caught. It is much more indirect, since this movement of micro-elements, including all the specific codes of the matters of cinematic expression except the segmentary codes of the larger narrative units, seems always more or less to escape the narration, whereas it is in fact constantly constructing it. To the extent that, destined by its very nature to specify itself essentially in a gradual progression across relatively small segments, it gives the illusion of ceaselessly closing in on itself, *as if stamped with a kind of symbolic atopia by its material specificity and the extreme fragmentation of its semantic contents.* But the indirectness of the effect of symbolization is precisely what constitutes its strength. Much more pregnant, since it is incessant, irrepressible, it constantly produces and reproduces, and produces because it reproduces, the major rhyme of the narration, of the story (*histoire*) become narration (*récit*). Like the narration, it resolves because it repeats, and repeats because it resolves, constantly directing itself towards its meaning from the starting point of its lack of meaning ("Le Blocage symbolique," op cit, p. 348, my italics).

It is in the relation of repetition to resolution, therefore, that cinematic specificity can be recuperated by the narrative. But not entirely, and the problems that this raises for analysis indicate precisely the points at which the fissures of the system can be spoken. First, the concept of repetition itself which for Freud indicates exactly the demonic insistence of the drive, repetition being the sign of an instance which will not be integrated into a constructed historicity. Second, the elision in the coupling resolution/repetition of the points of rupture which constantly undercut the micro-elemental system. Third, the inescapable "symbolic atopia" of the filmic substance of expression, which is a function of its *material* specificity.

What then is the cinematic code which dominates the segment in which the aggression of a false imposition of identity is objectified into assault? The segment is structured according to the basic opposition of shot and counter-shot which sustains a dialectic of vision (the look) alternating between the observing subject and the object of his vision. The code occults the position of the camera by setting up an opposition between two terms: the observer and the observed. What is seen is the subject himself and what he sees. The opposition is however a lure *in its very structure*. Firstly, the camera has to identify not only with the subject (Thornhill) in order to show what he sees, but also with the object of vision in order to show the subject. The series can therefore only be structured by a partial activation of the potentially aggressive reversal of its system. Secondly, the fact that the camera must identify with both terms of the opposition, and in the place of one of them cannot be assimilated to a subjectivity, reveals its presence *prior* to the point at which it disengages from that opposition, cancels the observer's centrality and subjects the observer and the observed to a gaze whose signified is attack. The opposition shot/counter-shot therefore contains its own principle of instability prior to the moment of its activation.

The process therefore mimes the dialectic of the imaginary relation, while demonstrating:

that this relation is reversible (it is this which Lacan defines as the paranoiac alienation of the ego):

that the subversion of the imaginary polarization is not only a function of the fact that the subject is looked at from the point of its own projection, but that the look can in itself be externalized (delusion of being photographed—cf "A Case of Paranoia Running Counter to. . . ." op cit).

The dominant cinematic code of the micro-segment reveals both the potential subversion of the system in the moment of its structuration, and, where it breaks, the fact that the intervention of difference is the point of disruption of the code. What needs to be looked at is the way in which the symbolization bars the repetitions of the micro-system, even as it is appropriated as the means of (an imaginary) resolution on the level of narrative content.

The process whereby the dialectic of the look culminates in the release of its aggressivity is demonstrated again in Bellour's breakdown of the Bodega Bay sequence of *The Birds* (*Cahiers du Cinéma*, n. 216, October 1969, English translation from the BFI Educational Advisory Service). In this instance the terms are duplicated as the sequence begins with the opposition between Melanie Daniels as subject and the object of her look, and then introduces as reply (response to the gift of the love-birds) the look of Mitch Brenner whose object is Melanie herself. I will not cover the segment in detail but point out a few points of the analysis which seem to be symptomatic of difficulties that can be read across into the narrative.

At the point where Melanie Daniels is attacked by the gull, the analysis identifies the attack with the reciprocal gaze of Mitch Brenner whose dominant mobility has determined the structure of the preceding shots of the sequence. The gull therefore represents a type of male violation. But this identification is challenged by the fact that Melanie sees Mitch but does not see the gull, which is shown in an anticipatory shot presented only to the spectator. The introduction of an object which is not seen reintroduces the elusion of the subject's centrality which we have found to be latent to the opposition itself, but it leaves the gull without cause, unless the latter can be read in the meeting of looks which syntagmatically generates the attack. The gull would not in that case represent an active male sexuality, but the suspension of its possibility which dilutes it into a relation of caring ("Are you all right?" etc...). The gull releases the aggressivity latent to the miming of looks between the protagonists, and takes up the place of persecutory object; but the narrative content of that opposition (the developing sexual relationship between Melanie Daniels and Mitch Brenner) is subverted in that moment.

Furthermore, a retrospective reading of the segment according to the alternations which it constructs (alternation between Mitch and Melanie in the shot) produces, if that alienation is followed through and past the point at which a second shot of the gull breaks the opposition, Mitch in the place of Melanie in the shot of the attack itself. In this position, as Bellour points out, it is Melanie herself who is united with the gull. The sequence therefore contains a potential reversal (the gull is Mitch—the gull is Melanie) which shows, firstly, that the aggressivity is a function of the alternation and not derived from one of its terms, and secondly, that the object of the attack can be fused with the subject of attack by applying the principle of reversibility back along the syntagm. This fusion latent to the first sequence of the film in which the birds are revealed as aggressive, anticipates the transition within the narrative from attack to persecution (Melanie Daniels accused of evil and bringing the birds).

The symbolic atopia of the filmic substance of expression is therefore a function of its grounding in an imaginary structuration; the fact that the latter contains its own principle of instability can be referred to the paranoid characterization of that structure and its attendant aggressivity, and also to the fact that the imaginary is always threatened by an intervening symbolization. In *North by Northwest*, the symbolic resolution fuses with the imaginary captation of the marital couple, which assures its ideological stability. In *The Birds*, the situation is more complex, because the film internalizes the paranoia latent to the cinematic codification.

The Hermeneutics of Delusion

Unlike *North by Northwest* (the detective story which becomes an investigation into the nature of the woman's sexuality) or *Psycho* (detection into a crime whose source is the collapse of sexual polarization), *The Birds* has no conventional detective content. The film's own tension works between the foreknowledge of the spectator (title of the film), the relative foreknowledge of the main characters (increasing anticipation of attack) and the resistance to knowledge, first of the town and then of the external world. The latter are linked by a series of narrative displacements (Annie Hayworth retrospectively, Mitch Brenner whose displacements in themselves constitute an alternation, and Melanie Daniels, the single journey), and then by a succession of partially abortive attempts at recall (telephone, newspaper, radio) which set up a paradigm of communication systems through the film comparable to that established for means of locomotion in *North by Northwest*.

The system of communication is also the possibility of the action (Melanie phones in order to trace Mitch), as well as its primary instigator (Melanie Daniels goes to the birdshop to collect a mynah bird which should talk, which doesn't talk, which she will have to teach to talk). The film therefore starts on a default symbolization displaced onto the absent bird, and then onto the love-birds ("Do you happen to have a pair of birds that are just friendly?"). Its objective could be said to be the establishment of intercourse—sexual consummation between Mitch and Melanie (never represented—the final energy passes between Melanie and Lydia), and the restoration of links between San Francisco and Bodega Bay. The fact that the latter is achieved can be taken as a resolution (with reservations which will be discussed below), but what is most important is the fact that the restoration constitutes an act of persuasion which convinces of the reality of the attack, and disperses it (the birds have started to attack Santa Rosa). The hermeneutic trajectory of *The Birds* is a process of conviction which has achieved its course when the external world recognizes aggressivity in the real.

This is the crucial importance of the scene in the café (significantly omitted in Truffaut's summary of the plot in an elision that kills Annie Hayworth at the point of the first attack of the birds on the school)[4] which shifts between different points of recognition and resistance (recognition by the drunkard and the hysterical mother, resistance by Mrs. Bundy whose desexualization is represented by her age and physical appearance), until the attack itself forces a cognizance which turns the investigation from the reality into its cause—Melanie Daniels. Note that in this moment, all the men have been evicted from the image which shows the group of women crowded together as the support of "the woman" who comes forward to accuse.

It is from the moment when the town recognizes the birds that Melanie Daniels's own relationship to their reality status starts to shift. During this scene a different challenge to the reality of the birds (the birds as hallucination) is depicted by Melanie frantically flaying her arms against the birds whose distance or separation is represented by the glass of the phone-booth itself. Glass, which represents the point of identification of the object which has not yet struck, here assimilated to the act of communication itself which, in the form of the human eye, it already represents symbolically. The relationship between the glass and vision is punned constantly throughout the film—Michele's cracked glasses, the schoolroom windows, the discovery of Dan Fawcett, and, symptomatically in a shot only just recorded during a viewing, the shattered glass on the window of the pick-up truck which opens into the camera's field of vision as Lydia rushes—speechless—out of Fawcett's house. Melanie in the phone-booth therefore condenses all these images, and establishes the glass as the anticipatory image of a severed communication (her own speechlessness—bar the negative of withdrawal—at the end of the film), and of the fighting off of an object whose place in the real is no longer assured (known). A play too on the potential transgression of the screen barrier itself. Hitchcock gives a second anticipation of this moment of hallucination: the camera retreats on Melanie as she recoils on the sofa during the penultimate attack of the birds, revealing a space whose signified is nothingness.

We can ask what generates the attack by referring back to the material specificity of the cinematic code of expression, which we have seen too to be resistant to symbolization, fixing subjects in frozen positions which release an aggressivity only matched by that produced when this fixity is challenged in itself. It is of course in the narrative, in the challenge to the imaginary stranglehold which characterizes the relationship of mother and son—Lydia and Mitch Brenner—the son being one of the "two kids" (exciting a laugh in response from Melanie) who live in the house across the bay.

And it is fully compatible with the constraints of the cinematic narrative space that at one level it should comment that relation. Note for example the set of semantic oppositions which characterizes the dialogue between Annie Hayworth and Melanie Daniels when the former describes the mother's intervention/obstruction in the sexuality of her son. Mrs. Brenner is not a jealous, possessive woman, she is a woman who is afraid; she is not afraid of someone taking Mitch, but of someone giving Mitch ("the one thing she can't give him—love"); she is not afraid of losing Mitch, but only of being abandoned. Within the terms of this opposition, it is Lydia's fear which pre-empts that released by the attack of the birds themselves, and her fear is in each case of an activity; not of the passive remove of her son, but of the intervention of a term which signifies for her an active abandonment rather than a simple loss, abandonment being the aggressive counterpart of remove. Loss has therefore been activated, and it is the possibility of its realization which produces the attack of the birds—Melanie brings the love-birds to Bodega Bay and signifies her intervention into the original dyad. (Annie's and Lydia's response to the designation of the love-birds is identical—"Love-birds" "I see"—and also puns on the visual metaphor of the film.)

We should also note that loss of the object and abandonment by the object are multiply and inversely represented through the film. For the mother afraid of being abandoned by her son, there is the daughter who was ditched by her mother (Melanie Daniels); and for the loss of which the mother is not afraid, there is the loss of the husband, the dead father, whose picture hangs (in a gesture dear to Hitchcock) over the family drama. That the mourning for the dead husband is not complete is indicated during the only dialogue between Melanie and Lydia in the film, and in the delusion of his continued presence which she describes. There is, therefore, an incomplete mourning in the film, which is the beginning, or pretext, of Lydia's own fear (the end of Mitch's relationship with Annie is justified in terms of the recent death of the father), and the birds are also inscribed in this space—the body of the bird which falls from the picture of the father which has been knocked out of place, and the bird wrought in iron of the firegrid taken obliquely in the shots of Lydia lying in her bed.

It seems important that out of the imaginary relation which constitutes a repression of sexuality, the subject is defined as a child. The attack of the birds precipitates the sexuality back into the terms of a caring, a dilution the "consummation" of Mitch and Melanie's relationship (which significantly takes place at the point where Lydia discovers the body of Fawcett)—"Oh, be careful, please!" "And you be careful"—through the school itself, and through the position of Cathy who mediates between the three terms of Melanie, Lydia and Mitch (actually sitting up into the shot where Lydia articulates the substitutive denigration of her son: "If only your father was here!"). Again at the one point where it is not Melanie's own look but that of the child which anticipates or signifies the presence of the birds (the attack on the children's party), the moment is directly preceded by Melanie's self-placement as child: "Well, maybe I ought to go and join the *other* children." The attack from the sky conjoins on the subject a deferment of sexuality and an inscription of relations within a framework of protection and dependence. The effect of the aggression is therefore revelatory of its source.

The birds therefore emanate from the inherent instability of the film's own system, overdetermined in this instance by a series of narrative relations which direct the energy of the film around the woman, while also using those positions to comment on its own system of repression; by doing so it subsumes the excess of its own aggressivity into a meta-(psycho-)analysis defined as an act of knowledge. That the film is unable to cope with the aggressivity it releases is most clearly indicated by the resolution.

The Resolution

On two counts the resolution of *The Birds* is abortive. First, the "psychosis" of Melanie Daniels; second, the dominance of the birds visually and on the sound track in the final image. The latter is a function of the paradox that for the world to be convinced of the attack, the birds must be seen to be real, so that re-establishment of communication authenticates the reality of the horror. Yet, if the birds dominate the final image, there is nonetheless a partial resolution within the terms of the oppositions set up by the narrative. The conclusion represents Mitch's self-assertion against Lydia, by his insistence that they leave Bodega Bay and go to San Francisco. To do this he must himself get through the birds, and bring the car which is to be the means of escape to the house. By leaving for San Francisco, Mitch forces together the two opposed terms of his sexuality, Bodega Bay, the place of his repression, and San Francisco, the place of his sexual autonomy. San Francisco is also the place of his activity as lawyer. For Bodega Bay, this activity constitutes a transgression and is classified as illicit. (Mitch spends his time in the state detention cells), since it is the law itself which is suspended in the relation between mother and son (Lydia: "Never mind the law").[5]

The end of the film represents a second resolution which refers this time to the nature of Melanie's sexuality. Remember that Melanie is first defined as a "practical joker," seen in court for having broken a plate glass window (cf p. 145), and is therefore presented as the opposite term to the law. Melanie is therefore defined in the first part of the film *as* transgression. What the narrative then does is to inscribe this transgression in a wild psychology (also dear to Hitchcock, compare the casual denegation of the Oedipal configuration in the dialogue with Annie) which defines her as a motherless child, thereby opening up the space into which Lydia herself can be inserted. The first six shots of the final ten of the film (starting with the first shot inside the car) alternate between the close shots of Lydia holding Melanie and the close-up of Melanie's own face registering a scarcely perceptible smile in response to the holding of the mother. The series is broken once, by the insert of Melanie's bandaged hand grasping the hand of Lydia, a kind of long-distance echo and reparation of the insert which showed blood on Melanie Daniel's finger after the first attack of the gull.

I would suggest therefore that there is a resolution—the radio the departure, the reconciliation—but this only at the expense of the woman. By defining her sexuality as reckless, her intervention into a more absolute transgression can in itself be presented as a violation, which then unleashes the aggressivity of which she is object/cause. What the birds achieve therefore is the subduing of Melanie Daniels into the place of infant (the non-speaking child). It is important that the coded repetitions of the final shots gravitate around Melanie and Lydia, while the camera simply holds on the birds whose insistent presence leaves open and outside this structuration the residual aggressivity of the film.

The Scream

I have not discussed any sequence of the film in detail but rather chosen to suggest some of the ways in which the latent structure of one of its systems of codification can be read across the narrative in the moment at which it tends toward rupture. Essential to this is the constant falling away of the text's own sexuality from the constraints of the code, its effect of dispersion of the system itself (the attack of the gull is generated by *and* breaks the dialectic of the look). I have already mentioned the shattered glass of the pick-up truck which opens into the field of vision following the discovery of Dan Fawcett, and the absence in it of any coordinating link with the narrative other than the dispersion or contagion of the horror. In the narrative sequence prior to the attack in the attic, at the end of the attack of the birds on the outside of the house, there is another moment which seems to be suspended in the same space.

When Mitch has blocked off the door through which the birds are breaking, a brief shot holds Melanie in the doorway watching Mitch off-screen; in the next shot Melanie and Mitch are seen together and move into the living-room, the camera trucking right to follow them. At the point where Cathy and Lydia, seated in a background chair, move into the shot, the lights go out in the house and there is a scream (discernible as such on the sound-track and recorded on the continuity). Immediately after this, the pitch of the sound of the birds is raised, blurring partly into the scream which it echoes and sustains. It is clear from the faces and the expressions of the four characters in the shot that none of the people in the house is the source of the scream. The scream is disembodied, marking along with the extinction of the lights (to which it also seems to come as response) the impossibility of holding the four characters in the shot, the clash of the couple man and woman with that of the mother and child. The scream also cuts across the film space into the response which it elicts from the spectator. It is also a woman's scream, the displaced sound of the woman victim of the birds who are to attack her from the bed in the attic, in an assault characterized only by the flapping of wings and the absence of the cry.[6]

Melanie Daniels therefore moves from one position outside the law to another in which her ex-centricity is juxtaposed to the assumption of the situation by the speaking voice of America (the radio). In *North by Northwest*, the symbolic resolution hung on a moment of "narrative waste" in which Eve revealed the true nature of her sexuality and secured the trajectory for ideology. The episode stalled the action in a film characterized above all by the speed of its movements, and was objected to for that reason in production. In *The Birds*, the woman's sexuality is also redefined as she moves from practical joker to infans. Through a euphemism this regressive trajectory conceals its own transgression and is assimilated to the legitimized family unit. ("Someone ought to tell her she'd be gaining a daughter"). But the position of the woman is not only located in this movement of Melanie, but also in the generalized dispersion of the feminine throughout the film, whether stressed (the image of the women in the café) or as an aside (the names of the boats on the quay—Maria, Maria 2, Donna, Frolic). The woman is not only the point of an identification, the place of a recognizable and silent image, but also the site of this constant dispersion which challenges the text's own reading of its libidinal space. The woman in this sense is not only the cause but also the effect of the horror, silenced, the rupture of her own category which can only be represented as one side of a bound (maternal) relation at the same time as it is dispersed across the film space. It is precisely that dispersion, the other face of the woman as infans, which reveals the splitting points of the re-absorption of the family unit into the (paternal) voice of America.

Comment

The article raises a number of problems. These concern chiefly the position of women in relation to paranoia taken both as a structure latent to the film system and also as a mechanism of neurosis (cf below) vehiculed by the narrative of the film in question. Taken in the first sense, paranoia is a pre-Oedipal structure of aggressivity which threatens the stabilization of symbolic positions in so far as they constitute the social overdetermination of the subject's self-cohesion in the imaginary. It refers therefore to a structure (imaginary) and an energy attendant on that structure (aggressivity), and the relationship between them could be said to preempt the inherent tendency to fissure of any symbolic system. Taken in the second sense, paranoia refers to a clinical phenomenon which veers constantly between neurosis and psychosis, and whose structure can only be posed theoretically through a concept of post-Oedipal sexuality in relation to that of regression and fixation. In the remarks that follow I will try to indicate how these two aspects of paranoia can be related to the position of woman inside symbolic systems, and how this position should be privileged in the discussion of contradictions within a specific ideological form. I should stress that these remarks are tentative; they represent an attempt to deal with difficulties that emerge from the article and which I hope can be developed through further discussion and comment.

    1.   The reading of paranoia offered in the article is based first on Lacan's concept of the imaginary dialectic. The predominance of the visual register in the Lacanian formulation had made it possible to read that formulation into certain specific codes of the filmic substance of expression. I suggest in the article that this has been done at the expense of those aspects of the phenomenon which cannot be retrieved for a concept of full specularity but which are no less essential to the phenomenon in that they indicate the points of its own rupture. This refers to the aggressivity of the imaginary dialectic, and in the reading of shot/reverse-shot I am using paranoia in this sense. It is clear that, taken in this sense, the structure of paranoia is not sexually differentiated but refers to the reversibility of an ego-structure which is restricted to two terms. In its effective form this is the relation of infant to image and of the mother to infant in so far as the latter is the object of her desire (her intervention introduces a third term but assigns it a place as image). The terms of the Oedipal configuration are present in the imaginary relation, but they are *unassumed* (in both senses of the word). When referring the concept of paranoia to a specific code of the filmic substance of expression, I am using it as a reference to the fundamental reversibility of the imaginary dyad and not to the effective positions of the relation (mother and child). Any number of sexual positions can be charted over that basic dialectic. It is my argument that in *The Birds* there is a tension at work between the recognizable narrative content of the code (man and woman—seduction etc.) and this intrinsic property of the code (its imaginary structuration) which in fact refers on two counts to a relation held elsewhere in the narrative between mother and child (Mitch and Lydia, Melanie and her mother [Lydia]). This can obviously only be understood as a process of *over-determination*; I am not positing a general coincidence between narrative relations of the type presented in *The Birds* and the latent structuration of the code.

    2.   The relationship of the woman to the imaginary does not only hold at this level. The imaginary also contains the realm of pre-Oedipality to which the sexuality of the woman is bound; this not only because of her negative relation to the privileged signifier of difference in the patriarchy but also because the Oedipal normativization which is expressive of that relation demands of her the relinquishment of the primordial object which necessarily persists. This is true of both sexes, but for the boy the substitution can follow the lines of a sexual equivalence. The sliding off of feminine sexuality from its socially determined genital and reproductive position is not just a function of

the component nature of sexuality but also contains a repressed reference to the pre-Oedipal relation between the mother and the girl-child. The imaginary dialectic is one of the sites of that reference.

This has two implications for the relation of woman to paranoia. First, in that the woman has a privileged relation to the imaginary dyad, she is bound to the principle of reversibility which it contains (this is simply the other side of my earlier point on the effective form of the imaginary relation). Second, in so far as the woman's relation to the symbolic order is determined negatively, so her relationship to significance is dystonic. It does seem that the emphasis on the imaginary in the discussion of film as a specific ideological form must address itself to the relation of woman to that register, since that relation is in itself a comment on the impossibility of stabilizing positions in the symbolic. It is therefore crucial when talking of film's constant replay of loss and retrieval and the possibility of articulating that loss to transform the position of the spectator of film, to remember that the negativity in question is now only accessible through the sexual differentiation which has overlaid the primary severance.

3.   The woman is centered in the clinical manifestation of paranoia as position. Paranoia is characterized by a passive homosexual current, and hence a "feminine" position in both man and woman. In the case of Schreber, the attack actually transforms his body into that of a woman; this is necessary because the "state of voluptuousness," which in his delusion is demanded of Schreber by God, is not restricted for the woman to the genitals but is dispersed over the whole body ("dispersed over it from head to foot," Freud: *Standard Edition*, op. cit, Vol. XII, p. 33), and is constant (extension in time and space as a reference to woman's relation to a non-genital, i.e. un-normativized sexuality). The attack itself is sexually ambivalent—apparition of the foreclosed phallus in the real (Schreber is to be inseminated by God) but also the penetration of the body by feminine tissue; God is also identified by Schreber with the sun which causes difficulties in the German precisely because it is a feminine noun. More important, the mechanism of paranoia involves a regression from "*sublimated homosexuality to narcissism*"... "*a fixation at the stage of narcissism*" (p. 72), that is, the delusion of persecution stems from the subject's narcissistic relation to his or her body when the components of sexuality have cohered but have taken the subject's own body as their object. The implications of the mechanism of paranoia for narcissism lead straight into Freud's paper "On Narcissism" (1914) on which Lacan bases his concept of the imaginary.

For the woman it is the infantile image of the mother which lies behind the delusion of persecution even where the persecutor is apparently a male. In the case which I mention in the article ("A Case of Paranoia Running Counter to the Psycho-Analytic Theory of the Disease") the woman regressively identifies with the mother in order to free herself from the primary homosexual attachment; the mother is then released as voyeur and persecutor into the place where the child once was at the moment of the primal scene. Narcissism is referred here not only to the choice of object but also to the process of identification itself; it then reappears, as in the case of Schreber, in the symptom of the delusion.

4. Freud states in this case that the neurotic manifestation is determined not by the patient's present-day relation to the mother but by the infantile relation to the earliest image of the mother. The tension between relation and image can be located in the narrative content of *The Birds* in the gradual overlapping of Mitch's relation to his mother and Melanie to hers, whose culmination is represented by the shots of the final sequence which I mention in the article. Furthermore, the nature of the resolution—containment by the mother signals obliquely the possibility of Melanie's relationship to Mitch, but silences her and reiterates the delusion—seems to me articulate of the conceptual relation here posited by Freud: "These then are phenomena of an attempted advance from the new ground which has as a rule been regressively acquired; and we may set alongside them the efforts made in some neuroses to regain a position of the libido which was once held and subsequently lost. Indeed we can hardly draw any conceptual distinction between these two classes of phenomena" (ibid, p. 271). It is important that for the girl Oedipal normativization is always achieved on the basis of such a regressive identification. We can say what *The Birds* produced in the narrative is this advance (resolution) *as* regression; and the latter pushed to its most extreme form. In my article I suggest that the state of Melanie and this reiteration of the delusion slides into the space of a psychosis which is the undercurrent to the film's system, and cannot be held to the narrative relations through which it is simultaneously placed. Within that conventional narrative space, the dislocation which I have assigned to this place of the woman can necessarily only take the path of a regression. To say this in relation to film is to assign the possibility of fixation to the film-system which acts out on the level of narrative in the film I have discussed the regressive paradigm of its own substance; on another level, this is nothing other than one of the components of its own history.

5. Finally, and more simply, I ask the question, why is the woman attacked? If it seems that I am repeating a question which I have been asking throughout this Comment, it is simply that I am bound to acknowledge that the aggression on the woman's body cannot invariably be read, even in the Hitchcock canon, in the way I have described. For the act of aggression can also be an act of disavowal by the man, the inscribing on the woman's body of the signifier of difference (literally in *Frenzy*—cf. the shot after the first strangulation) which the violation in itself represents. The attack on the woman in this sense is the inverse expression of the resistance which I have described from her place in the above remarks. To say that there are also

other films in which the resolution of a male identity charts the disintegration of that of the woman (*The Wrong Man*) is merely to point to another version of the same difference.

Notes

1.   Cf. also "A Case of Paranoia Running Counter to the Psycho-analytic Theory of the Disease," *Standard Edition*, Vol. XIV: the woman *hears* herself being *photographed*.

2.   Cf. also Lacan on the difference between paranoia and the dream: "One could say that, unlike dreams, which must *be interpreted*, the delirium is in itself *an act of interpretation* by the unconscious," *De la psychose paranoïaque dans ses rapports avec la personnalité* (Paris 1932, republished 1975), p. 293.

3.   Melanie Daniels does not at this point look directly into the camera; her look is off-screen front (implication of the spectator) and to the place of Mitch Brenner (shot/reverse-shot); this duality raises the whole problem of the sexual differentiation of the structure of aggressivity (see Comment below).

4.   It seems worth giving the whole of Truffaut's summary here: "Melanie Daniels (Tippi Hedren), a wealthy snobbish playgirl, meets Mitch Brenner (Rod Taylor), a young lawyer, in a San Francisco bird shop. Despite his sarcastic attitude, she is attracted to him and travels to Bodega Bay to take two small lovebirds as a birthday present to his little sister, Cathy. As she nears the dock in a rented motor boat, a seagull swoops down at her, gashing her forehead. Melanie decides to stay, spending the night with Annie Hayworth (Suzanne Pleshette), the local schoolteacher. Annie warns Melanie that Mitch's mother, Mrs. Brenner, is jealous and posses-sive of her son. The next day, at Cathy's outdoor birthday-party, the gulls swoop down on the picnicking children and that evening hundreds of sparrows come swooping down the chimney, flying all round the house and causing considerable damage. The following morning Mrs. Brenner goes to visit a farmer near by and finds him dead, with his eyes gouged out. That afternoon, when Melanie discovers an alarming assembly of crows gathered outside the school, she and Annie organize the children's escape. As Melanie escorts them down the road, Annie is trapped behind and sacrifices her life in order to save Cathy. Melanie's courage during these trials inspires Mitch's love and his mother's approval of their romance. That evening Melanie and the Brenners board up the windows of their home just in time to protect themselves from the enraged birds which drive suicidally against the house, tear at the shingles and gnaw at the doors to get at the people inside. After peace returns, Melanie hearing a sound upstairs goes up to the attic to investigate. There she finds herself in a room full of birds which attack her savagely. Finally rescued by Mitch, the girl is in a state of shock. Taking advantage of a momentary lull, Mitch decides to flee. Between the house and the garage and as far as the eye can see, thousands of birds wait in ominous array as the little group emerges from the battered house and moves slowly towards the car" (François Truffaut: *Hitchcock*, London 1967, p. 9).

5.   Except where it takes the form of interrogation by the mother of the son; cf. of the scene in the kitchen.

6.   I realized after working on the film that a detailed breakdown of the soundtrack is called for; most striking is the way in which the birds tend to enjoin silence on their object.

10

Enunciation and Sexual Difference

Janet Bergstrom

Introduction

There is a great deal of confusion at the moment about the aims, methods, scope and general importance of a particular kind of film analysis known as textual analysis. Within the rather broad range of critical approaches which might, given current usage, be called textual analysis, this article is being written as an introduction to the work of Raymond Bellour, Thierry Kuntzel and Stephen Heath, whose close analyses of films or parts of films have been of fundamental importance for *Camera Obscura*. These studies have been important both insofar as they investigate and demonstrate how meaning is produced in the classical film, and as they have helped to clarify and specify the systematic mapping of sexual difference—and therefore of the woman's function—onto the logic of narrative events, symbolization and figuration, and as they have attempted to understand the symbolic weight of the production of those figures, given as natural and therefore as necessary to a particular order of fiction film.

Textual analysis is a general term, but it is borrowed for film studies from a specific context—French literary critical theory which, from structuralism through two subsequent phases of semiology, reoriented the aims and methods of interpretation according to a series of theories of the *text* (therefore *textual* analysis) and *reading* as a critical activity. At the beginning of the interview which follows this article, Raymond Bellour outlines his view of the changes operated on the structural model (Saussure/Lévi-Strauss) in favor of psychoanalytic theory as a model to account for the production of meaning in terms of the subject. The insistence in this second phase on *structuring* (the *production* of meaning) rather than on virtual *structures* or patterns in a text is seen by Bellour as a shift in emphasis rather than, as has sometimes been implied, a rejection of what structuralism had brought to critical theory.

The shifts in emphasis and terminology can be seen very clearly in the progression of Roland Barthes's work, which has come around again and again to the concepts of the text, reading and the relationship between the object and the activity of analysis. Stephen Heath's reading of Barthes sees this progression as a constant movement of displacement—*Vertige du déplacement* is the title of his book—of the levels and object of analysis through the notions of pleasure and morality, "an ethics of style." Heath's study doesn't speak directly to the intersection of Barthes's work with film analysis. It remains to be shown how this work has been *rethought*—not applied in some mechanical way—for and through film analysis. Here the analyses of Bellour, Kuntzel and Heath are instructive in that they demonstrate a fundamental *reconceptualization* of Barthes's strategies of interpretation to account for the specificity of film. At this point, it may be useful to recall a few terms developed in Barthes's work which will be encountered again in the context of these filmic analyses.

Barthes's distinction between the *work* and the *text* distinguished the physical object (the work, e.g. the book) from the text, which is described as a "methodological field," "a process of demonstration," that which is "held in language," which "only exists in the movement of a discourse," and "experienced only in an activity of production" ("From Work to Text," p. 157).[1] The theory of the text is practically indistinguishable from literary theory in Barthes's work and beyond that, "the theory of the Text cannot but coincide with a practice of writing (*écriture*)" (p. 164). This means modern writing, modern in Barthes's sense, as opposed to classical, readable writing, as explained in *The Pleasure of the Text* and *S/Z* and as exemplified, perhaps, in the different modes of their writing.

With the publication of *S/Z* in 1970, a book whose importance for film analysis cannot be overestimated, Barthes shifted his earlier emphasis on the structural study of narrative to a demonstration of the step by step structuring of the classical narrative's meanings according to five broad codes or systems of meaning: (a) the deployment of the narrative's actions; (b) its posing, complicating and resolution of enigmas (the hermeneutic code); (c) the tracing of its symbolic structures; (d) the cultural knowledge it assumes its reader to share; and (e) the connotations it reiterates.[2]

> To study this text down to the last detail is to take up the structural analysis of narrative where it has been left till now: at the major structures; it is to assume the power (the time, the elbow room) of working back along the threads of meaning, of abandoning no site of the signifier without endeavoring to ascertain the code or codes of which this site is perhaps the starting point (or the goal); it is (at least we may hope as much, and work to that end) to substitute for the simple representative model another model, whose very gradualness would guarantee what may be productive in the classic text (*S/Z*, p. 12).

The gradualness of the critical itinerary through Balzac's *Sarrasine*, the way the quotation of the text is broken into with what is almost simultaneously commentary, theory and interpretation, the illuminating, clarifying, yet almost teasing way the analysis proceeds, mimicking the text's unfolding, little by little revealing a comprehensible logic which is already determined for the writer, the use of a "case-study" (*Sarrasine*) to stand for a class phenomena (the classic text)—these features of *S/Z* bear a striking resemblance to Freud's case studies and dream analyses.

Similarly the concept of reading in Barthes recalls the psychoanalytic model. In the section "How Many Readings?" Barthes replies: "We must further accept one last freedom: that of reading the text as if it has already been read." And in the section "Reading, Forgetting":

> I [the reader] am not hidden within the text, I am simply irrecoverable from it: my task is to move, to shift systems whose perspective ends neither at the text nor at the "I"; in operational terms, the meanings I find established not by "me" or by others, but by their *systematic* mark: there is no proof of a reading other than the quality and endurance of its systematics; in other words, than its functioning (p. 10).[3]

For Christian Metz the distinction that corresponds in many ways to Barthes's work vs. text is that between the *text* (e.g. the film, what Barthes would call the work) which is the physical object and the *textual system*. The text might be larger than a film (e.g. a genre) or smaller (e.g. a relatively autonomous segment). The textual system, on the other hand, "has no physical existence; it is nothing more than a logic, a principle of coherence. It is the intelligibility of the text, that which must be presupposed if the text is to be comprehensible" (*Language and Cinema*, p. 75). To be perfectly clear, Metz says, "What the cineaste constructs is the text, while the analyst constructs the system" (p. 74). The study of textual systems is called by Metz the study of filmic writing (*écriture*).

The central distinction Metz makes in *Language and Cinema* (1970) is not between text and textual system, but between the analysis of *codes* and the analysis of *textual systems*, the complementary areas into which the semiotics of the cinema is divided. To study the cinematographic language system is to study the specific codes, those the cinema doesn't share, for the most part, with the other arts, as they occur in numerous film-texts. To study a textual system, on the other hand, is to analyze a film in the organization of, ideally, all its codes, specific and non-specific.[4] The notion of a textual system is posed by Metz more or less in the abstract in *Language and Cinema*. The examples he gives are schematic and condensed;[5] the three chapters devoted to this area are primarily designed to set it apart as an object of study from the codes, the book's main theoretical object. Subsequently it has been convenient to adopt this distinction, as modified slightly in "The Imaginary Signifier," as does the recent bibliography by Roger Odin, *Dix années d'analyses textuelles de films,* or Michel Marie's article "L'analyse textuelle" in the semiological handbook *Lectures du film* (1976).

It might be said that ever since the publication of Bellour's seminal shot by shot analysis of a sequence from *The Birds* in 1969, the motivating question for textual analysis has been: what is a textual system? In this article, even before Metz had placed the study of textual systems within a methodological framework, Bellour demonstrated the systematic deployment of three specific codes within a delimited narrative action whose advance was shown to depend on condensations and displacements on different levels across the three codes. Subsequently the textual analyses of Bellour, Kuntzel and Heath (*Touch of Evil*) have been directed toward the logic of the movement and production of meaning in classical film, and thus its tendency toward systems, symmetry and the effect of homogeneity. The notion of system with respect to a film has broadened throughout and because of the development of this work on particular films, which are taken as examples of the classical American cinema. Bellour, for example, now prefers to speak of a textual volume in order to avoid misunderstandings about the possibility of reducing a film's systems to a structural schema and to suggest the myriad effects of mirroring across all levels that constitute the classical film.[6] A chart may be very useful as a summary, but the emphasis is on the itinerary through a film's systems.

The emphasis is also on the activity of film analysis: how to proceed. This is the explicit aim of Heath's "Film and System: Terms of Analysis," with its example of *Touch of Evil.* Heath's analysis adopts Metz's perspective on textual systems and the distinction between the specific and non-specific codes in order to question them, measure them against their object: "What is given is, as it were, an analysis in progress, in the process of the construction—in response to its object—of method and concept" (p. 7). In the development of Kuntzel's work, in particular, one can see an attention to a correlative question: how can a film's tendency to construct systems, its systematicity, best be presented? What position should the analyst adopt toward the film-text, on the one hand, and the reader (the "spectator"), on the other? Questions of presentation are by no means merely decorative. The mode of presentation has an important relationship to the method of analysis and the theoretical perspectives and priorities of the film analyst. The problem is how to demonstrate the functioning of abstract systems by means of concrete details.

The fundamental interdependence between film theory and textual analysis must be understood. There has been a constant and vitalizing exchange of ideas according to differences in perspective between textual analysis and film theory as it is being written outside of specific analyses. The importance of this exchange is acknowledged as clearly in these articles as it is in Metz's work; one need only glance at the continual cross-referencing as a kind of index.[7]

Another reciprocal relationship, perhaps less obvious, can be seen between theories of the apparatus as proposed by Metz and Baudry and the increasing understanding of the fiction-effect through analyses of enunciation and the spectator position in particular classical films. The question here is: where does the classical film's *fascination* come from? The imaginary project of classical cinema is seen to coincide with its economic objectives, the production of desire amounting to a "massive investment in the subject" in Heath's words (p. 10).

> It is precisely the figure of the subject as turning point (circulation) between image and industry (poles of the cinematic institution) which demands study in the analysis of films. The hypothesis, in short, is that ideology depends crucially on the establishment of a range of "machines" (of institutions) which move— transference of desire—the subject ("sender" and "receiver") in a ceaseless appropriation of the symbolic into the imaginary, production into fiction (p. 8).

Bellour's most recent work on the relationship between hypnosis and the cinematic institution, which has come out of specific textual studies of classical literature and film (Alexandre Dumas and Fritz Lang), is proposed as a continuation of the metapsychological work of Metz and Baudry on the apparatus.[8] His most recent film analyses—on *Marnie* and *Psycho*—show that the functioning of the classical fiction film depends on structures of perversion: voyeurism and fetishism. Kuntzel's textual analyses have extended the investigation of the comparison between film and dreams by Metz and Baudry to the demonstration of a productive analogy between the dreamwork (condensation and displacement), secondary elaboration, the work of figuration and the production of meaning in specific film-texts. He has suggested, through specific examples, the relationship of disavowal to the apparatus and, by analogy with the phantasy of the primal scene, the relationship between knowledge, power and vision in the classical cinema, a relationship predicated on an idealist conception of vision.

This is not to suggest that there are not important differences in the work of Bellour, Kuntzel and Heath. There are also other directions within textual analysis that are important to *Camera Obscura*. Among them: articles published in *Cahiers du Cinéma*, from the collective analysis of *Young Mr. Lincoln* (1970) to the recent essays on the relationship between history and fiction by Jean-Louis Comolli and François Géré (*Hangmen Also Die, To Be or Not To Be, La Marseillaise*); the shot by shot analysis of a sequence from *The General Line* by Jacques Aumont; the analyses of style and ideology in *Muriel* by Claude Bailble, Michel Marie and Marie-Claire Ropars and in *October* by Pierre Sorlin and Marie-Claire Ropars, designated by the analysts as avant-garde texts.[9] All of these articles are concerned with the relationship between form and meanings as systematized to constitute a film. They may be differentiated in this broad way from studies which are restricted to the descriptions of stylistic features. "Formalist" studies (in this sense) can be valuable sources of information which can serve as the basis for further analyses so long as the stylistic elements are shown to function systematically in the given film or group of films. Examples of such articles would be the analyses of Japanese film by David Bordwell and Kristin Thompson and by Edward Branigan, or the description of *Ballet mécanique* in Standish Lawder's *The Cubist Cinema*.[10]

There are numerous reasons for the confusion about textual analysis and the consequent resistances to such studies. Much of the influential work so far has been published outside the United States. The translation lag makes important French articles unavailable to many. Moreover, translations appear outside of their original context, out of chronological order, and are scattered among numerous publications. Bellour's seminal analysis of *The Birds* is still only available in English in mimeographed form from the British Film Institute.[11] The analyses themselves are difficult, however, partly because Bellour and Kuntzel tend to leave their methodological objectives implicit; while Heath is explicit, he makes few concessions to someone in need of an introduction. And—although there is much here of importance to film theory, specifically to questions of women and representation, it is impossible to reduce these studies to schematic arguments or information. What they have to teach us about the classical film, and about cinema as an institution, is learned in the process of working through them. It is not possible to read them like discursive essays. They demand another kind of attention, a constant referencing of the details of the already-seen film to the lines of the analysis, with the aid of frame enlargements and other approximations to quotation. It is hoped that this article will help to encourage people to work through this important material. It is proposed as a reading.

II.   Bellour

> . . . Mitch is the mediator, Hitchcock's main double, in the investigation he is conducting into the desire which speaks in Melanie's look.
>
> > "*The Birds*: Analysis of a Sequence"

All of Bellour's work in film analysis can be seen as an attempt to come to terms with a fascination, a fascination with the logic of the movement of narrative in classical film, especially the American classical cinema.[12] His analyses attempt to demonstrate, on different levels, the functioning of an abstract system—the textual system—by means of concrete details, instances of the codes actualized, what Bellour calls the "material abstraction" of film.[13] The pattern and the direction of the interaction of the codes, shot by shot, produces the narrative, *forms* it; the textual system is the logic of this trajectory, a system of systems. This fascination centers, for Bellour, on a number of doubling (or mirroring or rhyming) operations.[14] In "The Obvious and the Code," Bellour quotes Metz's observation that classical cinema

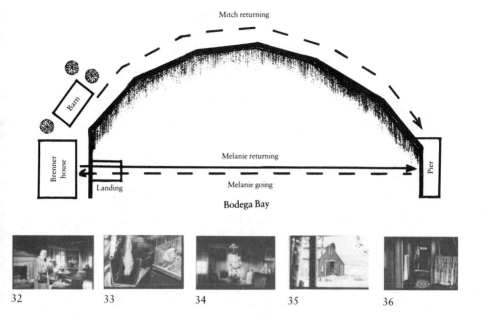

Mitch returning

Barn

Brenner house

Landing

Melanie returning

Melanie going

Bodega Bay

Pier

32   33   34   35   36

is constructed primarily by sequences rather than built up shot by shot. "It is the sequence (and not the shot) which is its preoccupation, its constant problem."[15] While this is true, Bellour says, "the organic material of this preoccupation is the prior set of formal, hierarchically-ordered relations between the shots" (p. 8). "Take as the example," his article begins, "twelve shots from *The Big Sleep*."

Both his analyses of *The Birds* (1969) and *The Big Sleep* (1973) are offered as examples of how meaning in the classical film is "materialized" shot by shot within the segment, which is taken as the basic narrative unit.[16] In the article on *The Birds*, three systems are followed, formulated as binary oppositions, through the 81 shots that make up the segment: framing (close/ distant), camera movement (still/moving), and point of view (seeing/seen). Bellour calls them "the series of the most marked pertinences, . . . deliberately restricted in number" (p. 3). They will later, after *Language and Cinema*, be referred to as specific codes.

The segment advances through the orchestration of these oppositions, an advance which is characterized by a constant effort toward balance and symmetry on the one hand (repetition) and dissymmetry on the other (differ- ence), without which there would be no narrative development. The segment is first broken into two parts, each of which is organized in mirror fashion, i.e. symmetrically around a center. Series A forms Melanie's trip by motor boat across Bodega Bay to Mitch's house where she leaves the love-birds, an invitation to Mitch in the guise of a birthday present for his sister, Cathy (the center of the series), back to her boat, where she waits, watching and half-hiding. Series B is organized around Mitch. Its beginning overlaps with the last part of series A: from her boat Melanie watches Mitch go from the

The Birds: shot list of the Bodega Bay segment (Melanie Daniels's trip to the Brenners's house)

Group 1: Departure:
3. MELANIE drives from background right, around a street corner to foreground.
4. MELANIE driving down a slope, out foreground right.
5. MELANIE parks her car, gets out of the car holding cage. Camera pans to jetty.
6. MELANIE enters the field, foreground left to face the fisherman.
7. THE FISHERMAN staring at Melanie; he moves offscreen down. She hands him cage.
8. THE FISHERMAN helps her down. She disappears offscreen down.
9. THE FISHERMAN bending over straightens up, shakes his head, goes down ladder.
10. MELANIE seated in the boat. The fisherman comes down the ladder, starts motor.
11. THE FISHERMAN standing on the ladder looking after Melanie. Loud engine sound.
12. MELANIE piloting the boat (up camera) 1st of three shots.
13. MELANIE piloting the boat, moving left to right (engine noise lower).
14. MELANIE piloting the boat (moving towards the camera).

Group A1: the journey to the Brenners's house:
15. MELANIE still piloting the boat looking off foreground right (engine louder).
16. THE BRENNERS'S HOUSE. Mitch, Lydia, Cathy walking towards the truck.
17. MELANIE piloting the boat, watching offscreen right; she cuts off the motor.
18. THE BRENNERS'S HOUSE. All get in the truck except Mitch.
19. MELANIE watching the group. Silence, sound of water against the boat.
20. THE BRENNERS'S HOUSE. The truck drives off, left to right. Mitch runs to barn.
21. MELANIE looking to the right (Mitch). She begins to paddle towards platform.
22. THE BARN. Mitch opens the door and goes inside.
23. MELANIE paddling, towards camera, looks to the right.
24. THE PLATFORM seen from Melanie's POV. Forward movement.

Group A2: Melanie moves towards the house:
25. MELANIE paddling. She steps out of the boat, picks up the cage.
26. THE BRENNERS'S HOUSE. The barn door wide open. Water noises. *Birds.*
27. MELANIE smiling. The camera tracks backwards.
28. THE BARN. Large tree in foreground and retaining wall.
29. MELANIE smiling.
30. THE BARN behind the trees. Camera tracks.
31. MELANIE climbing up the steps.

Group A3: Melanie inside the house (Center A):
32. THE BRENNERS'S HOUSE.
33. [INSERT], Melanie's hand putting the note in front of the cage.
34. MELANIE moving inside the house.
35. THE BARN, seen by Melanie from inside the house.
36. MELANIE in the hallway.

Group A4: Melanie returning to the landing platform:
37. MELANIE leaving the house.
38. THE BARN, tree in the foreground (30).
39. MELANIE moves along the house, away from it.
40. THE BARN (27).

41. MELANIE walking rapidly towards the boat, looks back.
42. THE BARN.
43 MELANIE steps down from the deck to platform into the boat, looks to the left, she paddles away.
44. THE BARN.

Group A5/B1 (Departure):
45. MELANIE puts down the oar and hides behind the boat engine.
46. MITCH enter the house.
47. MELANIE watching the house.
48. THE BRENNERS'S HOUSE.
49. MELANIE watching intently.
50. MITCH comes out of the house and goes near the garage and stops to look.
51. MELANIE watching.
52. MITCH turns around, walks back to the house, stops and sees something.
53. MELANIE reacts by hiding a little more.
54. MITCH runs to the house (slight pan left).
55. MELANIE stands up and tries to start the motor.
56. MITCH comes out of the house with binoculars, sound of engine, BIRDS in foreground.
57. MITCH with binoculars. Sound of engine.

Group B2: Mitch observing Melanie (Center B):
58. MELANIE seen through binoculars. She finally gets the motor to run.
59. MITCH lowers his binoculars and smiles, runs out (loud bird cries).
60. MELANIE smiles and pilots the boat, moving to the left.

Group B3: Melanie and Mitch. She returns to the dock. He drives around:
61. MITCH runs to the truck on the side of the house.
62. MELANIE piloting the boat, still moving to the left.
63. MITCH driving away (rapid left right pan; engine same noise level).
64. MELANIE in the boat watching him. Camera in different position in the boat.
65. MITCH drives to the right in the background.
66. MELANIE reacting. Loud engine noise.
67. MITCH drives from left to right.
68. MELANIE watching him.
69. MITCH driving. 2 sail boats in the foreground.
70. MELANIE watching.
71. MITCH driving to the right. Following pan.

Group 2: Arrival:
72. MELANIE smiling.
73. MELANIE approaching the dock. Large fishing boat docked.
74. MELANIE smiling. Slows down the motor.
75. MITCH on the jetty.
76. MELANIE smiles. She tips her head slightly to the side (waiting for gull).
77. SEA GULL IN FLIGHT.
78. MELANIE, the bird flies from right to the foreground. Loud sound, not cry.
79. THE BIRD flies from the right.
80. MITCH strolling on the jetty.
81. MELANIE removes her hand.
82. MELANIE'S GLOVED HAND.
83. MITCH arrives and jumps into the boat.
84. MITCH helps Melanie climb out of the boat. They run across a man.

barn into the house and run back out looking for her. Its center is marked by Mitch looking into the camera with his binoculars, followed by his view of Melanie as she tries to start the motor of her boat, and reciprocal shots of each of them smiling. The second half of the series alternates shots of Mitch and Melanie as they return separately to the pier on the other side of the bay, Mitch by truck around the shore-line, Melanie by boat. As she is about to meet Mitch at the pier, Melanie is hit by a gull on the forehead. Mitch takes charge of her, ending the segment.

The mid-sections of series A and B are also the centers of extremely complicated formal systems as Bellour's analysis shows in convincing detail.[17] Formal balance is achieved by alternating series of codic choices, e.g. seeing/seen/seeing/seen/seeing. A break in the pattern of alternation on one level, e.g. point of view (seeing/seeing), is smoothed over by a continued alternation on another, e.g. camera movement. The alternation is *displaced*, Bellour says, to another level. For example, the center of series A (Melanie inside Mitch's house) is marked by a break in alternation on two levels: framing and the look (point of view). But a stable alternation on the level of camera movement not only carries the rhythm of the segment across these breaks, which are therefore not very noticeable because of the *displacement* of alternation from framing and point of view onto camera movement, it also *condenses* the prior and subsequent series of shots on its own level.

> Series A3 is in fact governed by the alternating opposition static/movement. This opposition is distributed through the five shots in the following way: movement/static/movement/static/movement. The first effect of this alternation is to condense in the central series the double alternation static/static and movement/movement which opposes the series A1 and A2 on the one hand and the series A4 and A5 on the other. It supplements the break introduced into the alternation seeing/seen on the one hand, and, its half-corollary, the framing on the other, thus making it possible to maintain the continuity of the relation of alternating opposition by displacing it to another level (p. 18).

This is the formal basis for the sense of natural continuity, of *obviousness* which Bellour will show in the series of close analyses begun here to be characteristic of the classical American film.

A similar example is given in Bellour's elegant analysis of a twelve-shot segment from *The Big Sleep*: during a short car-ride, a transitional lull between two dramatically charged scenes, Vivian and Marlowe admit their love for each other.

> The interest in this segment lies in its apparent poverty. Even an attentive viewer will not be sure to retain anything but the impression of a certain amount of vague unity. Questioned, he will very likely hazard the view that the segment consists of a long take supported by dialogue, or at best, of two or three shots (p. 7).

Why were twelve shots necessary? What is the effect of the variation in form?

As deceptive in its simplicity as the segment is in its obviousness, "The Obvious and the Code" shows how the "naturalness" of the narrative progression is made possible, as in *The Birds*, only by a systematic balancing of symmetries and dissymmetries shot by shot across six principle codes, three specific and three non-specific, in connection with significant elements of the narrative (called here, loosely, another code). It continues the previous article's investigation of the classical fiction-effect:

> But Hawks needed twelve shots to secure the economy of this segment. Undoubtedly that economy was designed in order not to be perceived, which is in fact one of the determining features of the American cinema. But it exists, and from it, the classic mode of narration draws a part of its power (p. 7).

Bellour draws a number of general conclusions from this analysis: (a) the high number of shots given the minimal action allows for discontinuity, variation; (b) this variation is limited, however, by a tendency toward repetition—shots repeated exactly or shots with certain elements repeated; (c) repetition ensures an effect of naturalness or smoothness despite the differences introduced in the codes, differences which advance the narrative; (d) thus a balance is sustained by the movement of the shots in the segment between repetition and variation, symmetry and dissymmetry across the codes (p. 16).

As in the segment from *The Birds*, here too the formal movement is symmetrical around a center. This movement, which was analyzed in both examples *within* the segment, is seen in the article's conclusion from the perspective of the larger work of segmentation in building up the film as a whole. Each of a film's segments seems to introduce and resolve its elements (stabilize itself formally) anew "by means of a suspension and folding effect, as if to allow the segment to close back on itself more effectively and leave the new fold the problem of unrolling its new elements" (p. 16). This folding-effect is "profoundly characteristic of the American cinema," though not restricted to it.

In his article on *Gigi* two years later ("To Analyze, To Segment"), where segmentation per se is addressed before its effects are shown through a multi-level description/analysis of *Gigi*, Bellour describes his series of textual analyses as having shown the repetition-resolution effect—the "effects of differential repetition which structure the development of the narrative" in rhyming or mirroring fashion—on different levels: the fragment (*The Birds*), the segment (*The Big Sleep*), the whole film (*North by Northwest*) and in *Gigi* a crisscrossing of these levels including narrative units larger and smaller than the segment.

> Segmentation, as we shall see, is a *mise en abîme*, a process which theoretically is infinite—which is not to say that it lacks meaning. By the shifted play which operates between its different levels, segmentation permits us to sense the increased plurality of textual effects (p. 336).

But this plurality is not without direction. Redundancy across different levels in the classical film serves to reinforce over and over again an effect of homogeneity and of symbolic closure.

The formal movement of symmetry and dissymmetry toward and away from a center is one mirroring operation of a series. More fundamental, because it includes the work of the codes as one of its terms, is the reciprocity Bellour emphasizes between mise-en-scène (as organized by the codes) and narrative.

44   45   46

The arrangement shown by the work of the codes is the same one that shapes the meaning of the fiction.

"The Obvious and the Code" (p. 14)

The systematic stockpiling of symmetries and dissymmetries throughout the filmic chain decomposed by generalized segmentation faithfully copies (because they, in fact, produce one another) the schema of familial relations which constitute the space of the narrative. [This is] a fundamental effect common to most American film.

"To Analyze, To Segment" (p. 344)

Between shot 44 and shot 56, Mitch Brenner discovers Melanie Daniels's presence. The plot, hitherto organized by the vision of one character, redoubles onto itself to respond to the dual vision. The center is then displaced, and after the moment in which Mitch sees Melanie, becomes *also* the four shots 56–60 (B2) in which the two see that they have been seen. The sequence conforms to the equation: one character, one center only, two characters, two centers. It would be more accurate to say: one single mobile center, which slips beneath the scene and sustains the development of the script with an architectural slide.

"*The Birds*: Analysis of a Sequence" (p. 19)

This relationship of complementarity has already been implied by the fact that the formal series are organized around narrative events. It should not be thought that the codes are somehow, on their own, forming symmetrical patterns which happen to correspond to repetitions and variations in the plot. Rather, the codes are to an extent narrativized from the outset in these analyses. And the way that the narrative bears on them is shown, throughout Bellour's work, to be fundamentally tied to sexual difference as it is represented in the classical film. The movement of Bellour's work can most clearly be seen as an effort to understand how this relationship is determining, and

56

57

58

what this has to do with the captivation of the spectator by the classical fiction-effect.

If the segment from *The Birds* is organized on the narrative/structural level around a repetition (the trip out, the trip back) with a difference (the trip made by one, the trip made by two), with the resolution of the segment marked by the meeting of the two terms, it is more than relevant, yet so obvious as to be taken for granted, that the terms are female and male, that the trips are organized for the purpose of initiating a courtship (the formation of a couple), and that the eventual meeting—delayed by the time of the return trips, suspense before climax—is marked by an aggression staged literally against the body of the woman: as she is about to reach Mitch, Melanie is struck on the forehead by a gull. Again, repetition and difference: whereas it was first a question of love-birds, Melanie's gift through his sister to Mitch, it is secondly, after Mitch has seen the love-birds and their obvious significance, a question of the gulls which act out in their initial attack a response to Melanie's gift and the invitation her physical presence holds out to Mitch (p. 25).

Although point of view is introduced into the analysis as one system among others, by the end of the analysis it has been clearly shown to be more important than the others. As Melanie has been first subject, then object of "the birds" (she brings the love-birds, she is attacked by the gull), this same "reversibility" applies to the look. Melanie's look effectively controls the fiction through the alternation between "Melanie seeing/what Melanie sees" until the point at which she is caught in the double-iris of Mitch's binoculars, unable to return his look because she is trying to start the motor of her boat. These "rhymes" are linked according to Bellour's interpretation: series A was marked by Melanie's initiative, her gift; series B is centered on the reversal of the look which leads to the exchange of looks, and then smiles, between Mitch and Melanie. This exchange introduces the "wild birds"—in the image (shot 56), wheeling overhead, and in the sound (shot 59), their "murderous shrieks" presaging, at the moment Mitch lowers his binoculars and smiles, the attack on Melanie in shot 78, after which, her smile erased, she becomes the object of Mitch's look. A complementary pair of detail shots illustrate once again repetition and difference, in this case formal repetition marked by symbolic difference. The first, inside the house (shot 33) shows Melanie's gloved hands tearing up a gift card addressed to Mitch and replacing it with

171

59   60   61

78   79   80

one addressed to Cathy. Its formal counterpart (shot 82) details Melanie's
gloved hand, her index finger stained with blood after the gull's attack. The
first shows the nature of the gift, Bellour says, the second its effect (p. 29).

Why this should be the effect of Melanie's gift is given only a veiled
explanation. Bellour describes the effect as "symbolic punishment" for her
look.

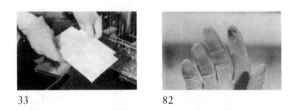

33   82

. . . the symbolic punishment which strikes [Melanie] in Mitch's look in the
metaphorical form of the killer birds has from the beginning spoken in her own
look, in the first metaphor which her indiscretion proposed to Mitch with the
symbolic gift of the love-birds. If Mitch's look reverses and precipitates the
sequence, Melanie's look guides it and organizes it until the moment of the
meeting (p. 29).

Her look has been wounded, for it is only metaphorically, and for the sake of the
rest of the plot, that the gull does not strike her eyes (p. 30).

The object of the scene is to show Melanie subjecting by her look and subjected
to a look. It could be given a reversible title: *the vision of Melanie Daniels* (p.
33).

The two shots 33 and 57 are united in the symbolic violence of this last close-up
[shot 82, the blood on Melanie's glove], in which a common look [i.e. it is seen
by Mitch and Melanie together] marks the effect of the gift, the fact that it is

impossible for Mitch and Melanie to see each other as seen without opening up a dual and murderous relationship (p. 32).

Melanie is punished for her look because it is through the alternation "Melanie seeing"/"what Melanie sees" that her sexual invitation is narrativized. But Melanie's look is itself controlled—by the organizer of these formal and narrative systems, the *metteur en scène*, and it is the fascination expressed by his look that will engage Bellour's critical attention increasingly.

It is Hitchcock, by means of the camera-eye, who sees through the eyes of now one, now the other of his characters. He identifies with both Mitch and Melanie, but not in the same way.

> There is no doubt that Hitchcock identifies with Mitch, who interrogates Melanie's look and allows himself to be bewitched by it, but there is even less doubt that Hitchcock identifies with Melanie, whose eyes bear the phantasy whose effects Hitchcock narrates and analyzes in that purely narcissistic art which mise en scène is for him (p. 38).

Bellour calls Hitchcock's direction narcissistic. He will call it perverse in subsequent articles: perverse not only on account of Hitchcock's voyeurism—his trademark is an excessive use of point of view shots—but more significantly because of the way he gains access to the scene that stimulates his voyeuristic pleasure. It is through the woman's eyes, both structurally and symbolically—here as will be shown in the analyses of *Marnie* and *Psycho*—that the man's desire is aroused, not only through her literal viewpoint, but perhaps even more through the sight of the woman absorbed by an imagined desire, looking. Only on this condition, Bellour says, are "perversion and morality linked" in the typical Hitchcockian scenario of guilt and false guilt, mistaken identity and true identity, thereby making it possible for the *director's* phantasy to be acted out through fictional delegates.[18]

For Hitchcock is introduced at the end of the analysis as "another character" and his phantasy as another kind of oblique explanation for the violence directed against the body of Melanie Daniels. In "Le blocage symbolique," Bellour suggests that Hitchcock's fictional moments in *North by Northwest* and *The Birds* provide a quasi-material link between the principle of the mise-en-scène, which he personifies, and the symbolic chain of events the narrative will play out, through a direct identification with his fictional counterparts. Thornhill, like Mitch, *acts out* the scenario *for* Hitchcock: "Thornhill accomplishes what Hitchcock can't expect through a symbolic transfer which the film as imaginary discourse makes possible" (p. 343). Likewise, ". . . Mitch is the mediator, Hitchcock's main double, in the investigation he is conducting into the desire which speaks in Melanie's look" (p. 35). The desire in her look is necessary to the fiction, but only so that it can be subjected to a masculine look speaking for a parasitical desire. The fisherman who held Melanie in a sustained look as her boat departed for Mitch's house is another double, a relay for both Mitch and Hitchcock. By extension, in a corresponding way, these fictional doubles, as well as Hitchcock himself taken as the principle for his textual organization, act *in the place of* the spectator—and his perhaps more interested double, the film analyst.[19]

Phantasy, not fantasy: it is a specific Freudian construct that is meant, and Bellour characterizes it in "Le blocage symbolique" as central to the fiction-effect of the classical American cinema. The beauty of *North by Northwest* as a model for analysis, in a purer and more abstract way than *The Birds*, is that the series of enigmas which carry the suspense-spy-detective story forward (the hermeneutic code)—e.g. who is Kaplan? who is agent no. 2? who is Eve?—is seen to coincide exactly with the symbolic code, under the pressure of *the* detective story whose locus classicus, according to Freud, Lévi-Strauss and Lacan, is the *Oedipus Rex*. It is not a question of psychoanalyzing Thornhill in "Le blocage symbolique," but of showing how the textual organization of the film corresponds in all its details—on the level of actions, enigmas, and mise-en-scène—to a scenarization of the Oedipus complex and the castration complex.[20]

> "Come on, Mrs. Thornhill." These words show clearly how the transgression of the adventure ends with the sanction of bourgeois marriage, but that the limit where desire is fixed can't be recognized except in the transgression of the adventure as test and place of truth: the loss of identity, the guilt which determines, from the initial mistake, the adventure as crossroads of the enigma, thus leading the hero from ignorance to knowledge, from lack to possession, from misrecognition to recognition of a (socialized) desire (pp. 238–39).

The analysis falls mainly into two parts.[21] The first traces Thornhill's symbolic itinerary through its narrative instances: the symbolic murder of the ideal father (Kaplan-Townsend), the change in object-choice from the infantilizing, phallic mother to the "duplicitous" Eve, who in the same scene saves Thornhill from the law by hiding him in her sleeping compartment on the train and sends him to his death—her note to Vandamm leads directly to the cornfield sequence. Thus the first kiss between Eve and Thornhill is "murderous," linking sexuality and death literally. Eve is the pivotal figure for Thornhill. The tests which he successfully passes—threats to his life, mysteries solved—serve to reestablish his true identity, thus absolving him from guilt in the eyes of the law, and simultaneously to transform Eve, the embodiment of transgressive, threatening sexuality as Vandamm's agent into the image of bourgeois domesticity. Thornhill comes to achieve a positive identification with the law (he helps the CIA materially by restoring the stolen microfilm) and to constrain his desire for Eve within socially-defined limits. The direction of *North by Northwest* is thus from negativity to positivity, from lack to possession, i.e. toward the happy ending, the successful resolution of the Oedipus complex for the masculine subject, and accession into the symbolic.

This drama of love, death and identity is played out most spectacularly in the cornfield sequence where Thornhill expects the resolution of his unstable identity in the person of Kaplan, but thanks to Eve is subjected to the threat of death. The formal analysis of this sequence, which is very detailed and equal in length to the preceding section, gives priority again to point of view as an organizing system. The moments of attack coincide with Thornhill's loss of vision (an interruption of the alternation seeing/seen), indicating his loss of mastery of the object, his loss of identity.[22] Between the segment and the whole film there is a homology of systems dominated by the paradigm of "means of locomotion," which both carry the narrative forward (materialize it) and symbolize it. Cars, trucks, buses and an airplane signal to the fore-warned spectator Eve's duplicity and the threat of death (symbolic castration) for Thornhill. The famous last images of the film (in the nick of time, Thornhill pulls Eve up from the precipice of Mt. Rushmore into his sleeping compartment with the words, "Come on, Mrs. Thornhill," as their train is entering a tunnel) underscore emphatically the positive resolution of sexuality as a *problem*.

Eve is first duplicitous. As a double-agent she combines sexuality and the threat of death. She shows that she has two sides: first phallic, she becomes domestic, Thornhill's double, his mirror-image. He saves her—for marriage. Eve, therefore, has a role to play for every stage of Thornhill's Oedipal itinerary.

> And what strikes me as absolutely fundamental in this perspective is that the American cinema is entirely dependent, as is psychoanalysis, on a system of representations in which the woman occupies a central place only to the extent that it's a place assigned to her by the logic of masculine desire.
>
> "Alternation, Enunciation, Hypnosis," (p. 93)

The central place accorded the woman by the logic of masculine desire is the starting place for the analyses of *Marnie* and *Psycho*, where the relationship of this logic both to the organization of the mise-en-scène and the narrative is formulated in terms of enunciation, Hitchcock's role becoming that of the enunciator. The operational value of Hitchcock within the analysis becomes clearer here. First, it is obvious that even in the article on *The Birds*, it was a question of considering Hitchcock's films as a group, a system, a text. The segment analyzed was an example of a kind of textual organization particular to Hitchcock; as such, its analysis led to generalizations which applied beyond his films to the classical American cinema as a larger system, Hitchcock's films being taken as an extreme (perverse) example of highly conventionalized formal and thematic preoccupations. Second, if Hitchcock's obsessions are of interest, it is clearly because they have interested very large audiences. Textual analysis tries to account for this shared fascination, first in the specific terms of a filmic system, then in terms of the general fictional apparatus of the classical cinema. Third, Hitchcock's particular use of point of view shots marks the conventionally vacant place of enunciation in the classical cinema. Bellour shows how in *Psycho* he emphasizes almost by way of visual diagrams the voyeuristic and sadistic relationship of the camera and the implicated spectator to the body and the look of the woman (e.g. Norman's "bulging eye" directed at Marion through a peep-hole before the shower scene). In his analysis of *Marnie*, Bellour examines the fetishistic aspect of the apparatus through Hitchcock's relationship, as enunciator ("pure image power"), to the image. Both articles are concerned with the *conditions of possibility* of enunciation in terms of the scopic drive (the relationship of the look to desire and lack) and identification. The enunciator-character-spectator oscillates between being and having the women-image: "the two processes of identification which transfix the spectator: identification with the camera, identification with the object (the perpetual dialectic between being and having: identification and object choice)" (p. 79).[23]

In the article on *Marnie*, this is immediately expressed by Bellour as violence, aggression against the woman: the credits initiate a "symbolic possession"—"Alfred Hitchcock's *Marnie*." Marnie is constituted and possessed as image, *reduced to image* by the very principle of the enunciation. Her enigmatic first appearance follows these credits. We see a woman only from behind, walking away from the camera on a train platform. We guess and will soon know that this is Marnie. The second time we see her comes in response to scene II, in narrative terms, as a partial realization of the imaginary picture Strutt has created for the police of his former secretary, helped by Mark Rutland's appreciative memories of her. *Formally* it is a direct reply to Mark's pensive look into the camera which ends the scene.

> Mark is daydreaming about this woman whose virtual image he has helped to create. The *real* image that follows repeats exactly the beginning of shot 1 and occurs as if to materialize his thoughtful look, taking the place of the traditional subjective shot (p. 71).

As in the first scene, but now as if the object of Mark's look, Marnie walks away from the camera, this time down a hotel corridor. A moment later Hitchcock steps out of one of the rooms, looks first after her and then toward

the camera, making both a *formal* and *logical* bridge similar to Mark's look, which bridged scenes II and III, between scenes III and IV where, as if in response to Hitchcock's look, we see Marnie in her hotel room, changing her identity (the social security cards) and her "looks" (she washes the dye out of her hair). Only now do we see Marnie's face. She looks almost into the camera and, according to Bellour's description, "admires the triumphant image of a split identity" in the mirror. "Following the segmentation of the name, the segmentation of the body completes Marnie's change of identity" (p. 80). This time it is Marnie's own look that bridges the scenes (IV to V), as if she looks to her own fragmented body.

Segmentation is the word we are used to seeing in Bellour's work refer to the cutting up of the filmic chain into narrative units, the very work of fictional construction. Here it describes the systematic fragmentation of the woman's image, the woman reduced to image, submitted to the control of the image-maker. The analysis shows how the fetishization of Marnie is equally central to Mark's fascination with her and to the logic of the enunciation—here in terms of the organization of "images" (real and imaginary), seen as already determined by the apparatus through the "fetishistic position" of the cinematic signifier.

> Mark's single-minded desire for Marnie is aroused by this relationship between himself and the image. . . . The fetishistic operation, thus amplified, is transferred from the director to the character who takes his place, to the extent that thus is accomplished a return to the narrative's initial condition of possibility; the essentially fetishistic position of the cinematic signifier (pp. 71–72).

The woman is central—Marnie, Marion, Melanie—insofar as the woman's desire is the central *problem* or challenge for the male protagonist (and the director, etc.). Her desire, as evidenced by her look, narrativizes the possibility and therefore the problem of sexual difference. The narrative then moves to reduce the image of the woman's sexuality as a threat, thus the work of fetishization: the pleasure of seeing the woman's body in pieces, a guarantee of the safety (coherence, totality) of the man's. Fetishism is thus directly linked to the logic of the enunciation by Bellour. For the male protagonist, the challenge of the woman's desire is to make it mirror his. The related enigmas which make Marnie at the same time fascinating to Mark and the central character of the film—her compulsion to steal and her frigidity—will be resolved by a cathartic experience staged by Mark in order to reconstruct her image as his wife. Sexual desire, first displaced to desire for Marnie's neurotic symptoms, can be rechannelled toward marriage because an image of domesticity is available that reduces the woman to the man's complement, his double. Sexual difference is thus eliminated, disavowed.

In *Psycho* the reconstruction of the woman's image is taken to an extreme: Norman has literally "fetishized his mother to death." Marion is only the center of the fiction (a subject of desire) in order to carry the fiction to a "masculine" subject who will be substituted for her as the character the fiction is centered around: Marion's theft and her getaway move the fiction until the psychotic subject of desire, by murdering her, becomes the protagonist. "In *Psycho* woman, the subject of neurosis, becomes the object of the psychosis of which man is the subject" (p. 112). Bellour takes pains to emphasize that woman as subject of desire is strictly subjected to and *used* by a desire which envelops hers.

Similarly to the way in which Marnie's body and her own look had been used to create a formal bridge between scenes in the examples given above, as the object of quasi-subjective shots attributable to Mark, then Hitchcock, then herself, Marion functions as a formal bridge between the first and second parts of *Psycho* (as Bellour defines them). Point of view, again, is the crucial agent, and it is implicated by Bellour's use of words as an explicitly sexual agent.

> However in order to go from one man to another [Sam to Norman] and from one position to another [neurosis to psychosis], the camera must also embody (*faire corps avec*) the woman and adopt (*se marier*) her look, conserving a strong identification—diegetic, of course, but more specifically specular, determined by the organization of the point of view—with the subject it has taken as its object. . . . In conformity with its basic path, that of perverse structuration, the transformation from neurosis to psychosis is brought about by woman, who is both its foundation and its indispensable form (p. 118).

Although the woman's vision has structured the fiction's movement toward the Bates Motel, the series of shot/reverse-shot exchanges between Norman and Marion as she attempts to rent a room for the night are already weighted in terms of power in favor of the masculine subject. In response to Jacqueline Rose's argument in "Paranoia and the Film System" that there is a component of aggression inherent in the shot/reverse-shot structure because of its restaging of aspects of the mirror phase, and that this aggressive component is potentially active for both parties of the exchange, Bellour emphasizes that the classical cinema is:

> a system in which the aggressive element can never be separated from the inflection it receives from sexual difference, and the attribution of this difference to the signifier that governs it. In other words, it is directed from the man towards the woman, and that difference which appears due to woman is nothing but the mirror-effect of the narcissistic doubling that makes possible the constitution of the male subject through the woman's body. . . (p. 118–19).

Within the confines of this logic, the woman's aggression against the man comes only as a reaction to his prior violence toward her.[26]

Within this massive, imaginary reduction of sexual difference to a narcissistic doubling of the masculine subject, there would seem to remain the woman's potential for sexual pleasure apart from the male protagonist: her pleasure for herself. However for Bellour, those scenes in Hitchcock's films which are there precisely to show the woman's pleasure alone function in a more perverse way than the use of the woman's body as object or vehicle to fuel the enunciative machine.

> Within this configuration, one things seems to me to be essential, namely that it is through woman's pleasure (*jouissance*) that the perverse projection and psychotic inscription are carried out (just as it is through her actions, her body, her look, that the film moves from one scene to the next).
> "Psychosis, Neurosis, Perversion," (p. 121).

For Bellour the "high point" of the enunciation of *Marnie* (of the initial setting into place of the fiction's elements) is the moment when Marnie half-smiles at herself in the mirror (and into the camera) "absorbed in her desire for her own image" (p. 81); i.e. her desire is for her image which is also the reduced and fetishized object of desire of Strutt and Mark. In *Psycho* the corresponding scene is the first part of Marion's shower. The quality of Bellour's description testifies, perhaps, to the fascination the scene holds from the point of view of the enunciation of masculine desire.

> The emphasis on Marion's pleasure in the shower goes well beyond all diegetic motivation: close-up shots of her naked body alternate with shots of gushing water; she leans into the stream, opens her mouth, smiles, and closes her eyes in a rapture that is made all the more intense because it contrasts with the horror that is to come, but also because the two are linked together. By a subtle reversal, the pleasure that Marion did not show in the opening love scene at last appears. However the pleasure is for herself (even if it can only be so for the camera, because of the image-nature assigned to her by the camera); it takes the form of narcissistic intimacy which poses, for men, the question of sexual pleasure itself, with woman's body instituted as its mythical site (p. 121).

Given the nature of this system of representations, Bellour says, which Freudian and Lacanian psychoanalysis account for so accurately, the woman's narcissistic pleasure is shown not only *for the pleasure of* the man (in this case it is figured in the film: Norman is watching Marion through a peep-hole) but is also shown as that which *will be assimilated to* masculine desire by the end of the film—one way or another. Bellour's statement continues:

> The masculine subject can accept the image of woman's pleasure only on condition that, having constructed it, he may inscribe himself and recognize himself within it, and thus reappropriate it even at the cost of its (or her) destruction (p. 121).[27]

Once again sexual difference, in this case through the question of feminine pleasure, is implicated within structures of identification and vision which serve to efface difference in favor of the masculine subject. With respect to the steady movement of Bellour's work toward demonstrating the overdetermination of this principle, two points are important to bring out, and will lead to a kind of conclusion.

(1)   The system of identifications Bellour is outlining, which depends heavily on the negotiation of vision in the classical film, is historically determined and culturally circumscribed. Thus qualified, it is this system that Bellour contends necessitates the Oedipal wish-fulfillment of the American classical cinema.[28] (He amplifies these views in the interview in Chapter 11 of this book.)[29]

(2)   Bellour is attempting to suggest different kinds of identification for the male and female spectator, i.e. to begin to include sexual difference as a factor in the analysis. For example, he suggests that Marnie's look into the mirror:

> extends to the male spectator (the camera held by Hitchcock, Mark, Strutt) the deferred orgasm (*jouissance*) of desire for an object; for any woman spectator who, for all practical purposes is alienated by this structure, she stimulates an identificatory desire (p. 81).

At this present stage of Bellour's work, he has brought together identification, vision and pleasure (fascination) in a way that suggests direct connections with the most important work being done in the area of film and psychoanalytic theory by feminists. On the one hand, his analysis of structures of fascination in the classical film is more complicated than in Laura Mulvey's "Visual Pleasure and Narrative Cinema" in that pleasure in looking in Bellour's work is taken within mechanisms which depend only in part on visual perception. It is, once again, the "*desire* which speaks in Marnie's look" which is the object of Mitch's and Hitchcock's investigation, not primarily her body as scopic object or fetish. The woman's desire is crucial to the logic of the enunciation of Hitchcock's films, Bellour contends (this is possibly his most insidious point) and he extends this description to the classical American cinema generally. Secondly, as the quotation above indicates, Bellour attempts to take the woman spectator into account differently than the male spectator when analyzing these structures of fascination, unlike in Mulvey's article where the spectator within phallocentrism is implicitly equated with the male spectator.

But if Bellour's work has progressively elaborated ideas which Mulvey, who was writing from a different perspective, placed at the center of her argument, and if Bellour has extended them in the process of demonstrating how these structures of fascination work within specific films, the resulting picture of the classical cinema is even more totalistic and deterministic than Mulvey's. Bellour sees it as a logically consistent, complete and closed system. (See, for example, the final sections of the interview in Chapter 11.)

It is with respect to identification that Bellour's discussion is less complicated than his work itself would lead one to expect. In fact, the *movement* of his work seems to be exactly *toward* a more complex consideration of identification and sexual difference in terms of specific fictional situations. However at this point masculine and feminine are still conceived of as fixed poles ("the male spectator," "any woman spectator"; or see the interview, p. 195), despite the fact that he talks about a constant oscillation of the spectator between object choice and identification (the active and passive scopophilia Mulvey describes), which must depend on an implicit theory of bisexual response, and despite the fact that the films themselves suggest a confusion of sexual boundaries. Wouldn't Norman's scenario have to read something like this? When he meets Marion, it is as the son to an available woman. When he watches her in the shower, Norman is the son watching his mother (Marion) imagining himself as the mother's lover ("the imaginary and ungraspable relation (*entre-deux*) of the primal scene"[30]); when Norman, impersonating his mother, kills Marion, it is as the mother killing a rival for her son's affection, the inverse manifestation of the incestuous desire which precedes the psychotic embodiment. In Norman's case it is at the price of psychosis that he can want to have the woman and be the woman at the same time. Each shift necessitates corresponding changes in the imaginary identifications of the other characters in the scenario. However this exchange and/or doubling of roles is not restricted to psychosis; it is *characteristic of* the structure of the phantasy.[31] Bellour begins to approach the question of partial or changing identifications, but only in terms of Norman's psychosis[32] (or, even more sketchily, Marnie's "split personality").

Freud devoted a chapter to identification in *Group Psychology and the Analysis of the Ego* (1922), preceded by this description: "there do exist other mechanisms for emotional ties, the so-called *identifications*, insufficiently-known processes and hard to describe . . ." After all the close work in film analysis that has led up to this point, it is now possible and absolutely necessary to complicate the question of identification as it functions in the classical film, first of all in terms of the realization that spectators are able to take up multiple identificatory positions, whether successively or simultaneously. Freud's case studies of the Wolfman or of Dora, among others, demonstrate this point at length. Jacqueline Rose's reexamination of the case of Dora ("Dora—Fragment of an Analysis") brings out some of the implications of the shifting of sexual identifications within a woman's history for attempting to say what "the woman's desire" is. A greater attention to the movement of identifications—whether according to theories of bisexuality, power relationships (as in *S/Z*) or in some other terms—seems to be the next logical step in attempting more accurately to account for the quality of our involvement as spectators. Whether arguing for a "counter" cinema or in terms of understanding the mechanisms of the fiction film, it is necessary to avoid a strictly biological male/female dichotomy while acknowledging the lived experience of women and men *generally* in our culture to be different.

In conclusion: Bellour's work has given us not only a flexible methodological model for performing detailed and specific analyses of narrative film, but a theoretical model of the classical cinema according to numerous axes. Not only has he shown us a great deal about the production of meaning in general in the classical film, with particular attention to cinematic specificity, but in doing so he has accorded the structural and symbolic role of the woman increasing importance. If Bellour's analysis of symbolic structures in the American cinema reveals a particular interest ("If I've wanted to go to the furthest possible point in understanding the power and subtlety of this textual pressure, it's quite simply because I myself am caught in it."),[33] there remains the question of the woman spectator's pleasure in the classical film, the woman now, which raises all the problems of identification just outlined. Understanding the determinants of the pleasure a woman can take in specific fictional situations is important both in itself and insofar as many filmmakers working as feminists are experimenting with the possibilities of narrative form. The direction of Bellour's analyses, although leading to a deterministic view of the function of women in classical film (which has not yet been acknowledged adequately within film theory) is also a beginning. The very preciseness of his work on identification, vision and pleasure might be the basis for continued work on the classical film from the point of view of its undeniable potential for arousing pleasure in women spectators—perhaps including, or perhaps aside from, the woman's masochism and/or sadism which Bellour quickly introduces into the discussion in the interview to explain the woman's pleasure (p. 195). It seems probable that this research will begin by attempting to find a more complex view of identification through analyses of specific films. It is not a question of positivizing the American cinema, but of understanding its mechanisms by coming to terms with our relationship as spectators and film analysts to it and to the seductiveness of the image in general.

Notes

1.   Roland Barthes, "From Work to Text," *Image, Music, Text* trans. Stephen Heath (New York: Hill and Wang, 1977), p. 157.

2.   Barthes also refers to these codes as (a) the code of actions, the voice of empirics, the proairetic code; (b) the hermeneutic code, the voice of truth; (c) the symbolic field; (d) cultural or referential code, voice of science, the gnomic code; (e) semes or connotative signifieds, voice of the person. (From the "Summary of Contents" of *S/Z*, pp. 261–63.)

3.   To make this comparison about methods of interpretation is not to suggest that the aims of Freud and Barthes are the same. The systematics of Freud's interpretations help to substantiate his description of mental processes; at the same time, his theories of mental processes serve an explanatory function within the interpretations. Freud's theories are among several systems of explanation used by Barthes, whose emphasis is on the multiple systems of meaning potentially operating in a text, rather than in the text as a symptom of mental process.

4.   Without going into an extensive explanation, suffice it to say that what Barthes means by code in *S/Z* would correspond to something like a bundle of codes in Metz's sense. It is also important to notice that the *grand syntagmatique* is distinct from the other codes Metz discusses in that it is a system with all its component parts known. Any actual syntagm will correspond to one of the types of the *grand syntagmatique*. This is *not* true of the codes of lighting, camera movement, or point of view shots, for example.

5.   Metz can summarize the textual system of *Intolerance* as follows:

> No matter what its (conscious or unconscious) motivations, the system of *Intolerance* is defined by the close association, which it makes itself, between a certain use of parallel montage and a certain manner of understanding fanaticism. . . . What is distinctive in the system of *Intolerance* is neither the parallel montage nor the humanitarian ideology, both of which appear elsewhere, nor even a unique use of parallel montage or a unique version of the humanitarian ideology, for nowhere (and above all not in *Intolerance*) can one find one without the other, the active fashioning of one by the other, the exact point—the only point—where these two structures succeed, in every sense of the word, in "working" together. (*Language and Cinema*, pp. 110 and 112.)

A series of shorter examples of textual systems follow, for example:

> —Reflections on memory, on forgetfulness *and* circular construction with the omnipresence of the "chronological" in montage, in the varieties of photographic exposition and luminosity: *Hiroshima mon amour* by Alain Resnais (p. 113).

6.   See my interview with Raymond Bellour, in particular the section, "Segmentation and *La Grande Syntagmatique*," "Alternation, Segmentation, Hypnosis," *Camera Obscura* nos. 3–4 (Summer, 1979).

7.   See, for example, Metz's revision of his notion of textual system in "The Imaginary Signifier," where he writes of the close relationship of his work with the textual analyses of Bellour and Kuntzel, with whom he edited *Communications* 23 (*Psychanalyse et Cinéma*), where the article was published along with Bellour's "Le blocage symbolique" and Kuntzel's "Le travail du film, II." See also the introductory chapter to Bellour's *L'Analyse du film* which is a history of the development of the textual analysis of films in France, again stressing the interrelationship between his work and that of Metz and Kuntzel, to whom the book is dedicated.

8.   See the last section of the interview with Bellour.

9.   *Cahiers du Cinéma* collective text, "John Ford's *Young Mr. Lincoln*," *Screen* (autumn, 1972), pp. 5–44; originally published in August–September 1970, *Cahiers du Cinéma* 223; "*Morocco* de Josef von Sternberg," *Cahiers du Cinéma* 225 (novembre-decembre, 1970), pp. 5–13.

Jean-Louis Comolli and François Géré, "Deux fictions de la haine: 1) *Les bourreaux meurent aussi* (*Hangmen Also Die*)," *Cahiers du Cinéma* 286 (mars, 1978); 2) "*To Be or Not To Be* (part 1)," *Cahiers du Cinéma* 288 (mai, 1978); 3) "*To Be or Not To Be* (part 2)," *Cahiers du Cinéma* 290–291 (juillet-août, 1978). Comolli and Géré, a historian, are collaborating on a book on Renoir's *La Marseillaise* and the Popular Front. They presented some of this work at the Centre univérsitaire américain du cinéma in Paris in the spring of 1978.

Jacques Aumont, "Un rêve soviétique," *Cahiers du Cinéma* 271 (novembre, 1976), pp.

26–44. Aumont, Eisenstein's principle French translator, has also just published an important study of Eisenstein's films, *Montage Eisenstein* (Paris: Editions Albatros, 1979).

Claude Bailble, Michel Marie and Marie-Claire Ropars, *Muriel* (Paris: Ed. Galilée, 1974).

Pierre Sorlin and Marie-Claire Ropars, *Ecriture et Idéologie I: Analyse filmique d'Octobre d'Eisenstein* (Paris: Editions Albatros, 1976).

Many more articles are listed in Roger Odin's *Dix années d'analyses textuelles de films: Bibliographie analytique* (1977).

10.   Kristin Thompson and David Bordwell, "Space and Narrative in the Films of Ozu," *Screen* (summer, 1976), pp. 41–73.

Edward Branigan, "The Space of Equinox Flower," *Screen* (summer, 1976), pp. 74–105.

Standish Lawder, *The Cubist Cinema* (New York: New York University Press, 1975).

11.   The mimeographed translation is available for the price of postage from the British Film Institute, 127 Charing Cross Road, London WC 2, England. It lacks the frame enlargements and diagram of the set which were published with the article in *Cahiers du Cinéma* and which are reprinted here.

12.   The classical American cinema is, generally speaking, the Hollywood cinema of the 30s, 40s and 50s. The codes or conventions which are characteristic of this cinema are the object of the textual analyses of Bellour, Kuntzel and Heath, among others, and of Metz's semiology. See the interview with Bellour for the relationship between the classical cinema and the 19th century novel.

13.   Raymond Bellour, "*The Birds*: Analysis of a Sequence," BFI mimeographed translation, p. 1. (See note 11 above.)

14.   "Hence the rather precise word 'rhyme' which I have used exclusively to denote very powerful formal homologies," Ibid., p. 1.

15.   Christian Metz, "Ponctuations et démarcations dans le film de diégèse," *Essais sur la signification au cinéma, II* (Paris: Klincksieck, 1973), especially pp. 126–29.

16.   Scene, sequence and segment are used interchangeably at various points of Bellour's work. That is to say that unless the term is specified further, it is not meant to refer to a specific unit of Metz's *grande syntagmatique*. However as basic units of narration, as are Metz's various types of syntagmas, they are distinguished by Bellour from the "fragment" which does not have any analytical status but designates an arbitrarily broken-off "piece." Although he called the article on *The Birds* "Analysis of a Sequence" when he published it, Bellour now calls it the analysis of a fragment in keeping with the above distinction. The basic units of narration are determined in accordance with the criteria Metz outlined in "Ponctuation et démarcation dans le film de diégèse." See, for example, Bellour's "To Analyze, To Segment," pp. 336–37.

17.   The translation provided by the BFI does not include the frame enlargements which were published with the article in *Cahiers du Cinéma*.

18.   Raymond Bellour, "Le blocage symbolique," *Communications* 23 (Paris: Seuil, 1975), p. 235; "Psychosis, Neurosis, Perversion," *Camera Obscura/3–4*, p. 106.

19.   For a more extended analysis of Hitchcock's appearances, see "Hitchcock, The Enunciator," *Camera Obscura/2* (fall, 1977), pp. 72–78.

20.   For explanations of the Oedipus complex and the castration complex, see the entries in J. Laplanche and J.-B. Pontalis, eds., *The Language of Psychoanalysis* (New York: W. W. Norton, 1973).

21.   Kari Hanet's summary of the article in the *Edinburgh '76 Magazine* ("Bellour on *North by Northwest*," pp. 43–49) doesn't give an adequate sense that the formal analysis of the cornfield sequence balances and is a necessary complement to Bellour's description of Thornhill's Oedipal trajectory on the level of the plot (the signifieds). Unfortunately, it also gives the impression of dogmatism, whereas the French version (which is 100 pages long as opposed to the six page summary) is always carefully nuanced and more suggestive than insistent on the ultimate

significance of the narrative details taken individually. For a partial account of the analysis of the cornfield sequence, see Jacqueline Rose, "Paranoia and the Film System," *Screen* (winter, 1976/77), pp. 85–104. This article is reprinted in Chapter 10 of this book.

22.   It is this point which interests Jacqueline Rose in "Paranoia and the Film System," see especially pp. 145–48 in this book.

23.   Compare these processes of identification to the two forms of scopophilia (active and passive) which Laura Mulvey describes after Freud in "Visual Pleasure and Narrative Cinema," *Screen* (autumn, 1975), pp. 8–10. This article is reprinted in Chapter 4.

24. .   Please refer to the frame enlargements in *Camera Obscura2*, pp. 88–91.

25.   See Christian Metz, "The Imaginary Signifier," *Screen* (summer, 1975), especially pp. 67–75.

26.   E.g. the murder of the rapist in *Blackmail* or in *Shadow of a Doubt*, the niece Charlie pushing her uncle Charlie off the train as he is trying to kill her by pushing her off the train, a tour de force of narrative doubling. In *Marnie* "the theft displays itself as the other side of sex: the woman's reply to the aggression, perpetuated through the image, which she experiences as object" (p. 70). See also "Hitchcock, The Enunciator," p. 79 and "Psychosis, Neurosis, Perversion," p. 112.

27.   Bellour's footnote following this passage reads: "*Marnie* in this respect deals with the reappropriation of the image, whereas *Psycho* deals with its destruction." "Psychosis, Neurosis, Perversion," p. 128.

28.   Proposing the Oedipal phantasies of the American classical cinema in terms of wish-fulfillment may be something of a response to the beginning of Jacqueline Rose's "Paranoia and the Film System": "This paper emerges from the need to query a semiotic practice which assimilates its own systematicity to an institutionalized psychoanalytic exigency—integration into the Symbolic through a successful Oedipal trajectory" (p. 141 in this book).

29.   See also his article on Dumas, "Un jour, la castration," *L'Arc 71* (1978), pp. 9–23.

30.   "Psychosis, Neurosis, Perversion," p. 121.

31.   This is one of the main points Elisabeth Lyon takes up in her study of Marguerite Duras's *India Song*, "The Cinema of Lol V. Stein," *Camera Obscura*, no. 6 (fall 1980); also in this volume, Chapter 15. For the definition of phantasy in this technical sense, see *The Language of Psycho-Analysis*, pp. 314–19.

> Phantasy: Imaginary scene in which the subject is a protagonist, representing the fulfillment of a wish (in the last analysis, an unconscious wish) in a manner that is distorted to a greater or lesser extent by defensive processes. . . . (a) Even where they can be summed up in a single sentence, phantasies are still scripts (*scénarios*) of organized scenes which are capable of dramatization—usually in visual form; (b) The subject is invariably present in these scenes . . ., (c) It is not an *object* that the subject imagines and aims at, so to speak, but rather a *sequence* in which the subject has his own part to play and in which permutations of roles and attributions are possible. . . . (d) In so far as desire is articulated in this way through phantasy, phantasy is also the locus of defensive operations: it facilitates the most primitive of defense processes, such as turning round upon the subject's own self, reversal into the opposite, negation and projection. (e) Such defenses are themselves inseparably bound up with the primary function of phantasy, namely the mise en scène of desire—a mise en scène in which what is prohibited (*l'interdit*) is always present in the actual formation of the wish (pp. 314 and 318).

See also Catherine Clément, "De la méconnaissance: fantasme, texte, scène," *Langages 31* (septembre, 1973).

32.   "Such (to complete the psychiatrist's speech) might be the motivations behind the genealogy of the case: the reiterative passage from the former murder (that of the mother) to the murder of Marion of which Norman-the mother is the agent, emphasizing in both cases, given an original identificatory fantasy, the literally impossible desire for possession and fusion that is at stake" (pp. 119–20).

33.   See the interview, p. 95.

11

Alternation, Segmentation, Hypnosis: Interview with Raymond Bellour—An Excerpt

Janet Bergstrom

Fictional Representation, the Woman's Symbolic Position, Enunciation

Janet Bergstrom: Already in the collective book *Le Western* (1966), while other contributors chose elements like "Indian attack," "sheriff's office," "fistfight," "gambler," or "ranch" to discuss and place, of the many elements in the "*Mythologies*" section of the book, you chose to write about "woman." And in this article one finds already closely linked an analysis of the woman's symbolic position as crucial in determining the narrative structure, the system of fictional representation carried over from the 19th century novel, and enunciation as the *principe producteur* of the narrative. Could you sketch the development of this matrix of interests, perhaps in terms of your ideas about what constitutes a textual system, throughout your work?

Raymond Bellour: Your question gives a lot of importance, retrospectively, to a quite modest and by now very old article in which I tried to set up a kind of comparative chart of the great feminine figures brought into play by the western. It seemed to us at the time that one way to get closer to the stylistic and ideological reality of the genre was to bring together a set of partial approaches, in a manner somewhat inspired by the example of Barthes's analyses of socio-cultural reality in his *Mythologies*.

I've been particularly interested in the problem of the representation of the woman, which is much more than a mere mythology among others. I was struck by a statement of Anthony Mann's: "In fact a woman is always added to the story because without women a western wouldn't work." This remark touches on something very profound. On the one hand it conforms with the purely historical fact that there were women in the West, that the economic, territorial and family system obviously required the presence of women, since what was involved was the creation of a society. But Mann's remark also tells us something much more important: namely, that the narrative couldn't function if this place assigned to the woman in the diegesis and in the representation of society weren't at the same time metaphoric, that is a place which assigns to her a specific role in the set of representations organized by the film.

Janet Bergstrom: And it's the woman's symbolic role that gives her this structural importance.

Raymond Bellour: Yes, and we must specify exactly what that means. Going back to the example of the western there is thus a whole organized circuit of feminine representations (the young heroine, the mother, the saloon girl, the wife, etc.) without which the film cannot function—in two ways, which articulate the two places, real and metaphorical, that I've talked about. On the one hand, the function of the woman in the organization and the motivations of the narrative is far more determining than is often thought (examples: in *The Searchers*, it's the kidnapping of a little girl by the Indians which gets the narrative started and which sustains it to the end; in *The Naked Spur*, it's the presence of Janet Leigh at Robert Ryan's side which determines, as much and even more than the reward on his head, the vicissitudes and above all the final twist of the scenario). On the other hand, the western is subtended from one end to the other by what one can all the problematic of marriage. If you think about it, you notice that after a certain situation posed at the start as a problem or as an enigma, the film gradually leads to a final solution which allows the more or less conflicting terms posed at the beginning to be resolved, and which in the majority of cases takes the form of a marriage. I've gradually come to think that this pattern organizes—indeed, constitutes—the classical American cinema as a whole, but I first became aware of it through the western, where one might have thought a priori that it played a less determining role. If you take westerns as different as those of John Ford and Anthony Mann, Samuel Fuller or Delmer Daves, you notice that the problematic of the formation of the couple is absolutely central in all of them (in *The Searchers*, there is the marriage of Jeffrey Hunter and Vera Miles, and in *The Naked Spur*, the marriage of James Stewart and Janet Leigh).

Let's take for example William Wyler's *The Westerner*. It shows very well how the territorial formation of Texas is absolutely determined by the formation of the couple. The segmentation (*découpage*) in the film carries the repetition-resolution effect to an exemplary point. First shot: a map of Texas, in a fixed shot. Last shot: another map of Texas, starting from which a backward camera movement discloses the conjugal bedroom where the heroine is moving toward the window, followed by her young husband who is holding her by the waist—the wild, untamed hero whose matrimonial education is the subject of the film. The hero's fate is shaped by the feminine figure, but only to the extent that the representations organized around this figure allow for the two of them to be inscribed together in a symbolic framework.

Janet Bergstrom: And these symbolic representations are linked, in your opinion, to a system of representations which constitute the 19th century novel?

Raymond Bellour: Indisputably. It has often been said, generally speaking, that the classical American cinema continued in the 20th century the great tradition of the 19th century European novel. But once you have pointed out that filiation, which is obvious . . .

Janet Bergstrom: By obvious you mean . . .

Raymond Bellour: I mean that the American cinema, like the 19th century novel, very clearly sets into play an art of narrative founded on representation, conflict, enigma, hermeneutics, suspense, all the things that Barthes defined so well in *S/Z*. That's why, incidentally, so many 19th century novels have been able to be adapted directly to the screen by the American cinema, without for a moment breaking the continuity with films adapted from recent works or made from original scenarios, which on the whole continue to belong to this tradition. What we must try to understand is the basis of this filiation, which is manifested by a certain formal unity in the broadest sense, in the functioning of the textual systems. (We should obviously, if we want a minimum of precision, qualify things here quite a bit. The first thing is to understand that from the novel to the cinema there occurs a kind of displacement: film comes to satisfy a general demand for narrativity which the novel today fulfills only in part, which it has turned away from—at least the more serious novels have—even if it continues to serve it. Next, this displacement is effected at the price of a certain levelling of the text which is clear in the adaptations of the great classical novels. The novels are in fact more diversified, more different from each other than the films. The American cinema is a machine of great homogeneity, due to its mode of production which is both mechanical and industrial. In this sense it exists at the level of maximum narrativity which in the 19th century was that of the serialized novel—the latter being precisely the point at which literature became an industry.)

But it nevertheless remains true that we can speak of a profound unity, founded on a general system of fiction, between the 19th century novel and the classical cinema (above all the American cinema). This unity seems to me to be due essentially to a certain type of articulation between the imaginary and the symbolic as it has been systematically elaborated by Freudian and Lacanian psychoanalysis, starting with the socio-historical situation opened up by the simultaneous development of the bourgeoisie, of industrial capitalism and of the nuclear family. This unity, this very strong articulation between the American cinema and the 19th century novel, seems to me therefore to be the result of a general, socially and historically determined phenomenon of representation founded on a scenarization of the psychic conflicts caused by the massive presence of the Oedipus complex and the castration complex. That's why this scenarization is organized around a very insistent and very strong representation of the feminine figure, starting from the relatively new situation of difference and identity, or what I call the structure of narcissistic reduplication, which, since the 19th century, has manifestly ruled over the relations between the two sexes.

Desire and the Law in the Western

Janet Bergstrom: In your essays in *Le Western* you weren't yet speaking from within a psychoanalytic framework. Since your analysis of *The Birds* (1969) you have become increasingly taken within the interests you are talking about now. Could we go back a few steps?

Raymond Bellour: Well, to try and clarify things a bit I'll start with an example that will be a good link between the two, since it's a western: it's once again *The Westerner*. Just now we saw how the film is organized around a territorial path: that of the couple, which represents as such both Texas (it occupies a parcel of Texas land) and more generally the United States, or the national community that Texas represents. But this parcel of land can be materially occupied by the couple only if it is occupied symbolically. Obviously, that's the basic thing. Let's try to see what it means. The film brings into play four characters: the hero, Cole Martin (Gary Cooper), the judge, Roy Bean (Walter Brennan), and two women—Lily Langtree (Lilian Bond), a famous actress in the West, and the heroine Janet Ellen Mathews (Doris Davenport), who will become Cole's wife at the end of the film. What is the condition that makes the final marriage possible? That is really the question asked by the film. We can answer it as follows: at the end, the hero must accept as his own a positive relationship between desire and the law; that means that he must accept the woman, who is the object of desire, but without eluding the threat of castration that looms doubly, in her and through the father.

The hero: an adventurer, apparently outside desire and outside the law. When the film opens he is about to be condemned to death for the theft of a horse that he didn't steal by the Judge Roy Bean who represents the derision of the law, the law as unrestrained and non-symbolized desire. The young woman, who tries to testify on behalf of the hero, can do nothing against the speedy justice of Roy Bean: she is one of the farmers terrorized by the judge (he prevents them from farming so that he can have grazing land for his herds, acquired by a series of thefts). One thing alone saves Cole: Roy Bean's passion for Lily Langtree, whose posters cover the walls of the saloon. Cole claims he knows her and that he owns a lock of her hair, which he holds out as a bait for the judge. Here the narrative substitutes the two women for each other: to make good on his promise to the judge, Cole asks Ellen on one of his visits to her to give him a lock of her hair which he cuts off with a great stroke of the scissors. In return, he makes the judge promise to respect the farmers' land. This pact, once it's sealed, accelerates the formation of the couple: first kiss of Cole and Ellen. But in vain: Roy Bean burns down the farmland and Ellen's father dies in the fire at his farm. Cole is then obliged to resolve the terms of the conflict by choosing his side. To that end the narrative uses a show given by Lily Langtree in the next town. The judge, dressed in full military uniform and thus carrying to its extreme the derision of the law, has bought up all the seats so that he can be the only spectator at the show. But instead of Lily, it's Cole who appears on stage when the curtain rises. Gunfight: the judge is fatally wounded. Cole carries him to Lily's dressing room so that he can pay her his respects; her idealized image gradually fades out to signify his death. Total fadeout, followed by the reappearance of the couple in the conjugal bedroom.

Why this narrative logic, why this play of relations and substitutions, if not to allow the hero to stabilize his desire, which functions in relation to the woman, the image of the woman, within a social and historical space. On the one hand, Cole must find himself inscribed within a filiation over which he must triumph: that is why his relationship with Roy Bean, placed under the sign of a confrontation between men (drinking bouts, fistfights) is metaphorically marked as a father-son relationship (Roy Bean constantly refers to Cole as "son"). The bad father (the idealized father according to Freud and Lacan) must die, in the final confrontation, so that the couple can be formed; he even has his double, his reverse image: the good father (Ellen's father, the dead father, the symbolic father according to Lacan), who makes possible the entry into the genealogy, the continuity between generations. On the other hand, the two women must be identical through the metaphor of the lock of hair: the actress, a double image comprising both lawless sexuality and extreme idealization (in the sense in which Freud speaks of it in the chapter on "Love and Hypnosis" in *Group Psychology and the Analysis of the Ego*), the woman as the very image of castration; and the heroine who reverses the image, through whom the masculine subject will find, in contrast, the positivity of a regulated sexuality and a measured idealization, the woman who permits the fixation of his desire—in a word its symbolization—through the conjunction of his entry into the social order and the internalized, finally

The Westerner (William Wyler, 1940)

bearable image of his own castration. It's the movement from the adventurer, lawless and faithless as we say in French (*sans foi ni loi*), to the husband, the future father and good citizen. (In this case we have a film with a "happy ending." But even films that "turn out badly," either because of internal tension within the couple or through a romantic idealization of the ill-starred lovers, are obviously complementary forms of the same problematic.)

This type of progression, which I've of course outlined much too quickly in a film like *The Westerner*, seemed to me exemplary when I saw the film for the first time two years ago. But I think that it struck me so strongly only because I had gradually realized by then that the majority of American films were thoroughly subject to a kind of symbolic pressure. The American cinema thus finds itself enacting, in what is at once a very direct and indirect way, the most classic paradigms elaborated for the subject of Western culture by Freudian psychoanalysis. Its massive attempt at socio-historical representation is basically shaped by the type of subjectivity, and above all by the type of scenarization of subjectivity, whose logic was first recognized and imposed by psychoanalysis.

My constant surprise, while I was working on *North by Northwest*, was to discover to what degree everything was organized according to a classic Oedipal scenario which inscribed the subject, the hero of the film, in a precise position in relation to parricide and incest, and to observe that his itinerary, his trajectory—that is, the succession of actions which constitute the film—corresponded to a strict psychic progression and had as their function to engage the hero in the symbolic paths of Oedipus and of castration: namely, in this instance, to make him accept the symbolization of the death of the father, the displacement from the attachment to the mother to the attachment to another woman. Which simply means accepting the place of the subject in the Western family as it massively constituted itself during the 19th century. And what strikes me as absolutely fundamental in this perspective is that the American cinema is entirely dependent, as is psychoanalysis, on a system of representations in which the woman occupies a central place only to the extent that it's a place assigned to her by the logic of masculine desire.

The Woman's Symbolic Position, Enunciation, the Logic of Masculine Desire

Janet Bergstrom: It was that aspect you concentrated on in your analyses of *Marnie* and *Psycho*.

Raymond Bellour: Yes. In these two analyses (the first segments of *Marnie* and *Psycho* as a whole), I tried to assess how, in two films in which women occupy a central place (Marnie is the heroine, and Janet Leigh is the star of *Psycho*), this place was determined by properly filmic means according to a very precise logic of enunciation: the same logic which in classical psychoanalysis is founded on a necessary differentiation between masculine and feminine sexuality, in order to finally fall back on the dominant model of masculine sexuality.

This gets crystallized in a particularly striking way in Hitchcock's films, but I think it's a determining factor in the America cinema as a whole. Of course one would have to draw fine distinctions between specific directors, genres, periods or films. But a number of precise analyses (of Hawks's films, of Minnelli, of Lang, of westerns, of musical comedies, of horror films, films of the fantastic, etc.) show clearly that the central place assigned to the woman is a place where she is figured, represented, inscribed in the fiction through the logical necessity of a general representation of the subject of desire in the film, who is always, first and last, a masculine subject.

Janet Bergstrom: And more and more you mark that subject as the enunciator.

Raymond Bellour: The term "enunciator" as I use it marks both the person who possesses the right of speech within the film, and the source (*instance*) toward which the series of representations is logically channelled back. Metz has very rightly invoked, as far as the Hollywood film or fiction film is concerned, Benveniste's distinction between story (*histoire*) and discourse (*discours*), and he has shown that the fiction film is a film that always tends to disguise itself as story by effacing its own marks of enunciation. But I think it's important to point out that this effacement, which can be more or less strong (in American cinema, it's probably least strong in the films of Hitchcock), is precisely the means, at once subtle and powerful, whereby a very strongly marked process of enunciation manifests itself, which defines and structures a certain subject of desire.

Janet Bergstrom: You might say that there are three levels operating here: first, the male characters within Hitchcock's films who very often act as relays for his point of view (as you show in your analysis of *Marnie*); second, Hitchcock as enunciator, *le sujet du désir du film, le sujet masculin,* the director; third, the male film analyst. Would you agree that, at a second remove from the fiction, you as the male film analyst continue this same fascination with a particular logic of desire and the law, which continues to accord the woman a place only insofar as she is an accessory to the male's Oedipal trajectory?

Raymond Bellour: That's a very difficult question—first because it's difficult in itself, second because it hides a trap.

Janet Bergstrom: I'm asking about your motivation because I can't imagine a woman carrying out an analysis like "*Le blocage symbolique,*" that is, having the same investment in following step by step, in minute detail, the Oedipal trajectory of the male hero. The desire to carry out the analysis must be linked to the logic of the enunciation as you construct it, or perhaps reconstruct it. You must have an interest in interrogating this *sujet du désir du film.*

Raymond Bellour: Obviously. That's exactly what I had in mind when I chose the words *blocage symbolique* (symbolic blocking) as a title, for they try to delimit the effect of endless interlocking and reflection which gets established between the different levels and the different dimensions of the filmic text, thus conferring a maximum textual expansion of the psychic trajectory of the hero. If I've wanted to go to the furthest possible point in understanding the power and subtlety of this textual pressure, it's quite simply because I myself am caught in it. It was as the subject whose desire is the prisoner of this machinery that I tried to demonstrate its functioning. In this sense the desire to analyze cannot help but manifest a certain ambiguity, since the analysis repeats the movement of the film in order to understand it, until inevitably it sets up a kind of second *blocage* in the writing itself, in the systematicity of the analysis. But in another sense it's also the only condition under which a certain *déblocage* (unblocking) can really occur, for me: by showing, in a way at once broad and precise, how and why and to what points this *blocage* occurs.

Oedipus and Castration

Janet Bergstrom: In the recent article on Dumas published in *L'Arc* ("Un jour, la castration"), you made a distinction between two Oedipal structures: (1) the structure which is the basis of human society, the universal prohibition on incest; and (2) the structure which psychoanalysis accounts for and which motivates the systems of representation that constitute the 19th century novel and classical film. You become increasingly critical of this second "complex."

Raymond Bellour: My studies of certain 19th century literary works (in particular the Brontës and Dumas's cycle of novels on pre-revolutionary and revolutionary France: *Joseph Balsamo, Le Collier de la reine, Ange Pitou, La Comtesse de Charny*) enabled me to understand and to experience concretely how during the 19th century a set of representations became elaborated largely founded, for a variety of historical reasons, on a profound transformation of the status of subjectivity. (This point is borne out not only by Foucault's "archeological" works but by the works of historians of collective mentalities and representations such as Philippe Ariès, Norbert Elias, or Jean-Yves Guiomar). This involves at the same time what seems to me a major reversal as far as psychoanalysis is concerned: to work in a psychoanalytic perspective on texts that more or less immediately precede the moment when psychoanalysis itself makes it appearance and becomes constituted allows one to understand psychoanalysis historically, to effect certain cleavages, to relativize the basic postulates which in psychoanalysis are endowed with a transcendental value of retrospective and atemporal truth. It especially allows one to see the Oedipus complex, and the castration complex which is linked to it, in a historical dimension. In this sense my work is part of a more general movement taking place in France, characterized by a certain putting into question and putting into perspective of psychoanalysis. One finds this in various forms and above all in various "tones" in the work of Deleuze and Guattari, Foucault, and Castel, as well as in a feminist like Luce Irigaray, all of whom are attempting to question the status of psychoanalysis in order to understand how we find ourselves today in a society where it has taken on such importance. What I try to do in this book on Dumas is to understand the historical crystallization of a certain number of representations which from the 19th century on became increasingly internalized, in particular the representations tied to the problematic of the family and to the imaginary relationship between the sexes.

Janet Bergstrom: Although you are critical of this system of symbolic representations, when I read your articles, I feel a greater and greater sense of claustrophobia and frustration at being trapped within your reconstruction of it. As a consequence, it is hard to see what future textual analyses of classical film could bring, in your view, to an understanding of how women function there since all possibilities collapse into one: the woman plays one or another role with respect to the male hero as he works through his conflicts about desire and the law.

Raymond Bellour: How can I answer you? It seems to me that the classical American cinema is founded on a systematicity which operates very precisely at the expense of the woman, if one can put it that way, by determining her image, her images, in relation to the desire of the masculine subject who thus defines himself through this determination. Which means that the woman too finds herself involved, for herself, in relation to desire and the law, but in a perspective which always collapses the representations of the two sexes into the dominant logic of a single one. If women want to and are able to do analyses of these films and find representations both of themselves and of the relations between the sexes which will satisfy them, by all means let them do so: I would be very eager to see the results, even though I can't help feeling a bit skeptical. The great American fiction films constitute a universe with which I felt and still feel completely taken and fascinated, even if it's in a different way. "I loved the cinema. I don't love it anymore. I love it still."— that's what Metz used to say, most aptly, in trying to situate in a general way his relationship to the cinema-object and the place of theoretical work in the management of this relationship. Analysis has been for me a kind of distantiation, a disentangling of the fascination, which can only be effected through the reconstruction of what founds it, that is the reality of *blocage* in the very power of its textual development. If you, as a woman, don't find you have a place in this, I can perfectly well understand it. But you ought to ask yourself about what seems to attract you too so strongly in these films, and also about the attention you accord to my work. To put it a bit hastily, for of course things are somewhat more complicated than that, I think that a woman can love, accept and give a positive value to these films only from her own masochism, and from a certain sadism that she can exercise in return on the masculine subject, within a system loaded with traps. All of which is far from being negligible!

Janet Bergstrom: I can see how this follows from your line of reasoning, but I think the play of identifications in classical film allows for more possibilities than that. (See Chapter 9 in this book.)

12

Caught and *Rebecca*: The Inscription of Femininity as Absence

Mary Ann Doane

Historically, Hitchcock's *Rebecca* (1940) and Ophuls's *Caught* (1949) bracket a decade in which many films were aimed at a predominantly female audience. They are instances of a broad category of films frequently referred to as the "woman film" or "womans' picture." This label implies that the films are in some sense the "possesson" of women and that their terms of address are dictated by the anticipated presence of the female spectator. Both presuppositions are problematic in light of contemporary film theory's investigation of positions offered by the film to the spectator—an investigation which stresses psychical mechanisms related primarily to the male spectator—voyeurism, fetishism, even identification. In this context, Hollywood narratives are analyzed as compensatory structures designed to defend the male psyche against the threat offered by the image of the woman. A crucial unresolved issue here is the very possibility of constructing a "female spectator," given the cinema's appeal to (male) voyeurism and fetishism.

Nevertheless addressing themselves to the perhaps illusory female spectator, the "women's films" are based on an idea of female fantasy which they themselves anticipate and in some sense construct. Interestingly, the problematic of female fantasy is most frequently compatible with that of persecution—by husband, family, or lover (both *Rebecca* and *Caught* can be aligned with this description). The films manifest an obsession with certain psychical mechanisms which have been associated with the female (chiefly masochism, hysteria, and paranoia). All of them attempt in some way to trace female subjectivity and desire. Nevertheless, because this attempt is made within the traditional forms and conventions of Hollywood narrative—forms which cannot sustain such an exploration—certain contradictions within patriarchal ideology become apparent. This makes the films particularly valuable for a feminist analysis of the way in which the "woman's story" is told.

Caught and *Rebecca* are especially interesting, even exemplary, because each of them contains a scene in which the camera almost literally enacts the repression of the feminine—the woman's relegation to the status of a signifier within the male discourse. The camera movements in these scenes can be described as hysterical—frantically searching for, retracing the path of, the lost object, attempting to articulate what is, precisely, not there. As such, the camera movements have the status of symptoms. The symptom gives access to, makes readable, the work of repression and hence indicates the process of transition from one system in the apparatus to another. In a way, the symptom can be seen as manifesting the severity of the repression or the force of the energy attached to the repressed idea which "breaks through" to the surface. In film theory and criticism, this scenario provides a means of accounting for perversion within the norm by positing the paradoxical possibility of the "hysterical classical text."[1] The hysteria frequently attributed to the female protagonist in the "woman's film" proliferates, effecting a more general "hystericization" of the text as body of signifiers.

It is quite appropriate that Laura Mulvey, in her influential essay on visual pleasure, limits her discussion to a Hollywood Cinema populated by male protagonists acting as relays in a complex process designed to insure the ego-fortification of the male spectator.[2] Yet there is a sense in which the "woman's film" attempts to constitute itself as the mirror image of this dominant cinema, obsessively centering and recentering a female protagonist. It thus offers resistance to an analysis which stresses the "to-be-looked-at-ness" of the woman, her objectification as spectacle according to the masculine structure of the gaze. Hence it becomes crucial in an investigation of the "woman's film" to trace the vicissitudes of the process of specularization. One assumption behind the positing of a female spectator (that is, one who does not assume a masculine position with respect to the reflected image of her own body) is that it is no longer necessary to invest the look with desire in quite the same way. A certain despecularization takes place in these films, a deflection of scopophilic energy in other directions. The aggressivity which, as Jacqueline Rose has demonstrated,[3] is contained in the cinematic structuration of the look is released or, more accurately, transformed into a narrativized paranoia (most apparent in films tinged by the gothic such as *Rebecca, Gaslight,* and *Dragonwyck* where it is a question of the husband's murderous designs, but also evident in *Caught*). This sub-class of the "woman's film" clearly activates the latent paranoia of the film system described by Rose.

Thus the metaphor of paranoia may prove even more appropriate for a delineation of the "woman's film" than that of hysteria. As Freud points out in his analysis of Dr. Schreber, whose most striking symptom is his assumption of the position body of the woman, paranoia is systematically disintegrative.[4] Hysteria condenses, paranoia decomposes. In this respect, both *Caught* and *Rebecca*, by privileging moments in which the cinematic apparatus itself undergoes a process of decomposition, situate themselves as paranoid texts. Both films contain scenes of projection in which the image as lure and trap is externalized in relation to the woman. The films dis-articulate the components of the apparatus which construct the woman as "imaged"—camera, projector, and screen—and incorporates them within the diegesis as props. In this *mise-en-scène* of cinematic elements, camera, projector and screen are explicitly activated as agents of narrativity, as operators of the image.

Yet, this gesture of disarticulation does not preclude an elaboration of the woman's relation to spectacle. In fact, the desire of the woman in both films is to duplicate a given image, to engage with and capture the male gaze. In *Caught*, the image is that of a woman in a mink coat; *Rebecca*, that of "a woman of thirty-six dressed in black satin with a string of pearls." And in both films, movie projection scenes act to negate each of these appropriations of an image, to effect a separation on both literal and figurative levels between the woman and the image of her desire (always situated as a desire to be desired or desirable, hence as subordinate).

The background of the credit sequence in *Caught* is constituted by a series of pages in a fashion magazine, slowly flipped over in synchronization with credit changes to reveal women posing in front of monuments and art works, women posing in the latest fashions (stills 1–2). Merging with the body proper of the film, this background becomes the first shot, its incorporation within the diegesis signaled by the addition of voice-over and pointing fingers, metonymic signifiers of female desire (stills 3–5). The voices-over—"I'll take this one," "That one," "This one's for me"—are the indexical actualizations of the female appetite for the image, an appetite sustained by the commodity fetishism which supports capitalism. And the ultimate commodity, as here, is the body adorned for the gaze. The logic of this economics of desire culminates in the final magazine image of the scene, a sketch of a woman modeling a fur coat, the unmediated signifier of wealth (still 7). The camera marks its significance by tracking back at this moment (accompanied by the voice-over, "I'd rather have mink") to incorporate within its image the two women whose fantasies are complicit with the fashion industry (still 8). Signifier of economic success, the fur coat (which becomes mink, aligning itself with Leonora's desire) is the site of a certain semantic wealth in the text, re-surfacing again and again to mark the oscillations of female subjectivity. In the image, significantly, it is a sketch which replaces the human model as support of the coat. The fur coat overpowers the body, given only as trace.

The first scene initiates the trajectory along the line of an investigation of the contradictions and convolutions of female spectatorship. Owners of the look in this instance, the woman can only exercise it within a narcissistic

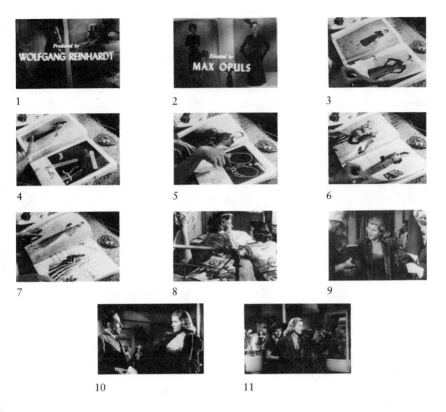

1   2   3

4   5   6

7   8   9

10   11

framework which collapses the opposition between the subject and the object of the gaze—"This one's for me." The woman's sexuality, as spectator, must undergo a constant process of transformation. She must look, as if she were a man with the phallic power of the gaze, in order to be that woman. There is a necessary movement or oscillation between the periphery of the image to its center and back again. The convolutions involved here are analogous to those described by Julia Kristeva as "the double or triple twists of what we commonly call female homosexuality": "'I am looking, as a man would for a woman': or else, "I submit myself, as if I were a man who thought he was a woman, to a woman who thinks she is a man.'"[5] For the female spectator exemplified by Maxine and Leonora in this scene, to possess the image through the gaze is to become it. The gap which strictly separates identification and desire for the male spectator (whose possession of the cinematic woman is at least partially dependent upon an identification with the male protagonist) is abolished in the case of the woman. Binding identification to desire (the basic strategy of narcissism), the teleological aim of the female look demands a becoming and hence, a dispossession. She must give up the image in order to become it—the image is *too* present for her.

And this is precisely the specular movement traced by *Caught*. Within the space of two scenes, the look is reversed—Leonora (Barbara Bel Geddes)

199

dons the mink coat and adopts the pose of the model, soliciting the gaze of both male and female spectators (stills 9–11). She now participates in the image, while her dispossession is signaled by the rhythmic chants which punctuate her turns, "$49.95 plus tax." The economics of sexual exchange are on display, for it is not only the coat which is on the market. Leonora receives an invitation to the yacht party at which she will later meet millionaire Smith Ohlrig (Robert Ryan) and, as her friend Maxine points out in the face of Leonora's resistance to the invitation, "How else do girls like us get to meet guys like Smith Ohlrig?" When Leonora actually marries Ohlrig, her transformation into the image is completed by the newspaper montage sequence announcing the wedding, framing and immobilizing her in the photograph (stills 12–14).

These three moments of the narrative trajectory—defining the woman as, successively, agent, object and text of the look—would seem to be self-contained, to exhaust the potential variations of Leonora's relation to the image. Yet, the film recovers and re-writes its own beginning in the projection scene, situating Leonora once more in the place of the spectator. But this time she is explicitly located as a spectator who refuses to see, in a cinema delimited as male. By the time of the projection scene, Leonora is fully in place: she owns the mink coat and no longer has to model it. Her alienation from the cinematic apparatus is manifested by the fact of her exclusion, her positioning on the margins of the process of imaging. The cinema which Ohlrig forces her to attend is described only as the "movies for my new project" and all of its spectators, except Leonora, are male (a situation which Leonora attempts to resist with the excuse she weakly presents to Ohlrig immediately preceding the screening, "... so many men."

The first shot of the sequence, with a marked keystone effect, presents the first image of Ohlrig's documentary, which appears to be a kind of testament to the technological power of industrial enterprise (still 15). Ohlrig positions himself as the most prominent spectator, his gaze held by the image, the projector's beam of light emanating from behind his head (stills 16–17). The images celebrating machinery and its products are, however, only a prelude to the image which really fascinates Ohlrig—his own (his excitement contained in the anticipatory voice-over which assumes the language of the cinéphile, "Wait 'til the next shot") (still 18). The relation between the image and himself is articulated at this moment by a pan rather than a cut, the camera movement apparently motivated by the shadow of a figure crossing in front of the screen to sit next to Ohlrig (stills 19–20).[6]

It is at this point—the moment of Ohlrig's most intensely narcissistic fascination—that Leonora's off-screen laugh breaks the mirror relation between Ohlrig and his image. Within this shot, Ohlrig turns to face Leonora, acting as a pivot for the displacement of the spectator's attention from the movie screen to the woman as screen. Assuming his quasi-directional power. Ohlrig stops the projector and lights Leonora, transforming her from voice

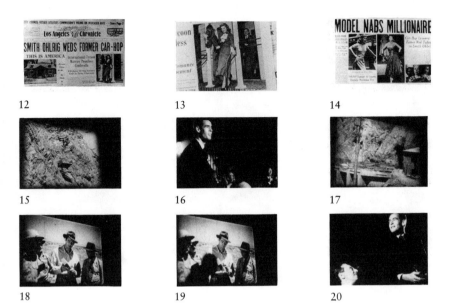

12   13   14

15   16   17

18   19   20

into image (stills 21–22). This shot imitates a shot/reverse shot series which dominates the sequence, the deployment of space inscribing a hyperbolized distance between Ohlrig and Leonora (still 23). The reverse shot here, with Leonora in the foreground on the left and Ohlrig in the background on the right, is a crucial condensation of sexual and cinematic positions and invites a number of comments. (1) The keystone effect characterizing the projected documentary image shown previously together with Leonora's placement in this shot retrospectively situate the point of view on the screen as coincident with hers. Nevertheless, both her laugh and the fact that she faces *away* from the screen indicate her refusal of this position as spectator, the marked absence of that diegetic spectatorial gaze which would double and repeat that of *Caught*'s own spectator. Leonora's glance is averted from Ohlrig and his cinema. (2) The *mise-en-scène* situates the screen directly behind Leonora's head (lending it the beatific power of a halo), just as, in the previous and following shots, the projector is situated directly behind Ohlrig's head. There is a kind of sexual cinematographic symmetry which the shot/reverse-shot sequence rigorously respects. Leonora's face emerges from the confines of the screen as though the medium had suddenly gained a three-dimensional relief. In a perverse movement, the close-up of the woman is simultaneously disengaged from the diegetic screen and returned to it. (3) The eye-lines attributed to the two characters are staggered in relation to one another. The directions of their looks are correct but the planes of the image are not (i.e. in an image with no illusion of depth, they could be, would be, looking at each other). As it is, however, Ohlrig becomes the displaced and dislocated spectator of Leonora's image, the *mise-en-scène* articulating a difficulty in the gaze.

The remaining shots of the shot/reverse-shot sequence frame a dialogue

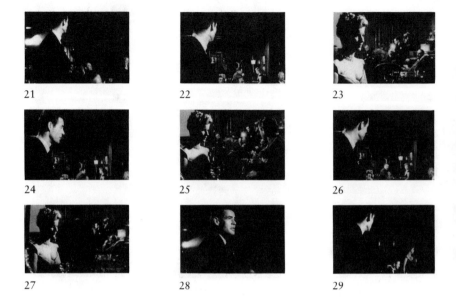

21 22 23

24 25 26

27 28 29

in which Ohlrig attempts to ascertain Leonora's guilt (stills 24–25). He immediately assumes, in paranoid fashion, that her laugh is a response to his own image—the last image of his film presented in the scene. But Leonora's guilt lies rather in not watching, in dissociating her entertainment from the screen and laughing instead at something said by the man sitting next to her. Ohlrig eliminates the competition, which is both sexual and cinematic (stills 26–27), and resumes his cinema at the expense of Leonora—blackening her image in order to start the show (still 28). Leonora, however, leaves, asserting her final alienation from his spectacle despite his orders that she stay (still 29). Invisible support of a cinema which excludes her, Leonora demonstrates by means of her exit the force of that silent complicity. For without her presence, Ohlrig cannot continue the show. After emptying the theater, he paces back and forth, his rage punctuated by the beam of the projector (stills 30–32).

The projection sequence as a whole marks an important turning point in the narrative. The interruption of the filmic flow of images within the diegesis, here as in *Rebecca*, is the metaphor for the disintegration of a short-lived family romance. Spectator of a cinema whose parameters are defined as masculine, Leonora is dispossessed of both look and voice. Yet, the trajectory which traces her dispossession in relation to the image is not completed until the end of the film. For, when Leonora leaves Ohlrig as a result of this scene, she takes a piece of the image with her—the mink coat, signifier of her continuing complicity in the process of imaging.

Hitchcock's *Rebecca* also contains a crucial scene in which the film effects a decomposition of the elements which collaborate in making the position of female spectatorship an impossible one. The home movie se-

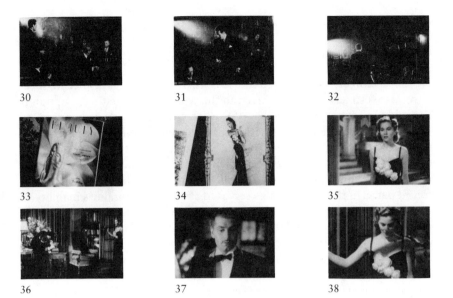

30   31   32

33   34   35

36   37   38

quence depicts a process of projection constituted as an assault on the diegetic female spectator. This scene as well is preceded by the delineation of female desire in relation to the fixed image of the fashion magazine. A preface to the projection scene, the shot of the fashion magazine whose pages are slowly turned is here unlocalized (stills 33–24). Unlike *Caught*, *Rebecca* elides the establishing shot which would identify the woman as viewer and, instead, dissolves immediately to her transformation into the image, an image she had previously promised Maxim (Laurence Olivier) she would never appropriate for herself—that of a woman "dressed in black satin with a string of pearls" (still 35). The character played by Joan Fontaine (who is never given a proper name) enters the cinema in the hope of becoming a spectacle for Maxim (stills 36–38) but is relegated to the position of spectator—spectator of the images Maxim prefers to retain of her, those taken on their honeymoon.

The length of this essay precludes the possibility of an in-depth analysis of this sequence[7] but it is necessary to make several points relating it to the sequence from *Caught*. (1) Maxim, like Ohlrig, is in control of both lighting and projection (stills 39–40), while the *mise-en-scène* frequently positions the projector or itself *between* Fontaine and Maxim as a kind of barrier or limit to their interaction (still 41). (2) The movie projected is a proper "home movie," unlike that of *Caught*, the logic of its syntax hence supposedly more arbitrary, linking disparate shots designed to capture pregnant moments for a private family history. (Maxim says at one point, "Won't our grandchildren be delighted when they see how lovely you were?") The images of Fontaine feeding geese constitute a denial of the image she has constructed for herself by means of the black evening dress, while Maxim's binoculars give him a mastery over the gaze even within the confines of the filmic image (stills 42–43).

Like *Caught*, the projected movie is interrupted twice, displacing spectatorial investment from the screen to the woman. The first interruption is caused by a film break (stills 44–45) which coincides with and appears to negate Fontaine's remark, "I wish our honeymoon could have lasted forever." When Maxim attempts to fix the film the interruption is prolonged by the entry of a servant who reveals the discovery that a china cupid is missing—a cupid Fontaine had broken and hidden earlier in the film. This forced pause in the home movies serves to emphasize Fontaine's inability to deal with the servants, to fully assume her position as mistress of Manderley, in short, to effectively replace Rebecca. The home movies are resumed but this deficiency in her image, her discomfort in the evening gown chosen to imitate Rebecca, leads to the second interruption of the screening. When Fontaine suggests that Maxim must have married her so that there would be no gossip, he abruptly walks between Fontaine and the screen, blocking the image with his body and effectively castrating her look (stills 46–48). Substituting himself for the screen, he activates an aggressive look back at the spectator, turning Fontaine's gaze against itself. The absolute terror incited by this violent re-organization of the cinematic relay of the look is evident in her eyes, the only part of her face lit by the reflected beam of the projector (stills 49–51). Furthermore, the image revealed as he finally moves out of the projection beam to turn on the light is that of himself, once again holding the binoculars (stills 52–53). (4) All of these aggressions and threats are condensed in the penultimate shot of the sequence which constitutes the most explicit delineation of projection as an assault against the woman. The projection light reflected from the screen fragments and obscures Fontaine's face (stills 54–55), contrasting it with the clarity, coherency and homogeneity proffered by the home movie image of the next shot. The camera positions itself so as to coincide with the diegetic projector and slowly tracks forward towards the final image of the couple together, taken, as Maxim points out, by an autonomous camera mounted on a tripod (stills 56–57). At this point, the rule dictating that the home movie conform to an arbitrary and contingent syntax is broken by the insertion of a cut to a closer shot of the couple (a cut, furthermore, interrupting a shot still supposedly taken by an autonomous camera [stills 58–59]). The cut guarantees a certain rhetorical finesse, a satisfying closure which demonstrates the stability of the couple and simultaneously sutures the diegetic film to the larger film. For the camera continues to track forward until the edges of the screen disappear and the home movie coincides with *Rebecca* itself.

It is as though in both *Caught* and *Rebecca*, the diegetic film's continuous unfolding guaranteed a rather fragile binding of the drives in the heterosexual unit of the harmonious couple. Its interruption, in each inst-

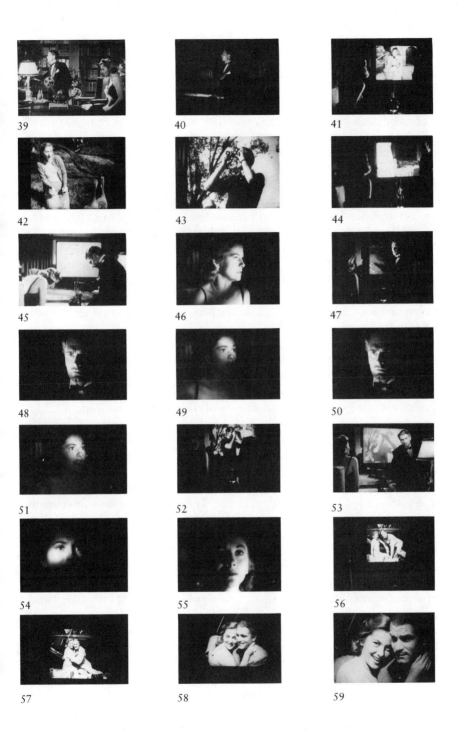

39　40　41

42　43　44

45　46　47

48　49　50

51　52　53

54　55　56

57　58　59

ance, signals the release of aggressive tendencies. In this way, the films play out the problematic of paranoia in its relation to the process of imaging and, simultaneously, the institution of marriage. As Rose points out, paranoia is "The aggressive corollary of the narcissistic structure of the ego-function."[8] The "woman's films" as a group appear to make a detour around or deflect the issue of spectacle and the woman's position (an obsession of the dominant cinema addressed to the male spectator), and hence avoid the problem of feminine narcissism. Yet, this narcissism returns and infiltrates the two texts by means of a paranoia which is linked to an obsession with the specular. The projection scenes in both films are preceded by the delineation of a narcissistic female desire—the desire to become the image which captures the male gaze. Nevertheless, it is as though the aggressivity which should be attendent on that structure were detached, in the projection scenes, and transferred to the specular system which insures and perpetuates female narcissism—the cinematic apparatus. Thus, the aggressivity attached to her own narcissism is stolen and used against the woman; she becomes the object rather than the subject of that aggression.

The desire to be looked at is thus transformed into a fear of being looked at, or a fear of the apparatus which systematizes or governs that process of looking. From this perspective, it is interesting to note that in the only case of female paranoia Freud treats, as described in "A Case of Paranoia Running Counter to the Psychoanalytical Theory of the Disease," the woman's delusion concerns being photographed. During lovemaking with a male friend, a young woman hears a noise—a knock or tick—which she interprets as the sound of a camera, photographing her in order to compromise her. Freud doubts the very existence of the noise, "I do not believe that the clock ever ticked or that any noise was to be heard at all. The woman's situation justified a sensation of throbbing in the clitoris. This was what she subsequently projected as a perception of an external object."[9] Female paranoia thus finds its psychoanalytic explanation in the projection of a bodily sensation from inside to outside, in a relocation in external reality.

Projection is a mechanism which Freud consistently associates with paranoia. Yet, he is reluctant to make it specific to paranoia, since it is present in more "normal" provinces such as those of superstition, mythology and, finally, the activity of theorizing. For Freud, projection is instrumental in formulating the very condition of the opposition between internal and external reality, between subject and object. For projection enables flight (from the "bad object") and the possibility of a refusal to recognize something in or about oneself.[10] The invocation of the opposition between subject and object in connection with the paranoid mechanism of projection indicates a precise difficulty in any conceptualization of female paranoia—one which Freud does not mention. For in his short case history, what the woman projects, what she throws away, is her sexual pleasure, a part of her bodily image. The sound of her own body throbbing becomes the click of the camera, the capture of her image. For the female spectator in the cinema, on the other hand, the spectator so carefully delineated in *Caught* and *Rebecca*, the problem is even more complex. In the cinematic situation, in the realm of the image, the distinction between subject and object effected by projection is not accessible to the female spectator in the same way as to the male. For Leonora and Maxine in *Caught* and the Joan Fontaine character in *Rebecca*, the pictures in fashion magazines demonstrate that to possess the image through the gaze is to become it. And becoming the image, the woman can no longer have it. For the female spectator, the image is *too* close—it cannot be projected far enough. The alternatives she is given are quite literally figured in the two films: (1) She can accept the image, full acceptance indicated by the attempts to duplicate it (by means of the mink coat or the black silk dress); or (2) She can repudiate the image (voluntarily in *Caught*, unwillingly in *Rebecca*). The absoluteness of the dilemma is manifested in the mutual exclusivity of its terms—a condition which does not mirror that of the male spectator, who, like Sean Connery in *Marnie* (as described by Mulvey), can "have his cake and eat it too." As a card-carrying fetishist, the male spectator does not have to choose between acceptance or rejection of the image; he can balance his belief and knowledge. Deprived of castration anxiety, the female spectator is also deprived of the possibility of fetishism—of the reassuring "I know, but even so. . . ."

To the extent that the projector scenes in *Caught* and *Rebecca* mobilize the elements of a specular system which has historically served the interests of male spectatorship, they are limit-texts, exposing the contradictions which inhabit the logic of their own terms of address as "women's films." The relation between the female body and the female look articulated by the two films (a relation which always threatens to collapse into the sameness of equivalence), together with the over-presence of the image, indicate a difficulty in the woman's relation to symbolization. Sexuality, disseminated in the classical representation across the body of the woman, is for her non-localizable. This is why psychoanalytic theory tells us she must be It rather than have It. As Parveen Adams points out, the woman does not represent lack: she lacks the means to represent lack.[11] According to the problematic elaborated by *Caught* and *Rebecca*, what the female viewer lacks is the very distance or gap which separates, must separate, the spectator from the image. What she lacks, in other words, is a "good throw."

Although the projection scenes in *Caught* and *Rebecca* do deconstruct, in some sense, the woman's position relative to the process of imaging, there is a missing piece in this *mise-en-scène* of cinematic elements—projector and screen are there but the camera is absent. In *Rebecca* the home-movie camera is briefly mentioned to justify the final shot, but in neither film is the camera visualized. The camera is, of course, an element whose acknowledgment would pose a more radical threat to the classicism which ultimately these texts fully embrace, particularly if the camera whose presence was acknowledged were non-diegetic. Yet, while it is true that indications of the presence of a camera are missing in the projection scenes, it is possible to argue that inscriptions of the camera are displaced, inserted later in the films to buttress a specifically male discourse about the woman. Paradoxically, in each of the films the camera demonstrates its own presence and potency through the very absence of an image of the woman. In a frantic, almost psychotic search for that image, the camera contributes its power to the hallucination of a woman.

In *Rebecca*, there is a scene late in the film which exemplifies the very felt presence of the woman who is absent throughout the movie, the woman whose initials continually surround and subdue the Joan Fontaine character—Rebecca. It is the scene in which Maxim narrates the story of Rebecca, despite his own claim that it is unnarratable ("She told me all about herself—everything—things I wouldn't tell a living soul"). The camera's very literal inscription of the absent woman's movements is preceded by a transfer of the look from narrator to narratee. Maxim, standing by the door, looks first at the sofa, then at Fontaine, then back at the sofa (still 60). Fontaine turns her glance from Maxim to the sofa, appropriating his gaze (still 61). From this point on, the camera's movements are very precisely synchronized with Maxim's words; when he tells Fontaine that Rebecca sat next to an ashtray brimming with cigarette stubs, there is a cut to the sofa, empty but for the ashtray (still 62); as he describes Rebecca rising from the sofa, the camera duplicates that movement (still 63) and then pans to the left—purportedly following a woman who is not visible (stills 64–65). In tracing Rebecca's path as Maxim narrates, the camera pans more than 180 degrees (stills 66–67). In effect, what was marked very clearly as Maxim's point of view, simply transferred to Fontaine as narratee, comes to include him. The story of the woman culminates as the image of the man.

Caught makes appeal to a remarkably similar signifying strategy in a scene in which Leonora's absence from the image becomes the strongest signified—the scene in which her empty desk is used as a pivot as the camera swings back and forth between Dr. Hoffman (Frank Fergusson) and Dr. Quinada (James Mason) discussing her fate. The sequence begins with a high angle shot down on Leonora's desk (still 68), the camera moving down and to the left to frame Dr. Hoffman, already framed in his doorway (still 69). Moving from Hoffman across the empty desk, the camera constructs a perfect symmetry by framing Dr. Quinada in his doorway as well (stills 70–71). The middle portion of the sequence is constituted by a sustained crosscutting between Hoffman and Quinada, alternating both medium shots and close-ups (stills 72–76). The end of the sequence echoes and repeats the beginning, the camera again pivoting around the absent woman's desk from Quinada to Hoffman and, as Hoffman suggests that Quinada "forget"

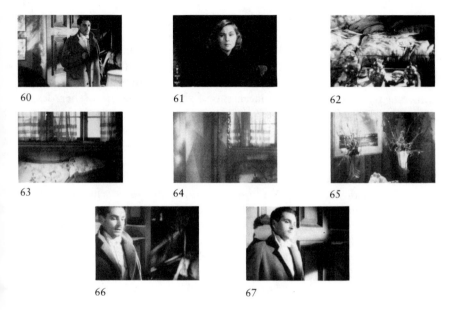

60   61   62

63   64   65

66   67

Leonora, back to the empty desk, closing the sequence with a kind of formal tautology (stills 77–80). The sequence is a performance of one of the over-determined meanings of the film's title—Leonora is "caught," spatially, between an obstetrician and a pediatrician (other potential readings include the theme of "catching" a rich husband which initiates the film, the fact that Leonora is "caught" in her marriage by her husband who wants to keep her child or that she is "caught" between Smith Ohlrig and Larry Quinada).

In tracing the absence of the woman, the camera inscribes its own presence in the film as phallic substitute—the pen which writes the feminine body. The two scenes demonstrate the technical fluency of the camera in narrating the woman's story, extended to the point of ejecting her from the image. In its foreclosure of a signifier—here, the woman's body—from the symbolic universe, the camera enacts its paranoia as a psychosis. It is as though, in a pseudo-genre marked as the possession of the woman, the camera had to desperately reassert itself by means of its technical prowess—here embodied in the attribute of movement. The projection scenes discussed earlier effect a cleavage, a split between the image of the woman's desire (linked to stills—photographs or sketched without movement) and what is projected on the screen (in *Caught*, the machinery of industry, capitalist enterprise; in *Rebecca*, the images of Maxim's memory of her before the black satin dress). In each case, it is the man who has control of the projector and hence the moving image. Thus the films construct an opposition between different processes of imaging, along the lines of sexual difference: female desire is linked to the fixation and stability of a spectacle refusing the temporal dimension, while male desire is more fully implicated with the defining characteristic of the cinematic image—movement. The two scenes in which the camera inscribes the absence of the woman thus accomplish a double negation of the feminine—through her absence and the camera's movement, its continual displacement of the fixed image of her desire. Invoking the specific attributes of the cinematic signifier (movement and absence of the object) around the figure of the woman, the films succeed in constructing a story about the woman which no longer requires even her physical presence.

Nevertheless, each of the films recovers the image of the woman, writing her back into the narrative. At the end of *Caught*, in a scene which echoes the earlier one pivoting on Leonora's empty desk, her image is returned to the diegesis. Inserted, almost accidentally it seems, between two shots of Dr. Hoffman and Dr. Quinada who are once more discussing her, is an image of Leonora in which the camera stares straight down at her lying in a hospital bed (stills 81–82). In *Rebecca*, Joan Fontaine's full appropriation of Rebecca's position toward the end of the film coincides with the abolition of even the traces of Rebecca's absent presence. In the final shot of the film, the initial R which decorates the pillow of her bed is consumed by flames. This denial of the absent woman and the resultant recuperation of presence form the basis for the reunification and harmony of the couple which closes the film.

The closure in *Caught*, however, is less sure, the recuperation more problematic.[12] The oppressiveness of the *mise-en-scène* toward the end of the film is marked. This is particularly true of the scene inside an ambulance, in which sirens wail as Dr. Quinada tells Leonora how free she can be if her child dies. The claustrophobic effect of the scene issues from the fact that there are two simultaneous movements toward Leonora—as the camera moves gradually closer and closer, framing her more tightly, Dr Quinada repeats its movement from another direction (stills 83–88). By the end of the shot he appears to have nearly smothered her with his body. Leonora is caught in the pincers of this double movement as Quinada tells her, "He (Smith Ohlrig) won't be able to hold you . . . Now you can be free." The camera's movement explicitly repeats that of Dr. Quinada in its domination, enclosure, and framing of the woman. In the next scene, in which the image of Leonora in a hospital bed is inserted between two shots of the doctors, the camera literally assumes Dr. Quinada's position in the ambulance, aiming itself directly down at Leonora (still 82). Dr. Quinada has just been informed by Dr. Hoffman in the hallway that the baby has died and his reply, the same words he used in the ambulance—"He can't hold her now—she's free"—constitutes the voice over Leonora's image.

But Leonora's ultimate "freedom" in the last scene is granted to her by Dr. Hoffman when he tells the nurse to take her mink coat away with the statement, "If my diagnosis is correct, she won't want that anyway." With the rejection of the mink coat comes the denial of the last trace of the image in its

68 69 70 71 72 73 74 75 76 77 78 79 80

relation to Leonora. By means of the doctor's diagnosis, she becomes instead of an image, an element in the discourse of medicine, a manuscript to be read for the symptoms which betray her story, her identity. It is appropriate that the final scene in *Caught* takes place in a hospital. For the doctor, as reader or interpreter of that manuscript, accomplishes the final de-specularization proposed by the text's own trajectory and the terms of its address. The final image of the film consists of the nurse slinging the mink coat over her shoulder and taking it away down the hospital corridor.

The movement of the narrative is thus from the representation of the mink coat which sparks desire to the rejection of the "real thing" (a rejection really made "on behalf" of the woman by the doctor). One could chart the elaboration of female subjectivity in the film according to the presence or absence of the mink coat. At the beginning of the film, Leonora's only desire is to meet a man rich enough to allow her to return to her home town with two mink coats—"One for my mother and one for me." A cut from Leonora at

Dorothy Dale's School of Charm pretending that a cloth coat is mink to a tilt upwards along the mink coat she models in a department store in the next scene establishes her rise on the social scale. When she leaves Smith Ohlrig after the projection scene discussed earlier, she takes her mink coat with her and the coat immediately signals to Quinada her alliance with an upper class. Yet, when she briefly returns to Ohlrig after quitting her job as Quinada's receptionist, she realizes that he has not changed and, as she calls Dr. Quinada on the phone, Leonora tells Franzi, "I'm through with that coat." Dr. Quinada subsequently buys Leonora a cloth coat, an action which initiates their romance. The opposition cloth/mink governs the economic thematics of the text.

The mink coat is thus the means by which the specular is welded to the economic—it functions both as an economic landmark of Leonora's social position and as the articulation of the woman's relation to the spectacle and the male gaze. The textual meditations upon the sexed subject and the class subject merge imperceptibly, Leonora's desire to own the mink coat is both narcissistic and socially economically ambitious. Yet, the text attempts to prove the desire itself to be "wrong" or misguided since the man she marries in order to obtain the coat is dangerously psychotic. Dr. Quinada, unlike Smith Ohlrig, is a member of her own class; hence, Leonora's understanding of her own sexuality is simultaneous with her understanding and acceptance of her class position.

In *Rebecca*, the situation is somewhat similar, with important deviations. Generic considerations are here much stronger since *Rebecca* belongs more clearly to a group of films infused by the gothic and defined by a plot in which the wife fears her husband is a murderer. In films like *Rebecca*, *Dragonwyck*, and *Undercurrent*, the woman marries, often hastily, *into* the upper class; her husband has money and social position which she cannot match. The marriage thus constitutes a type of transgression (of class barriers) which does not remain unpunished. The woman often feels dwarfed or threatened by the house itself (*Rebecca*, *Dragonwyck*). A frequent reversal of the hierarchy of mistress and servant is symptomatic of the fact that the woman is "out of place" in her rich surroundings. Nevertheless, in films of the same genre such as *Suspicion*, *Secret Beyond the Door*, and *Gaslight*, the economic sexual relationship is reversed. In each of these, there is at least a hint that the man marries the woman in order to obtain her money. Hence, it is not always the case that a woman from a lower class is punished for attempting to change her social and economic standing. Rather, the mixture effected by a marriage between two different classes produces horror and paranoia.

By making sexuality extremely difficult in a rich environment, both films—*Caught* and *Rebecca*—promote the illusion of separating the issue of sexuality from that of economics. What is really repressed in this scenario is

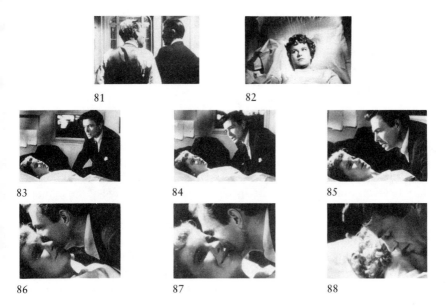

81 82

83 84 85

86 87 88

the economics of sexual exchange. This repression is most evident in *Caught* whose explicit moral—"Don't marry for money"—constitutes a negation of the economic factor in marriage. But negation, as Freud points out, is also affirmation: in *Caught* there is an unconscious acknowledgment of the economics of marriage as an institution. In the course of the film, the woman becomes the object of exchange, from Smith Ohlrig to Dr. Quinada.[13] A by-product of this exchange is the relinquishing of the posited object of her desire—the expensive mink coat.

There is a sense, then, in which both films begin with a hypothesis of female subjectivity which is subsequently disproven by the textual project. The narrative of *Caught* is introduced by the attribution of the look at the image (the "I" of seeing) to Leonora and her friend. The film ends by positioning Leonora as the helpless bed-ridden object of the medical gaze. In the beginning of *Rebecca*, the presence of a female subjectivity as the source of the enunciation is marked. A female voice-over (belonging to the Fontaine character) accompanies a hazy, dream-like image: "Last night I dreamed I went to Manderley again. It seems to me I stood by the iron gate leading to the drive. For a while I could not enter." The voice goes on to relate how, like all dreamers, she was suddenly possessed by a supernatural power and passed through the gate. This statement is accompanied by a shot in which the camera assumes the position of the "I" and, in a sustained subjective move-ment, tracks forward through the gate and along the path. Yet, the voice-over subsequently disappears entirely—it is not even resuscitated at the end of the film in order to provide closure through a symmetrical frame. Nevertheless, there *is* an extremely disconcerting re-emergence of a feminine "I" later in the film. In the cottage scene in which Maxim narrates the "unnarratable" story of the absent Rebecca to Joan Fontaine, he insists upon a continual use of direct quotes and hence the first person pronoun referring to Rebecca. His narrative is laced with these quotes from Rebecca which parallel on the soundtrack the moving image, itself adhering to the traces of an absent Rebecca. Maxim is therefore the one who pronounces the following statements "I'll play the part of a devoted wife". . . "When I have a child, Max, no one will be able to say that it's not yours". . . "I'll be the perfect mother just as I've been the perfect wife". . . "Well, Max, what are you going to do about it. Aren't you going to kill me?" Just as the tracking subjective shot guarantees that the story of the woman literally culminates as the image of the man, the construction of the dialogue allows Maxim to appropriate Rebecca's "I."[14]

The films thus chronicle the emergence and disappearance of female subjectivity, the articulation of an "I" which is subsequently negated. The pressure of the demand in the "woman's film" for the depiction of female subjectivity is so strong, and often so contradictory, that it is not at all surprising that sections such as the projection scenes in *Caught* and *Rebecca* should dwell on the problem of female spectatorship. These scenes internalize the difficulties of the genre and in their concentration on the issue of the woman's relation to the gaze occupy an important place in the narrative. Paranoia is here the appropriate and logical obsession. For it effects a confusion between subjectivity and objectivity, between the internal and the external, thus disallowing the gap which separates the spectator from the image of his/her desire.

In many respects, the most disturbing images of the two films are those which evoke the absence of the woman. In both films these images follow projection scenes which delineate the impossibility of female spectatorship. It is as though each film adhered strictly to the logic which characterizes dream work—establishing the image of an absent woman as the delayed mirror image of a female spectator who is herself only virtual.

Notes

1. For an example of this use of the concept of hysteria in film analysis, see Geoffrey Norwell-Smith, "Minnelli and Melodrama," *Screen*, 18:2 (Summer 1977), pp. 113–118. I have discussed this idea of perversion within the norm more fully in "The 'Classical Hollywood Text' as Norm and Symptom," paper presented at Clark/Luxembourg Film Conference, Luxembourg, May 1980.

2. Laura Mulvey, "Visual Pleasure and Narrative Cinema," *Screen*, 16:3 (Autumn 1975), pp. 6–18. Reprinted as Chapter 4 in this book.

3. Jacqueline Rose, "Paranoia and the Film System" *Screen*, 17:4 (Winter 1976–7), pp. 85–104. Reprinted as Chapter 10 in this book.

4. Sigmund Freud, *Three Case Histories* (New York: Collier Books, 1963), p. 149.

5. Julia Kristeva *About Chinese Women*, trans. Anita Barrows (New York: Urizen Books, 1977), p. 29.

6. The figure is Franzi, Ohlrig's rather slick public relations man and secretary who is endowed with characteristics stereotyped as homosexual. Thus, an intensification of the representation of male bonding (as in the predominantly male audience of Ohlrig's cinema) immediately precedes the threatening laugh of the only female spectator present.

7. The sequence is composed of fifty shots; this brief analysis covers only twenty-five of these.

8. Rose, p. 86; p. 142 in this book.

9. Freud, "A Case of Paranoia Running Counter to the Psychoanalytical Theory of the Disease," in *Sexuality and the Psychology of Love* (New York: Collier Books, 1963), p. 104.

10. See J. Laplanche and J. B. Pontalis, *The Language of Psychoanalysis*, trans. Donald Nicolson-Smith (New York: Norton, 1973), pp. 349–356. Laplanche and Pontalis define projection as having a sense "comparable to the cinematographic one: the subject send out into the external world an image of something that exists in him in an unconscious way. Projection is here defined as a mode of *refusal to recognize (méconnaissance)* . . ."

11. "Representation and Sexuality," *m/f*, no. 1, pp. 66–67.

12. An acknowledgement of the difficulties with the ending of *Caught* can be found in Ophuls's remarks about the film: "I worked for MGM, I made *Caught*, which I quite like. But I had difficulties with the production over the script, so that the film goes off the rails toward the end. Yes, the ending is really almost impossible, but up until the last ten minutes it's not bad." Paul Willeman, ed. *Ophuls* (London: British Film Institute, 1978), p. 23.

13. In the generic sub-category to which *Rebecca* belongs, the "paranoid" woman's film, there are frequently two major male characters, one evil or psychotic, the other good and heroic. The woman, as in Lévi-Strauss's fable of the constitution of society, is exchanged from one to the other. In *Rebecca* this is not quite the case. Nevertheless, Maxim is a composite figure and therefore incorporates both character-types—both sane and insane, rich but with middle-class tastes (e.g. the Joan Fontaine character). At the end of the film, Fontaine finds a harmonious re-unification with the sane Maxim, whose strongest symbol of wealth—Manderley—burns to the ground.

14. The vicious quality of such a gesture is mitigated by the fact that Rebecca, in contradistinction to the Joan Fontaine character, is isolated as the evil, sexually active woman.

13

Woman's Stake: Filming the Female Body

Mary Ann Doane

We know that, for want of a stake, representation is not worth anything
　　　　　　　　　　　　　　　　　　　—Michèle Montrelay

To those who still ask, What do women want?" the cinema seems to provide
no answer. For the cinema, in its alignment with the fantasies of the voyeur,
has historically articulated its stories through a conflation of its central axis of
seeing/being seen with the opposition male/female. So much so that in a
classical instance such as *Humoresque*, when Joan Crawford almost violently
attempts to appropriate the gaze for herself, she must be represented as
myopic (the moments of her transformation from spectacle to spectator thus
captured and constrained through their visualization as the act of putting on
glasses) and eventually eliminated from the text, her death equated with that
of a point of view. Cinematic images of woman have been so consistently
oppressive and repressive that the very idea of a feminist filmmaking practice
seems an impossibility. The simple gesture of directing a camera toward a
woman has become equivalent to a terrorist act.

　　This state of affairs—the result of a history which inscribes woman as
subordinate—is not simply to be overturned by a contemporary practice that
is more aware, more self-conscious. The impasse confronting feminist film-
makers today is linked to the force of a certain theoretical discourse which
denies the neutrality of the cinematic apparatus itself. A machine for the
production of images and sounds, the cinema generates and guarantees
pleasure by a corroboration of the spectator's identity. Because that identity
is bound up with that of the voyeur and the fetishist, because it requires for its
support the attributes of the "noncastrated," the potential for illusory mastery of the signifier, it is not accessible to the female spectator, who, in buying
her ticket, must deny her sex. There are no images either *for* her or *of* her.

There is a sense in which Peter Gidal, in attempting to articulate the relationship between his own filmmaking practice and feminist concerns, draws the most logical conclusion from this tendency in theory:

> In terms of the feminist struggle specifically, I have had a vehement refusal over the last decade, with one or two minor aberrations, to allow images of women into my films at all, since I do not see how those images can be separated from the dominant meanings. The ultra-left aspect of this may be nihilistic as well, which may be a critique of my position because it does not see much hope for representations for women, but I do not see how, to take the main example I gave round about 1969 before any knowledge on my part of, say, semiotics, there is any possibility of using the image of a naked woman—at that time I did not have it clarified to the point of any image of a woman—other than in an absolutely sexist and politically repressive patriarchal way in this conjuncture.[1]

This is the extreme formulation of a project which can define itself only in terms of negativity. If the female body is not necessarily always excluded within this problematic, it must always be placed within quotation marks. For it is precisely the massive reading, writing, filming of the female body which constructs and maintains a hierarchy along the lines of a sexual difference assumed as natural. The ideological complicity of the concept of the natural dictates the impossibility of a nostalgic return to an unwritten body.

Thus, contemporary filmmaking addresses itself to the activity of uncoding, de-coding, deconstructing the given images. It is a project of de-familiarization whose aim is not necessarily that of seeing the female body differently, but of exposing the habitual meanings/values attached to femininity as cultural constructions. Sally Potter's *Thriller*, for instance, is a rereading of the woman's role in opera, specifically in Puccini's *La Bohème*, in terms of its ideological function. Mimi's death, depicted in the opera as tragedy, is rewritten as a murder, the film itself invoking the conventions of the suspense thriller. In Babette Mangolte's *The Camera: Je/La Caméra: Eye*, what is at stake are the relations of power sustained within the camera-subject nexus. The discomfort of the subjects posing for the camera, together with the authority of the off-screen voice giving instructions ("Smile," "Don't smile," "Look to the left," etc.), challenge the photographic image's claim to naturalism and spontaneity. And, most interestingly, the subjects, whether male or female, inevitably appear to assume a mask of "femininity" in order to become photographic (filmable)—as though femininity were synonymous with the *pose*.[2] This may explain the feminist film's frequent obsession with the pose as position—the importance accorded to dance positions in *Thriller*, or those assumed by the hysteric in Terrel Seltzer's *The Story of Anna O.*—which we may see as the arrangements of the body in the interests of aesthetics and science. In their rigidity (the recurrent use of the tableau in these films) or excessive repetition (the multiple, seemingly unending caresses of the woman's breasts in Mangolte's *What Maisie Knew*), positions and gestures are isolated, deprived of the syntagmatic rationalization which, in the more classical text, conduces to their naturalization. These strategies of demystification are attempts to strip the body of its readings. The inadequacy of this formulation of the problem is obvious, however, in that the gesture of stripping in relation to a female body is already the property of patriarchy. More importantly, perhaps, the question to be addressed in this: what is left after the stripping, the uncoding, the deconstruction? For an uncoded body is clearly an impossibility.

Attempts to answer this question by invoking the positivity or specificity of a definition have been severely criticized on the grounds that the particular definition claims a "nature" proper to the woman and is hence complicit with those discourses which set woman outside the social order. Since the patriarchy has always already said everything (everything and nothing) about woman, efforts to give those phrases a different intonation, to mumble, to stutter, to slur them, to articulate them differently, must be doomed to failure. Laura Mulvey and Peter Wollen's *Riddles of the Sphinx*, for instance, has been repeatedly criticized for its invocation of the sphinx as the figure of a femininity repressed by the Oedipal mythos. Femininity is something which has been forgotten or repressed, left outside the gates of the city; hence, what is called for is a radical act of remembering. The radicality of that act, however, has been subject to debate. As Stephen Heath points out,

> The line in the figure of the sphinx-woman between the posing of a question and the idea that women are the question is very thin; female sexuality is dark and unexplorable, women, as Freud puts it, are that half of the audience which is the enigma, the great enigma. This is the problem and the difficulty—the area of debate and criticism—of Mulvey and Wollen's film *Riddles of the Sphinx* where the sphinx is produced as a point of resistance that seems nevertheless to repeat, in its very terms, the relations of women made within patriarchy, their representation in the conjunction of such elements as motherhood as mystery, the unconscious, a voice that speaks far off from the past through dream or forgotten language. The film is as though poised on the edge of a politics of the unconscious, of the imagination of a politics of the unconscious ("what would the politics of the unconscious be like?"), with a simultaneous falling short, that politics and imagination not yet there, coming back with old definitions, the given images.[3]

What is forgotten in the critical judgment, but retrieved in Heath's claim that "the force remains in the risk"—the risk, that is, of recapitulating the terms of patriarchy—is the fact that the sphinx is also, and crucially, subject to a kind of filmic disintegration. In the section entitled "Stones," the refilming of found footage of the Egyptian sphinx problematizes any notion of perceptual immediacy in refinding an "innocent" image of femininity. In fact, as the camera appears to get closer to its object, the graininess of the film is marked, thus indicating the limit of the material basis of its representation.

Thriller (Sally Potter, 1979)

Most of this essay will be a lengthy digression, a prolegomenon to a much needed investigation of the material specificity of film in relation to the female body and its syntax. Given the power of a certain form of feminist theory which has successfully blocked attempts to provide a conceptualization of this body, the digression is, nevertheless, crucial.

The resistance to filmic and theoretical descriptions of femininity is linked to the strength of the feminist critique of essentialism—of ideas concerning an essential femininity, or of the "real" woman not yet disfigured by patriarchal social relations. The force of this critique lies in its exposure of the inevitable alliance between "feminine essence" and the natural, the given, or precisely what is outside the range of political action and thus not amenable to change. This unchangeable "order of things" in relation to sexual difference is an exact formulation of patriarchy's strongest rationalization of itself. And since the essence of femininity is most frequently attached to the natural body as an immediate indicator of sexual difference, it is this body which must be refused. The body is always a function of discourse.

Feminist theory which grounds itself in anti-essentialism frequently turns to psychoanalysis for its description of sexuality because psychoanalysis assumes a necessary gap between the body and the psyche, so that sexuality is not reducible to the physical. Sexuality is constructed within social and symbolic relations; it is most *un*natural and achieved only after an arduous struggle. One is not born with a sexual identity (hence the significance of the concept of bisexuality in psychoanalysis). The terms of this argument demand that charges of phallocentrism be met with statements that the phallus is not equal to the penis, castration is bloodless, and the father is, in any case, dead and only symbolic.

Nevertheless, the cap between body and psyche is not absolute; an image or symbolization of the body (which is not necessarily the body of biological science) is fundamental to the construction of the psychoanalytical discourse. Brief references to two different aspects of psychoanalytic theory will suffice to illustrate my point. Jean Laplanche explains the emergence of sexuality by means of the concept of propping or *anaclisis*. The drive, which is always sexual, leans or props itself upon the nonsexual or presexual instinct of self-preservation. His major example is the relation of the oral drive to the instinct of hunger whose object is the milk obtained from the mother's breast. The object of the oral drive (prompted by the sucking which activates the lips as an erotogenic zone) is necessarily displaced in relation to the first object of the instinct. The fantasmatic breast (henceforth the object of the oral drive) is a metonymic derivation, a symbol, of the milk: "The object to be rediscovered is not the lost object, but its substitute by displacement; the lost object is the object of self-preservation, of hunger, and the object one seeks to refind is an object displaced in relation to that first object."[4] Sexuality can only take form in a dissociation of subjectivity from the bodily function, but the concept of a bodily function is necessary in the explanation as, precisely, a support. We will see later how Laplanche de-naturalizes this body (which is simply a distribution of erotogenic zones) while retaining it as a cipher. Still, the body is there, as a prop.

The second aspect of psychoanalysis which suggests the necessity of a certain conceptualization of the body is perhaps more pertinent, and certainly more notorious, in relation to a discussion of feminism: the place of the phallus in Lacanian theory. Lacan and feminist theorists who subscribe to his formulations persistently claim that the phallus is not the penis; the phallus is a signifier (the signifier of lack). It does not *belong* to the male. The phallus is only important insofar as it can be put in circulation as a signifier. Both sexes define themselves in relation to this "third term." What is ultimately stressed here is the absolute necessity of positing only one libido (which Freud labels masculine) in relation to only one term, the phallus. Initially, both sexes, in desiring to conform to the desire of the other (the mother), define themselves in relation to the phallus in the mode of "being." Sexual difference, then, is inaugurated at the moment of the Oedipal complex when the girl continues to "be" the phallus while the boy situates himself in the mode of "having." Positing two terms, in relation to two fully defined sexualities, as Jones and Horney do, binds the concept of sexuality more immediately, more directly, to the body as it expresses itself at birth. For Jones and Horney, there is an essential femininity which is linked to an expression of the vagina. And for Horney at least, there is a sense in which the little girl experiences an empirical, not a psychic, inferiority.[5]

But does the phallus really have nothing to do with the penis, no commerce with it at all? The ease of the description by means of which the boy situates himself in the mode of "having" one would seem to indicate that this is not the case. And Lacan's justification for the privilege accorded to the phallus as signifier appears to guarantee its derivation from a certain representation of the bodily organ:

> The phallus is the privileged signifier of that mark in which the role of the logos is joined with the advent of desire. It can be said that this signifier is chosen because it is the most tangible element in the real of sexual copulation, and also the most symbolic in the literal (typographical) sense of the term, since it is equivalent there to the (logical) copula. It might also be said that, by virtue of its turgidity, it is the image of the vital flow as it is transmitted in generation.[6]

There is a sense in which all attempts to deny the relation between the phallus and the penis are feints, veils, illusions. The phallus, as signifier, may no longer *be* the penis, but any effort to conceptualize its function is inseparable from an imaging of the body. The difficulty in conceptualizing the relation between the phallus and the penis is evident in Parveen Adams's explanation of the different psychic trajectories of the girl and the boy.

> Sexuality can only be considered at the level of the symbolic process. This lack is undifferentiated for both sexes and has nothing to do with the absence of a penis, a physical lack.
> Nonetheless, the anatomical difference between the sexes does permit a differentiation within the symbolic process. . . . The phallus represents lack both for boys and girls. But the boy in having a penis has that which lends itself to the phallic symbol. The girl does not have a penis. What she lacks is not a penis as such, but the means to represent lack.[7]

The sexual differentiation is permitted but not demanded by the body and it is the exact force or import of this "permitting" which requires an explanation. For it is clear that what is being suggested is that the boy's body provides an access to the processes of representation while the girl's body does not. From this perspective, a certain slippage can then take place by means of which the female body becomes an absolute tabula rasa of sorts: anything and everything can be written on it. Or more accurately, perhaps, the male body comes fully equipped with a binary opposition—penis/no penis, presence/absence, phonemic opposition—while the female body is constituted as "noise,"[8] an undifferentiated presence which always threatens to disrupt representation.

This analysis of the bodily image in psychoanalysis becomes crucial for feminism with the recognition that sexuality is inextricable from discourse, from language. The conjunction of semiotics and psychoanalysis (as exemplified in the work of Lacan and others) has been successful in demonstrating the necessity of a break in an initial plenitude as a fundamental condition for signification. The concept of lack is not arbitrary. The fact that the little girl in the above description has no means to represent lack results in her different relation to language and representation. The work of Michèle Montrelay is most explicit in this issue: ". . . for want of a stake, representation is not worth anything."[9] The initial relation to the mother, the determinant of the desire of both sexes, is too full, too immediate, too present. This undifferentiated plenitude must be fissured through the introduction of lack before representation can be assured, since representation entails the absence of the desired object. "Hence the repression that ensures that one does not think, nor see, nor take the desired object, even and above all if it is within reach: this object must remain lost."[10] The tragedy of Oedipus lies in his refinding of the object. And as Montrelay points out, it is the sphinx as the figure of femininity which heralds this "ruin of representation."

In order for representation to be possible then, a stake is essential. Something must be threatened if the paternal prohibition against incest is to take effect, forcing the gap between desire and its object. This theory results in a rather surprising interpretation of the woman's psychic oppression: her different relation to language stems from the fact that she has nothing to lose, nothing at stake. Prohibition, the law of limitation, cannot touch the little girl. For the little boy, on the other hand, there is most definitely something to lose. "He experiments, not only with chance but also with the law and with his sexual organ: his body itself takes on the value of stake."[11]

Furthermore, in repeating, doubling the maternal body with her own, the woman recovers the first stake of representation and thus undermines the possibility of losing the object of desire since she has, instead become it.

> From now on, anxiety, tied to the presence of this body, can only be insistent, continuous. This body, so close, which she has to occupy, is an object in excess which must be "lost," that is to say, repressed, in order to be symbolized. Hence the symptoms which so often simulate this loss: "there is no longer anything, only the hole, emptiness . . ." Such is the *leitmotif* of all feminine cure, which it would be a mistake to see as the expression of an alleged "castration." On the contrary, it is a defense produced in order to parry the avatars, the deficiencies, of symbolic castration.[12]

There are other types of defense as well, based on the woman's imaginary simulation of lack. Montrelay points to the anorexic, for instance, who diminishes her own body, dissolving the flesh and reducing the body to a cipher.[13] Or the woman can operate a performance of femininity, a masquerade, by means of an accumulation of accessories—jewelry, hats, feathers, etc.—all designed to mask the absence of a lack.[14] These defenses, however, are based on the woman's imaginary simulation of lack and exclude the possibility of an encounter with the symbolic. She can only mime representation.

Montrelay's work is problematic in several respects. In situating the woman's relation to her own body as narcissistic, erotic, and maternal, Montrelay insists that it is the "real of her own body" which "imposes itself," prior to any act of construction.[15] Furthermore, she does, eventually, outline a scenario within which the woman has access to symbolic lack, but it is defined in terms of a heterosexual act of intercourse in which the penis, even though it is described as "scarcely anything," produces the "purest and most elementary form of signifying articulation."[16] Nevertheless, Montrelay's work points to the crucial dilemma confronting an anti-essentialist feminist theory which utilizes psychoanalysis. That is, while psychoanalysis does theorize the relative autonomy of psychic processes, the gap between body and psyche, it also requires the body as a prop, a support for its description of sexuality as a discursive function. Too often anti-essentialism is characterized by a paranoia in relation to all discussions of the female body (since ideas about a "natural" female body or the female body and "nature" are the linchpins of patriarchal ideology). This results in a position which simply repeats that of classical Freudian psychoanalysis in its focus upon the little boy's psychic development at the expense of that of the little girl. What is repressed here is the fact that psychoanalysis can conceptualize the sexuality of both the boy and the girl *only* by positing gender-specific bodies.

Even more crucially, as Montrelay's work demonstrates, the use of the concepts of the phallus and castration within a semiotically oriented psychoanalysis logically implies that the woman must have a different relation to language from that of the man. And from a semiotic perspective, her relation to language must be deficient since her body does not "permit" access to what, for the semiotician, is the motor-force of language—the representation of lack. Hence, the greatest masquerade of all is that of the woman speaking (or writing, or filming), appropriating discourse. To take up a discourse for the woman (if not, indeed, by her), that is, the discourse of feminism itself, would thus seem to entail an absolute contradiction. How can she speak?

Yet, we know that women speak, even though it may not be clear exactly how this takes place. And unless we want to accept a formulation by means of which woman can only mimic man's relation to language, that is, assume a position defined by the penis-phallus as the supreme arbitrer of lack, we must try to reconsider the relation between the female body and language, never forgetting that it is a relation between two terms and not two essences. Does woman have a stake in representation or, more appropriately, can we assign one to her? Anatomy is destiny only if the concept of destiny is recognized for what it really is: a concept proper to fiction.

The necessity of assigning to woman a specific stake informs the work of theorists such as Luce Irigaray and Julia Kristeva, and both have been criticized from an anti-essentialist perspective. Beverley Brown and Parveen Adams, for example, distinguish between two orders of argument about the female body which are attributed, respectively, to Irigaray and Kristeva:

> We can demand then: what is this place, this body, from which women speak so mutely?

Two orders of reply to this question can be distinguished. In the first there is an attempt to find a real and natural body which is pre-social in a literal sense. The second, more sophisticated reply, says that the issue at stake is not the actual location of a real body, but that the positing of such a body seems to be a condition of the discursive in general.[17]

Although the second order of argument is described as "more sophisticated," Brown and Adams ultimately find that both are deficient. I want briefly to address this criticism although it really requires an extended discussion impossible within the limits of this essay. The criticisms of Irigaray are based primarily on her essay, "That Sex Which Is Not One,"[18] in which she attempts to conceptualize the female body in relation to language/discourse, but independently of the penis/lack dichotomy. Irigaray valorizes certain features of the female body—the two lips (of the labia) which caress each other and define woman's auto-eroticism as a relation to duality, the multiplicity of sexualized zones spread across the body. Furthermore, Irigaray uses this representation of the body to specify a feminine language which is plural, polyvalent, and irreducible to a masculine language based on restrictive notions of unity and identity. Brown and Adams claim that "her argument turns upon the possibility of discovering that which is already there—it is a case of 'making visible' the previously 'invisible' of feminine sexuality."[19] While there are undoubtedly problems with the rather direct relation Irigaray often posits between the body and language, her attempt to provide the woman with an autonomous symbolic representation is not to be easily dismissed. Irigaray herself criticizes the logic which gives privilege to the gaze, thereby questioning the gesture of "making visible" a previously hidden female sexuality. Her work is a radical rewriting of psychoanalysis which, while foregrounding the process of mimesis by which language represents the body, simultaneously constructs a distinction between a mimesis which is "productive" and one which is merely "reproductive" or "imitative"—a process of "adequation" and of "specularization."[20] An immediate dismissal of her work in the interests of an overwary anti-essentialism involves a premature rejection of "the force that remains in the risk."

The criticism addressed to Kristeva, on the other hand, is directed toward her stress on pre-Oedipal sexuality, allying it with a femininity whose repression is the very condition of Western discourse.[21] For Kristeva, the woman's negative relation to the symbolic determines her bond with a polymorphous, prelogical discourse which corresponds to the autonomous and polymorphous sexuality of the pre-Oedipal moment. Brown and Adams formulate their criticism in these terms: "Setting up this apolitical autonomy of polymorphous sexuality is, in effect, the positing of sexuality as an impossible origin, a state of nature, as simply the eternal presence of sexuality at all."[22] However, pre-Oedipal sexuality is not synonymous with "nature"; it already assumes an organized distribution of erotogenic zones over the body and forms of relations to objects which are variable (whether human or nonhuman). Both male and female pass through, live pre-Oedipality. Hence, pre-Oedipality can only be equated with femininity retrospectively, *après coup*, after the event of the Oedipal complex, of the threat of castration, and the subsequent negative entry into the symbolic attributed to the woman. Insofar as Kristeva's description of pre-Oedipality is dependent upon notions of the drive, it involves a displacement of sexuality in relation to the body. As Laplanche points out, the drive is a metonymic derivation from the instinct which is itself attached to an erotogenic zone, a zone of *exchange*.

> The drive properly speaking, in the only sense faithful to Freud's discovery, *is* sexuality. Now sexuality, in its entirety, in the human infant, lies in *a movement which deflects the instinct, metaphorizes its aim, displaces and internalizes its object, and concentrates its source on what is ultimately a minimal zone, the erotogenic zone.* . . . This zone of exchange is also a zone for care, namely the particular and attentive care provided by the mother. These zones, then, attract the first erotogenic maneuvers from the adult. An even more significant factor, if we introduce the subjectivity of the first "partner": these zones *focalize parental fantasies* and above all *maternal fantasies*, so that we may say, in what is barely a metaphor, that they are the points through which is *introduced into the child that alien internal entity* which is, properly speaking, the *sexual excitation*.[23]

The force of this scenario lies in its de-naturalization of the sexualized body. The conceptualization of the erotogenic zone as a zone of exchange demonstrates that the investment of the body with sexuality is always already social. Since it is ultimately *maternal* fantasies which are at issue here, it is apparent that, without an anchoring in the social, psychoanalysis can simply reiterate, reperform in its theorization, the vicious circle of patriarchy.

The rather long digression which structures this essay is motivated by the extreme difficulty of moving beyond the impasse generated by the opposition between essentialism and anti-essentialism. In the context of feminist film theory, both positions are formulated through a repression of the crucial and complex relation between the body and psychic processes, that is, processes of signification. From the point of view of essentialist theory, the goal of a feminist film practice must be production of images which provide a pure reflection of the real woman, thus returning the real female body to the woman as her rightful property. And this body is accessible to a transparent cinematic discourse. The position is grounded in a mis-recognition of signification as outside of, uninformed by, the psychic. On the other hand, the logical extension of anti-essentialist theory, particularly as it is evidenced in Gidal's description of his filmmaking practice, results in the absolute exclusion of the female body, the refusal of any attempt to figure or represent that body. Both the proposal of a pure access to a natural female body and the rejection of attempts to conceptualize the female body based on their contamination by ideas of "nature" are inhibiting and misleading. Both positions deny the necessity of posing a complex relation between the body and

Riddles of the Sphinx (Laura Mulvey and Peter Wollen, 1977)

psychic/signifying processes, of using the body, in effect, as a "prop." For Kristeva is right—the positing of a body *is* a condition of discursive practices. It is crucial that feminism move beyond the opposition between essentialism and anti-essentialism. This move will entail the necessary risk taken by theories which attempt to define or construct a feminine specificity (not essence), theories which work to provide the woman with an autonomous symbolic representation.

What this means in terms of the theorization of a feminist filmmaking practice can only be sketched here. But it is clear from the preceding exploration of the theoretical elaboration of the female body that the stake does not simply concern an isolated image of the body. The attempt to "lean" on the body in order to formulate the woman's different relation to speech, to language, clarifies the fact that what is at stake is, rather, the syntax which constitutes the female body as a term. The most interesting and productive recent films dealing with the feminist problematic are precisely those which elaborate a new syntax, thus "speaking" the female body differently, even haltingly or inarticulately from the perspective of a classical syntax. For instance, the circular camera movements which carve out the space of the mise-en-scène in *Riddles of the Sphinx* are in a sense more critical to a discussion of the film than the status of the figure of the sphinx as feminine. The film effects a continual displacement of the gaze which "catches" the woman's body only accidentally, momentarily, refusing to hold or fix her in the frame. The camera consistently transforms its own framing to elide the possibility of a fetishism of the female body. Chantal Akerman's *Jeanne Dielman, 23 Quai du Commerce—1080 Bruxelles* constructs its syntax by linking together scenes which, in the classical text, would be concealed, in effect negated, by temporal ellipses. The specificity of the film lies in the painful duration of that time "in-between" events, that time which is exactly proper to the woman (in particular, the housewife) within a patriarchal society. The obsessive routine of Jeanne Dielman's daily life, as both house-wife and prostitute, is radically broken only by an instance of orgasm (corres-ponding quite literally to the "climax" of the narrative) which is immediately followed by her murder of the man. Hence, the narrative structure is a parodic "mime" that distorts, undoes the structure of the classical narrative through an insistence upon its repressions.

The analysis of the elaboration of a special syntax for a different articula-tion of the female body can also elucidate the significance of the recourse, in at least two of these films, to the classical codification of suspense. Both *Jeanne Dielman* and Sally Potter's *Thriller* construct a suspense without expectation. *Jeanne Dielman*, although it momentarily "cites" the mechan-ism of the narrative climax, articulates an absolute refusal of the phatic function of suspense, its engagement with and constraint of the spectator as consumer, devourer of discourse. *Thriller*, on the other hand, "quotes" the strategies of the suspense film (as well as individual films of this genre—for example, *Psycho*) in order to undermine radically the way in which the woman is "spoken" by another genre altogether, that of operatic tragedy. This engagement with the codification of suspense is an encounter with the genre which Roland Barthes defines as the most intense embodiment of the "generalized distortion" which "gives the language of narrative its special character":

> "Suspense" is clearly only a privileged—or "exacerbated"—form of distor-tion: on the one hand, by keeping a sequence open (through emphatic pro-cedures of delay and renewal), it reinforces the contact with the reader (the listener), has a manifestly phatic function; while on the other, it offers the threat of an uncompleted sequence, of an open paradign (if, as we believe, every sequence has two poles), that is to say of a logical disturbance, it being this disturbance which is consumed with anxiety and pleasure (all the more so because it is always made right in the end). "Suspense," therefore, is a game with structure, designed to endanger and glorify it, constituting a veritable "thrilling" of intelligibility: by representing order (and no longer series) in its fragility, "suspense" accomplishes the very idea of language. . . .[24]

It is precisely this "idea of language" which is threatened by both *Jeanne Dielman* and *Thriller* in their attempts to construct another syntax which would, perhaps, collapse the fragile order, revealing the ending too soon.

While I have barely approached the question of an exact formulation of the representation of the female body attached to the syntactical construc-tions of these films, it is apparent that this syntax is an area of intense concern, of reworking, rearticulating the specular imaging of woman, for whom, in the context of a current filmmaking, the formulation of a stake is already in process.

Notes

1.   Peter Gidal, transcription of a discussion following "Technology and Ideology in/through/and Avant-Garde Film: An Instance," in *The Cinematic Apparatus*, eds. Teresa de Lauretis and Stephen Heath, New York, St. Martins Press, 1980, p. 169.

2.   This calls for a more thorough dissection and analysis of the assumptions underlying the cliché that male models are "effeminate."

3.   Stephen Heath, "Difference," *Screen*, vol. 19, no. 3 (Autumn 1978), 73.

4.   Jean Laplanche, *Life and Death in Psychoanalysis*, trans. Jeffrey Mehlman, Baltimore, Johns Hopkins, 1976, p. 20.

5.   See, for example, "The Denial of the Vagina," in *Psychoanalysis and Female Sexuality*, ed. Hendrick M. Ruitenbeek, New Haven, College and University Press, 1966, pp. 73–87; and *Feminine Psychology*, ed. Harold Kelman, New York, W. W. Norton, 1967.

6.   Jacques Lacan, *Écrits: A Selection*, trans. Alan Sheridan, New York, W. W. Norton, 1977, p. 287.

7.   Parveen Adams, "Representation and Sexuality," *m/f*, no. 1 (1978), 66–67. Even if the phallus is defined as logically prior to the penis, in that it is the phallus which bestows significance on the penis, a *relation* between the two is nevertheless posited, and this is my point.

8.   I am grateful to Philip Rosen for this "representation" of the problem.

9.   Michèle Montrelay, "Inquiry into Femininity," *m/f*, no. 1 (1978), 89.

10.   *Ibid.*

11.   *Ibid.*, p. 90.

12.   *Ibid.*, pp. 91–92.

13.   *Ibid.*, p. 92.

14.   This description is derived from Lacan's conceptualization of masquerade in relation to femininity. See *Écrits: A Selection*, pp. 289–90. Lacan, in turn, borrows the notion of masquerade from Joan Riviere; see "Womanliness as Masquerade," in *Psychoanalysis and Female Sexuality*, pp. 209–20.

15.   Montrelay, p. 91.

16.   *Ibid.*, p. 98.

17.   Beverley Brown and Parveen Adams, "The Feminine Body and Feminist Politics," *m/f*, no. 3 (1979), 37.

18.   Luce Irigaray, "That Sex Which Is Not One," trans. R. Albury and P. Foss, in *Language, Sexuality, Subversion*, ed. Paul Foss and Meaghan Morris, Darlington, Feral Publications, 1978, pp. 161–72. This is a translation of the second essay in *Ce sexe qui n'en est pas un*, Paris, Minuit, 1977, pp. 23–32.

19.   Brown and Adams, p. 38.

20.   *Ce sexe qui n'en est pas un*, pp. 129–30.

21.   The critique of Kristeva is based on *About Chinese Women*, trans. Anita Barrows, New York, Urizen Books, 1977.

22.   Brown and Adams, p. 39.

23.   Laplanche, pp. 23–34.

24.   Roland Barthes, "Introduction to the Structural Analysis of Narratives," in *Image-Music-Text*, trans. Stephen Heath, New York, Hill and Wang, 1977, p. 119.

14

India Song/Son nom de Venise dans Calcutta désert: The Compulsion to Repeat

Joan Copjec

One no longer hears the term *profilmic event* (used or mentioned), although not such a very long time ago it was a commonplace of film theory. The term has been allowed to obsolesce as attention has shifted instead to the cinematic apparatus and its ideological inscription—to the scene, that is, of writing. The biological metaphor which defines this simple chronology is, of course, in a sense totally inapt. The profilmic event is not the vestigium, the trace, of a theoretical structure which declined—naturally. Rather the cinematic apparatus has been theorized precisely as an intervention between the profilmic— the natural—and the discourse of and about film.

The chronology has, in fact, been described differently, for example by Christian Metz, who in "The Imaginary Signifier" refers to it as a shift "from attention to the *énoncé* to concern for the *énonciation*."[1] *Énoncé* is best translated, as Ben Brewster does in his notes to Metz's essay, as "statement" and *énonciation* as "speech act"—or, one might add for reasons which will become clear, as "speech event." Metz's distinction here is related to the one he makes (following Benveniste) between history and discourse. Attention to the statement alone suppresses the sourse of the statement, makes of it an object, a found or historical (or profilmic) object which seems to come from nowhere. Concern for the speech act or event, on the other hand, uncovers the presence of a subject, a point of view, of the statement, locates it in a present moment, a *context* of speaker and speech, rather than a historical, an apersonal past.

There is, however, another linguistic distinction to which we can relate the terms of Metz's chronology. Metz himself does not note this relation, but

Roland Barthes, in his structural analysis of narratives, does. Barthes describes the contemporary concern for discourse as opposed to history.

> It is this formal person [the linguistic first person or enunciator] that writers today are attempting to speak and such an attempt represents an important subversion . . . for it aims to transpose narrative from the purely constantive plane, which it has occupied until now, to the performative plane, whereby the meaning of an utterance is the very act by which it is uttered: today, writing is not "telling" but saying that one is telling . . . which is why part of contemporary literature is no longer descriptive, but transitive. Striving to accomplish so pure a present in its language that the whole of discourse is identified with the act of its delivery. . . .[2]

The distinction—between constantive utterances, descriptive sentences which can be judged true or false as they have their referents outside themselves, that is, outside language; and performative utterances which have no truth value, but have instead a *force*, a power of effecting, of establishing themselves as, events—is taken from speech act theory.

It must be remembered that it is Barthes who makes this connection, and with reference to literature, between a distinction of French linguistic theory and one of Anglo-American speech act theory. The connection has not been made within French film theory, nor have the implications of this connection been examined by Barthes or film theorists. It is easy to see, however, how, historically, film theory which first formulated the profilmic as an *event* could come to share some common ground with linguists who define speech as an event. It seems that contemporary film theory began by substituting one event for another, by questioning the theoretical limitations of "profilmic" and not of "event." It progressed, like speech act theory, through a critique of the communications model of language which had preceeded it. Metz, in his second book, *Language and Cinema* had himself proposed a communications model of cinematic language, having five matters of expression, five technico-sensorial unities. Under the influence of debates around the cinematic apparatus, which raged in the film journals *Cinéthique* and *Cahiers du Cinéma*, however, he began a revision of his theory which meant, basically, a questioning of the scientific neutrality of the "channel" of cinematic communication, the apparatus, and an introduction of the subject of the enunciation, the performer of the film's utterance. It was Jean-Louis Baudry who most clearly argued, in "The Ideological Effects of the Basic Cinematographic Apparatus" and "The Apparatus," that the apparatus could not be granted a place apart, but must be examined in the context of its historical development, that is, in the context of the ideology which produced it as an effect. These articles must be read alongside those of Metz written during the same period. For Metz's work becomes a sympathetic response to Baudry, an extension and a clarification of many of Baudry's arguments. Indeed, it seems that the direction which film theory has taken can be traced back to these beginnings. The "subject" with which film theory is now concerned, for example, was introduced into theory at this precise moment, at the same time as, *through* the apparatus—through a metaphor which established a relationship between the psychic and the cinematic apparatus (which was defined not simply as the camera, but the whole machinery of relations and meanings, socio-psychic systems which construct the psyche).

The question which should be asked is how this metaphor, this particular historico-technical metaphor, has effected or precipitated the subject which is the reality of film theory. Film theory turned from consideration of its object as a reproduction of reality, the profilmic, and became a critique of this very notion of reproduction in order to consider film as an intervention, an event, which participated in the production of a subject. What remains unclear in the theory is how this production can be anything but a reproduction, how the cinematic apparatus, effect of an idealist, patriarchal ideology can produce, "effect" anything but a transcendent, male "subject." Speech act theory finds itself in the same position. A performative utterance (which is, in the end, the main kind which concerns these theorists, just as it is the only utterance admitted as evidence by American law) can only be said to have taken place, its saying is only said to be (or to make it) so, when it has appropriately, correctly, completely, intentionally, and consistently repeated, reproduced a conventional procedure. A performative, then, can not be either true *or* false because it can *only* be true, that is, according to the laws of logic, identical with itself.

Baudry, in fact, defines the force which activates and is activated by the cinematic apparatus as the "compulsion to repeat . . . a former condition," as "desire as such . . . the nostalgia for a former state." Cinema, therefore, is like a dream, the fulfillment of a wish for sameness, for "survival and . . . bygone periods," for a repetition of the oneness, the identity, of and with the beginning.[3] Metz also finds the parallel between cinema and dream telling (by which I intend all its possible senses), although he admits that cinema undergoes a process of secondarization further still than the dream. For him also the cinema is "motivated" by the *economy* of the pleasure principle; it is inaugural of a circuit of return. The cinema is, thus, by definition the production of "good objects," that is, pleasurable films. Metz recognizes the existence of filmic unpleasure, "bad objects" or bad films, but these are not "basic" to the institution of cinema, are simple "local failure[s]."[4]

In the same way Austin defines the difference between the "happy" functioning of a performative and the "unhappy" functioning, that is, the "failure" of a performative to take effect, to take place. He admits that "things can go wrong" and he accounts for these things by the "doctrine of the infelicities."[5] This doctrine *extenuates* the possibility of failure, bad illocutionary objects; by attributing them to "extenuating circumstances." Only successes are counted, failures are voided. The speech event in its total context is overdetermined to reproduce only itself. Compare this to Metz's definition of the institution as "auto-reproduction":

It is the specific characteristic of every true institution that it takes charge of the mechanisms of its own perpetuation—there is no other solution than to set up arrangements whose aim and effect is to give the spectator the "spontaneous" desire to visit the cinema and pay for his ticket. . . . In this way the libidinal economy (filmic pleasure in its historically constituted form) reveals its "correspondence" with the political economy. . . .[6][7]

For Austin it is finally the carrying out of the appropriate intentions of the speaker which is determinant of the performative. Although the presence within the speaker of certain thoughts, feelings, and intentions is listed as one of the conditions of the success of the performative, Austin stresses that this is not one circumstance among others, but *the* condition upon which the others depend. For Metz it is the carrying out of the intention of the institution which defines the success of the cinematic performance, "since the institution as a whole has filmic pleasure alone as its aim."[7]

And so we have the same old story—"cine-repetitions," as Raymond Bellour calls them; cinema repeats itself. For "beyond any given film, what each film aims at through the apparatus that permits it is the regulated order of the spectacle, the return of an immemorial and everyday state which the subject experiences in his dreams and for which the cinematic apparatus renews the desire."[8] Cinema accomplishes its aim primarily through narrative. Although, as narrative claims to repeat events which have already taken place, it is possible to define it as it defines itself, as "history," as a constantive utterance which his its referents outside and prior to itself; it may also be considered a force which insures the taking place of events. In this case there would be an implied performative "I sing" behind each narrative. This is what Barthes isolates as characteristic of contemporary narrative, and what Metz eventually proposes as well. But this direction is prepared for at the beginning by Metz, who takes up the study of the *grande syntagmatique* to rescue cinematic language from its "paradigmatic"—and here we would say constantive—"poverty." Narrative, from this perspective, does not merely refer to some prior reality; it predicates. The force of narrative is generated through repetitions which contain differences and, hence, space, mark out its limits, and produce its homogeneity. Bellour puts it succinctly: "Repetition saturates the narrative space."[9] That is, through systems of alternations (between shots and reverse shots, syntagmatic units, etc.), *mise-en-abyme* constructions, smaller units get locked into, absorbed by the larger unit of the complete narrative, its resolution. Just so does the performative take place, in and only in a total situation, a "saturated context," which is to say, one that is "exhaustively determined."[10] The performative takes place only as it is an exact repetition of a conventional procedure, uttered by a person fully conscious of and intending this procedure, absorbed, as it were, by the convention.

At the end of his analysis of cine-repetitions, Bellour includes a reference to Thierry Kuntzel's work on the "scene of repetition" in *King Kong*:

King Kong appears, provoking the full repetition of the cry; the cry, which is now the woman's real cry, was expected, remembered, and almost uttered by the viewer. The latter, of course, knows that he is "at the cinema" as Metz says. Yet, in the shadow of that knowledge the film does indeed repeat *his own* dream, his desire to dream.[11]

The *effect* of repetition is clearly identification—which brings with it this "purificatory effect," this catharsis. But we have heard this before: "A tragedy . . . is the imitation of an action that is serious and also . . . complete in itself . . . with incidents arousing pity and fear wherewith to accomplish its catharsis of such emotions."[12] And again: "It is clear that in their play children repeat everything that has made a great impression on them in real life and that in doing so they abreact the strength of the impression, . . . make themselves master of the situation."[13] As Philippe Lacoue-Labarthe has pointed out, the (speculative) philosophy of tragedy, of representation, has remained, since the beginning, a theory of tragedy's *effect*, of the catharsis of the "menace which the contradiction illustrated by the tragic conflict represented."[14] Repetition has this effect—of heterotautology. Of interiorizing difference, contradiction, distance, making them self-same. Of converting contradictions into "metaphysical pitch and toss,"[15] that is, into an idealization of movement itself whereby pitch is absorbed by toss, hurly by burly, fort by da, death by life, body by soul and so on and so forth. That is to say, into no movement at all, into similarity, the "at home" status of homeostasis.

One may find this argument *heimlich*, and pleasurable for that, for its familiarity. There is certainly no disputing this effect—the "subject effect," the "cathartic effect," the "performative effect": these *eventual effects*. And one may appreciate the advance of this argument which speaks in terms of forces, of knowledge in terms of relations of power rather than in terms of "true" or "false"; the foundation in psychoanalysis which also tells us that repetition is the reexperiencing of something identical, is a source of pleasure; the advance in considering language, rather than the body, as the "house of being," language rather than biology as destiny. For as this parallel consideration of film and speech act theory has intended to indicate, the exclusion of the profilmic by theory from film discourse is a repetition of the exclusion of the body—the external referent—from discourse in general.

Still there are some (not quite included in "one") who are not happy with this resolution. These "infelicities" are women. For it is they, finally, who are the difference, the external who are repeatedly excluded by the homeostatic system—the constant reproduction of the male by the patriarchal mechanisms of film, language. Film theory has turned from ontological analysis, a concern with essentialist questions about what is, to textual analyses of the effectivity of point of view, of the speech event. Yet the point of view and the structures of voyeurism, exhibition, identification which follow from it are always, repeatedly, male. Women, therefore, can not look, can not be represented—as women. They do not exist, according to Lacan, as women.

This very nonexistence is the effect of the repetition of the same. Women are not in a position to contest the force of this conclusion, the "male effect" of repetition. But they must and can find ways to break into this system, this theory, perhaps by first breaking from a theory of effects which remains in their imaginary—that is, consistent and plenitudinous—hold. Psychoanalysis can provide a model for this break, for it has progressed from the "happy" (I am tampering with Lacan's descriptive, "optimistic") days of catharsis upon the discovery, in the transference, of another kind of repetition, repetition in act, by which it recognized the significance of missed encounters, of events that never took place—in an infinity, a beyond, of the pleasure principle. And a before—by which we may be able to break cinema from the hold of the eternal return of the dream analogy: "If there is a 'beyond of the pleasure principle,' it is only consistent to grant that there was also a time before the purpose of dreams was the fulfillment of wishes."[16] Freud turned his attention to this beyond when he observed that certain of his patients, in their dreams or in their analysis, exhibited a compulsion to repeat traumatic experiences. It was this observation that forced Freud to supplement his theory of dreams so that it could include those dreams which did not fulfill wishes; to question the priority of the pleasure principle, the tendency of the psychic system towards constancy, and to assert instead a more radical tendency towards zero; to grant a metapsychological status to aggressiveness, that is, to affirm the existence of a death drive. The compulsion to repeat is definitely not, according to psychoanalysis, what Baudry describes. It is definitely not an attempt to return to a previous state of satisfaction; rather it is the return to a trauma which is conceived, psychoanalytically as it is medicosurgically, as a wound, a break in the protective skin which triggers catastrophe, misfortune throughout the whole of the organism.

This brings us once again to the question of the profilmic and of the body and their relation to discourse. Most philosophical, psychoanalytic theory has dismissed the essentialist assertion of a simple causal relation between the somatic and the psychic, in which the one is directly eventuated by the other, as theoretically unsound, politically useless. Yet the anti-essentialist position which eschews any but a parallel relation by which soma and psyche are seen to run along side by side, each totally the outside of the other (like two clocks wound by a cosmic grand*father*), ends up constructing a kind of monadology which is equally unsound, equally regressive politically. It seems that we must begin to specify a different kind of relation between these two terms, one which focuses on the breaks between them, in order to prepare the way for an introduction of women, the outside, into the systems which repeat their absence. It is important to recognize, however, that this will be no easy task, that it will often look like a return to biologism. Freud himself, who began psychoanalysis with the study of hysteria, that is, the study of the relationship of soma to psyche, came back, in *Beyond the Pleasure Principle*, to a reconsideration of this same relationship between the biological and the psychological organism. But he passed, as we have said, from a study of catharsis, which is precisely a freeing or clearing a place of dead bodies, to a study, simultaneous with *Beyond the Pleasure Principle*, of "The Uncanny," which is the place of the return of bodies once dead.

The pleasure principle would be, according to Freud's definition, on the side of the *heimlich*, the canny which is "friendly, intimate, homelike; the enjoyment of quiet content, etc., arousing a sense of peaceful pleasure and security as in one within the four walls of this house," rather than the *unheimlich*, the uncanny. An example of such domestic pleasure: "A careful housewife who knows how to make a pleasing *Heimlichkeit* (*Häuslichkeit*) out of the smallest means."[17]

Marguerite Duras reused, cited in its entirety, the sound track from her previous film, *India Song*, in the making of *Son nom de Venise dans Calcutta désert*. The second film merely adds a new visual track, consisting almost completely of images of the deserted, deteriorating Rothschild palace near Reims (no human figures appear until the final minutes of the film) to this already-paid-for sound track. A frugal gesture, surely—and some would find *Som nom de Venise* pleasurable to watch (few have even had the chance to see it, however, so seldom is it screened)—but clearly an economic failure. An homage, it would seem, to the death drive rather than the pleasure principle. Bellour has included the "remake" among his list of cine-repetitions (cine-pleasures), noting that it is a particularly "triumphant" form, for it simultaneously repeats and interlocks its historical past and its historical present. But Duras is no careful housewife and her "remake" is directly ruinous of the very image of "home," of the *heimlich* notion of historical context. The repetition which is involved in the making of *India Song/Son nom de Venise*, this doubling of the "*son*," alientates the name, here a place name, from itself. Replaces the singularity of name, origin, place—familiarity, finally—in the uncanny of "*désert*." Naming is an effect of repetition, but Duras's films desert the *da* of repetition, the "here" of the *énonciation*, of the speech event, the effect of mastery, for the *fort* of alienation. Hers are not films of illusionary effects, but of the lost causes of repetition, of the xenopathology of the proper, the home.

That I suggest *India Song/Son nom de Venise* be read in tandem with *Beyond the Pleasure Principle*, as an example of the repetition compulsion delineated there, will perhaps surprise no one. Certainly not those familiar with Duras's other works. Marie-Claire Ropars-Wuilleumier has isolated from these, three novels (*Le Ravissement de Lol V. Stein, Le Vice-Consul, L'Amour*) and three films (*La Femme du Gange, India Song, Son nom de Venise*) which she refers to as the *cycle durassein*.[18] Each of these works cycles around, repeats, and disfigures the same "protextual" event, the ball at S. Thala, the Michael Richardson-Lol V. Stein-Anne Marie Stretter configuration. I am also suggesting, however, that all of Duras's films, from

Hiroshima Mon Amour to *Le Camion*, display the workings of this compulsion, extend their analyses, like Freud's own, from a recognition of traumatic war neuroses to a theory of the drives, beyond the pleasure principle. Like Freud also, the films displace the trauma from the immediacy of the present, the present unfolding of the film, exteriorize it in some vague profilmic, make of it an event which never takes place. *Le Camion*, in which Dépardieu and Duras read the script of a film that they would have made had they had the economic means, is most ostensibly concerned with this not-taking-place of the profilmic, but *India Song*, which substitutes the reception of the middle section for the traumatic ball at S. Thala, and *Son nom de Venise*, which substitutes other images for even this substitution, defer, take the place *of* the profilmic event, preventing it from taking place. The profilmic maintains a genitive relation to the film, but it is partitive rather than possessive.

The question the films and their repetitions compel us to ask is *where* can we locate possession when it is defined by an utterance which can not hold its own, but rather must always depend for its meaning on its context—is always only partial, ideologically inscribed? The performative utterance which distinguishes itself from the constative does so by virtue of the fact that it is in possession of its own referent, which means that something is being done at the moment of the person's uttering. But when Austin allows himself to "step out into the desert of comparative precision," he momentarily loses track of this person who utters. Although the performative usually takes the form of the first-person singular, present indicative, active (as in Benveniste's "discourse"), sometimes this active and singular first person's presence is not indicated grammatically (or lexicographically) in the sentence. In other words, sometimes there is no "I" to indicate the utterance's source, who is thus left out of the "picture," or the "speech-situation." When this happens, when the purely grammatical context is not sufficient to define the "happiness" of the performance, Austin, who is at this point marking his break from "obsessional logicians," looks to the extra-grammatical, to another context, for clues. The speaker, not present in the grammatical sense, is "referred to" (Austin places the phrase in quotation marks to indicate his distance, the difference he implies by his use) in verbal utterances by the physical-speaking presence, in written utterances by the signature, of the source of the utterance. The utterance is thus "tethered" to its source, whose word becomes its bond. Derrida's critique of speech act theory, in "Signature, Event, Context" ("Sec"), ends with this discussion of signatures. There are, no one will deny, effects of signature observable in everyday life, but Derrida is interested in the xenopathology (the alterity tied to repetition), rather than the effect of these effects. In order for a signature to be effective, it must have a recognizable, that is, a repeatable form, and it must be able to function in the absence of the signatory. The pleasure, the constancy of the signature effect—the recognizability and economic circulation it ensures—is thus marked by the absence, even the radical absence—the death—of the signatory. The utterance func-

Son nom de Venise dans Calcutta désert (Marguerite Duras, 1976)

tions in the absence not only of its source, but also of its referent and its context. These absences are not merely "infelicities," but the condition, the mark of any utterance, any sign, oral or written. The identity or identifiability of a sign, that is, depends upon its being recognizable outside its source, referent, context—in their absence. Identity, therefore, is assured only by otherness, the otherness of the sign to itself. By way of clarification Derrida offers this:

> By virtue of its essential iterability, a written syntagma can always be detached from the chain in which it is inserted or given without causing it to lose all possibility of functioning, if not all possibility of "communicating," precisely. One can perhaps come to recognize other possibilities in it by inscribing it or *grafting* it onto other chains. No context can entirely enclose it.[19]

It is this "untetherability" of the utterance which constructs it from the beginning in repetition and in otherness and suspends its source in the position of receiver.

The nosology of voices in *India Song*, the tabulation of the different disturbances between them and the visual images of the film, has been undertaken elsewhere.[20] It is sufficient to recall here that the voices are not "tethered" to the visual images as utterance to source, and so when one of the final, and most "authoritative" voices of the film is identified as Duras's own, it barely has the effect of "signature," barely closes a full meaning over the images. *Son nom de Venise* further attenuates this effect by contextualizing the voices differently. Placed within a film that images the hollows of deserted rooms, empty spaces, the voices become uncanny echoes of voices themselves.

They become, that is, the acoustic equivalents of the mirror reflections which reverberate through the previous film, which are so endemic to it that they make *India Song* a reverberation of itself. Duras has turned the canniness from her four-walled house, made it uncanny, by covering one of these walls with a mirror. The function of mirrors, of course, is to allow the self to observe itself. But the doubling, the repetition, which mirrors perform in order to serve the self's narcissistic regard and, hence, its self-protection, entails[21] an exteriorization as well which makes the self foreign to itself, makes it its own aggressor. It is the central section of *India Song* which has the highest concentration of mirror images. For this section is a series of alternating exterior and interior shots, and all the interiors are of the physical space of the drawing room, which has a mirrored rear wall. The diegetic space of this section is that of a reception, of the "pursuit of Anne-Marie Stretter, her hunting down by death, by . . . the Vice-Consul of Lahore."[22] Anne-Marie *Guardi*-Stretter, one should say, her Venetian name, a command to look, doubled by a foreign name and on *that* account hunted down by death. It is in this section—obedient to all the laws of classical beauty, laws of repetition, symmetry, harmony, in which perception is doubled, precisely a *reception*— that the primary object of narcissism, Anne-Marie Guardi-Stretter, is suspended in the space of a mirror, and is there, in the mirror, met by the principle of death. Her mirror image, which stands between her and the Vice-Consul, does not protect, but is turned instead to receive the bearer of her extinction. The Vice-Consul, exiled by a xenophobic, conservative society, invades it, nevertheless, as one of its own invited guests.

As we pass from a discussion of the relationship of the sound to the image track, of the "disembodied voices," their disembodiment from one film and grafting onto another, to a discussion of the diegetic space of bodies and sounds, we pass to an important criticism which is sometimes lodged against the work of Duras. Though everywhere her disjunctive use of sound and image is acknowledged as "progressive," her films are sometimes accused of replaying a regressive essentialism. The sensuousness of the images, the mysterious rhythms and silences of speech which yoke women to a sublime language of madness and love, the forests which are symbolic of the priority of nature, all suggest, so the interpretation goes, that it is the natural body which is the real voice of the films and that we are being asked to listen to its direct speech. Besides reiterating the point of this essay, that the disjunction, through doubling, of speech from itself renders direct speech—the full presence of speech to a total context within which it takes place—impossible, something more must be said about this relation of body to speech, and of body to speech act theory.

Bodies act, but do speeches . . . act? *Do* they, really, or is this just a metaphor? Perhaps not, since even psychoanalysis through its own metaphor, the transference, asserts that we can do things with words, cure things with talk. Derrida's critique of speech act theory is founded in psychoanalytic theory, its concept of the unconscious which undoes Austin's concept of context as a fully determinable entity. This unconscious is the effect of speech, of the rupture from the body which is the condition of speech and of representation in general. To say, however, that this rupture excludes the body from speech and from the psyche which speech structures, to say that the somatic and the psychic bear no relation to each other is to misread the theory which began with Freud and his compulsive return to the biological order. It is in the works of the French psychoanalysts, Jean Laplanche and

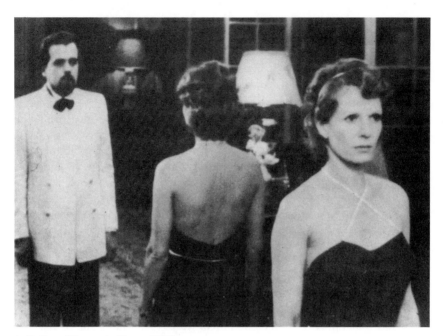

India Song (Marguerite Duras, 1975)

J.-B. Pontalis, and the Hungarian, Nicholas Abraham, that we find the most extended analyses of the somatic-psychic relationship which is inherent in Freud's theories. Abraham, in "The Shell and the Kernel," deals directly with this relationship as it is developed in *The Language of Psycho-analysis* and Derrida introduces himself (his own theoretical complicity) and Abraham's work in "Me-Psychoanalysis," and "Fors." Briefly, the relation, specified in all these works, between the two terms, soma and psyche, is one of mission, of psychical representatives, delegates, and foreign service. Laplanche and Pontalis define "psychical representative" in their dictionary of psychoanalysis:

> This term cannot be understood save by reference to the concept of *instinct*—a concept which in Freud's view bridges the gap between the somatic and the mental. On the somatic side, the instinct has its source in organic phenomena . . . but at the same time, by virtue of its aim and of the objects to which it becomes attached, the instinct undergoes a "vicissitude" that is essentially psychical in nature. This borderline position of the instinct no doubt accounts for Freud's calling upon the notion of representative—by which he means a kind of *delegation*—of the soma within the psyche . . . though in principle he is nothing more than the proxy of his mandator, the delegate . . . enters into a new system of relationships which is liable to change his perspective and cause him to depart from the directives he has been given.[23]

Laplanche, in *Life and Death in Psychoanalysis*, extends this Freudian analogy into a detailed account of anaclisis,[24] or, as he translates it, "propping"—the process by which the drive leaning on the instinct, much as

239

a delegate leans on the mandator by performing its function, deviates metaphorically from its aim and metonymically from its object. The deviation is caused by fantasy, the introjection, the reflection, of a scene of satisfaction into the subject. The fantasy is, of course, not the scene itself, but a representation which points to its absence. The instinct, turned away from the vital order of the biological towards the object of the displacement, is turned onto the subject itself, wherein the fantasy resides, to become the drive. It is this moment of reflection which constitutes sexuality, which is nothing else but this perverse movement, this deflection of instinct by fantasy. And as the fantasy disjoins the biological subject who needs from the sexual subject who desires, as it is an *infraction*, a trauma, it is the first psychic pain. The sexual drive which emerges from the fantasy is thus established as primarily masochistic. The ego is the first fantasmatic, the first sexual, object which is produced. In defining the *limits* of the psychic apparatus (as its surface, which is contiguous with the body and everything else outside, and its form, which is a metaphor of the body) it also defines the threshold through which pain breaks. The ego, then, which is the ballast of the psychic system, that which binds energies and seeks equilibrium by maintaining them at a certain minimal level, seeks, in short, the preservation of the system, introduces a masochism which threatens the system with annihilation.

From this brief summary we can make two important points about the relationship of the body to the psychic apparatus: although we cannot say that the body causes the psyche, we can say that it has a structuring function, is its organizing metaphor; body and psyche are related through the radical *insufficiency* of the former. The biological fact of prematuration entails that the satisfaction of the infant is attainable only from the field of another, or more precisely, of others, since the supplementary field of the other, the body's context, can never be saturated, determined fully. Desire corresponds to what Derrida, in "Sec," calls *restance*, a neologism translated as "nonpresent remainder." It is a metonym, the contiguous margin of body and psyche, the measure of their difference, their inadequation.

Baudry, in "Ideological Effects," links his project to Derrida's by citing his essay "Freud and the Scene of Writing." The two projects are, indeed, generally consonant—both attempt to define the ideological stake of the Western metaphysical tradition in maintaining a concept of an originating subject and—specifically in these essays—both are concerned with the relationship between the historico-technical fact of the nonpsychic apparatus and the analogy with the psychic apparatus which it makes possible. But there are also important differences. Baudry describes the "return effect" in cinema as the repetition of a time when "representation and perception were not yet differentiated." Derrida's essay, on the other hand, is a direct refutation of such a distinction, is "polemical on the very threshold of what we persist in calling perception."[25] Perception is, according to his reading of Freud, from the very first, repetition and representation, which is to say that it exists only as a relationship of the body to otherness. Desire is, for Baudry, a "nostalgia for a state in which desire has been satisfied through the transfer of a perception to a formation resembling hallucination which seems to be activated by the cinematic apparatus."[26] Derrida would disagree, insisting instead upon his concept of *restance*. Desire has definitely never been satisfied; it is instead that which is missed by satisfaction. This error, in considering desire as a matter of sufficiency rather than insufficiency, is compounded by Baudry's further, concluding speculation that unconscious desire represents itself to the subject through the cinematic apparatus. By folding this summary statement over his own analysis of the ideology of scientific invention, the system of science, he begins to undermine his project. Desire becomes an originating force with an attainable end and systems of ideology are given an unconscious aim. The cinematic apparatus becomes, once again, a tool that restores the integrity of the subject, supplies the subject's demand. Derrida avoids this incipient anthropomorphism by relating the technical apparatus of the writing pad to the insufficiency of the psychic apparatus, by exposing its supplementary (rather than complementary) status. The invention becomes the effect of the psyche's Being-in-the-worldness, its insertion into an otherness upon which it depends. It is proof of the psyche's inability to maintain itself even as it is the psyche's metaphor. There may be no way of getting around the observation that the apparatus fulfills an ancient dream of man, but at least we can see by Derrida's analysis that this dream is itself a psychic supplement, the indication within the subject of its unfulfillment.

It may be necessary to add that the target of this essay is neither Metz nor Baudry, both of whose work has made some of these arguments possible, has propelled the valuable work of textual analysis as well as the work on the apparatus. Rather it is an attempt to locate those points to which the *reductio ad absurdum* of their arguments attaches itself. In "The Uncanny," Freud quotes and affirms this important observation of Otto Rank: "The 'immortal soul' was the first 'double' of the body. This invention of doubling as a preservation against extinction has its counterpart in the language of dreams, which is fond of representing castration by a doubling or multiplication of the genital symbol."[27] It is important to guard against a tendency in film theory to make of language or the cinematic apparatus an "immortal soul" with a life all its own, unthreatened by the death drive, to guard against a "multiplication of the genital symbol" by subscribing to a nominalism that begins with and repeats endlessly the name of the father. This can only be done by recognizing that language and the apparatus are constructed out of relations of otherness, which means also, of otherness to the body. To say that there is no outside of language, no extra-textual, is not to say that there is an inside which is not Imaginary. Being, in short, is no more housed in language than it is in the body; it resides rather in the otherness of body and language each to the other. Otherness, death, the body are the preconditions of language and are operant there, represented in its repetitions. What is most compelling about the compulsion to repeat is the way it returns difference always at the expense of the same. And desire is the xenogenetic offspring as well as the compulsion of this difference of repetition. It is always as other, in some other place, that desire is. Therefore, as Lacan is fond of repeating, the question which it poses for the subject is not *what* (this is a question for demand), but *where* it desires.

Laplanche makes a crucial distinction between the hallucination of satisfaction and satisfaction through hallucination. Hallucination of satisfaction, "the reproduction of the pure feeling of discharge even in the absence of discharge," is, in fact, impossible to conceive. For what need would provoke the organism to hallucinate if satisfaction were self-contained? Satisfaction through hallucination, "by virtue of *the very existence* of the hallucinatory phenomena,"[28] implies the insufficiency of the organism which must supplement itself, introduce into itself fantasmatic objects produced by the symbolizing mechanisms of hallucination. Those theorists who maintain that at the cinema only men can look would have to deny this very existence of cinema, of representation in general, would have to ask us to believe that we hallucinate satisfaction.

The cinema of Marguerite Duras not only exists, but exists to point out the very conditions of its existence. It makes a statement against a patriarchal monadology by representing the xenophobia at work within pleasure itself. To call it essentialist by merely pointing to its mysterious rhythms and its silences is to invoke an argument which may itself be essentialist. It is to ignore the importance as well as the limits of context, the predicative movement of conflict. For the mysterious, the exotic of place, is set precisely and conflictually within the familiar of the same, and the repetition of trauma, of difference, within the repetition of pleasure. It presents not a cinema of the sublime, of the sublimity of desire, but rather of the limits of the pleasure principle to which desire attests, through its disjunction of image and sound, a hendiadys of desire.

Notes

1.   Christian Metz, "The Imaginary Signifier," *Screen*, Vol. 16, no. 2 (Summer 1975), 14.

2.   Roland Barthes, *Image-Music-Text*, trans. Stephen Heath, New York, Hill and Wang, 1977, p. 114.

3.   J.-L. Baudry, "The Apparatus," *Camera Obscura*, no. 1 (1976), 108, 121.

4.   Metz, pp. 18–19.

5.   J. L. Austin, *How to Do Things with Words*, Cambridge, Harvard Univesity Press, 1962. p. 14.

6.   Metz, p. 19.

7.   *Ibid.*

8.   Raymond Bellour, "Cine-Repetitions," *Screen*, vol. 20, no. 2 (Summer 1979), 71.

9.   *Ibid.*, p. 70.

10. Jacques Derrida, "Signature, Event, Context," *Glyph 1*, Baltimore, Johns Hopkins University Press, 1976.

11. Bellour, pp. 71–72.

12. Aristotle, *Poetics*, 1449b.

13. Sigmund Freud, *Beyond the Pleasure Principle*, trans. James Strachey, New York, W. W. Norton, 1961, p. 11.

14. Philippe Lacoue-Labarthe, "The Caesura of the Speculative," *Glyph 4*, Baltimore, Johns Hopkins University Press, 1978, p. 66.

15. Frank Kermode, *The Sense of an Ending*, New York, Oxford University Press, 1967, p. 83. This phrase is quoted from L. C. Knights by Kermode, whose own book remains one of the best considerations of the way beginnings are absorbed by ends.

16. Freud, *Beyond the Pleasure Principle*, p. 27.

17. Sigmund Freud, "The Uncanny," in *On Creativity and the Unconscious*, New York, Harper and Row, 1958, p. 126.

18. Marie-Claire Ropars-Wuilleumier, *L'Avant-Scène Cinéma*, no. 225 (April 1979), 5.

19. Derrida, p. 182.

20. Marie-Claire Ropars-Wuilleumier in her introductory essay in *L'Avant-Scène* and "The Disembodied Voice (*India Song*)," *Yale French Studies*, no. 60 (1980). Also Michel Marie, "La parole dans le cinéma français contemporain: l'exemple d'*India Song*," and Marie-Françoise Grange, "Un système d'écriture: *India Song*," both in *Ça cinéma*, no. 19 (1979). See also Elizabeth Lyon's "The Cinema of Lol V. Stein," *Camera Obscura*, no. 6 (1980), reprinted as Chapter 15 in this book. Although this article focuses more on the primal scene of fantasy and less on the voices that narrate it, I include it here to indicate the extensive work that has already been done on the text of *India Song*. While my essay supports the work of textual analysis, it is obvious that it does not engage in it, even as it is committed to the analysis of one textual nexus. It inserts itself instead in the space of otherness opened up by textual analysis—its insistence, in principle, on the way particular texts *disturb* codes of cinema, their authority, binding, and finitude, the way they differ from the very codes which maintain their identity—inserts itself as a kind of contextual analysis.

21. Part of the context, the total speech act which defines the performative, are the other propositions which the performative proposition "entails." To say that *p* entails *q* is to say that the truth of *q* is not in conflict with the truth of *p*. Those schooled in this type of logic will find the Freudian concept on the death drive, which is entailed by the pleasure principle, difficult to grasp.

22. Marguerite Duras, "Notes on *India Song*," *Camera Obscura*, no. 6 (1980), 45.

23. J. Laplanche and J.-B. Pontalis, *The Language of Psycho-analysis*, New York, W. W. Norton, 1973, pp. 364–65.

24. As it is translated by Laplanche and by psychoanalysis generally, *anaclisis* comes from the Greek verb, *anaklino*, which means "to lean one thing against another," "to lean back." In fact, Liddell and Scott define it as a noun which is derived from the verb, *anakaleo*, which means "to call up, especially the dead; to call back, especially from exile." This definition seems more appropriate and accurate.

25. Derrida, "Freud and the Scene of Writing," in *Writing and Difference*, ed. and trans. Alan Bass, Chicago, University of Chicago Press, 1978, p. 113.

26. Baudry, p. 121.

27. Freud, "The Uncanny," p. 141.

28. Jean Laplanche, *Life and Death in Psychoanalysis*, trans. Jeffrey Mehlman, Baltimore and London, Johns Hopkins University Press, 1976, p. 71.

15

The Cinema of Lol V. Stein

Elisabeth Lyon

I

... this word, which does not exist, is nonetheless there: it awaits you just
around the corner of language, it defies you—never having been used—to raise
it, to make it arise from its kingdom, which is pierced on every side and through
which flows the sea, the sand, the eternity of the ball in the cinema of Lol V.
Stein.

Le Ravissement de Lol V. Stein

India Song is part of what has been called in Marguerite Duras's work the
"Indian" cycle,[1] a group of three novels and three films which all transform
and repeat a single story. That story, like the "cinema of Lol V. Stein" (from
the novel in which it first appears), turns around a scene which is at once an
"eternity" and eternally absent: the ball at S. Thala. Although the novels
(*Le Ravissement de Lol V. Stein, Le Vice-Consul, L'Amour*) were written
first, in Duras's work perhaps more than in other filmmakers similarly
engaged, the films (*La Femme du Gange, India Song, Son nom de Venise
dans Calcutta désert*) are not reducible simply to translations into cinematic
terms of those fictions. Both the novels and the films are taken in the same
effort of remembering—through the imaginaries of the characters, narrators,
Duras, and the spectator or reader—making it impossible to find a real event
from which the imaginary stories would follow. The scene of the ball,
although it becomes a kind of signifying knot across which the fantasy of
India Song is later put into play, never attains the status of a true event or

an original trauma. It is always already fantasmic as it is told by the narrator at the beginning of *Le Ravissement de Lol V. Stein* (1964):

> Here then in full and all mixed together, both this false impression [*faux semblant*] which Tatiana Karl tells about and what I have been able to imagine about that night at the town beach casino. Following which I shall relate my own story of Lol Stein.[2]

The story begins then already shot through with the holes and gaps of someone else's memory. But the transformations and repetitions within *Le Ravissement de Lol V. Stein* and the subsequent novels and films do nothing to fill these gaps, but rather open up new ones or enlarge those already there.

The story of Lol V. Stein recedes somewhat to the background of Duras's next novel in this cycle. *Le Vice-Consul* (1966), on which *India Song* is partially based, takes place in Calcutta and focuses primarily on Anne-Marie Stretter and Michael Richardson. Lol's story circulates through the novel in fragmented references to *Le Ravissement de Lol V. Stein* and is taken up in some ways by the figures of the mad beggarwoman and the Vice Consul, whose stories also become mixed and identified with that of Anne-Marie Stretter. The novel *L'Amour* (1971) reopens the story of Lol V. Stein in S. Thala with the return of Michael Richardson many years later to the fantasmic scene of the ball. It is from this matrix of madness and fantasy that Duras later drew the film *La Femme du Gange* (1972).[3]

The story of Anne-Marie Stretter and Michael Richardson as it is first told in *Le Vice-Consul* was subsequently developed in several different kinds of work: besides the novel, Duras wrote a play (*India Song, texte-théâtre-film*, 1973) and directed two films, *India Song* (1975) and *Son nom de Venise dans Calcutta désert* (1976) which plays the same sound track as *India Song*, but replaces the image track with scenes of a deserted mansion, its ruined facades and rooms emptied of people until the very end. As in *Le Vice-Consul*, the story of Lol V. Stein continues to circulate through the films: off-screen, the voices of two young women in the beginning tell the story of the ball at S. Thala, echoing and at some points actually citing, in a *mise en abyme* of memory, both *La Femme du Gange* and *Le Ravissement de Lol V. Stein*.

The scene of the ball at the beginning of *Le Ravissement de Lol V. Stein* describes a kind of substitution operated through an exchange of looks in which the couple Lol V. Stein and her fiancé Michael Richardson is replaced by the couple Anne-Marie Stretter and Michael Richardson. At the moment of that substitution, however, the couple becomes a threesome, Lol being inextricably bound to them by her look, as the spectator in the scene, a witness to her own no-longer-being-there, her own absence. It is the fantasy of being able to see herself not being there in precisely that play of substitutions set up at the ball that Lol seeks to repeat throughout the rest of the novel. But like the repetitions and transformations that occur elsewhere intertextually in this cycle of novels and films, repetition is not therapeutic: it leads to neither resolution nor cure, but rather to an uncanny effect of familiarity and difference.

II

> What is fascination if not, so to speak, the temperate or mild form of the feeling of strangeness or of unbelievable familiarity (*Unheimlichkeit*) which is called forth when there is before me (or in what there is before me, in the *Gegenstand*) something unknown but nevertheless at the root of my identity, like a stranger to my self.
>
> Moustapha Safouan

Duras was once asked why the character of Anne-Marie Stretter fascinated her. She replied that when she was very young and living in Indochina, a new embassy official, perhaps named Stretter, moved into town with his wife and two little girls. A short time after their arrival, Duras learned that a young man had committed suicide because of his love for this woman.

> In any case, it's like the primal scene that Freud talks about. Perhaps this is my primal scene, the day I learned of the death of the young man. You see, this woman was a mother—good, sensible—and the two little girls always in white were her children, and this man, this husband, was a father. I had no father and my mother lived like a nun. This woman, the mother of these two little girls who were my age, possessed a body which had the power of death.[4]

Duras describes being attracted by the extraordinary paleness of this woman, "invisible" yet seen by Duras riding around in her limousine and at the embassy tennis courts where Duras's brother used to play because "he was handsome and played well," but from which she was excluded.

The interest of Duras's response to a question of fascination lies less in its final explanatory value than in its suggestiveness—her comments are less proof of an origin of her fascination than of another scene in which it is replayed. Her references here to original fantasies,[5] of which the primal scene is one, finds a certain resonance in the rest of her work. In many ways the ball scene has the status of an original fantasy, a kind of primal scene of the Indian cycle, in which a scene is reconstructed *après coup* across the imaginary registers of seen and heard, by people who may or may not have seen or heard anything. Like the primal scene, then, the ball scene is first of all a fantasy. And like the ball scene, the original fantasy analogously marks a vanishing point in psychoanalytic theory. For psychoanalysis, like the subject it describes, is tempted by a fantasy of origins, wishing as it does to construct an origin or an original moment in the history of the subject, a moment which lies at once beyond that history and in it.

The question of the origin of the fantasy is one which is difficult to settle. Jean Laplanche and J.-B. Pontalis have addressed this question in, among other places, an article which appeared in *Les Temps modernes* whose title indicates the complexity of the problem: "Fantasme originaire, fantasmes des origines, origine du fantasme."[6] If, from the beginning of his work on hysteria and on the origins of hysterical fantasies, Freud finds himself repeatedly caught between the oppositions real-imagined, objective-subjective, it is not necessarily due to an inadequate conceptualization of the problem, but to the complex and ambiguous relationship of real to imagined in the fantasy.

Freud first mentions the primal scene in a case history entitled "A Case of Paranoia Running Counter to the Psychoanalytic Theory of the Disease" (1915). In a remarkable condensation, the patient, a young woman, claimed to have been photographed while making love, hearing what she imagined to be the click of a camera while in a compromising position with her lover. Freud concludes that she probably never heard a noise, having projected as the perception of an external object what was in all probability the beat of her clitoris. Earlier in this same paper, however, leading to a discussion of "primal fantasies," Freud decides that the actual status of the noise, real or imagined, is unimportant.

> I do not for a moment imagine, of course, that if the unlucky noise had not occurred the delusion would not have been formed; on the contrary, something inevitable is to be seen behind this accidental circumstance, something which was bound to assert itself compulsively in the patient just as when she supposed that there was a *liaison* between her lover and the elderly superior, her mother-substitute. Among the store of unconscious phantasies of all neurotics, and probably of all human beings, there is one which is seldom absent and which can be disclosed by analysis: this is the phantasy of watching sexual intercourse between the parents. I call such phantasies—of the observation of sexual intercourse between the parents, of seduction, of castration, and others— "primal phantasies" . . .[7]

Freud goes on to correct himself, saying that "it is doubtful whether we can rightly call the noise 'accidental' " since such noises are an integral part of the fantasy of listening and an indication of the primal scene—the noise of parental intercourse which wakes the child and/or the noise by which the child is afraid he will betray himself. Here, the oppositions real-imagined have become displaced, as the question of the origin of the fantasy becomes circular. What is imagined to be at the source of the fantasy, the origin of its subsequent elaboration—in this case, a noise—is at once an integral part of the original fantasy, a mark of the primal scene: ". . . the origin of the fantasy is integrated in the very structure of the original fantasy."[8]

In psychoanalytic theory, the origin of the notion of fantasy comes about through Freud's work on hysteria. It was through his analysis of hysterical fantasies that the categories of real and imagined began to be displaced and, at the same time, where he was forced to attempt an account of the desire of the hysteric. From a theory of sexual seduction by a father or a father-figure, a more realist conception of primal scenes, Freud, in a long and complex development, began to elaborate a theory of primal fantasies which were not reducible to the lived experience of the subject. In a letter to Fliess on September 21, 1897, Freud confesses "the great secret that has been slowly dawning on me in the last few months: I no longer believe in my *neurotica*. ..."[9] He had begun to question whether the scenes of seduction, systematically and pervasively recounted by hysterics, had actually taken place. Although Freud remained convinced that seduction did in fact occur in a number of cases, he was equally convinced that it was not as frequently real as he had first thought.

The question of the desire behind the fantasy and of the role of the subject in it remain, but are taken up again in " 'A Child is Being Beaten': A Contribution to the Study of the Origin of Sexual Perversions" (1919). Basing his analysis on the cases of four women, Freud reconstructs the syntactical permutations of the fantasy "a child is being beaten."

> The little girl's beating-phantasy passes through three phases, of which the first and third are consciously remembered, the middle one remaining unconscious. ... In the first and third phantasies the child who is being beaten is always someone other than the subject; in the middle phase it is always the child herself; in the third phase it is almost invariably only boys who are being beaten. The person who does the beating is from the first her father, replaced later on by a substitute taken from the class of fathers.[10]

The child, then, is not only the subject looking but takes up positions *in the scene*. This kind of slipping of the subject among various positions, various identifications, is characteristic of the structure of the fantasy and of the complexity of the desire it stages. Returning to Laplanche and Pontalis and to the fantasy of seduction of the hysteric,

> ... "A father seduces a daughter" might perhaps be the summarized version of the seduction fantasy. The indication here of the primary process is not the absence of organization, as is sometimes suggested, but the peculiar character of the structure, in that it is a scenario with multiple entries in which nothing shows whether the subject will be immediately located as *daughter;* it can as well be fixed as *father,* or even in the term *seduces.*"[11]

The fantasy of seduction is only one of the original fantasies, but it has in common with the others its relation to origins, a claim to represent a response to those major enigmas which confront the child. Original fantasies are at the same time, then, fantasies of origins. They dramatize moments of emergence: the primal scene replays the origin of the individual; the fantasy of seduction pictures the emergence of sexuality; and fantasies of castration represent the origin of sexual difference.

Analogously, the ball scene, as the original fantasy, the fantasy of origins and the origin of the fantasy of the Indian cycle, makes the beginning of a history.

III

> The principle of classical film is well known: the end must reply to the beginning; between one and the other something must be set in order; the last scene frequently recalls the first and constitutes its resolution.
>
> Raymond Bellour

Although *India Song* is not a classical film, it does conform in certain important aspects to the classical model: it is composed, rather classically, of three parts, three large movements; there is, also along the lines of the classical model as Bellour has described it, a symbolic folding of the last part onto the first, but one which here, instead of constituting the resolution of the first scene, continues the narrative circulation it puts into play.

The story of *India Song* is that of the last days/weeks/months of Anne-Marie Stretter's life and of her love affair with Michael Richardson in India during the 1930s. It takes place in Calcutta, where Anne-Marie Stretter is living as the wife of the French ambassador to India, and on an island in the Delta during the season of the summer monsoon. The story is told by voices whose faces are never seen, gradually taking shape through what they remember, "having known or read of this love story long ago. Some of them remember it better than others. But none of them remembers it completely. And none of them has completely forgotten it."[12] Around this story, but off-screen, is another—that of the misery of Calcutta, hunger and leprosy. There are two characters who are explicitly part of this off-screen story: the mad beggarwoman, who is heard but never seen; and the Vice Consul, who is both seen and heard, but remains in social and diplomatic exile.

The three-part composition of the film traces a story which is always already history when the film begins: embedded in the telling of the story of Anne-Marie Stretter is the triple inscription of her death—spoken by the voices in the past tense at the beginning, as part of the *already-there (déjà-là)* of the space of the film; in the recurring image of an "altar" to a recent death—flowers, a photograph, incense; and finally at the end of the film when the voices tell of Anne-Marie Stretter's suicide.

India Song is the *mise en scène* of what could be called a *fantasmatic*—that structuring activity which shapes and orders the life of the subject.[13] It is the work of the fantasy which gives the story its contours, its structure:

—in the *mise en abyme* of beginnings, endings, origins;
—in the slipping and mixing, the circulation, of identification;
—in its answer to the question of desire.

The first part of the film (shots 1–27) puts into play a circulation of positions and identities, beginning with the I/eye who is looking and the beggarwoman and ending with the Vice Consul and an idea of death. The voices of two young women, at times indistinguishable from one another, tell the stories—the *already-there* of the fiction—of the beggarwoman, Anne-Marie Stretter, Michael Richardson, Lol V. Stein and the Vice Consul. The identities are mixed in a kind of fantasmic blend across the registers of seen and heard (*entendu*),[14] projecting—here recalling Freud's study of "A Case of Paranoia . . ." (see above)—one onto the other, one into the other.

IV

Shot 1 (5″).
White credits on black.

Shot 2 (3′52″).
Credits continue over an image of the setting sun, then stop. A woman is singing in an Asian language—the song of Savannakhet sung by the beggarwoman. The song stops and the voices begin.[15]

Voice 1: A beggarwoman.
Voice 2: Mad.

V1: Yes.
V2: Yes, I remember. She stays around the riverbanks. She comes from Burma.

The beggarwoman begins to sing again, then stops.

V1: She's not Indian. She comes from Savannakhet. Born there.

The song begins again and continues intermittently.

V2: She's been walking for ten years. One day, she comes to the Ganges.
V1: Yes. She stays.
V2: That's right . . . Twelve children die while she walks to Bengal.
V1: Yes. She leaves them, sells them, forgets them. Becomes barren on the way to Bengal.

The beggarwoman sings alone, then the voices begin again.

V2: Savannakhet, Laos.
V1: Yes. Seventeen years. She's pregnant, seventeen years old. She's driven away by her mother. She leaves. She asks how to get lost. No one knows.

The beggarwoman continues to sing intermittently, then begins to babble, stops and the voices begin again.

V1: They were together in Calcutta.
V2: The white woman and the other one?
V1: Yes. During the same years . . .

The first position taken up by the I/eye of the camera during the second shot—the look toward the setting sun—is one which is off-screen: that of the beggarwoman and the voices of the two women which identify her and tell her story, both excluded from the scene and on the side of seeing, as are we. The stories of Anne-Marie Stretter and the beggarwoman also begin to be woven together ("They were together in Calcutta. . . ."), beginning a series of positions taken up, linked in a play of identity and difference.

Shot 3 (56″).
"India Song" is heard, played on the piano. An interior at night. On a black piano, a lamp and a photograph of a young girl. On the keyboard a musical score. A servant in Hindu dress enters and places a bouquet of flowers next to the photograph, lights a candle and some incense, leaves.

Shot 4 (59″).
Slow pan from right to left over some black cloth, jewels, a red dress, a red hair piece.
"India Song" continues.

V1: He had followed her to India.
V2: Yes. He left everything for her. In one night.
V1: The night of the ball?
V2: Yes.
V1: Michael Richardson was engaged to a girl from S. Thala, Lola Valérie Stein . . .

V2: They were to have been married in the autumn. Then there was the ball, the ball at S. Thala.

V1: She had arrived at the ball late in the middle of the night, dressed in black . . .

"India Song" continues on the piano.

Shot 5 (10″).
Photograph of a young girl in black, some flowers, incense, three half-filled champagne glasses. The smoke from the incense rises.

V1: What love at the ball, what desire.

These three shots begin to trace the *already-there* of the fiction: we see, for the first time, what will be the recurring image of the "altar"—the photograph, flowers, incense; and we hear, also for the first time, the story of what is already in this cycle a recurring scene: the fantasy of the ball at S. Thala.

The image of the photograph introduces another dimension into the temporal *mise en abyme* of the fiction. In the logic of the film, it comes to represent the death of Anne-Marie Stretter (metonymically, as part of the "altar"), marking that death as ever-present through repetition in the present, the *being-there* of the film. A little later however, the voices tell us about her death in the past tense, making it part of the *already-there* of the fiction. Although still caught up in the present of the film (the *being-there*), the photograph is a condensation of the two temporalities at work in *India Song:* "What we have is a new space-time category: spatial immediacy and temporal anteriority, the *here-now* and the *there-then*."[16] The time of the photograph, then, its *having-been-there*, joins the fantasmic *already-there*, the past of the fiction, to the present of the film.

Between the shots of the photographs (shots 3 and 5), the voices begin to remember the story of the ball, looping the film once again back onto the *already-there* of the fiction. The fantasy of the ball is accompanied by music, "India Song," and is told over a slow, lingering pan of Anne-Marie Stretter's *things,* personal things—clothing, hair pieces, jewels—detached from her body and strewn about as if she no longer had any use for them. This image, somewhere between voyeurism and melancholia, is one of a series in the film which, through an activity of looking in relation to loss, wants to shape the story into a fantasy of looking.

Shot 6 (15″).
On the right, a lighted chandelier, reflected in a rectangular mirror placed behind it on a mantle. In front of the mirror, a small clock with red flowers on either side. "India Song" continues on the piano.

V2: That light.
V1: The monsoon.
V2: The dust . . .
V1: Central Calcutta.

Shot 7 (17″).
Reframing of the clock in the center, the mirror behind it (reflecting another mirror) and the red flowers on either side; the reverse of the previous shot. Above, a chandelier whose reflections play off one another in a *mise en abyme* between the mirrors.
"India Song" stops.

V2: Isn't there a smell of flowers?
V1: Leprosy.
V2: Where are we?

Shot 8 (1′29″).
Blue sky, then a pan of the exterior of a mansion, scaffolding under a window, crumbling walls, shuttered windows; pan left to right to a dark green forest, framed at the end of the shot in a low angle against the blue sky.

V1: The French Embassy in India.
V2: That distant noise . . .
V1: The Ganges.
Silence.
V1: After her death, he left India?
V2: Yes.
V1: Her tomb is in the English cemetery?
V2: Yes.
Silence.
V1: She died there, in the islands. One night, found dead . . .
Silence.
V2: A black Lancia speeds along the road to Chandernagor. . . . It was then that she first . . .
V1: Yes.

Shots 6 to 8 return to the play of identification and substitution being set up in this part, linking in a series of questions and answers: the light—the monsoon; the dust—central Calcutta; the smell of flowers—leprosy; a distant noise—the Ganges. These terms recur throughout the film and are mixed and blended by the voices with the identities of Anne-Marie Stretter and the beggarwoman. This mirroring effect, the play of identity and difference set up by the voices, has a counterpart in the image: shots 6 and 7, both framed across mirrors, present the same objects, reframed and reflected. In the middle of the next shot, the voices talk about Anne-Marie Stretter's death, her tomb in the English cemetery, over an image of the ruined façades and broken windows of what appears to be an abandoned mansion, but is identified as the French Embassy ("Where are we?" "The French Embassy in India.").

Shot 9 (3'2").
Semi-circular pan, right to left, of the drawing room; beginning in a corner with a rose-colored sofa, panning across some French doors opening onto a park, the piano with the lamp, flowers, photograph and incense. A young man in a white suit, looking toward off-screen right, is reflected in a mirror against which he is leaning and which also reflects the piano, the objects on it and the French doors. The camera stops panning at the mirror, where a young man and woman are reflected dancing (Anne-Marie Stretter and Michael Richardson). The couple stops dancing. The young man in white turns his head to the right and the woman of the couple moves away slightly and turns.

V1: What are you afraid of?

Long silence.

V2: Anne-Marie Stretter.

Long silence.

V2: They used to dance at night?
V1: They're dancing.

"India Song" begins again, played on the piano.

V1: Why are you crying?
   I love you so much I can't see anymore, can't hear, can't live. . . .

Shot 10 (21″).
The stone steps of a stairway in the park, brightly lit. A shadow comes and goes near the bottom step, then disappears.
"India Song" continues.

Shot 11 (1′5″).
Anne-Marie Stretter, Michael Richardson and the young man in white all looking to the right toward the park, through the open French doors. Anne-Marie Stretter exits through the doors, the two men follow her.
V1: You know, lepers burst like sacks of dust.
V2: [They] don't suffer?
V1: No. Not a thing. Laugh.
Long silence.
Voice of the beggarwoman: Savannakhet! Savannakhet!
V1: She's there, on the banks of the Ganges, under the trees. She has forgotten.

Uncannily, the dialogue of the voices over shot 9 recalls *La Femme du Gange,* where the voices of two young women speak to each other, occasionally commenting on the image, but more frequently trying to reconstruct, to remember the scene of the ball and the stories of Anne-Marie Stretter, Lol V. Stein, and Michael Richardson. Also like *La Femme du Gange,* the voices here speak of their love for each other in words which seem to float between the stories they are telling and their own.

With shot 9, we see a pan of the drawing room, a glimpse of the couple dancing (Anne-Marie Stretter and Michael Richardson), caught in a paradoxical past-present moment ("They used to dance in the evenings"/ "They're dancing"), a moment complicated by being also a filmed reflection, introducing the possibility of an absent or displaced presence into the already complex temporal scheme.

This absent presence is continued in the next shot (shot 10) with a shadow approaching the stairs then retreating—the beggarwoman?—recalling, again, a very similar shot in *La Femme du Gange,* with the difference that in the earlier film the "shadow" revealed itself to be Lol V. Stein.

During shot 11, the voices once more take up the play of substitutions— "lepers burst like sacks of dust"—and introduce a phrase ("[they] don't suffer")[17] which becomes a refrain linking various positions set up in the first movement. Meanwhile, Anne-Marie Stretter, Michael Richardson and the young man—the spectator in the scene—move outside, their attention drawn by the cries of the beggarwoman.

Shot 12 (56″).
Anne-Marie Stretter, Michael Richardson and the young man outside in front of the Embassy residence. They walk slowly toward the camera and exit to the left.

Shot 13 (12″).
In the distance, 'a man in white, standing near a small lake in the park.
V2: The French Vice Consul in Lahore.
V1: Yes, in disgrace in Calcutta.

Shot 14 (28″).
Anne-Marie Stretter, Michael Richardson, the young man walk down the stairs; in the background, the façade of the Embassy residence.

Shot 15 (41″).
Return to 13.
The man in white (the Vice Consul) walks slowly along the edge of the lake, stops, then leaves.
V1: Has he come back into the park?
V2: Yes, he comes every night.

Shot 16 (28″).
The deserted tennis courts, some benches, a red bicycle seen through a wire mesh fence.
The Vice Consul enters from the left, passes the bicycle, stops to look at it, then exits to the right.

V2: The deserted tennis courts.
V1: Anne-Marie Stretter's red bicycle.

Shot 17 (24″).
The Vice Consul walking in the park. The camera pans left to right with his movement. He stops and looks to the right.

Shots 12 to 17 present a series of exterior shots, the only ones in the film in which Anne-Marie Stretter appears. The first four form an alternation between the three characters walking (Anne-Marie Stretter, Michael Richardson, the young man, in shots 12 and 14) and the Vice Consul (shots 13 and 15), who is introduced by the voices during shot 13. This alternation sets up spatial parallels between Anne-Marie Stretter and the Vice Consul which will converge, briefly, at the end of the first movement. Their eventual meeting is prefigured, metonymically, in shot 16 where we see the Vice Consul walking by the deserted tennis courts and lingering over Anne-Marie Stretter's red bicycle, an object which is invested with some of the same value as the more personal effects seen in shot 4.

Shot 18 (3'1").
Reflected in a large rectangular mirror, the piano (with musical score, flowers, lamp, photograph) and three open French doors.
A servant, dressed in white, enters and lights the lamp on the piano. He walks toward the mirror, which still reflects him, and then enters the frame at the right, doubled by his reflection. He lights another lamp next to the mirror, then exits. From the left, Anne-Marie Stretter enters, closing her black peignoir around her. She exits at the right edge of the frame and reappears, reflected in the background by the mirror, walking toward the open doors. She goes outside, then re-enters, still seen reflected in the mirror, stops near the piano where she looks for a long time at the photograph. She then looks at herself in the mirror and exits to the left.

V2: Where is the one dressed in black?
V1: Out, every evening. She comes back when it's dark. The Embassy's black Lancia has just entered the park.

The beggarwoman begins to sing.

V2: You know, she hunts at night in the Ganges, for food.

Long silence.

V1: Dead in the islands.
V2: Her eyes blinded with light, dead.
V1: Yes, there, under a stone. Around her, a bend in the Ganges.

Silence, then Beethoven's variation #14 on a theme by Diabelli begins on the piano.

Shot 19 (1'27").
From a high angle, Anne-Marie Stretter in her black peignoir, stretched out on her stomach on the floor.
Reflected in the mirror, in the background, a man in white comes down the stairs, stops.
The Beethoven variation continues on the piano.

V1: Four o'clock. Black night.
V2: No one can sleep.
V1: No one.
V2: The heat . . . impossible . . . terrible.
V1: Another storm . . . approaching Bengal.
V2: Coming from the islands.
V1: The mouth of the river. Inexhaustible.

V2: What's that sound?
V1: Her weeping.
V2: [She] doesn't suffer, does she?
V1: She neither. A leper . . . of the heart.

Shot 20 (54″).
The camera pans over a fragment of a red dress against some rose-colored material, a red hairpiece, a silver belt, then in a sweeping movement, it pans over black, obscuring the edges of the frame, then back to the red dress.
The Beethoven variation continues.

Shot 21 (4′45″).
Return to 19.
The man seen in shot 19, Michael Richardson, is now stretched out next to Anne-Marie Stretter, leaning on his elbow, looking at her. She turns over onto her back, uncovering her breast.
In the background, the young man seen in shots 9, 11, etc., enters through a doorway, walks in front of the mirror, leaves, then re-enters and sits down near Anne-Marie Stretter and Michael Richardson on the floor.
The Beethoven variation continues.

V2: [She] can't bear it.
V1: No, she can't bear it . . . can't bear India.

The voices are silent.

V1: She's sleeping.
V2: He loved her more than anything in the world.
V1: Even more.

The music stops.

V1: Michael Richardson started a marine insurance company in Bengal so that he could stay in India.
V2: Listen . . . Ganges fishermen . . .

Silence.

V1   What darkness, what heat, relentless, deathly.

Silence.

V1:   (*As if reading*) From behind the indoor plants in the bar, she watches
        them. It was only at dawn, when the lovers were going towards the door
        of the ballroom, that Lola Valérie Stein uttered a cry.

Sounds of water.

V1:   Couldn't hear anymore, couldn't see.

V2:   With this crime behind them . . .

Sounds of water continue. A siren can be heard in the background.

V1:   Yes.

V2:   Rain.

V1:   Yes . . . cool . . .

Silence. The piano begins to play Beethoven's variation again.

V1:   The music, it was in Venice. A hope in music . . .

V2:   She never gave up playing?

V1:   No.

Silence. The music continues.

V2:   (*Pronouncing each syllable*) An-na Ma-ri-a Guar-di.

V1:   Yes . . .

Silence.

V2:   The first marriage, the first post . . .?

V1:   Savannakhet, Laos. She's married to a French colonial official. She's
        eighteen.

V2:   Ah yes . . . a river . . . she's sitting by a river. Already. Looking at it.

V1:   The Mekong.

V2:   She's silent, crying?

V1:   Yes. They say: "She can't get acclimated. She'll have to be sent back to
        Europe."

V2:   [She] couldn't bear it, even then?

V1:   Even then.

V2:   Those iron gates around her?

V1:   The park of the chancellery.

V2:   The sentries?

V1:   Official.

V2:   Even then [she] couldn't bear it.

V1:   No.

The music stops.

V1:   One day, a government launch stops: Monsieur Stretter is inspecting the
        posts on the Mekong.

V2:   He takes her away from Savannakhet?

V1:   Yes. Takes her with him.

Shot 22 (33″).
Anne-Marie Stretter's nude breast, surrounding by the black peignoir. Beads
of sweat form on the skin as she breathes.

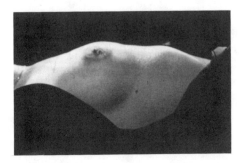

V1: (*Continuing*) Takes her with him for seventeen years through the capitals
of Asia. You find her in Peking, then in Mandalay, in Rangoon, Sydney.
You find her in Lahore. Seventeen years. You find her in Calcutta. Calcutta: she dies.

During shots 18 and 19, the voices continue the work of substitution,
linking through almost imperceptible alternations, the identities of Anne-
Marie Stretter and the beggarwoman: shifting from "the one dressed in
black" to "she hunts at night" to "Dead in the islands." The refrain "[She]
doesn't suffer" returns to link Anne-Marie Stretter with leprosy: "A leper
. . . of the heart."

There are several levels of redundancy between the spatial and temporal
schemes at work in shot 18: the uncanniness of watching Anne-Marie Stretter
looking at the photograph which has been associated with the "altar" to her
death and then at herself in the mirror; the voices meanwhile speak of her
in the past tense ("Dead in the islands"). The effect of absent presence has
a spatial counterpart produced by the placement of the mirror in the room,
in which Anne-Marie Stretter disappears from the view of the camera,
reappearing seconds later, caught as a reflection.

Shots 20 and 22 continue the series that began with shot 4, shaping a
fantasy of looking. The first (shot 20) is very similar to shot 4: a pan over
Anne-Marie Stretter's *things*—the jewels, the hairpiece, the red dress, black
cloth (the peignoir we saw earlier?). But here, after panning over the objects
strewn across a rose-colored sofa, there is a sweeping movement of the
camera over black, blending the edges of the frame with the object, confusing
the looked at with the frame of the look. Then, in an upward sweep, the
frame is regained against the rose of the sofa and the red dress.

Shot 21 returns us to the heat, "relentless, deathly," of Calcutta while
the voices take up again the *already-there* of the fiction (the ball—"this crime
behind them"), at times seeming to slip back to that past, seeing Lol *looking*
("From behind the indoor plants in the bar, she watches them."), seeing
Anne-Marie Stretter in Savannakhet, sitting by the Mekong, or surrounded

by the iron gates of the chancellery. The story of Anne-Marie Stretter is more explicitly linked here to that of the beggarwoman—both of them beginning their trajectories across Asia at Savannakhet.

Anne-Marie Stretter's movement from Savannakhet to Calcutta is traced in the next shot (shot 22) over the image of her nude breast, an image which marks the deathly heat by the beads of sweat forming on her skin. The stories of the beggarwoman and Anne-Marie Stretter have become parallel: one, eighteen years old, married, unhappy; the other, seventeen years old, pregnant, driven away; both beginning in Savannakhet and ending in Calcutta.

Like the two shots (4 and 20) which precede it in this series, the image of Anne-Marie Stretter's breast, although on a more abstract level, is about a fantasy of looking, a slipping of subject and object, of the look and the looked at. The breast, as a signifier in psychoanalytic theory, has in common with both the look and the fantasy a relation to loss. In the history of the subject, the object of the infant's "primal hallucination," in which he seeks to reproduce the experience of satisfaction in the absence of the real object (the milk), is in fact not the *real* object but the *lost* object "linked with the very earliest experiences of the rise and resolution of desire"[18]—the breast as signifier.

It is the work of the fantasy to try to "cover the moment of *separation* between *before* and *after* . . . between the two stages represented by real experience and its hallucinatory revival, between the object that satisfies and the sign [the breast] which describes both the object and its absence. . . ."[19] The fantasy originates in the continually renewed and repeated moment of separation, making its appearance along with sexuality which, split off from the non-sexual functions (such as feeding) which provided its object, becomes auto-erotic.

The fantasy not only has its origins at the same time as auto-eroticism, in loss, but is the *mise en scène* of the subject in relation to loss—to the experience of separation and to an impossible desire for a lost object. Both the look and the breast have in common their status as signifiers of loss (*l'objet petit a* in the Lacanian algebra), those objects which have been separated from or have fallen off from the body and which stand for the experience of separation. Within this, both the fantasy and the look permit a kind of reciprocity, a circulation and return: the fantasy, in the slipping among positions of subject and object, blurs those distinctions within its own structure; and the look always includes not only *seeing* but *being seen*.[20]

The fantasy of looking, then, could be said to be the desire to see loss, to see what is by definition that to which the subject can have no access, but through which, at the same time, the subject is marked. In the context of a reading of the other two shots in this series—somewhere between voyeurism and melancholia—the image of the breast traces out that middle ground.

The distinctions between looking and looked at that began to be confounded in shot 20, here find a mythical moment of reciprocity—recalling in a singularly overdetermined way, Lol's desire to see herself not being there.

Shot 23 (18″).
From a high angle, Anne-Marie Stretter, Michael Richardson and the young man stretched out on the floor.
In the extreme foreground, half off-screen, the back of a man in a white jacket.

V2: The other man who's sleeping?
V1: Passing through. A friend of the Stretters.

The piano begins playing the Beethoven variation again.

V1: She belongs to whoever wants her. Gives her to whoever will have her.
V2: Love.

Shot 24 (25″).
Against a black background, the Vice Consul stands facing the camera, looking.
The piano music continues.

V1: Yes . . . splendor.
V2: (*Pronouncing each syllable*) An-ne Marie Stret-ter written on her tomb?
V1: An-na Ma-ria Guar-di, erased.

The music stops.

Shot 25 (27″).
Return to 23.
The Vice Consul, seen again from the back, exits.
Anne-Marie Stretter sits up and looks beyond the camera.

V1: Every night . . . looks at her.

Piano music begins again softly.

V2: He never spoke to her?
V1: No, never went near . . .

Shot 26 (37″).
The deserted tennis courts and the red bicycle leaning against the fence. The
Vice Consul enters from the left and stops near the bicycle, touches it, and
turns to face the camera.

V2: The male virgin of Lahore.
V1: Yes.

The music stops.

Shot 27 (1′2″).
Return to 25.
Anne-Marie Stretter, sitting up, continues to look off-screen in the direction
of the camera. She lies down again.

The light dims and goes out. The bodies are vaguely outlined in the darkness. The beggarwoman's song can be heard in the distance.

V2:   Those flickering lights?
V1:   The crematories.
V2:   They're burning those who've starved to death?
V1:   Yes. It's going to be daylight soon. (Pause) He fired a gun. One night, from his balcony in Lahore, he fired at the lepers in the Shalimar gardens.
V2:   [He] couldn't bear it.
V1:   No.
V2:   India—couldn't bear India?
V1:   No.
V2:   What couldn't he bear about it?
V1:   The idea.

The last term to be brought into the play of identification and difference, which began with shot 2, is the Vice Consul in a series of five alternating shots. The manipulation of a classic instrument of identification, shot/reverse-shot, in which the look of the camera is placed in an axis identical to that of the spectator, occurs only once in the film, at the end of the first movement. After the image of the breast, we see, from a high angle, Anne-Marie Stretter, Michael Richardson and the friend stretched out on the floor (shot 23). In the extreme foreground, half off-screen, is the Vice Consul. The next shot is a medium close-up of his face, looking beyond the camera (shot 24). Shot 25 goes back to the camera set-up of 23, the Vice Consul turning and leaving at the edge of the frame. Anne-Marie Stretter then sits up and looks beyond the camera, in the direction of his exit (shot 25). The Vice Consul is then seen wandering around the deserted tennis courts, lingering near Anne-Marie Stretter's red bicycle (shot 26). The last shot (shot 27) of this series, the last in the first movement of the film, goes back to the set-up of shots 25 and 23—Anne-Marie Stretter is looking off-screen then lies down again. The voices talk of the crematories where they burn the bodies of those who have died of starvation. They then tell the story of the Vice Consul (already begun over shot 13). Through the voices, the Vice Consul becomes identified with death: Anne-Marie Stretter's tomb (shot 24); the generalized death permeating India, but never seen—the crematories (shot 27 which, like shots 23 and 25, is identified with the Vice Consul's look, his point of view); and an act of death—firing on the lepers in Lahore (shot 27).

The look of the camera which coincides with the axes of the looks of Anne-Marie Stretter and the Vice Consul establishes a relation of doubling, ensuring their eventual substitution, underlined by the cries of the beggar-woman, the references to death, and the refrain "[she] doesn't suffer" and its slightly displaced opposite "[he/she] can't bear it." In this final, fatal condensation the last term is put into play in the series of positions taken up during this movement of the film. The trajectory might be written as follows, keeping in mind that each moment along the way is less precisely located than it is continually repeated and blended with the others: the I/eye of the camera—the beggarwoman—Anne-Marie Stretter—the Vice Consul—death.

V

For us, the most important thing about the reception, its essence as it were, was the pursuit of Anne-Marie Stretter, her hunting down by death, by the bearer of that feminine element, the Vice Consul of Lahore.

Marguerite Duras

The first part of the film sets up a circulation among positions of subject and object, the look and looked at, characteristic of the structure of the fantasy where the subject is at once included in the scene and excluded from it. Each of the terms put into play during the first movement, from the I/eye who is looking to death, has the status of an absent presence complicated by the temporal scheme—the relation of the *already-there* of the fiction to the *being-there* of the film. This absent presence is the mark of a kind of reciprocity, of a joining of inclusion/exclusion: Anne-Marie Stretter and the Vice Consul are literally present in the scene, but they are also linked with those positions which are literally absent, excluded from the scene—the beggarwoman and the I/eye who is looking. Each term, then, is both present and absent, in the scene and excluded from it, an exemplary version being Anne-Marie Stretter's death and the image of the photograph which is its emblem.

This play of inclusion/exclusion is written into the very structure of the fantasy, as Lacan has formulated it: ($ ◊ a) (which reads: the barred subject; desire of/for/to; *petit objet a*).[21] The losange (*le poinçon*, the "punch" in the middle of the formula), even on the level of its *shape*, includes the possibility of a circulation which links inclusion/exclusion. To indicate that circular process, Lacan provides the losange with a "vectorial direction": ◇.[22] But the losange can also be read as the joining of the signs for inclusion and exclusion ($<$ and $>$) signifying, then, the circulation among positions of subject and object in the fantasy, where the subject plays a role not only as an observer but as a participant in his own fantasy.

The second part of *India Song* (shots 28–59), the center of the film, is the reception scene. The voices of the guests, men and women, talk about what they observe at the reception and tell what they remember of the stories, the backgrounds, of Anne-Marie Stretter, Michael Richardson, the Vice Consul and the beggarwoman. The guests remain off-screen throughout the reception which takes place in a drawing room of the Embassy residence. We see Anne-Marie Stretter, Michael Richardson, the Vice Consul, the friend of the Stretters (from part one) and a young attaché passing through or dancing, accompanied by various kinds of music and the voices of the unseen guests speaking among themselves. From time to time, we hear conversations taking place among some of the five characters we see on the screen— between Anne-Marie Stretter and the young attaché or the Vice Consul, for example—but we never see them speaking: "while they are speaking, their lips remain silent."[23]

The reception scene continues the work of the fantasmatic, continuing that circulation which began in the first part, and at the same time, carving out in the center of the film, like the losange of the fantasy, an absent presence. The entire scene is an alteration from shot to shot between images of the exterior of the Embassy—the façades, the park, tennis courts—and the drawing room. Within this, all of the scenes of the drawing room are organized around a mirror placed at one end of the room, opposite the camera (similar to shot 9). The position of the mirror in the scene produces a temporal and spatial gap in the image into which the characters disappear as they enter and dance across the room, leaving the field of the camera only to reappear a few seconds later reflected in the mirror. An absence, then, is written into the filmed present in the actual filming of the scene by the triangulation of the look of the camera—mirror—object.

This part of the film is organized in a pattern of alternation: from shot to shot and interior to the image, the mirror in the drawing room effecting a kind of alternation *manqué*. As in the first movement, the alternation here between inside and outside (one might as easily say inclusion and exclusion) leads to the final encounter at the end of the evening (at the end of the second movement) between Anne-Marie Stretter and the Vice Consul, an encounter that has been in preparation from the beginning. But unlike the encounter at the end of the first part of the film, where Anne-Marie Stretter and the Vice Consul are linked together by a manipulation of shot/reverse-shot, the scene (shot 52) is filmed in a long, slow pan of the camera, retracting in reverse the movement of shot 9, where we first saw Anne-Marie Stretter dancing, reflected in the mirror, with Michael Richardson. The alternation which leads to this final encounter, between the interior shots of the drawing

room and the exterior tracking shots or pans of the buildings and the park, represents not only the literal alternation interior/exterior, but also the positions that Anne-Marie Stretter and the Vice Consul have taken up in the fiction: each included in the scene of the fiction, but each at the same time linked with positions in "exile"—the Vice Consul, in diplomatic and social exile in Calcutta for his crime, yet still invited by Anne-Marie Stretter to the reception; and Anne-Marie Stretter herself, linked by her history to that of the beggarwoman who is in her own form of exile as an "untouchable." The scene of their encounter, filmed in a single shot across the kind of repressed alternation that the mirror produces, fuses Anne-Marie Stretter and the Vice Consul in a common space of exile.

Anne-Marie Stretter's "exile"—which has come to mean her death by her identification with "the bearer of that feminine element, the Vice Consul"—is prefigured again in the last shot of the second movement (shot 59). Surrounded by the guest, the young attaché, Georges Crawn and Michael Richardson, Anne-Marie Stretter is sitting partially stretched out on a sofa. The Vice Consul, who horrified the guests during the reception by his presence and by his encounter with Anne-Marie Stretter, has been driven away. With her, he had been the center of attention during the reception; at

the end he is present only by the sound of his voice, off-screen, crying: Anna Maria Guardi. During the shot, his cries become more and more distant, the

Beethoven variation that was heard in the first movement of the film is heard again, and two voices, a man's and a woman's, describe the scene. The trajectory which began in the first part of the film with the I/eye who is looking and ended with an identification with death, here finds those two points condensed in the *fascinum:* "it is that which has the effect of arresting movement and, literally, of killing life."[24] Anne-Marie Stretter is fixed by the look in a pose, like a still-life where nothing moves but the light which dims and brightens again like slow breathing.

The second movement of the film continues the circulation that began in the first, at the same time condensing even further the play of identity and difference set up among the I/eye who is looking, the beggarwoman, Anne-Marie Stretter, the Vice Consul and death, which has become their common denominator. Like the losange in Lacan's formulaic designation of the fantasy —◊— this circulation turns around an empty center which in the film takes the shape of an absent presence: in the *mise en scène* effected by the mirror; in the temporal disjunction produced by characters who are *heard* speaking, but never *seen* speaking; in the complicated status of each of the successive positions taken up in the first part; and, finally, in the (almost) literal center of the second movement, an image of the photograph (shot 40), a mark of the absent presence of Anne-Marie Stretter and of the two temporalities of the film—the *already-there* and the *being-there.*

VI

The third movement (shots 60–74) of the film responds in some ways to the first: if the first movement puts into play a fantasmatic, the third both continues that circulation and is its signature. There are similarities between the two: two voices—this time a man's and a woman's—talk about what they are seeing and about what they remember of Anne-Marie Stretter's story; the "mood" of the last part is also similar to that of the first— the long nights, the heat, flowers, incense—but this time situated at the ambassador's residence on an island in the Delta.

The work of signature begins with the voices: the man's voice (Dionys Mascolo) asks questions, can't remember at first, while the woman's seems to know, sees what we and he can't see, seems to remember it all. Duras has called these two voices "the authors, the motors ... of the story,"[25] a particularly appropriate comment because that distinctive voice, marked by its difference from other voices heard in the film, is her own.

There is also an effect of symbolic folding of the last part onto the first, forming a frame around the empty center, giving the film the shape of the losange of the fantasy: ◊. The folding of the last part onto the first is constructed across four specific shots, two in each part.

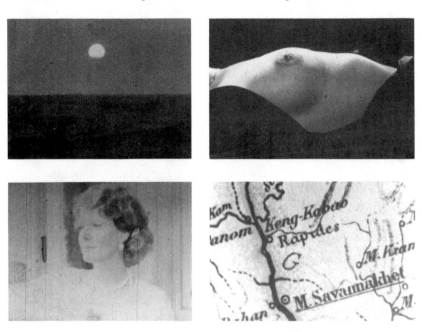

Shot 2: The look toward the setting sun during which the voices tell the story of the beggarwoman: born in Savannakhet, begins walking ten years ago (west, it's easy to figure, toward the setting sun) and has twelve children who die along the way. By the time she reaches the Ganges she is barren.

Shot 22: The image of Anne-Marie Stretter's nude breast; the voices speak of her trajectory across Indochina to India, for seventeen years through the capitals of Asia: Savannakhet, Peking, Mandalay, Rangoon, Sydney, Lahore, Calcutta.

Shot 62: A blinding white light is coming in through a window next to which Anne-Marie Stretter is sitting with her entourage. The voices of two women (one is Duras) tell the story:

V1: It was a September evening during the summer monsoon on the islands in 1937. In China the war was continuing. Shanghai had just been bombed. The Japanese were still advancing. In the Asturias the battle was raging, they were still fighting.

V2:   (Duras): The throat of the Republic has been cut. In Russia, the revolution is betrayed.

V1:   The Nuremberg Congress had just taken place.

Shot 73: The last shot before the credits at the end: a tracking shot of a map of India and Indochina. There are no voices, but "India Song" is played on the piano. The shot begins at some islands on the coast of India (where the last part of the film takes place) and moves to Rangoon, Mekong and finally Savannakhet.

The trajectories of Anne-Marie Stretter and the beggarwoman, told in the present tense by voices at the beginning of the film, are then retraced in reverse as history at its end. Within that join, *India Song,* like the fantasy, dramatizes an imaginary history of the subject, but one which, nevertheless, is marked by traces of time (analogously, the importance of the role of the maid in some of Freud's analyses, a role which depends on a specific familial and relational structure and is a mark of the social and economic milieu of the time). The geographical and historical notations make *India Song* a dated scene, providing a symbolic structure, a frame in which subjectivity and history meet in the scene of the fantasy. By the end of the last part the fiction has folded back onto itself, the two temporalities of the film condensing— the *already-there* of the fiction joining the *being-there* of the film as Anne-Marie Stretter leaves (shot 71) to accomplish that death that has been at once inexorably present in the film and the condition of its *mise en scène.*

VII

That is precisely what I recognize in the ravishing of Lol V. Stein, where Marguerite Duras turns out to know without me what I teach.

Jacques Lacan

To return to dreams and hysteria, isn't this exactly the question which reveals itself in the dream of the hysteric . . . who dreams that her own wish was not fulfilled, through an identification with the woman she posited as her sexual rival. Her desire, therefore, being the desire for an unsatisfied desire . . .

Jacqueline Rose

Returning briefly to the formula of the fantasy, we have seen how the losange signifies the circulation of the subject through positions inside and outside the scene of his fantasy. However, the losange not only marks that circulation, but in relation to the other terms in the formula ($ \$ \Diamond a $) is the screen which radically separates the subject from the lost object. The fantasy is not only the *mise en scène* of desire, but the *mise en scène* of an impossible desire—the desire for that to which the subject can have no access. It is in this impossibility that any moment of reciprocity (as in shot 22) has to be mythical and, further, why it is said that desire and prohibition go hand in hand.[26]

It is in the *mise en scène* of this impossibility—the desire for an unsatisfied desire—that the structure of the fantasy again rejoins the fantasy of *India Song*. The film replays that circulation around an absence, an empty center, a circulation which even in the moments it rejoins itself—the folding of the last part onto the first—it has simply accomplished that which was always already there (Anne-Marie Stretter's death), but lost to itself.

Although it is not here a question of hysteria or of desire and identification in hysteria, it was from a matrix of hysterical fantasies—Lol, Dora—that the question of desire was opened in the film and in psychoanalytic theory, but it is from their difference that our fascination with *India Song* derives. The film does not propose itself as a corrective to psychoanalysis, but it does take up and interrogate, within the terms of psychoanalytic theory, within the structure of a fantasmatic, the question of desire. If *India Song* proposes to us a reading of psychoanalytic theory, it is insofar as the film, like the fantasy, is the *mise en scène* of desire, not its object, displacing the question of the content of that desire back onto the question itself.

Notes

1. This analysis is indebted to the meticulous work of Marie-Claire Ropars-Wuilleumier who is responsible for the complete découpage of *India Song* (and *Son Nom de Venise dans Calcutta désert*), including a transcription of the sound track, published in *L'Avant Scène Cinéma*, no. 225 (April 1979).

2. Marguerite Duras, *The Ravishing of Lol Stein*, trans. Richard Seaver (New York: Grove Press, 1966), p. 4.

3. For a brief discussion/description of the film, see Elisabeth Lyon, "*Woman of the Ganges*," *Camera Obscura*, no. 2 (Fall 1977).

4. François Barat and Joël Farges, eds., *Marguerite Duras* (Paris: Editions Albatros, 1975), p. 85.

5. The decision in this article (apart from citations) to use the word "fantasy" instead of "phantasy," the term sometimes employed in English to translate a distinction between conscious and unconscious fantasies, has been made for the following reasons outlined by Jean Laplanche and J.-B. Pontalis:

> The proposal to eliminate the unfortunate confusion by the graphological device (using "ph" for unconscious fantasies and "f" for the daydream type) has been declared at times to be real progress, the result of half a century of psychoanalysis. Whether or not this distinction is in fact justified, it seems undesirable to use it in translations of Freud's work. It betrays little respect for the text to render words such as *Phantasie* or *Phantasieren*, which Freud invariably employed, by different terms according to the context. Our opposition to this terminological and conceptual innovation rests on three grounds: (i) the distinction should not be introduced into translations of Freud's work, even if the interpretation of his thought were correct; (ii) this interpretation of Freud's thought is incorrect; (iii) this distinction contributes less to the study of the problem than Freud's concept. "Fantasy and the Origins of Sexuality," *The International Journal of Psycho-Analysis* 49 (1968), part 1, p. 11, footnote 24.

6. This article first appeared in French in *Les Temps modernes* 19 (1964), no. 215.

7. Sigmund Freud, "A Case of Paranoia Running Counter to the Psychoanalytic Theory of the Disease," in *The Standard Edition of the Complete Psychological Works of Sigmund Freud*, ed. and trans. James Strachey (London: The Hogarth Press, 1958), vol. 14, p. 269. *The Standard Edition of the Complete Psychological Works of Sigmund Freud* is hereafter abbreviated to *S.E.*

8. Laplanche and Pontalis, "Fantasy and the Origins of Sexuality," p. 10.

9. Freud, *S.E.*, vol. 1, p. 259.

10. Freud, " 'A Child is Being Beaten': A Contribution to the Study of the Origin of Sexual Perversions," *S.E.*, vol. 17, p. 195–196.

11. Laplanche and Pontalis, "Fantasy and the Origins of Sexuality," p. 14.

12. Marguerite Duras, *India Song*, trans. Barbara Bray (New York: Grove Press, 1976), p. 145.

13. ". . . It is the subject's life as a whole which is seen to be shaped and ordered by what might be called, in order to stress this structuring action, 'a phantasmatic' (*une fantasmatique*). This should not be conceived of merely as a thematic—not even as one characterized by distinctly specific traits for each subject—for it has its own dynamic, in that the phantasy structures seek to express themselves, to find a way out into consciousness and action." Jean Laplanche and J.-B. Pontalis, *The Language of Psycho-Analysis*, trans. Donald Nicholson-Smith (New York: Norton, 1973), p. 317.

14. In French, *entendu* has the sense of both heard and understood: ". . . Hearing is also . . . the history of the legends of parents, grandparents, and the ancestors: the family *sounds* or *sayings*, this spoken or secret discourse, going on prior to the subject's arrival, within which he must find his way. Insofar as it can serve retrospectively to summon up the discourse, the noise . . . can acquire this value." Laplanche and Pontalis, "Fantasy and the Origins of Sexuality," p. 10–11.

15. All the dialogue is taken from Marie-Claire Ropars-Wuilleumier's découpage of the film (see note 1). The translation is at times my own and, where possible, taken from *India Song*, trans. Barbara Bray (New York: Grove Press, 1976), originally published in French as *India Song—texte-théâtre-film* (Paris: Gallimard, 1973).